Jane's

Aircraft
Recognition Guide

Fifth edition published in 2007 by Collins

HarperCollins*Publishers*
77-85 Fulham Palace Road
Hammersmith
London W6 8JB
UK

www.collins.co.uk

HarperCollins*Publishers* Inc
10 East 53rd Street
New York
NY 10022
USA

www.harpercollins.com

www.janes.com

ISBN-13 978-0-00-725792-8

Layout: Susie Bell
Editorial: Louise Stanley, Jodi Simpson

Printed and bound by Printing Express, Hong Kong

Aircraft
Recognition Guide

Günter Endres and
Michael J. Gething

Collins

Contents

Civil Prop Airliners

Civil Utility Aircraft

Business Jets and Turboprops

Private Light Aircraft

Civil Helicopters

Combat Aircraft

Military Training Aircraft

Combat Support Aircraft

Military Helicopters

Picture credits

Foreword

This latest edition of *Jane's Aircraft Recognition Guide* has again been revised with many new photographs, new aircraft types (which have entered service since the last issue or are about to receive their airworthiness certificates), and silhouettes for each throughout the book. The information has been sourced from *Jane's All the World's Aircraft, Jane's Aircraft Upgrades,* and *Jane's World Air Forces*. As befits a guide bearing the Jane's marque, we have updated the entries, hopefully correcting the few (human) mistakes, which had still crept into the last edition.

Let us remind the reader what exactly this book sets out to provide and, also, what it does not. It is an aide memoire for individuals interested in aviation who visit airfields, airports, or air shows to assist with the identification of the aircraft they will see. It sets out to illustrate a very wide variety of aircraft and helicopters likely to be found at such locations and events around the world.

It is not a pocket-sized edition of *Jane's All The World's Aircraft*, however. To this end, there are no entries for the likes of Unmanned Aerial Vehicles or the multitudinous variety of light general aviation, sports, or homebuilt aircraft produced in single figures, which would fill a book twice this size.

Readers should note, however, that specifications remain rounded up or down to one decimal place (in the case of metric) and without fractions (in imperial measures). After all, at the distances involved in aircraft recognition, what difference can 0.04m or ¾ inch make in identifying the type of aircraft? We can well remember that, during the mid-1960s, the skill was to detect the subtle differences between the Boeing 707, Convair 880, and DC-8 airliners, all three types being of the same overall size and configuration, in order to confirm identity.

Indeed, it is identification of aircraft types that is the raison d'être for this minor tome. While aircraft recognition goes back almost one hundred years, it has only been practised as an "art form" since the Second World War when, with radar in its infancy, visual identification of "ours" and "theirs" was a vital requirement for air defense.

In the UK, this skill resided, principally, in the Royal Observer Corps, which was an integral part of the RAF's reporting and control organization. In the latter years of the 20th century, its importance faded and the corps was disbanded in 1991. The fascination with aviation, however, be it civil or military, remains as strong as ever. Indeed, its popularity as an enthusiast pastime in the UK, much of continental Europe, and the United States continues unabated.

Another trend that has arisen in recent years is the contraction of the aerospace business itself, leading to a vast reduction in the number of aircraft manufacturers. In parallel, there has been the longevity, well beyond original plans, of many types of aircraft.

Thus we see many aircraft flying built by companies that no longer exist… but the DC-3 Dakota/C-47 Skytrain will forever be a Douglas rather than a Boeing product (via the McDonnell Douglas Corporation). In applying "common sense" to this contraction of the industry, aircraft are labeled with what we believe is the obvious manufacturer, with either the original or current name in parentheses afterwards. Hence we have the Aerospatiale Alouette III rather than the original Sud Aviation or current Eurocopter identity.

The overall rule applied is that, if production has ceased, the main manufacturer name is prime, with the current holder of design authority secondary. Where a manufacturer has been taken over during production of a type, the new company name is used with the original name secondary.

Our revised recategorisation of the many types remains. For instance, several advanced jet trainers have a light ground-attack role and previously were included as Combat Aircraft. Such types now reside under Military Training Aircraft, where their prime role is better reflected. We have also, where applicable, included the military versions of a basic civil type under its latter category, if it is mainly a civil aircraft, and vice versa. This has reduced the number of essentially duplicate entries between military and civil types.

Another feature of the aerospace industry is the quantum growth in the use of initials for all manner of long-winded names, titles, and techniques, as well as shorthand phrases, only some of which are in common usage. Most of these comprise the lingua franca of aviation. Mindful that many readers may have this book as their first-ever reference to aircraft and aviation, we have updated the Glossary, which allows these sometimes incomprehensible abbreviations and acronyms to be decoded and explained.

In compiling this book, we acknowledge the considerable assistance of the many public relations personnel of the aerospace industry and operators (civil and military) whom we have consulted for information and photographs. You are too numerous to single out, but you know who you are and we thank you.

Within the Jane's and HarperCollins organizations, we thank Jo Agius, Sean Howe, Michael Johnson, Louise Stanley, and Kate Whithead for their help.

We would also like to thank those of our peers who have provided the few elusive images to complete this guide: *Air Forces Monthly*, Patrick Allen, Gerd Beilfuss, Brian Bartlett, Art Berett, Piotr Butowski, Samuel Chy, Horacio J. Claria, Tomas Coelho, Barry Crompton, Elias Daloumis, Rainer Eixenberger, Andy Graff, Grzegorz Holdanowicz, Jamie Hunter, Paul Jackson, Dmitry Kudryn, David McIntosh, Toni Marimon, Tony Marlow, Felix Mayer, Shawn Miller, Lothar Müller, John Olafson, Thomas Posch, Nigel Steele, Michael Stroud, Henry Tenby, Tsen Tsan Tung, Theodore Valmas, Paolo Valpolini, Alan Warnes, Sokol Ymeri and Harima Yoshihiro.

Gunter Endres and Michael J. Gething, January 2007

Civil Jet Airliners

Airbus A300 FRANCE/GERMANY/SPAIN/UK

Twin-turbofan medium-haul airliner

First flown on October 28, 1972, the A300 was the first aircraft to be built by the multinational Airbus consortium. The introduction into service in June 1984 of the A300-600 represented a major step up, featuring advanced technologies including a two-crew cockpit. Total delivered: 555 (ordered 561).

SPECIFICATION (A300-600R):

ACCOMMODATION: 2 + 361
CARGO/BAGGAGE: 147.4 m³ (5206 cu.ft)
MAX SPEED: M0.85 (484 kt; 895 km/h)
RANGE: 4160 nm (7700 km)

DIMENSIONS:
WINGSPAN: 44.8 m (147 ft 1 in)
LENGTH: 54.1 m (177 ft 5 in)
HEIGHT: 16.5 m (54 ft 3 in)

VARIANTS:
A300B2-100: Baseline model with GE CF6-50 turbofans
A300B2K: Krüger flaps and higher T-O weight
A300B2-200: Redesignation of A300B2K
A300B4-100: Increased range capability
A300B4-200: Higher T-O weight
A300B4-300: Introduced P&W JT9D turbofans
A300B4-600: Two-crew cockpit
A300B4-600R: Two-crew and increased range
A300C4-200: Convertible version of A300B4
A300C4-600: Convertible version of A300B4-600
A300F4-200: All-cargo version of A300B4-200
A300F4-600F: All-cargo version of A300B4-600R
Many early B2 and B4 models converted to cargo

FEATURES:
Low/swept wing with small winglets; twin underwing GE CF6-80C2 or P&W PW4000 turbofans; swept tailfin and low-set tailplane; wide-body fuselage

Airbus A310 FRANCE/GERMANY/SPAIN/UK

Twin-turbofan short/medium-haul airliner

Shorter version of A300, developed at the instigation of Swissair and Lufthansa, with major innovations including a new advanced-technology wing, smaller horizontal tailplane, and digital two-crew cockpit. First flown on April 3, 1982, and entered service with Lufthansa on April 12, 1983. Total delivered: 255 (ordered 260).

SPECIFICATION (A310-300):

ACCOMMODATION: 2 + 280
CARGO/BAGGAGE: 102.0 m³ (3605 cu.ft)
MAX SPEED: M0.85 (484 kt; 895 km/h)
RANGE: 4350 nm (8050 km)

DIMENSIONS:

WINGSPAN: 43.9 m (144 ft 0 in)
LENGTH: 46.7 m (153 ft 1 in)
HEIGHT: 15.8 m (51 ft 10 in)

VARIANTS:

A310-200: Baseline model
A310-200C: Convertible passenger/cargo version
A310-300: Increased fuel capacity and range, plus wingtip fences
A310-300ER: Additional center tanks for extra long range
Many early aircraft since converted to cargo with some also operating as MRTT

FEATURES:

Low/swept wing with wingtip fences; twin underwing CF6-80, JT9D, or PW4000 turbofans; swept tailfin and low-set tailplane; wide-body fuselage

Airbus A318 FRANCE/GERMANY/SPAIN/UK

Twin-turbofan short-haul airliner

Short-bodied version of single-aisle A319, formally announced at the Farnborough Air Show in September 1998. Final assembly started at Hamburg on August 9, 2001, with first flight with P&W engines on January 15, 2002 and with CFM56-5s on August 29, 2002. Entered service with Frontier Airlines on July 29, 2003. Total delivered: 36 (ordered 90).

SPECIFICATION:

ACCOMMODATION: 2 + 129
CARGO/BAGGAGE: 21.9 m³ (773 cu.ft)
MAX SPEED: M0.82 (470 kt; 870 km/h)
RANGE: 1500 nm (2778 km)

DIMENSIONS:
WINGSPAN: 34.1 m (111 ft 10 in)
LENGTH: 31.5 m (103 ft 3 in)
HEIGHT: 12.6 m (41 ft 3 in)

VARIANTS:
A318-100: Baseline aircraft
A318 Elite: Business jet variant with seating for 14–18 passengers

FEATURES:
Low/swept wing with winglets; twin underwing P&W PW6000 or CFM56-5 turbofans; swept tailfin and low-set tailplane

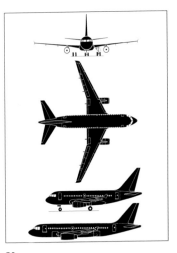

Airbus A319 FRANCE/GERMANY/SPAIN/UK

Twin-turbofan short-haul airliner

Short-fuselage version of A320, officially launched in June 1993 and first flown at Hamburg on August 29, 1995. Entered service with Swissair on April 30, 1996. First ACJ (Airbus Corporate Jetliner) variant was announced at 1997 Paris Air Show and made its maiden flight on November 12, 1998. First delivery to customer November 8, 1999. A319LR delivered to PrivatAir May 2004. Total delivered: 930 (ordered 1497).

SPECIFICATION:

ACCOMMODATION: 2 + 145
CARGO/BAGGAGE: 27.6 m3 (976 cu.ft)
MAX SPEED: M0.82 (470 kt; 870 km/h)
RANGE: 1830 nm (3390 km)

DIMENSIONS:
WINGSPAN: 34.1 m (111 ft 10 in)
LENGTH: 33.8 m (111 ft 0 in)
HEIGHT: 11.8 m (38 ft 7 in)

VARIANTS:
A319-100: Baseline passenger model
A319LR: Intercontinental version with up to four additional fuel tanks and ACJ features
ACJ: Corporate jet with typically 58 passengers and customer-specific interior

FEATURES:
Low/swept wing with winglets; twin underwing CFM56-5 or IAE V2500 turbofans; swept tailfin and low-set tailplane

Airbus A320 FRANCE/GERMANY/SPAIN/UK

Twin-turbofan short-haul airliner

First member of single-aisle Airbus family launched on March 23, 1984. Maiden flight with CFM56-5 engines at Toulouse on February 22, 1987, and with IAE V2500 engines on July 28, 1988. First deliveries with CFM56 engines to Air France on March 28, 1988. Adria Airways took first V2500-powered aircraft on March 18, 1989. Total delivered: 1663 (ordered 2700).

SPECIFICATION:

ACCOMMODATION: 2 + 180
CARGO/BAGGAGE: 38.8 m³ (1370 cu.ft)
MAX SPEED: M0.82 (470 kt; 870 km/h)
RANGE: 2800 nm (5185 km)

DIMENSIONS:

WINGSPAN: 34.1 m (111 ft 10 in)
LENGTH: 37.6 m (123 ft 3 in)
HEIGHT: 11.8 m (38 ft 9 in)

VARIANTS:

A320-100: Initial version, only 21 built
A320-200: Standard version featuring wingtip fences and wing-center fuel tank
A320 Prestige: Executive variant
A320 'Enhanced': Proposed upgrade with new cabin, improved aerodynamics and winglets
MPA 320: Proposed maritime patrol version
Freighter conversions planned with Russian industry for first deliveries in 2011

FEATURES:

Low/swept wing with winglets; twin underwing CFM56-5 or IAE V2500 turbofans; swept tailfin and low-set tailplane

Airbus A321 FRANCE/GERMANY/SPAIN/UK

Twin-turbofan short-haul airliner

Stretched version of A320 launched on November 24, 1989. First flight with V2530 lead engine on March 11, 1993, followed by CFM56-powered alternative in May that year. Type entered service with Lufthansa on March 18, 1994. Alitalia took delivery of first CFM56-powered model on same day. Total delivered: 371 (ordered 649).

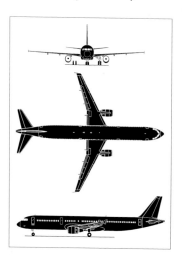

SPECIFICATION:

ACCOMMODATION: 2 + 220
CARGO/BAGGAGE: 52.0 m³ (1838 cu.ft)
MAX SPEED: M0.82 (470 kt; 870 km/h)
RANGE: 2325 nm (4306 km)

DIMENSIONS:
WINGSPAN: 34.1 m (111 ft 10 in)
LENGTH: 44.5 m (146 ft 0 in)
HEIGHT: 11.8 m (38 ft 9 in)

VARIANTS:
A321-100: Initial version
A321-200: Extended range with additional center tank (ACT), reinforced structure, and higher-thrust engines

FEATURES:
Low/swept wing with winglets; twin underwing CFM56-5 or IAE V2500 turbofans; swept tailfin and low-set tailplane

Airbus A330 FRANCE/GERMANY/SPAIN/UK

Twin-turbofan medium/long-haul airliner

Developed simultaneously with four-engined A340. Launched on June 5, 1987, and made its first flight with GE CF6-80 engines on November 2, 1992 and with Rolls-Royce Trent 700s on January 31, 1994. Entered service with Air Inter in January 1994. Total delivered: 447 (ordered 674).

SPECIFICATION (A330-300):

ACCOMMODATION: 2 + 440
CARGO/BAGGAGE: 46,715 kg (102,958 lb)
MAX SPEED: M0.86 (493 kt; 912 km/h)
RANGE: 5620 nm (10,400 km)

DIMENSIONS:
WINGSPAN: 60.3 m (197 ft 10 in)
LENGTH: 63.7 m (208 ft 11 in)
HEIGHT: 16.8 m (55 ft 3 in)

VARIANTS:
A330-200: Shortened fuselage, extended range
A330-200F: New long-haul freighter
A330-300: Baseline version
A330 Enhanced: Improved model with FBW-controlled rudder, flightdeck with new LCDS, and updated passenger cabin
A330MRTT: Proposed aerial tanker/transport

FEATURES:
Low/swept wing with winglets; twin underwing GE CF6-80, P&W PW4000, or Rolls-Royce Trent 700 turbofans; swept tailfin and low-set tailplane; wide-body fuselage

Airbus A340 FRANCE/GERMANY/SPAIN/UK

Four-turbofan long-haul airliner

Launched June 5, 1987, in a combined program with A330. First flight of -300 and -200 models on October 25, 1991, and April 1, 1992, respectively, followed by service entry with Lufthansa in January 1993. Stretched -600 first flown on April 23, 2001, and ultra-long-range A340-500 on February 11, 2002, entering service respectively with Virgin Atlantic on August 5, 2002, and Emirates on December 3, 2003. Total delivered: 337 (ordered 398).

SPECIFICATION (A340-300):

ACCOMMODATION: 2 + 440
CARGO/BAGGAGE: 45,915 kg (101,915 lb)
MAX SPEED: M0.86 (493 kt; 912 km/h)
RANGE: 7100 nm (13,150 km)

DIMENSIONS:
WINGSPAN: 60.3 m (197 ft 10 in)
LENGTH: 63.6 m (208 ft 8 in)
HEIGHT: 16.8 m (55 ft 3 in)

VARIANTS:
A340-200: Short-fuselage, longer-range version
A340-300: Higher-capacity version of A340-200
A340-300E: Extended range with additional center tank (ACT)
A340-500: Ultra-long-range stretch
A340-600: Further stretch, higher-thrust engines, and four-wheel central landing gear

FEATURES:
Low/swept wing with winglets; four underwing CFM56-5 or Rolls-Royce Trent 500 turbofans; swept tailfin and low-set tailplane; wide-body fuselage

Airbus A380 FRANCE/GERMANY/SPAIN/UK

Four-turbofan high-capacity long-range airliner

Development of this double-deck airliner was begun in April 1996, with formal launch as the A380 December 19, 2000. First metal was cut January 23, 2002, and first flight with R-R Trent engines took place April 27, 2005. First GP7200-powered aircraft flew August 25, 2006. Singapore Airlines to put passenger A380 into service 2007, and freighter June 2008. Total ordered: 166.

SPECIFICATION (A380-800):

ACCOMMODATION: 2 + 555
CARGO: 150,000 kg (330,690 lb) (-800F)
MAX SPEED: M0.89
RANGE: 8000 nm (14,815 km)

DIMENSIONS:

WINGSPAN: 79.7 m (261 ft 4 in)
LENGTH: 72.8 m (238 ft 8 in)
HEIGHT: 24.1 m (79 ft 0 in)

VARIANTS:

A380-700: Potential short-fuselage version
A380-800: Baseline passenger variant for 555 passengers in three classes
A380-800F: All-cargo version with 150-tonne payload capacity
A380-900: Potential stretch for up to 950 passengers in high-density configuration
A380 MRTB: Projected military version (multirole transport/bomber)

FEATURES:

Low/swept wings with winglets; four underwing Engine Alliance GP7200 or Rolls-Royce Trent 900 turbofans; swept high tailfin with swept low-set tailplane; double-deck fuselage

Antonov An-72/74 "Coaler" UKRAINE

Twin-turbofan light STOL transport

Developed as tactical transport replacement for the An-26 in service with the Soviet air force. The most significant design feature is the considerable increase in lift achieved through the Coanda effect whereby the engine exhaust gases are blown over the high wing's upper surface. First flown on August 31, 1977, but did not enter production until December 1989. Total delivered: 160+.

SPECIFICATION:

ACCOMMODATION: 3 + 68
CARGO: 10,000 kg (22,046 lb)
MAX SPEED: 380 kt (705 km/h)
RANGE: 1160 nm (2150 km)

DIMENSIONS:
WINGSPAN: 31.9 m (104 ft 8 in)
LENGTH: 28.1 m (92 ft 2 in)
HEIGHT: 8.7 m (28 ft 5 in)

VARIANTS:
An-72-100: Civilianized version
An-74: Improved MRT
An-74T-100: As -200, with navigator station
An-74T-200: Freight version with increased payload
An-74T-200A: Longer hold, roller conveyors, and loading winch
An74TK-100: As TK-200, with navigator and flight engineer station
An-74TK-200: Passenger/cargo convertible
An-24TK-200 Salon: Executive version for 10–16 passengers

FEATURES:
High/swept wings; twin ZMKB Progress D-36 turbofan engines mounted high on wing and close in to sides of fuselage; upswept rear fuselage with ramp/door; swept T-tail; tricycle landing gear retracting into large side fairings

Antonov An-74-300 UKRAINE

Twin-turbofan short-haul transport

Announced in mid-1998 and demonstrated for the first time at the Paris Air Show in June 2001 after making its maiden flight in April 2001. This new model differs considerably from the earlier An-74 version, most noticeably in the replacement of the overwing engines by conventionally podded engines under the wing. Certificated in September 2002.

SPECIFICATION:

ACCOMMODATION: 2 + 52
CARGO: 10,000 kg (22,046 lb)
MAX SPEED: 378 kt (700 km/h)
RANGE: 1890 nm (3500 km)

DIMENSIONS:
WINGSPAN: 31.9 m (104 ft 8 in)
LENGTH: 28.1 m (92 ft 2 in)
HEIGHT: 8.7 m (28 ft 5 in)

VARIANTS:
An-74T-300: Cargo transport
An-74TK-300: Baseline passenger transport
An-174: Proposed stretched fuselage

FEATURES:
High/swept wing with slight anhedral; twin underslung ZMKB Progress D-36 turbofan engines; upswept rear fuselage; swept T-tail; tricycle landing gear retracting into large side fairings

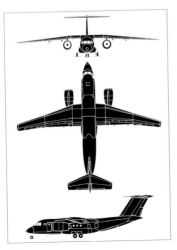

Antonov An-124 "Condor" UKRAINE

Four-turbofan outsize freight transport

Under development in the late 1970s as outsize freighter, capable of take-off and landing from unprepared fields and provided with front and rear loading access with fold-down hydraulic ramps. Prototype first flew on December 26, 1982 and the type entered service in January 1986. Set several world records for payload/distance flights. Total built to date: 55.

SPECIFICATION (An-124-100M):

ACCOMMODATION: 6 crew + 12 cargo handlers
CARGO: 150,000 kg (330,700 lb)
MAX SPEED: 467 kt (865 km/h)
RANGE: 2510 nm (4650 km)

DIMENSIONS:
WINGSPAN: 73.3 m (240 ft 6 in)
LENGTH: 69.1 m (226 ft 9 in)
HEIGHT: 21.1 m (69 ft 2 in)

VARIANTS:
An-124: Basic military transport
An-124-100: Standard civil transport
An-124-100M: As An-124-100, but with Western avionics and increased take-off weight
An-124-200: Proposed version with GE CF6-80C2 turbofans
An-124-300: Proposal with extended fuselage and wingspan and two-crew glass cockpit
Military models being converted for civil freighter use

FEATURES:
High/swept anhedral wing; four ZMKB Progress D-18T turbofans; clamshell doors aft of rear loading ramp; upward-opening nose section with fold-down ramp for front loading; retractable undercarriage with 24 main wheels

Antonov An-148

Twin-turbofan short-haul airliner

First revealed in September 2001, the first prototype of this new twin-jet made its maiden flight on December 17, 2004. Russian certification was expected by the end of 2006. Production is being undertaken by VASO in Russia. Total ordered: 41.

SPECIFICATION (An-148-100):

ACCOMMODATION: 2 + 70
CARGO/BAGGAGE: 11.8 m³ (417 cu.ft)
MAX SPEED: 470 kt (870 km/h)
RANGE: 1906 nm (3530 km)

DIMENSIONS:
WINGSPAN: 28.9 m (94 ft 10 in)
LENGTH: 29.1 m (95 ft 6 in)
HEIGHT: 8.2 m (26 ft 11 in)

VARIANTS:
An-148-100A: Short-haul derivative of An-148B
An-148-100B: Baseline version for up to 80 passengers
An-148-100E/E1: Longer range; additional fuel tanks
An-148-100E2: Executive configuration for 10–30 passengers
An-148-200A/B: Stretched versions for 100 passengers
An-148-C1: Small parcels transport
An-148-C2: Palletized cargo transport; cargo door
An-148T: Rear-loading ramp freighter

FEATURES:
High-mounted straight wing with slight anhedral; twin wing-mounted ZMKB Progress D-4360148 turbofans mid-mounted on rear fuselage; swept T-tail with high-set swept tailplane

BAe (BAC) One-Eleven UK

Twin-turbofan short-haul airliner

Decision to proceed with development of former Hunting H.107 project taken in March 1961. Prototype first flew on August 20, 1963, and type entered service with British United Airways on April 9, 1965. Later produced under license in Romania. Total delivered: 230 (in UK), 9 (in Romania).

SPECIFICATION (Series 500):

ACCOMMODATION: 119
CARGO/BAGGAGE: 20.1 m³ (710 cu.ft)
MAX SPEED: M0.82 (470 kt; 870 km/h)
RANGE: 1480 nm (2745 km)

DIMENSIONS:
WINGSPAN: 28.5 m (93 ft 6 in)
LENGTH: 32.6 m (107 ft 0 in)
HEIGHT: 7.5 m (24 ft 6 in)

VARIANTS:
Series 200: Initial version
Series 300: Increased fuel in center tank and structural modifications
Series 400: Based on Series 300 but optimized for U.S. operators
Series 475: Combining wings of Series 500 with fuselage of Series 400
Series 500: Stretched version with more powerful engines
Rombac 495: Romanian-built version of Series 475
Rombac 560: Romanian-built version of Series 500

FEATURES:
Low/swept wing; twin rear-mounted Rolls-Royce Spey turbofans; swept T-tail and tailplane; ventral airstairs

BAe 146/Avro RJ UK

Four-turbofan short-haul regional jet

Former Hawker Siddeley H.S.146 project relaunched on July 10, 1978, and first flown on September 3, 1981. Entered revenue service with Dan-Air on May 27, 1983. Avro RJ developed from 146, with major changes including uprated engines and digital avionics; first flight on March 23, 1992. Further improvements incorporated in RJX, first flown on April 28, 2001, but program abandoned in November 2001. Total delivered: 389 (219 BAe 146, 170 Avro RJ).

SPECIFICATION (RJ85):

ACCOMMODATION: 2 + 112
CARGO/BAGGAGE: 18.3 m³ (644 cu.ft)
MAX SPEED: M0.72 (412 kt; 763 km/h)
RANGE: 1080 nm (2000 km)

DIMENSIONS:
WINGSPAN: 26.3 m (86 ft 5 in)
LENGTH: 28.6 m (93 ft 8 in)
HEIGHT: 8.6 m (28 ft 3 in)

VARIANTS:
146-100: Baseline version with ALF 502 turbofans
146-200: Longer fuselage and higher weights
146-300: Further stretch for increased capacity
Statesman: Executive model
146-300ARA: Atmospheric Research Aircraft
146QC (Quick-change): Variant with large freight door
146QT (Quiet Trader): Conversion of new-build aircraft by Pemco. Being relaunched for secondhand aircraft with Romanian industry participation
RJ70: Short version for 70–94 passengers, LF 507 turbofans
RJ85: Lengthened version for 85–112 passengers
RJ100: Further stretch for 100–116 passengers

FEATURES:
High/swept wing; four underwing ALF 502 or LF 507 turbofans; swept T-tail and swept tailplane; retractable landing gear in fuselage panniers

Boeing 707/720 USA

Four-engined medium/long-haul airliner

First Boeing jet airliner to enter service. Prototype, designated 367-80, first flew on July 15, 1954. First 707 with longer fuselage and powered by four P&W JT3C-6 turbojets entered service with Pan American across the Atlantic on October 26, 1958. The 720 was similar in general appearance but with lighter structure, and slightly shorter fuselage matching that of the "short-body" 707-120. Total delivered (including military): 878 (707), 154 (720).

SPECIFICATION (707-320B):

ACCOMMODATION: 3 + 219
CARGO/BAGGAGE: 50.3 m³ (1775 cu.ft)
MAX SPEED: M0.94 (540 kt; 1000 km/h)
RANGE: 5000 nm (9265 km)

DIMENSIONS:
WINGSPAN: 44.4 m (145 ft 9 in)
LENGTH: 46.6 m (152 ft 11 in)
HEIGHT: 12.9 m (42 ft 5 in)

VARIANTS:
707-120: First production version available in both "long-body" and "short-body" versions, P&W JT3C turbojets
707-120B: More powerful development with JT3D turbofans
707-220: As -120 but powered by JT4A turbojets
707-320: Intercontinental range, increased wingspan, and longer fuselage
707-320B: More powerful JT3Ds
707-320C: Convertible with forward cargo door
707-320C: All-cargo version
707-420: As -320 with R-R Conway turbofans
720: basic model with P&W JT3C-7 turbojets
720B: Improved version with JT3D turbofans
Most 707s still in service have been converted to freighters

FEATURES:
Low/swept wings; four underwing P&W or Rolls-Royce turbojets or P&W JT3D turbofans; swept tailfin with antenna at top; low-set tailplane; small ventral fin (except -320B/C)

Boeing 717 USA

Twin-turbofan short-haul airliner

Announced at Paris Air Show in June 1991. Originally developed by McDonnell Douglas as MD-95, design was taken over by Boeing in 1997 and renamed. Prototype first flew on September 2, 1998, and type entered service with AirTran Airways in September 1999. Production ceased in 2006. Total delivered: 155.

SPECIFICATION:

ACCOMMODATION: 2 + 117
CARGO/BAGGAGE: 26.5 m³ (936 cu.ft)
MAX SPEED: M0.76 (438 kt; 811 km/h)
RANGE: 1920 nm (3556 km)

DIMENSIONS:
WINGSPAN: 28.5 m (93 ft 4 in)
LENGTH: 37.8 m (124 ft 0 in)
HEIGHT: 8.9 m (29 ft 1 in)

VARIANTS:
717-100: Proposed shorter version, shelved in 2003
717-100Lite: Proposed 75-seat variant, abandoned
717-200: Standard production version
717-300: Proposed "stretch" for around 130 passengers; never implemented
717 Business Express: Corporate 717-200

FEATURES:
Low/swept wings; twin rear fuselage-mounted Rolls-Royce Deutschland BR 715 turbofans; swept T-tail and tailplane

Boeing 727 USA

Three-turbofan short-haul airliner

Launched on December 5, 1960, and designed for maximum commonality with 707, permitting similar cabin layouts. Advanced aerodynamics and greater wing sweepback. First flown on February 9, 1963, and entered service with Eastern Air Lines on February 1, 1964. Total delivered: 1832.

SPECIFICATION (727-200):

ACCOMMODATION: 3 + 189
CARGO/BAGGAGE: 43.2 m³ (1525 cu.ft)
MAX SPEED: M0.95 548 kt (1014 km/h)
RANGE: 2370 nm (4392 km)

DIMENSIONS:
WINGSPAN: 32.9 m (108 ft 0 in)
LENGTH: 46.7 m (153 ft 2 in)
HEIGHT: 10.4 m (34 ft 0 in)

VARIANTS:
727-100: Initial production version
727-100C: Convertible passenger/cargo with reinforced flooring and large forward cargo door
727-100QC: Quick-change alternative with palletized seats
727-200: Stretched model replacing -100s as standard aircraft
727-200 Advanced: Further refinements and improved cabin interior
727-200F: Pure freighter with strengthened fuselage structure and windows blocked out
Many aircraft since fitted with "hushkits"

FEATURES:
Low/swept wing; three P&W JT8D turbofan engines, one atop and integral with tail and two on side of rear fuselage; highly swept T-tail and tailplane

Boeing 737-100/200 USA

Twin-turbofan short-haul airliner

Design of the "Baby" Boeing started on May 11, 1964, featuring a conventional layout with underwing engines. Made first flight on April 9, 1967, and entered service with launch customer Lufthansa on February 10, 1968. Original model quickly replaced by stretched version, which flew on August 8, 1967. Total delivered: 1144.

SPECIFICATION (737-200A):

ACCOMMODATION: 2 + 130
CARGO/BAGGAGE: 24.8 m³ (875 cu.ft)
MAX SPEED: M0.84 (481 kt; 890 km/h)
RANGE: 2530 nm (4688 km)

DIMENSIONS:
WINGSPAN: 28.4 m (93 ft 0 in)
LENGTH: 30.5 m (100 ft 2 in)
HEIGHT: 11.3 m (37 ft 0 in)

VARIANTS:
737-100: Original production version; only 30 built
737-200: Standard model with small fuselage stretch
737-200C: Convertible passenger/cargo with forward side door
737-200 Advanced: Improved technology
737-200C Advanced: Convertible alternative
737-200QC Advanced: Quick-change version with palletized seats

FEATURES:
Low/swept wing; twin underwing P&W JT8D turbofans in slim engine nacelles; swept tailfin and low-set tailplane

Boeing 737-300/400/500 USA

Twin-turbofan short-haul airliner

Stretched development of popular twin, incorporating advanced technology CFM56 engines and other improvements. First flown on February 24, 1984, and put into service by launch customer Southwest Airlines on December 7 that year. Longer and shorter derivatives added. Models replaced by next-generation 737s. Total delivered: 1988.

SPECIFICATION (737-400):

ACCOMMODATION: 2 + 170
CARGO/BAGGAGE: 30.2 m³ (1070 cu.ft)
MAX SPEED: M0.84 (481 kt; 890 km/h)
RANGE: 2500 nm (4633 km)

DIMENSIONS:
WINGSPAN: 28.9 m (94 ft 9 in)
LENGTH: 36.5 m (119 ft 7 in)
HEIGHT: 11.1 m (36 ft 6 in)

VARIANTS:
737-300: Initial baseline model
77-33: Corporate model
737-400: Longer variant with strengthened structure
737-500: Short-fuselage variant
Some aircraft, especially the 737-300, operated in all-cargo or quick-change configuration with suffix C

FEATURES:
Low/swept wing; large twin underwing CFM56-3 turbofans; swept tailfin with dorsal fin and low-set tailplane

Boeing 737-600/700/800/900 USA

Twin-turbofan short-haul airliner

Current "next generation" family, initially referred to as the 737X, with increased wing, new high-lift devices, and greater range and speed. Maiden flight was made on February 9, 1997, and the 737-700 was the first to enter service with launch customer Southwest Airlines in October that year. Total delivered: 2136 (ordered 3696).

SPECIFICATION (737-700):

ACCOMMODATION: 2 + 149
CARGO/BAGGAGE: 27.4 m³ (966 cu.ft)
MAX SPEED: M0.82 (470 kt; 870 km/h)
RANGE: 1540 nm (2852 km)

DIMENSIONS:
WINGSPAN: 34.3 m (112 ft 7 in)
LENGTH: 33.6 m (110 ft 4 in)
HEIGHT: 12.6 m (41 ft 3 in)

VARIANTS:
737-600: Smallest version equivalent to 737-500
737-700: Mid-size model equivalent to 737-300
737-700C: Quick-change with palletized seats
737-700ER: Extended range, wings and landing gear from larger 737-800
737-700IGW: Increased gross weight
737-800: More powerful engines, roughly equivalent to 737-400
737-900: Largest 737 version for 189 passengers
737-900ER: Increased capacity, longer range
BBJ: Boeing Business Jet based on the 737-700
BBJ 2: Boeing Business Jet based on the 737-800

FEATURES:
Low/swept wing (blended winglets on BBJ and some -800s); twin underwing CFM56-7 turbofans; swept tailfin with dorsal fin and low-set tailplane

Boeing 747-100/200/SP USA

Four-turbofan long-haul airliner

First wide-body airliner developed as a by-product of work done by Boeing on CH-X military transport requirement. Officially launched into production on July 25, 1966, and made first flight on February 9, 1969. Put into service by launch customer Pan American on the North Atlantic on January 21, 1970. Total delivered: 643.

SPECIFICATION:

ACCOMMODATION: 3 + 516
CARGO/BAGGAGE: 90,720 kg (200,000 lb)
MAX SPEED: M0.92 (525 kt; 973 km/h)
RANGE: 6600 nm (12,223 km)

DIMENSIONS:
WINGSPAN: 59.6 m (195 ft 8 in)
LENGTH: 70.7 m (231 ft 10 in)
HEIGHT: 19.3 m (63 ft 5 in)

VARIANTS:
747SP: Longer-range short-body derivative
747-100: Original production model
747-100B: Higher gross weight and strengthened structure
747-100SF: Cargo conversion with main-deck cargo door
747-100SR: Short-range version optimized for high T-O/landing cycles
747-200B: Increased fuel and uprated engines
747-200C: Passenger/cargo model with upward-hinged nose
747-200F: Freighter with upward-hinged nose
747-200M: Combi with large portside cargo door aft of wing

FEATURES:
Low/swept wings; four underwing GE CF6, P&W JT9D, or Rolls-Royce RB 211 turbofans; short upper deck; swept tailfin and low-set tailplane; wide-body fuselage

Boeing 747-300/400 USA

Four-turbofan long-haul airliner

Extended upper-deck development announced on June 12, 1980. Initially known as 747SUD (stretched upper deck) and 747EUD (extended upper deck), but first flown as 747-300 on October 5, 1982. Extensive changes, including a two-crew flight deck, resulted in the -400 model, first flown on April 29, 1988. Total delivered: 81 (-300); 656 (-400).

SPECIFICATION (747-400):

ACCOMMODATION: 2 + 568
CARGO/BAGGAGE: 113,000 kg (249,125 lb)
MAX SPEED: M0.88 (507 kt; 938 km/h)
RANGE: 7260 nm (13,445 km)

DIMENSIONS:
WINGSPAN: 64.4 m (211 ft 5 in)
LENGTH: 70.7 m (231 ft 10 in)
HEIGHT: 19.4 m (63 ft 8 in)

VARIANTS:
747-300: Initial upper-deck model
747-300M: Combi with rear portside cargo door
747-300SR: Short-range with extra windows
747-400: Extended wingtips with winglets, two-crew flight deck, and low-fuel-burn engines
747-400ER: Extended range with additional fuel
747-400ERF: Freighter version of -400ER with additional payload or range
747-400F: 747-200F fuselage with short upper deck combined with larger -400 wing
747-400M: Combi with rear portside cargo door
747-400 Domestic: High-density version with five additional upper-deck windows, no winglets
747-400SF: Freighter conversion
747-8: Stretched -400 for up to 500 passengers; first delivery in 2009
747-8F: Stretched -400F; first delivery in 2009

FEATURES:
Low/swept wing with large winglets (not on -300); four underwing GE CF6-80, P&W PW4000, or Rolls-Royce RB 211 turbofan engines; extended upper deck; swept tailfin and low-set tailplane; wide-body fuselage

Boeing 757 USA

Twin-turbofan medium-haul airliner

New-technology twin-engined 757/767/777 family announced in mid-1978. The 757 was the second to fly on February 19, 1982. Revenue services began by launch customers Eastern Air Lines on January 1 and by British Airways on February 9, 1983. Production ceased in November 2005. Total delivered: 1050.

SPECIFICATION (757-200):

ACCOMMODATION: 2 + 289
CARGO/BAGGAGE: 47.3 m³ (1670 cu.ft)
MAX SPEED: M0.86 (493 kt; 912 km/h)
RANGE: 3930 nm (7278 km)

DIMENSIONS:

WINGSPAN: 38.1 m (124 ft 10 in)
LENGTH: 47.3 m (155 ft 3 in)
HEIGHT: 13.6 m (44 ft 6 in)

VARIANTS:

757-200: Initial production version
757-200ER: Extended range with increased fuel
757-200M: Combi with forward upward-opening cargo door on portside
757-200PF: Package freighter with large forward cargo door, no windows
757-200SF: Special Freighter conversion for DHL
757-300: Stretched derivative

FEATURES:

Low/swept wing; twin underwing P&W PW2000 or Rolls-Royce RB 211 turbofans; swept tailfin with low-set tailplane; long, narrow fuselage

Boeing 767 USA

Twin-turbofan medium-haul airliner

Launched on receipt of United Airlines order on July 14, 1978, and made its maiden flight September 26, 1981. Initial service of P&W JT9D-powered aircraft with United Airlines on September 8, 1982, followed by GE CF6-80A-powered variant with Delta Air Lines on October 25, 1982. Total delivered: 947 (ordered 975).

SPECIFICATION (767-300ER):

ACCOMMODATION: 2 + 350
CARGO/BAGGAGE: 147.0 m³ (5190 cu.ft)
MAX SPEED: M0.86 (493 kt; 912 km/h)
RANGE: 5875 nm (10,880 km)

DIMENSIONS:
WINGSPAN: 47.6 m (156 ft 1 in)
LENGTH: 54.9 m (180 ft 3 in)
HEIGHT: 15.9 m (52 ft 0 in)

VARIANTS:
767-200: Basic model
767-200ER: Extended-range with center-section fuel tanks
767-300: Stretched model with strengthened landing gear
767-300BCF: Converted freighter with side cargo door; based on 767-300ER
767-300ER: Extended range with further increase in center tankage
767-300F: Pure freighter with forward portside cargo door, no windows
767-400ER: Stretched version with improved flight deck
KC-767: Aerial tanker/transport

FEATURES:
Low/swept wing; twin underwing GE CF6-80C2, P&W PW4000, or Rolls-Royce RB 211 turbofans; swept tailfin and low-set tailplane; wide-body fuselage; blended winglets available for retrofit on 767-300ER

Boeing 777 USA

Twin-turbofan long-haul airliner

Designed to fit between the 767 and the 747, and initially known as the 767-X, the fly-by-wire 777 was launched in October 1990 and made its maiden flight on June 12, 1994. First revenue service with United Airlines between London and Washington, D.C., took place on June 7, 1995. Total delivered: 604 (ordered 903).

SPECIFICATION (777-300):

ACCOMMODATION: 2 + 550
CARGO/BAGGAGE: 200.5 m³ (7080 cu.ft)
MAX SPEED: M0.89 (510 kt; 944 km/h)
RANGE: 5720 nm (10,593 km)

DIMENSIONS:
WINGSPAN: 60.9 m (199 ft 11 in)
LENGTH: 73.9 m (242 ft 4 in)
HEIGHT: 18.5 m (60 ft 9 in)

VARIANTS:
777-200: Baseline aircraft
777-200ER: Longer-range variant, formerly known as the 777-200IGW (increased gross weight)
777-200LR: Ultra-long range, optional auxiliary fuel tank
777-300: Stretched derivative with strengthened fuselage, inboard wing and landing gear
777-300ER: Ultra-long range, strengthened tail surfaces and wing, added wingtips
777F: Production freighter based on 777-200LR; first delivery 2008

FEATURES:
Low/swept wing (folding optional); twin underwing GE90, P&W PW4000, or Rolls-Royce Trent 800 turbofans; swept tailfin and low-set tailplane; wide-body fuselage

Boeing (McDonnell Douglas) MD-11 USA

Three-turbofan medium-haul airliner

Follow-on design to DC-10, similar in configuration but slightly larger and distinguished by the addition of wingtips, revealed at Paris Air Show in June 1985. Launched on December 30, 1986, and first flown on January 10, 1990. Went into service with Finnair on December 20, 1990. Total delivered: 200. Out of production.

SPECIFICATION (MD-11ER):

ACCOMMODATION: 2 + 410
CARGO/BAGGAGE: 633.7 m³ (22,380 cu.ft)
MAX SPEED: M0.945 (542 kt; 1003 km/h)
RANGE: 7240 nm (13,408km)

DIMENSIONS:
WINGSPAN: 51.6 m (169 ft 5 in)
LENGTH: 61.6 m (202 ft 2 in)
HEIGHT: 17.6 m (57 ft 8 in)

VARIANTS:
MD-11: Standard passenger version
MD-11C: Combi with rear portside main-deck cargo door
MD-11CF: Convertible passenger/freight model with front portside main-deck cargo door
MD-11ER: Extended-range version with removable auxiliary fuel tank in lower cargo hold
MD-11F: All-cargo model with no cabin windows
Most passenger aircraft are being converted to freighters

FEATURES:
Low/swept wing with winglets; three GE CF6-80C2 or P&W PW4000 turbofans, one near base of tailfin, the others on underwing pylons; swept tailfin and low-set tailplane; wide-body fuselage

Boeing (McDonnell Douglas) MD-80 USA

Twin-turbofan short-haul airliner

Development of the McDonnell Douglas DC-9 with refanned engines and other refinements, initially known as the DC-9 Super 80 Series. First flight on October 18, 1979, followed by the first revenue service with Swissair on October 5, 1980. Total delivered: 1191. Out of production.

SPECIFICATION (MD-82):

ACCOMMODATION: 2 + 172
CARGO/BAGGAGE: 35.5 m³ (1255 cu.ft)
MAX SPEED: M0.87 (500 kt; 925 km/h)
RANGE: 1877 nm (3476 km)

DIMENSIONS:
WINGSPAN: 32.8 m (107 ft 8 in)
LENGTH: 45.0 m (147 ft 8 in)
HEIGHT: 9.00 m (29 ft 6 in)

VARIANTS:
MD-81: Baseline model, formerly DC-9 Super 81
MD-82: Uprated engines with emergency thrust reverse; formerly DC-9 Super 82
MD-83: Further thrust increase and more fuel in cargo compartments; formerly DC-9 Super 83
MD-87: Shorter-fuselage version with extended tailfin
MD-88: Enhanced relative of MD-82 with EFIS, FMS, and IRS
MD-80 'Super Q': Noise reduction modification offered by Comtran and Jet Engineering
Blended winglets proposed by several companies to improve fuel efficiency

FEATURES:
Low/swept wings; twin rear-side fuselage-mounted P&W JT8D turbofans; swept T-tail and tailplane

Boeing (McDonnell Douglas) MD-90 USA

Twin-turbofan short-haul airliner

Stretched, high-technology MD-80 follow-on with IAE V2500 engines, improved cabin, and enlarged tailfin, launched on November 14, 1989. First flight on February 22, 1993, and service entry with Delta Air Lines on April 1, 1995. Total delivered: 114. Out of production.

SPECIFICATION (MD-90-30-ER):

ACCOMMODATION: 2 + 172
CARGO/BAGGAGE: 36.8 m³ (1300 cu.ft)
MAX SPEED: M0.76 (437 kt; 809 km/h)
RANGE: 2172 nm (4023 km)

DIMENSIONS:
WINGSPAN: 32.8 m (107 ft 8 in)
LENGTH: 46.5 m (152 ft 6 in)
HEIGHT: 9.3 m (30 ft 6 in)

VARIANTS:
MD-90-30: Baseline model
MD-90-30ER: Extended-range model with auxiliary fuel tank

FEATURES:
Low/swept wings; twin rear-side fuselage-mounted IAE V2500 turbofans; swept T-tail and tailplane

Bombardier Canadair CRJ100/200 CANADA

Twin-turbofan regional airliner

Developed from Challenger business jet with extended fuselage for regional airline operations. Formal go-ahead given on March 31, 1989, first flight on May 10, 1991. Initial delivery to Lufthansa CityLine on October 29, 1992. Total delivered: 1054.

SPECIFICATION (CRJ200ER):

ACCOMMODATION: 2 + 50
CARGO/BAGGAGE: 13.7 m³ (484 cu.ft)
MAX SPEED: M0.81 (465 kt; 860 km/h)
RANGE: 1645 nm (3046 km)

DIMENSIONS:
WINGSPAN: 21.2 m (69 ft 7 in)
LENGTH: 26.8 m (87 ft 10 in)
HEIGHT: 6.2 m (20 ft 5 in)

VARIANTS:
CRJ100: Original standard aircraft
CRJ100ER: Extended range derivative with additional fuel capacity
CRJ100LR: Long-range model with further fuel
CRJ200: Standard production aircraft
CRJ200ER: Extended range with optional increase in fuel capacity
CRJ200LR: Long-range variant
CRJ440: Version with 44 seats for U.S. market
Challenger 800: Executive transport for 5–19 passengers
Challenger 850: Corporate shuttle for 27–50 passengers

FEATURES:
Low/swept wings with winglets; high rear fuselage-mounted GE CF34 twin turbofans; swept T-tail and tailplane

Bombardier Canadair CRJ700/900 CANADA

Twin-turbofan regional airliner

Developed as 70-seat stretched derivative of CRJ200. First flown on May 27, 1999, with initial delivery to French regional Brit Air in February 2001. Further capacity increase to 90 seats in CRJ900, which made its maiden flight on February 21, 2001 and entered service with launch customer Mesa Air in January 2003. Total delivered: 266 (700), 75 (900); ordered 268 (700), 153 (900).

SPECIFICATION (CRJ700ER):

ACCOMMODATION: 2 + 78
CARGO/BAGGAGE: 23.3 m³ (824 cu.ft)
MAX SPEED: M0.83 (475 kt; 879 km/h)
RANGE: 1984 nm (3674 km)

DIMENSIONS:
WINGSPAN: 23.2 m (76 ft 3 in)
LENGTH: 32.5 m (106 ft 8 in)
HEIGHT: 7.6 m (24 ft 10 in)

VARIANTS:
CRJ700 Series 701: Standard 68-seat model
CRJ700 Series 705: Reduced capacity for U.S.
CRJ700ER: Extended-range model with increased weight and fuel
CRJ900: Minimum stretch for 86–90 passengers
CRJ900ER: Heavier extended-range model
CRJ900LR: Longer-range capability
CRJ900X: Stretch proposal for 98 passengers
Challenger 870: Corporate shuttle based on CRJ700
Challenger 890: Corporate shuttle based on CRJ900

FEATURES:
Low/swept wing with winglets; high rear fuselage-mounted GE CF34 twin turbofans; swept T-tail and tailplane

Embraer ERJ135/140/145 BRAZIL

Twin-turbofan regional airliner

Original development plans for regional twin-jet revealed at Paris Air Show in June 1989, but aircraft subsequently completely redesigned. First flight of ERJ145 on August 11, 1995, and first deliveries to U.S. launch customer Continental Express on December 19, 1996. Total delivered: 108 (135); 74 (140), 679 (145).

SPECIFICATION (ERJ145ER):

ACCOMMODATION: 2 + 50
CARGO/BAGGAGE: 14.8 m³ (521 cu.ft)
MAX SPEED: M0.78 (450 kt; 833 km/h)
RANGE: 1600 nm (2963 km)

DIMENSIONS:
WINGSPAN: 20.0 m (65 ft 9 in)
LENGTH: 29.9 m (98 ft 0 in)
HEIGHT: 6.8 m (22 ft 2 in)

VARIANTS:
ERJ135: Short-fuselage version
Legacy 600: Corporate variant of ERJ135
ERJ140: Mid-size version, primarily for U.S. market
ERJ145: Baseline model
ERJ145ER: Extended range with increased fuel
ERJ145EU: Customized for European operations
ERJ145LR: Long-range model with uprated engines and increased fuel
ERJ145XR: Extra-long range with other improvements
EMB-145SA: AEW version for Brazilian Air Force, designated R-99A
EMB-145RS: Remote-sensing version for Brazilian Air Force as R-99B

FEATURES:
Low/swept wing; twin rear fuselage-mounted Rolls-Royce Allison AE 3007A turbofans; swept T-tail with dorsal fin and swept tailplane

Embraer 170/175/190/195 BRAZIL

Twin-turbofan regional airliner

Higher-capacity development of ERJ145, announced February 1999. New design with podded wing-mounted turbofans and clean tail. First 170 (formerly ERJ170) rolled out October 28, 2001, with first flight February 19, 2002. Service entry immediately following FAA certification February 20, 2004. Embraer 175 flew on June 14, 2003, followed by 190 on March 12, 2004, and 195 on December 7, 2004. Total delivered: 125 (170), 53 (190), 3 (195).

SPECIFICATION (170):

ACCOMMODATION: 2 + 70
MAX SPEED: M0.80 (461 kt; 851 km/h)
RANGE: 1800 nm (3333 km)

DIMENSIONS:
WINGSPAN: 26.0 m (83 ft 4 in)
LENGTH: 29.9 m (98 ft 1 in)
HEIGHT: 9.7 m (31 ft 9 in)

VARIANTS:
170: Baseline version for 70 passengers
175: Stretch proposal for 78–86 passengers, reinforced wing, higher gross weight, enhanced management system
190: Further stretch for 98 passengers, strengthened landing gear
195: Lengthened fuselage for up to 108 passengers
Lineage 1000: Business jet for up to 19 passengers based on 190 model
Longer-range (LR) variants with additional fuel also offered

FEATURES:
Low/swept wing; twin underwing podded GE CFE34-8 turbofans; swept tailfin with small dorsal fin and swept tailplane

Fairchild Dornier 328JET GERMANY/USA

Twin-turbofan regional airliner

Jet-powered development of 328 turboprop aircraft, originally designated 328-300. Announced on February 5, 1997, and formally launched at Paris Air Show in June 1997. First flight on January 20, 1998; first delivery to Skyway Airlines in June 1999. Production was restarted by Avcraft Aerospace following bankruptcy of Fairchild Dornier, but Avcraft itself went bankrupt. Total delivered: 86.

SPECIFICATION (328JET):

ACCOMMODATION: 2 + 34
CARGO/BAGGAGE: 6.4 m³ (226 cu.ft)
MAX SPEED: M0.70 (405 kt; 750 km/h)
RANGE: 900 nm (1666 km)

DIMENSIONS:
WINGSPAN: 21.0 m (68 ft 10 in)
LENGTH: 21.3 m (69 ft 10 in)
HEIGHT: 7.2 m (23 ft 9 in)

VARIANTS:
328JET: Baseline regional transport for up to 34 passengers
Corporate Shuttle: High-density version for corporate transport
Envoy 3: Corporate version for up to 19 passengers

FEATURES:
High/straight wing with tapered leading edge; twin underwing P&WC PW300 turbofans; swept T-tail with dorsal fin and tapered tailplane

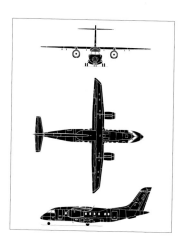

Fokker F28 Fellowship THE NETHERLANDS

Twin-turbofan regional airliner

Developed as a jet transport partner for the F27 turboprop, with first details published in April 1962. Made its maiden flight on May 9, 1967, and entered service with launch customer LTU of Germany on February 24, 1969. Total delivered: 241.

SPECIFICATION (F28 Mk 4000):

ACCOMMODATION: 2 + 85
CARGO/BAGGAGE: 15.8 m³ (560 cu.ft)
MAX SPEED: M0.75 (430 kt; 795 km/h)
RANGE: 1025 nm (1900 km)

DIMENSIONS:
WINGSPAN: 25.1 m (82 ft 3 in)
LENGTH: 29.6 m (97 ft 2 in)
HEIGHT: 8.5 m (27 ft 10 in)

VARIANTS:
F28 Mk 1000: Initial short-fuselage version for up to 65 passengers
F28 Mk 1000C: Convertible passenger/cargo model with large cargo door at front portside
F28 Mk 2000: Lengthened fuselage for up to 79 passengers
F28 Mk 3000: Short-fuselage model with new engines and increased span
F28 Mk 4000: Long-fuselage derivative for up to 85 passengers

FEATURES:
Low/swept wing; twin rear fuselage-mounted Rolls-Royce Spey turbofans; swept T-tail with dorsal fin and swept tailplane

Fokker 70/100 THE NETHERLANDS

Twin-turbofan short-haul regional airliner

New technology derivatives of F28, first announced on November 24, 1984, including new aerofoil, digital avionics, and greater use of composites. Prototype of Fokker 100 flew on November 30, 1986, with first delivery to Swissair on February 29, 1988. Smaller Fokker 70 made its first flight on April 2, 1993. Total delivered: 48 (70), 283 (100).

SPECIFICATION (Fokker 100):

ACCOMMODATION: 2 + 109
CARGO/BAGGAGE: 19.7 m³ (695 cu.ft)
MAX SPEED: M0.77 (441 kt; 816 km/h)
RANGE: 1550 nm (2870 km)

DIMENSIONS:
WINGSPAN: 28.1 m (92 ft 2 in)
LENGTH: 35.5 m (116 ft 6 in)
HEIGHT: 8.5 m (27 ft 10 in)

VARIANTS:
Fokker 70: Short-fuselage version for up to 79 passengers
Executive Jet 70: VIP/corporate shuttle version
Executive Jet 70ER: VIP/corporate shuttle with extended range
Fokker 100: Standard model for up to 109 passengers
Fokker 100CS: Corporate shuttle version
Fokker 100EJ: Executive conversion by Stork Aerospace with auxiliary fuel tank

FEATURES:
Low/swept wing; twin rear fuselage-mounted Rolls-Royce Tay turbofans; swept T-tail with dorsal fin and swept tailplane

Fokker 100

Ilyushin Il-62 "Classic" RUSSIA

Four-turbofan long-haul airliner

Developed to provide Aeroflot with long-haul jet airliner and unveiled on September 24, 1962, featuring four rear-mounted turbofan engines and high-tail layout. First flight on January 3, 1963, but did not enter service until September 15, 1967. Total delivered: 289.

SPECIFICATION (Il-62M):

ACCOMMODATION: 3 + 186
CARGO/BAGGAGE: 48.0 m³ (1695 cu.ft)
MAX SPEED: M0.85 (486 kt; 900 km/h)
RANGE: 4210 nm (7800 km)

DIMENSIONS:
WINGSPAN: 43.2 m (141 ft 9 in)
LENGTH: 53.1 m (174 ft 3 in)
HEIGHT: 12.4 m (40 ft 7 in)

VARIANTS:
Il-62: Initial production model with Kuznetsov NK-8 engines
Il-62M: Improved variant with Soloviev D-30KU engines
Il-62MK: Strengthened to permit operations at higher weights

FEATURES:
Low/swept wing; four rear-mounted NK-8 or D-30 turbofans, two on each side of the fuselage; swept T-tail and tailplane; prominent bullet fin fairing

Ilyushin Il-76 "Candid" RUSSIA

Four-turbofan medium/long-haul freighter

Developed in late 1960s to replace turboprop Antonov An-12 and made its first flight on March 25, 1971. Originally designed for and delivered to military customers, but many since converted for civil use. Low-rate production continues. Total built to date: c. 920.

SPECIFICATION (Il-76TD):

ACCOMODATION: 7 + 140 (troops)
CARGO: 50,000 kg (110,230 lb)
MAX SPEED: M0.77 (441 kt; 817 km/h)
RANGE: 1970 nm (3650 km)

DIMENSIONS:
WINGSPAN: 50.5 m (165 ft 8 in)
LENGTH: 46.6 m (152 ft 11 in)
HEIGHT: 14.8 m (48 ft 6 in)

VARIANTS:
Il-76MD: Incorporates improvements of Il-76TD
Il-76MDP: Firefighting version with two water/fire retardant tanks in hold
Il-76T: Civil conversion with additional fuel tankage
Il-76TD: Strengthened wings and center fuselage
Il-76TF: Civil-production version available from 1996; none sold
Plus several military models (which see)

FEATURES:
High/swept wing with slight anhedral; four Aviadvigatel D-30 turbofans; rear loading ramp/door; T-tail with swept-back tail surfaces; tricycle landing gear retracting into large side fairings

Ilyushin Il-86 "Camber" RUSSIA

Four-turbofan medium-haul airliner

First Soviet-built wide-body airliner intended as successor to Il-62, and first to have wing-mounted engines. Made first flight on December 22, 1976, and entered Aeroflot service on December 26, 1980. Performance shortfall resulted in curtailed production run. Total delivered: 103.

SPECIFICATION:

ACCOMMODATION: 3 + 350
MAX SPEED: M0.89 (512 kt; 950 km/h)
RANGE: 1944 nm (3600 km)

DIMENSIONS:
WINGSPAN: 48.1 m (157 ft 9 in)
LENGTH: 59.5 m (195 ft 4 in)
HEIGHT: 15.8 m (51 ft 10 in)

VARIANTS:
Il-86: Standard production model continuously updated but not redesignated
Il-87 "Maxdome": Airborne strategic command post version with large boat-shaped fairing above forward fuselage and large pod with ram air intake under each inner wing

FEATURES:
Low/swept wing; four underwing Kuznetsov NK-86 turbofans; swept tailfin and swept low-set tailplane; wide-body fuselage

Ilyushin Il-96 RUSSIA

Four-turbofan long-haul airliner

Developed from the Il-86 to provide improved performance and increased range, featuring a new supercritical wing and large winglets. Made its first flight on September 28, 1988, and entered Aeroflot service in early 1993. Program dogged by lack of funding and only 18 delivered to date.

SPECIFICATION (Il-96M):

ACCOMMODATION: 3 + 386
CARGO/BAGGAGE: 115.9 m³ (4094 cu.ft)
MAX SPEED: M0.86 (493 kt; 912 km/h)
RANGE: 6195 nm (11,482 km)

DIMENSIONS:
WINGSPAN: 60.1 m (197 ft 3 in)
LENGTH: 64.7 m (212 ft 3 in)
HEIGHT: 15.7 m (51 ft 7 in)

VARIANTS:
Il-96-300: Initial production version
Il-96PU: VIP model built for Russian president
Il-96-400: Stretched and extended-range passenger model
Il-96-400T: Freighter with cargo door forward of wing on portside

FEATURES:
Low/swept wing with large winglets; four underwing PS-90A turbofans; swept tailfin and low-set tailplane; wide-body fuselage

Lockheed L1011 TriStar USA

Three-turbofan medium-haul airliner

Developed to an American Airlines requirement for a high-capacity aircraft with transcontinental range and able to take off from comparatively short runways. First flown on November 17, 1970, the TriStar entered revenue service with Eastern Air Lines on April 26, 1972. Total delivered: 250.

SPECIFICATION (L1011-500):

ACCOMMODATION: 3 + 330
CARGO/BAGGAGE: 118.9 m³ (4200 cu.ft)
MAX SPEED: M0.84 (481 kt; 890 km/h)
RANGE: 5297 nm (9815 km)

DIMENSIONS:
WINGSPAN: 47.3 m (155 ft 4 in)
LENGTH: 50.1 m (164 ft 3 in)
HEIGHT: 16.9 m (55 ft 4 in)

VARIANTS:
L1011-1: Initial production version
L1011-50: Conversion of TriStar 1 with higher operating weight
L1011-100: Higher gross weight and fuel capacity
L1011-150: Conversion of TriStar 1 to increase range capability
L1011-200: Uprated engines and higher gross weight
L1011-250: Converted TriStar 1 with same engines as Model 500
L1011-500: Shorter fuselage, long range with aerodynamic improvements

FEATURES:
Low/swept wings; three Rolls-Royce RB 211 turbofans, two on pylons under wing, the third at base of and integrated with swept tailfin; low-set swept tailplane; wide-body fuselage

McDonnell Douglas DC-8 USA

Four-engined medium/long-haul airliner

First Douglas commercial jet launched in June 1955, featuring, like the Boeing 707, four turbojets under the wing. Made maiden flight on May 30, 1958, and entered service simultaneously with Delta Air Lines and United on September 18, 1959. Total delivered: 293.

SPECIFICATION (DC-8-50):

ACCOMMODATION: 3 + 179
CARGO/BAGGAGE: 39.4 m³ (1390 cu.ft)
MAX SPEED: M0.88 (505 kt; 934 km/h)
RANGE: 6078 nm (11,260 km)

DIMENSIONS:
WINGSPAN: 43.4 m (142 ft 5 in)
LENGTH: 45.9 m (150 ft 6 in)
HEIGHT: 12.9 m (42 ft 4 in)

VARIANTS:
DC-8-10: Initial production version for domestic routes
DC-8-20: Long range with more powerful P&W JT4A turbojets
DC-8-30: Intercontinental range with uprated engines
DC-8-40: Similar to Series 30 but with Rolls-Royce Conway engines
DC-8-50: Similar to Series 30 but with P&W JT3D turbofans
DC-8F-55: Freighter with cargo door and strengthened floor

FEATURES:
Low/swept wing; four underwing P&W JT3C or JT4A or Rolls-Royce Conway turbojets, or P&W JT3D turbofans; swept tailfin and low-set tailplane; auxiliary chin intakes

McDonnell Douglas DC-8 "Super Sixty" USA

Four-turbofan long-haul airliner

Launched in April 1965 as follow-on from one-size initial DC-8 series with considerably lengthened fuselage and various aerodynamic improvements. First flight made on March 14, 1966, with service entry on February 25 the following year. Total delivered: 263.

SPECIFICATION (DC-8-63):

ACCOMMODATION: 2 + 259
CARGO/BAGGAGE: 70.8 m³ (2500 cu.ft)
MAX SPEED: M0.91 (521 kt; 965 km/h)
RANGE: 4000 nm (7400 km)

DIMENSIONS:

WINGSPAN: 45.2 m (148 ft 5 in)
LENGTH: 57.1 m (187 ft 5 in)
HEIGHT: 12.9 m (42 ft 5 in)

VARIANTS:

DC-8-61: First stretched variant for 259 passengers
DC-8-62: Shorter fuselage than -61, ultra-long-range capability
DC-8-63: Combines long fuselage of -61 with powerplant of -62
Convertible (CF) and all-freighters (AF) available in all three models
DC-8-71: Re-engined Series 61 with new CFM56-2 turbofans
DC-8-72: Re-engined Series 62 with new CFM56-2 turbofans
DC-8-73: Re-engined Series 63 with new CFM56-2 turbofans

FEATURES:

Low/swept wing; four underwing P&W JT3D or CFM56-2 turbofans; swept tailfin and low-set tailplane; auxiliary chin intakes; long slim fuselage

McDonnell Douglas DC-9 USA

Twin-turbofan short/medium-haul airliner

Design studies of a short/medium-range aircraft with twin rear-mounted turbofans as partner to the DC-8 were released in 1962, leading to the official launch on April 8, 1963. First flight on February 25, 1965, with service entry with Delta following on December 8, that year. Total delivered: 976.

SPECIFICATION (DC-9-50):

ACCOMMODATION: 2 + 139
CARGO/BAGGAGE: 29.3 m³ (1034 cu.ft)
MAX SPEED: M0.87 (500 kt; 926 km/h)
RANGE: 1795 nm (3326 km)

DIMENSIONS:
WINGSPAN: 28.5 m (93 ft 5 in)
LENGTH: 40.7 m (133 ft 7 in)
HEIGHT: 8.5 m (28 ft 0 in)

VARIANTS:
DC-9-10: Initial production version with two engine options
DC-9-15MC: Multiple-change convertible with forward port cargo door
DC-9-15RC: Rapid-change version with roller floor and cargo door
DC-9-20: Hot-and-high model combining wings of Series 30 and short fuselage of Series 10
DC-9-30: Longer fuselage, uprated engines, and high-lift devices
DC-9-30CF: Convertible freighter, no cargo door, for small packages
DC-9-30F: Freighter with no windows, formerly DC-9-30AF
DC-9-40: Further stretch, uprated engines, and increased fuel
DC-9-50: Longest model with new interior
Plus military models under C-9A, C-9B and VC-9C designation (which see)

FEATURES:
Low/swept wing; twin rear fuselage-mounted P&W JT8D turbofans; swept T-tail and tailplane

McDonnell Douglas DC-10 USA

Three-turbofan medium/long-haul airliner

Developed from an American Airlines specification of March 1966 for a so-called "jumbo twin", but eventually became a larger capacity tri-jet. Launched in April 1968 and made its first flew August 29, 1970. Entered service with launch customer American Airlines on August 5, 1971. Total delivered (including military): 446.

SPECIFICATION (DC-10-30):

ACCOMMODATION: 3 + 380
CARGO/BAGGAGE: 103 m³ (3655 cu.ft)
MAX SPEED: M0.88 (505 kt; 934 km/h)
RANGE: 4000 nm (7413 km)

DIMENSIONS:
WINGSPAN: 50.4 m (165 ft 5 in)
LENGTH: 55.5 m (182 ft 1 in)
HEIGHT: 17.7 m (58 ft 1 in)

VARIANTS:
DC-10-10: Initial GE CF6-powered U.S. domestic
DC-10-10CF: Convertible, forward side cargo door
DC-10-15: Hot-and-high model with uprated engines
DC-10-30: Heavier and more powerful long-range model
DC-10-30CF: Convertible, forward side cargo door
DC-10-30ER: Extended range with higher weights and fuel capacity
DC-10-30F: Pure freighter without cabin windows
DC-10-40: Version with P&W JT9D turbofans, formerly Series 20
MD-10: Advanced freighter conversion with two-crew cockpit
Plus military KC-10A tankers (which see)

FEATURES:
Low/swept wing; three GE CF6 or P&W JT9D turbofans, two on underwing pylons, the third above rear fuselage near base of swept tailfin; swept low-set tailplane; wide-body fuselage; additional two-wheel landing gear on centerline of Series 30 only

SATIC Super Transporter (Beluga) FRANCE/GERMANY/SPAIN/UK

Twin-turboprop outsize freight transport

Announced in December 1990 as re-placement for Super Guppy to carry Airbus assemblies between manufac-turing plants. Based on Airbus A300-600 with enlarged unpressurized upper fuselage and upward-hinged door above flight deck. First flown September 13, 1994, and entered service in January 1996. Military cargolifter also proposed but future uncertain. Total built to date: 5.

SPECIFICATION:

ACCOMMODATION: 4
CARGO: 47,300 kg (104,279 lb)
MAX SPEED: M0.70 (401 kt; 742 km/h)
RANGE: 900 nm (1666 km)

DIMENSIONS:
WINGSPAN: 44.8 m (147 ft 0 in)
LENGTH: 56.2 m (184 ft 4 in)
HEIGHT: 17.2 m (56 ft 6 in)

VARIANTS:
A300-600ST: Basic and only model built to date

FEATURES:
Low/swept wing; twin GE CF6-80C2 turbofans; large cargo compartment with upward-opening nose section for front loading; flight deck below main cargo deck; raised fin and tailplane with large endplate fins

Tupolev Tu-134 "Crusty" RUSSIA

Twin-turbofan short-haul airliner

Rear-engined twin-turbofan development of the Tu-124, initially known as Tu-124A, started in early 1960s. Believed to have made its first flight in December 1963. Commercial services with Aeroflot began in September 1967. Total delivered: 850+.

SPECIFICATION (Tu-134A):

ACCOMMODATION: 3 + 96
MAX SPEED: M0.85 (485 kt; 897 km/h)
RANGE: 1630 nm (3020 km)

DIMENSIONS:
WINGSPAN: 29.0 m (95 ft 2 in)
LENGTH: 37.1 m (121 ft 7 in)
HEIGHT: 9.1 m (30 ft 0 in)

VARIANTS:
Tu-134: Initial production version with Soloviev D-30 turbofans
Tu-134A: Small stretch, uprated engines, and improved avionics
Tu-134A-3: Improved engines and new lightweight seats
Tu-134B: Spoilers for direct lift and forward-facing crew compartment
Tu-134B-1: Minor internal improvements
Tu-134B-3: Further internal revisions to increase seating
Plus various military models (which see)

FEATURES:
Low/swept wing; twin rear fuselage-mounted Soloviev D-30 turbofans; swept T-tail with dorsal fin and swept tailplane; early models have glazed nose

Tupolev Tu-154 "Careless" RUSSIA

Three-turbofan medium-haul airliner

Announced in spring 1966, the Tu-154 was designed to operate from poorly surfaced airfields. It made its first flight on October 4, 1968, and, after many proving and ad-hoc flights, entered commercial service with Aeroflot on February 9, 1972. Production now completed. Total delivered: 926.

SPECIFICATION (Tu-154M):

ACCOMMODATION: 3 + 180
CARGO/BAGGAGE: 43.0 m³ (1519 cu.ft)
MAX SPEED: M0.90 (515 kt; 953 km/h)
RANGE: 3723 nm (6900 km)

DIMENSIONS:
WINGSPAN: 37.6 m (123 ft 3 in)
LENGTH: 47.9 m (157 ft 2 in)
HEIGHT: 11.4 m (37 ft 5 in)

VARIANTS:
Tu-154: Initial production version
Tu-154A: Uprated engine, higher gross weight, and increased fuel
Tu-154B: Improved version with new avionics and cabin interior
Tu-154B-2: Western flight control and navigation system
Tu-154C: Freighter with forward portside cargo door and roller tracks
Tu-154M-LK-1: Head-of-state use
Tu-154M: More powerful D-30KU engines, redesigned lifting devices
Tu-156M: Cryogenic-fuel development

FEATURES:
Low/swept anhedral wing; three Soloviev D-30 rear-mounted turbofans, one each side of rear fuselage, third atop fuselage in base of tailfin; swept T-tail with bullet fin fairing and swept tailplane

Tupolev Tu-204/214 RUSSIA

Twin-turbofan medium-haul airliner

Developed to replace the Tu-154 and Il-62 and first announced in 1983. Conventionally designed aircraft with twin underwing turbofans and winglets, the Tu-204 made its maiden flight with PS-90AT engines on January 2, 1989. Initially used for freight, but first passenger flight operated by Vnukovo Airlines on February 23, 1996. Total delivered: 17.

SPECIFICATION (Tu-214):

ACCOMMODATION: 2 + 212
CARGO/BAGGAGE: 26.4 m³ (932 cu.ft)
MAX SPEED: M0.80 (459 kt; 850 km/h)
RANGE: 2591 nm (4800 km)

DIMENSIONS:
WINGSPAN: 41.8 m (137 ft 2 in)
LENGTH: 46.1 m (151 ft 3 in)
HEIGHT: 13.9 m (45 ft 7 in)

VARIANTS:
Tu-204: Basic model with PS-90A turbofans
Tu-204C: Basic freighter model
Tu-204-100: Extended-range version with additional fuel in wing
Tu-204-120: As -100, but with Rolls-Royce RB 211-535 turbofans
Tu-204-300: Shortened, longer-range derivative, formerly Tu-234
Tu-204-500: Enhanced version with smaller wing and higher MTOW under development
Tu-214: As -100, higher gross weight, formerly Tu-204-200
All models are available as freighters with C suffix

FEATURES:
Low/swept wing with large winglets; twin underwing Aviadvigatel PS-90A or R-R RB 211-535 turbofans; swept tailfin and low-set tailplane

Tupolev Tu-334 RUSSIA

Twin-turbofan short/medium-haul regional jet

Launched in 1986 as replacement for Tu-134, but funding shortages delayed first flight to February 8, 1999. Much commonality with Tu-204, incl-uding identical cockpit. Certification was expected by end of 2001, with service entry late 2002/early 2003, but this has been further delayed. Provisional certification obtained December 30, 2003, but aircraft not yet in production. Total ordered: 24.

SPECIFICATION (Tu-334-100D):

ACCOMMODATION: 2 + 102
CARGO/BAGGAGE: 16.2 m³ (572 cu.ft)
MAX SPEED: M0.77 (442 kt; 820 km/h)
RANGE: 2213 nm (4100 km)

DIMENSIONS:

WINGSPAN: 32.6 m (107 ft 0 in)
LENGTH: 31.8 m (104 ft 4 in)
HEIGHT: 9.4 m (30 ft 9 in)

VARIANTS:

Tu-334-100: Basic version with Ivchenko Progress D-436T1 engines
Tu-334-100C: Combi version
Tu-334-100D: Extended range, increased wingspan, and uprated engines
Tu-334-120: As -100, but R-R Deutschland BR710 turbofans
Tu-334-120D: As -100D, but R-R Deutschland BR710 turbofans
Tu-334-200: Extended fuselage and increased span; also known as Tu-354
Tu-334-200C: Freighter

FEATURES:

Low/swept wing with winglets; twin rear fuselage-mounted Ivchenko Progress D-436 or R-R Deutschland BR710 turbofans; swept T-tail with dorsal fin and swept tailplane

Yakovlev Yak-40 "Codling" RUSSIA

Three-turbofan short-haul regional jet

Designed to replace the Lisunov Li-2 and to operate from grass airfields. Made first flight on October 21, 1966, and entered passenger service with Aeroflot on September 30, 1968. Clam-shell thrust reverser added on center engine during production run. Total delivered: 1000+.

SPECIFICATION:

ACCOMMODATION: 2 + 32
MAX SPEED: M0.70 (401 kt; 742 km/h)
RANGE: 971 nm (1800 km)

DIMENSIONS:
WINGSPAN: 25.0 m (82 ft 0 in)
LENGTH: 20.4 m (66 ft 10 in)
HEIGHT: 6.5 m (21 ft 4 in)

VARIANTS:
Yak-40: Basic production model
Yak-40EC: Export version with Westernized avionics
Yak-40K: Passenger/cargo model
Yak-40V: Export version with AI-25T engines and higher gross weight

FEATURES:
Low/straight wing; three Ivchenko (Lotarev) AI-25 turbofans, two on side of rear fuselage, one atop at base of and integrated with tailfin; swept T-tail and tailplane; ventral access

Yakovlev Yak-42 "Clobber" RUSSIA

Three turbofan short/medium-haul airliner

Developed as medium-capacity aircraft for Aeroflot. Closely resembling in configuration the smaller Yak-40, the new type made its first flight on March 7, 1975, and began passenger flights in late 1980. Total delivered: 200+.

SPECIFICATION (Yak-42D):

ACCOMMODATION: 2 + 120
CARGO/BAGGAGE: 29.3 m³ (1035 cu.ft)
MAX SPEED: M0.76 (437 kt; 810 km/h)
RANGE: 1240 nm (2300 km)

DIMENSIONS:
WINGSPAN: 34.9 m (114 ft 6 in)
LENGTH: 36.2 m (118 ft 10 in)
HEIGHT: 9.8 m (32 ft 3 in)

VARIANTS:
Yak-42: Initial standard production model
Yak-42A: Improved version with increased fuel capacity and new Russian avionics
Yak-42D: Current production with increased range and forward passenger door
Yak-42D-100: Western avionics
Yak-42-200: Projected stretch for 150 passengers
Yak-42T: Projected freighter with cargo door

FEATURES:
Low/swept wing; three Ivchenko Progress D-36 turbofans, one on each side of rear fuselage, the third atop at base of and integrated with tailfin; swept T-tail and tailplane

Civil Prop Airliners

Airtech (EADS CASA/Indonesian Aerospace) CN-235

SPAIN/INDONESIA

Twin-turboprop short-haul airliner

Preliminary design began in January 1980, with one prototype built by each country. The Spanish-built model flew on November 11, 1983, followed by the Indonesian aircraft on December 30 that year. Merpati Nusantara Airlines put the type into commercial service on March 1, 1988. Total delivered (including military): 221.

SPECIFICATION (CN-235-200):

ACCOMMODATION: 2 + 44
CARGO/BAGGAGE: 5.3 m³ (187 cu.ft)
MAX SPEED: 240 kt (445 km/h)
RANGE: 860 nm (1593 km)

DIMENSIONS:
WINGSPAN: 25.8 m (84 ft 8 in)
LENGTH: 21.4 m (70 ft 3 in)
HEIGHT: 8.20 m (26 ft 10 in)

VARIANTS:
CN-235-10: Initial production aircraft with CT7-7A engines
CN-235-100: Improved CT7-9C with composite nacelles and enhanced systems; built in Spain
CN-235-110: As –100, but built in Indonesia
CN-235-200: Higher weight and increased range; built in Spain
CN-235-220: As –200, but built in Indonesia
CN-235-300: More powerful GE CT7-9C3 engines for improved hot-and-high performance
Civil versions are available in passenger, cargo, or quick-change layouts
Plus various military models (which see)

FEATURES:
High/straight wing; twin wing-mounted GE CT7 turboprops with four-bladed propeller; rear ramp/cargo door; swept tail unit with dorsal fin; straight low-set tailplane

Antonov An-24 "Coke" UKRAINE

Twin-turboprop short-haul airliner

First developed in 1958 to replace large numbers of piston-engined twins used on internal routes in the Soviet Union, and made its maiden flight in April 1960. Service entry with Aeroflot took place in September 1963. Type later license-produced in China as the Y-7. Total delivered: 1100+.

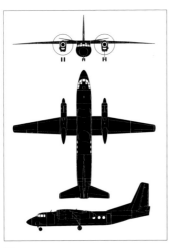

SPECIFICATION (An-24V):

ACCOMMODATION: 3 + 52
CARGO/BAGGAGE: 61.0 m³ (2150 cu.ft)
MAX SPEED: 243 kt (450 km/h)
RANGE: 1297 nm (2400 km)

DIMENSIONS:
WINGSPAN: 29.2 m (95 ft 10 in)
LENGTH: 23.5 m (77 ft 2 in)
HEIGHT: 8.3 m (27 ft 3 in)

VARIANTS:
An-24P: Firefighting version
An-24RT: As An-24T, but with auxiliary turbojets in starboard engine nacelle
An-24V: Initial production version with Ivchenko AI-24 engines
An-24V Series 2: Improved AI-24A engines, increased chord on wing center section and larger flaps
An-24RV: As An-24V, but with auxiliary turbojet
An-30: Optimized for aerial survey work
Plus many military derivatives under An-24, An-26, and An-32 designations (which see)

FEATURES:
High/straight wing; twin Ivchenko AI-24 turboprops with four-blade propellers; swept dorsal fin; slight dihedral on low-set tailplane

Antonov An-140 UKRAINE

Twin-turboprop short-haul transport

Announced at Paris Air Show in June 1993 as An-24 replacement and designed to operate from unprepared runways at all altitudes and in all weathers, with airline-style comfort. Conventional high-wing layout. First flight on September 17, 1997, with first deliveries to Odessa Airlines in March 2002. Built in Russia, Ukraine, and Iran. Total delivered: 12.

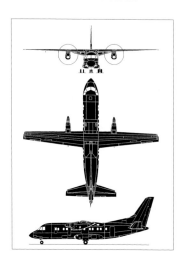

SPECIFICATION (An-140-100):

ACCOMMODATION: 2 + 52
CARGO/BAGGAGE: 9.0 m³ (318 cu.ft)
MAX SPEED: 310 kt (575 km/h)
RANGE: 1349 nm (2500 km)

DIMENSIONS:
WINGSPAN: 25.5 m (83 ft 8 in)
LENGTH: 22.6 m (74 ft 2 in)
HEIGHT: 8.2 m (26 ft 11 in)

VARIANTS:
An-140A: Basic regional airline version
An-140T: Proposed freighter with large portside cargo door
An-140TK: Convertible, similar to An-140T
An-140-100: Improved model with small increase in wingspan and MTOW
IrAn-140: Model being built under license in Iran by HESA
Plus several military models proposed

FEATURES:
High/straight wing; twin AI-30 turboprops with six-blade propellers; swept tailfin with large dorsal fin; low-set straight tailplane

Avions de Transport Régional ATR 42 FRANCE/ITALY

Twin-turboprop short-haul regional airliner

Jointly launched by Aerospatiale and Aeritalia in October 1981, the ATR 42 made its maiden flight on August 16, 1984. Deliveries began on December 3, 1985, to French regional Air Littoral, which began revenue service with the type on December 9. Command Airways became the first U.S. operator in March 1986. Total delivered: 390 (ordered 401).

SPECIFICATION (ATR 42-500):

ACCOMMODATION: 2 + 50
CARGO/BAGGAGE: 9.6 m³ (340 cu.ft)
MAX SPEED: 300 kt (556 km/h)
RANGE: 840 nm (1555 km)

DIMENSIONS:
WINGSPAN: 24.6 m (80 ft 8 in)
LENGTH: 22.7 m (74 ft 5 in)
HEIGHT: 7.6 m (24 ft 11 in)

VARIANTS:
ATR 42-300: Initial production version with PW120 turboprops
ATR 42-320: Optional PW121 engines for improved hot-and-high performance
ATR 42-400: Improved PW121As and six-blade propellers
ATR 42-500: More powerful PW127E engines, reinforced wings, and higher weights
ATR 42L: Freighter with lateral cargo door
ATR 42 Tube: Quick-change interior
ATR 42 Large Cargo Door: Upward-opening cargo door in front port fuselage
Plus several military derivatives

FEATURES:
High/straight wing; twin wing-mounted PW127E turboprops with four-bladed propeller; swept double-cranked fin and T-tail with straight tailplane

Avions de Transport Régional ATR 72 FRANCE/ITALY

Twin-turboprop short-haul regional airliner

Stretched version of ATR 42 announced at 1985 Paris Air Show and launched on January 15, 1986. First flight was made on October 27, 1988, and Finnish airline Karair received the first of the new type on October 27, 1989. Total delivered: 323 (ordered 436).

SPECIFICATION (ATR 72-500):

ACCOMMODATION: 2 + 74
CARGO/BAGGAGE: 10.6 m³ (375 cu.ft)
MAX SPEED: 275 kt (509 km/h)
RANGE: 910 nm (1685 km)

DIMENSIONS:

WINGSPAN: 27.1 m (88 ft 9 in)
LENGTH: 27.2 m (89 ft 2 in)
HEIGHT: 7.7 m (25 ft 2 in)

VARIANTS:

ATR 72-200: Original production version with PW124B turboprops
ATR 72-210: Improved hot-and-high performance with uprated PW127s
ATR 72-500: Higher weights and improved airfield performance; previously referred to as ATR 72-210A

FEATURES:

High/straight wing; twin wing-mounted PW127F turboprops with six-bladed propeller; swept double-cranked fin and T-tail with straight tailplane

BAe (Hawker Siddeley) 748 UK

Twin-turboprop short-haul transport

Developed from the Avro 748 high-wing design of the mid-1950s, but had adopted a low-wing configuration and Rolls-Royce Dart turboprops by the time of the first flight on June 24, 1960. Entered service with British airline Skyways in 1962. Total delivered: 379.

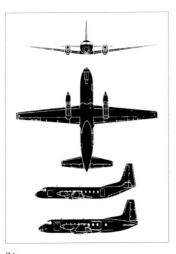

SPECIFICATION:

ACCOMMODATION: 2 + 58
CARGO/BAGGAGE: 9.55 m³ (337 cu.ft)
MAX SPEED: 244 kt (452 km/h)
RANGE: 926 nm (1715 km)

DIMENSIONS:
WINGSPAN: 31.2 m (102 ft 5 in)
LENGTH: 20.4 m (67 ft 0 in)
HEIGHT: 7.6 m (24 ft 11 in)

VARIANTS:
748 Series 1: Initial production version with Rolls-Royce RDa6 Dart engines
748 Series 2: Uprated Rolls-Royce RDa7 Dart engines
748 Series 2A: More powerful RDa7 Darts, a few with RDa8s
748 Series 2B: Improved and refined model with increased span, new engines and hushkit option
748 Series 2C: Series 2A with large cargo door in port rear fuselage
Super 748: Improved version with new cockpit and cabin interior
Plus military derivatives known as Andover and Coastguarder

FEATURES:
Low/straight wing; twin wing-mounted Rolls-Royce Dart turboprop engines with four-bladed propeller; stepped engine nacelles; tailfin with large dorsal fin; low-set tailplane

BAe ATP UK

Twin-turboprop short-haul regional airliner

Conceived as a stretched and modernized 748, the ATP (Advanced Turboprop) used the basic wing of the 748 with a longer fuselage of the same cross-section and new PW124 engines. It was announced in September 1982 and made its first flight on August 6, 1986. British Midland flew the first service on August 9, 1988. First converted freighter flew on July 10, 2002. Total delivered: 64.

SPECIFICATION:

ACCOMMODATION: 2 + 68
CARGO/BAGGAGE: 13.8 m³ (485 cu.ft)
MAX SPEED: 271 kt (502 km/h)
RANGE: 619 nm (1146 km)

DIMENSIONS:

WINGSPAN: 30.6 m (100 ft 6 in)
LENGTH: 26.0 m (85 ft 4 in)
HEIGHT: 7.6 m (24 ft 11 in)

VARIANTS:

ATP: Only production version
ATPF: Freighter conversion with large sliding cargo door in port rear fuselage
Jetstream 61: Improved version certificated on June 16, 1995, but never put into production

FEATURES:

Low/straight wing; twin wing-mounted PW127D turboprops with six-bladed propellers; swept tailfin with large dorsal fin; low-set tailplane

BAe Jetstream 31 UK

Twin-turboprop short-haul commuter

Originally a Handley Page product dating back to 1965, but major update was initiated by British Aerospace in December 1978. Exterior remained similar, but BAe introduced new technology propellers, revised cockpit, and new interiors and systems. First Jetstream 31 flew on March 28, 1980. German airline Contact Air took delivery on December 15, 1982. Total delivered: 381.

SPECIFICATION:

ACCOMMODATION: 2 + 19
CARGO/BAGGAGE: 2.5 m³ (89 cu.ft)
MAX SPEED: 263 kt (488 km/h)
RANGE: 680 nm (1260 km)

DIMENSIONS:

WINGSPAN: 15.9 m (52 ft 0 in)
LENGTH: 14.4 m (47 ft 2 in)
HEIGHT: 5.4 m (17 ft 8 in)

VARIANTS:

Jetstream 31: Basic production model
Jetstream 32: Significant improvements in performance and passenger comfort; also known as Jetstream Super 31
Jetstream 32EP: Enhanced-performance upgrade package
Jetstream 31EZ: EEZ patrol version
Corporate: Executive version for 9–10 passengers
Executive Shuttle: Executive company transport for 12 passengers
Plus quick-change and military trainers

FEATURES:

Low/straight wing; twin wing-mounted Garrett TPE331 turboprops with four-blade propellers; swept fin with mid-mounted tailplane

BAe Jetstream 41 UK

Twin-turboprop short-haul commuter

A stretched adaptation of the Jetstream 31 for up to 29 passengers, the Jetstream 41 was announced on May 24, 1989, and launched on a risk-sharing basis. It features uprated engines, EFIS, rear baggage door, and aerodynamic improvements. First flown on September 25, 1991, it entered service with Loganair and Manx Airlines, both of which took delivery on November 25, 1992. Total delivered: 106.

SPECIFICATION:

ACCOMMODATION: 2 + 29
CARGO/BAGGAGE: 6.2 m³ (218 cu.ft)
MAX SPEED: 295 kt (547 km/h)
RANGE: 775 nm (1434 km)

DIMENSIONS:
WINGSPAN: 18.4 m (60 ft 5 in)
LENGTH: 19.3 m (63 ft 2 in)
HEIGHT: 5.6 m (18 ft 5 in)

VARIANTS:
Jetstream 41: Basic airliner model
Jetstream 41F: Freighter conversion launched with capacity for 3–4 tonnes
Corporate Shuttle: Executive version for 8–14 passengers
Plus combi, quick-change and special role models

FEATURES:
Low/straight wing; twin wing-mounted Garrett TPE331 turboprops with five-blade propellers; swept fin with mid-mounted tailplane

Beech 99 USA

Twin-turboprop short-haul commuter

Developed from the twin-piston
Queen Air to enter the commuter
airline market. With a fuselage
lengthened to accommodate 15
passengers, the Beech 99 made its
first flight in December 1965 and
entered service with the aptly
named Commuter Airlines in May
1968. Total delivered: 239.

SPECIFICATION:

ACCOMMODATION: 2 + 15
CARGO/BAGGAGE: 1.7 m³ (60 cu.ft)
MAX SPEED: 268 kt (496 km/h)
RANGE: 578 nm (1072 km)

DIMENSIONS:
WINGSPAN: 14.0 m (45 ft 11 in)
LENGTH: 13.6 m (44 ft 7 in)
HEIGHT: 4.4 m (14 ft 5 in)

VARIANTS:
Beech 99: Initial production model with P&WC
PT6A-20 engines
Beech A99: More powerful PT6A-27 engines
Beech B99: Higher gross weight
Beech C99 Airliner: Improved version for dedicated
commuter-airline operations
Plus executive versions

FEATURES:
Low/straight wing; twin wing-mounted PT6A
turboprops with three-blade propellers; swept
tailfin and low-set swept tailplane

Beech 1900 USA

Twin-turboprop short-haul commuter

Developed for commuter market as successor to Beech 99. Two versions built, including the 13-seat Beech 1300, and the 19-seat 1900, based on the Super King Air, but with a lengthened fuselage. The 1900 made its maiden flight September 3, 1982 and entered service with Bar Harbor Airlines in February 1984. Total delivered: 248 (1900C); 690 (1900D).

SPECIFICATION (1900D):

ACCOMMODATION: 2 + 19
CARGO/BAGGAGE: 6.25 m³ (224 cu.ft)
MAX SPEED: 283 kt (524 km/h)
RANGE: 1476 nm 92,733 km)

DIMENSIONS:
WINGSPAN: 17.7 m (58 ft 0 in)
LENGTH: 17.6 m (57 ft 10 in)
HEIGHT: 4.7 m (15 ft 6 in)

VARIANTS:
1900C: Initial production version with passenger door forward and upward-hinged cargo door at rear portside
1900 Exec-Liner: Corporate model
1900C-1: Increased fuel capacity and redesigned fuel system
1900D: More powerful engines, stand-up cabin, and ventral strakes for improved stability
1900D Executive: Custom-designed executive interior
C-12J: 1900C-1 for Air National Guard mission support

FEATURES:
Low/straight wing; twin P&WC PT6A turboprops with four-blade propellers; swept fin and tailplane with taillets on underside near tip; stabilon each side of rear fuselage; ventral strake (1900D only)

Bombardier (DHC) Dash 7 CANADA

Four-turboprop short-haul STOL airliner

Developed by de Havilland Canada with the backing of the Canadian government, targeted primarily at serving downtown STOLports, and featured a high-wing layout and high-lift system. The aircraft took off on its first flight on March 27, 1975, and entered service with U.S. carrier Rocky Mountain Airways on February 3, 1978. Total delivered: 111.

SPECIFICATION:

ACCOMMODATION: 2 + 54
CARGO/BAGGAGE: 6.8 m³ (240 cu.ft)
MAX SPEED: 213 kt (427 km/h)
RANGE: 1170 nm (2168 km)

DIMENSIONS:
WINGSPAN: 28.4 m (93 ft 0 in)
LENGTH: 24.5 m (80 ft 6 in)
HEIGHT: 8.0 m (26 ft 2 in)

VARIANTS:
Series 100: Basic production model
Series 101: All-cargo or mixed version with large forward freight door in portside
Series 150: Higher weights and fuel increase for extended range
Series 151: All-cargo or mixed passenger/cargo derivative
IR Ranger: Ice reconnaissance model for Canadian government

FEATURES:
High/straight wing; four wing-mounted P&WC PT6A turboprops with four-bladed propellers; swept T-tail with large dorsal fin and straight tailplane

Bombardier (DHC) Dash 8 CANADA

Twin-turboprop short-haul regional airliner

Follow-on to the Dash 7 with similar external configuration, but only two powerful new P&WC PW100 engines. Launched in 1980, the Dash 8 first flew on June 20, 1983, and entered revenue service with NorOntair on December 19, 1984. Total delivered: 761 (ordered 843).

SPECIFICATION (Srs 300):

ACCOMMODATION: 2 + 56
CARGO/BAGGAGE: 8.0 m³ (280 cu.ft)
MAX SPEED: 285 kt (528 km/h)
RANGE: 700 nm (1297 km)

DIMENSIONS:
WINGSPAN: 27.4 m (90 ft 0 in)
LENGTH: 25.7 m (84 ft 3 in)
HEIGHT: 7.5 m (24 ft 7 in)

VARIANTS:
Srs 100: Initial production version with either PW120A or PW121 engines
Srs 100A: Restyled interior with more headroom
Srs 100B: PW121 standard for enhanced take-off/climb performance
Srs 200A: Faster and more powerful engines
Srs 200B: Improved engine for better hot-and-high performance
Srs 300: Extended wingtips and longer fuselage
Srs 300A: Improved payload/range performance
Srs 300B: Optional higher gross weight
Srs 300E: Further increase in performance at high temperatures
Srs 400: Final stretch for up to 78 passengers
Aircraft with noise and vibration suppression (NVS) System have Suffix Q

FEATURES:
High/straight wing; twin wing-mounted PW120 engines; swept T-tail with large dorsal fin and straight tailplane

Convair 580 USA

Twin-turboprop short-haul transport

During the late 1950s/early 1960s, many of the famous Convair 240/340/440 piston-engined airliners were converted to turboprop power. The most successful was the Convair 580, which first flew with Allison 501 engines on January 19, 1960, and entered airline service in June 1964. Total converted: 130.

SPECIFICATION:

ACCOMMODATION: 2 + 56
CARGO/BAGGAGE: 14.6 m³ (514 cu.ft)
MAX SPEED: 297 kt (550 km/h)
RANGE: 1970 nm (3650 km)

DIMENSIONS:

WINGSPAN: 32.1 m (105 ft 4 in)
LENGTH: 24.8 m (81 ft 6 in)
HEIGHT: 8.9 m (29 ft 2 in)

VARIANTS:

Model 580: Conversion of CV-340 and CV-440 with Allison 501D turboprops
Model 5800: Stretched conversion by Kelowna Flightcraft in Canada
Model 600: Conversion of CV-240 with Rolls-Royce Dart turboprops
Model 640: Conversion of CV-340 and CV-440 with Rolls-Royce Dart turboprops

FEATURES:

Low/straight wing; twin Allison 501 turboprops with four-blade propellers; curved tailfin with low-set straight tailplane

Douglas DC-3 USA

Twin-piston short-haul airliner

Design of this twin-engined airliner began in 1932 and led, via the DC-1 and DC-2, to the DC-3, which first flew on December 17, 1935. Some 430 were built for airliner use before WW II, when Douglas proceeded to build more than 10,000 for military use. After the end of the war, many found their way to commercial operators and several hundreds remain in service. Also built in USSR as the Lisunov Li-2.

SPECIFICATION:

ACCOMMODATION: 2 + 32
CARGO/BAGGAGE: 3.5 m³ (123 cu.ft)
MAX SPEED: 187 kt (346 km/h)
RANGE: 305 nm (563 km)

DIMENSIONS:
WINGSPAN: 29.0 m (95 ft 0 in)
LENGTH: 19.7 m (64 ft 6 in)
HEIGHT: 5.2 m (17 ft 0 in)

VARIANTS:
DC-3C: General designation for commercially operated versions
Super DC-3: Turboprop conversion
Plus many military variants under C-47, C-53, C-117, and R4D designations (which see)

FEATURES:
Low/tapered wing; twin wing-mounted P&W Twin Wasp piston engines; rounded tailfin with low-set tailplane; semiretractable landing gear with tailwheel

Douglas DC-4 USA

Four-piston medium-haul airliner

Larger and more advanced follow-up to the DC-3 with four engines and intercontinental range. It first flew in its definitive form on February 14, 1942, but was initially built for the U.S. forces as the C-54, before a dedicated civil version was produced after the war. Many war-surplus aircraft later found their way into commercial service.

SPECIFICATION:

ACCOMMODATION: 3 + 86
MAX SPEED: 244 kt (451 km/h)
RANGE: 1897 nm (3510 km)

DIMENSIONS:
WINGSPAN: 35 .8 m (117 ft 6 in)
LENGTH: 28.6 m (93 ft 10 in)
HEIGHT: 8.4 m (27 ft 6 in)

VARIANTS:
DC-4-1009: Civil version with accommodation for 44 passengers
DC-4-1037: Incorporated cargo door of C-54
DC-4M-1 North Star: Developed by Canadair with Rolls-Royce Merlin engines for Royal Canadian Air Force
DC-4M-2 North Star: Pressurized fuselage and square cabin windows
Plus more than 1000 built for the U.S. armed forces designated C-54

FEATURES:
Low/tapered wing; four wing-mounted P&W Twin Wasp piston engines; curved tailfin with large dorsal fin and low-set tailplane

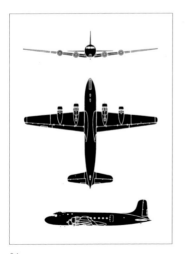

Douglas DC-6 USA

Four-piston medium-haul airliner

Successor to the DC-4 with substantially the same wing, but a lengthened fuselage, more powerful engines, and improved systems. The aircraft, as the XC-112, first flew on February 15, 1946, and entered airline service on April 27, 1947. Total delivered: 536.

SPECIFICATION (DC-6B):

ACCOMMODATION: 4 + 102
CARGO/BAGGAGE: 25.1 m³ (886 cu.ft)
MAX SPEED: 275 kt (509 km/h)
RANGE: 1650 nm (3058 km)

DIMENSIONS:
WINGSPAN: 35.8 m (117 ft 6 in)
LENGTH: 32.2 m (105 ft 7 in)
HEIGHT: 9.0 m (29 ft 3 in)

VARIANTS:
DC-6: Initial passenger version
DC-6A: Cargo model with lengthened and strengthened fuselage, two portside cargo doors, no cabin windows
DC-6B: Passenger equivalent of DC-6A
DC-6C: Convertible passenger/cargo model
Many passenger models later converted to cargo use with suffix F

FEATURES:
Low/tapered wing; four wing-mounted P&W Double Wasp piston engines; tall rounded tailfin with dorsal fin and low-set tailplane

Embraer EMB-110 Bandeirante BRAZIL

Twin-turboprop short-haul commuter

Developed in the 1960s to meet a requirement for the Brazilian Air Force, but later aimed at domestic commuter market. Built by EMBRAER, the first production Bandeirante (pioneer) with PT6A-20 engines flew on August 9, 1972, entering civil revenue service with Transbrasil on April 16, 1973. Total delivered: 494, including military versions.

SPECIFICATION (EMB-110P2):

ACCOMMODATION: 2 + 21
CARGO/BAGGAGE: 2.0 m³ (71 cu.ft)
MAX SPEED: 248 kt (459 km/h)
RANGE: 1060 nm (1964 km)

DIMENSIONS:
WINGSPAN: 15.3 m (50 ft 3 in)
LENGTH: 15.1 m (49 ft 7 in)
HEIGHT: 4.9 m (16 ft 2 in)

VARIANTS:
EMB-110C: First version for 15 passengers
EMB-110E/J: Seven-seat corporate transport
EMB-110P: Optimized for export with PT6A-27s and accommodation for 18 passengers
EMB-110P1: Mixed passenger/cargo model with aft freight-loading door and longer fuselage
EMB-110P1/41: Higher T-O weight to meet U.S. SFAR Pt 41
EMB-110P2: Airliner for up to 21 passengers
EMB-110P2/41: Optimized for U.S. SFAR Pt 41
Late changes to passenger comfort and handling resulted in the addition of suffix "A"
EMB-110S1: Geophysical survey version with wing-tip tanks
Plus a number of military versions under the EMB-110 and EMB-111 designations

FEATURES:
Low, straight wing; twin wing-mounted PT6A turboprops with three-bladed propellers; swept tailfin and low-set tailplane; ventral tailfin

Embraer EMB-120 Brasilia BRAZIL

Twin-turboprop short-haul commuter

Developed as a pressurized version of the Bandeirante for 30 passengers and officially launched in September 1979. The most notable external difference, apart from the length-ened fuselage, was a new T-tail. First flight was made on July 27, 1983 and the first production aircraft went into service in October 1985. Total delivered: 352.

SPECIFICATION:

ACCOMMODATION: 2 + 30
CARGO/BAGGAGE: 6.4 m³ (226 cu.ft)
MAX SPEED: 327 kt (606 km/h)
RANGE: 850 nm (1575 km)

DIMENSIONS:

WINGSPAN: 19.8 m (64 ft 11 in)
LENGTH: 20.1 m (65 ft 11 in)
HEIGHT: 6.4 m (20 ft 10 in)

VARIANTS:

EMB-120: Initial production model with P&WC PW115 engines
EMB-120RT: More powerful PW118s for reduced take-off
EMB-120ER: Aerodynamic improvements, re-designed cockpit, and higher cabin-comfort levels
Also available in all-cargo, combi and quick-change versions, and two military derivatives for AEW and remote sensing as the EMB-120SA and EMB-120RS respectively

FEATURES:

Low, straight wing; twin PW100 turboprops with four-blade propellers; all-swept T-tail with large dorsal fin

Fairchild F-27/FH-227 USA

Twin-turboprop short-haul airliner

License-built Fokker design intended as a DC-3 replacement. First U.S.-built production aircraft flew at Hagerstown, Maryland, on April 12, 1958, and entered service with West Coast Airlines on November 27, 1958. Total delivered: 207.

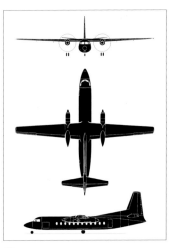

SPECIFICATION (F-27J):

ACCOMMODATION: 2 + 48
CARGO/BAGGAGE: 8.4 m³ (297 cu.ft)
MAX SPEED: 280 kt (520 km/h)
RANGE: 792 nm (1465 km)

DIMENSIONS:
WINGSPAN: 29.0 m (95 ft 2 in)
LENGTH: 23.5 m (77 ft 2 in)
HEIGHT: 8.4 m (27 ft 6 in)

VARIANTS:
F-27: Initial production model with Rolls-Royce Dart RDa6 engines
F-27A: Higher gross weight and uprated RDa7s
F-27B: Combi with forward side-loading cargo door, RDa6s
F-27F: As F-27A, for corporate use with more powerful RDa7s
F-27J: More powerful Dart RDa7 Mk 532-7 engines
F-27M: Dart Mk 532-7N engines, higher weight
FH-227: Stretched fuselage
FH-227B: Higher gross weight and strengthened structure

FEATURES:
High/straight wing; twin Rolls-Royce Dart turboprops with four-blade propellers; tailfin with large dorsal fin and low-set tailplane

Fairchild (Swearingen) Metro USA

Twin-turboprop short-haul commuter

Initially developed as a series of business aircraft by Ed Swearingen. Further refinements led to the Metro commuter aircraft, which first flew on August 26, 1969, and entered service in early 1971. In November that year, the Swearingen company was taken over by Fairchild, which continued to improve the aircraft until ceasing production in 1999. Total delivered (including military and corporate): 1053.

SPECIFICATION (Metro 23):

ACCOMMODATION: 2 + 20
CARGO/BAGGAGE: 5.05m² (179 sq.ft)
MAX SPEED: 290 kt (537 km/h)
RANGE: 540 nm (1000 km)

DIMENSIONS:
WINGSPAN: 17.4 m (57 ft 0 in)
LENGTH: 18.1 m (59 ft 5 in)
HEIGHT: 5.1 m (16 ft 8 in)

VARIANTS:
SA-226TC Metro: Initial production version
SA-226TC Metro II: Squared-off windows and optional rocket in tail for better hot-and-high performance
SA-226TC Metro IIA: Higher gross weight
SA-227AC Metro III: Uprated engines, increased wingspan with small wingtips, four-blade propellers
SA-227AC Metro IIIA: P&WC PT6A engines
Expediter: Large door in rear, reinforced floor
Metro 23: Improved final production model.
Each Metro version also produced in Merlin corporate configuration
C-26A: Transport for the U.S. National Guard
C-26B: Transport for the U.S. National Guard

FEATURES:
Low/straight wing; twin Honeywell (AlliedSignal) TPE331 or P&WC PT6A turboprops; three- or four-blade propellers; swept tailfin with large dorsal fin; mid-mounted swept tailplane

Fairchild Dornier 328 GERMANY

Twin-turboprop short-haul regional airliner

Growth version of 228 approved in late 1986, combining the TNT supercritical wing of the 228 with a new pressurized circular fuselage with stand-up cabin and T-tail; extensive use made of composites. First flight on December 6, 1991, and first delivery to Swiss regional Air Engiadina on October 21, 1993. Production halted in 2001 in favor of 328 JET. Total delivered: 112.

SPECIFICATION:

ACCOMMODATION: 2 + 33
CARGO/BAGGAGE: 6.3 m³ (223 cu.ft)
MAX SPEED: 335 kt (620 km/h)
RANGE: 900 nm (1666 km)

DIMENSIONS:
WINGSPAN: 21.0 m (68 ft 10 in)
LENGTH: 21.3 m (69 ft 10 in)
HEIGHT: 7.2 m (23 ft 9 in)

VARIANTS:
328-100: Initial production version
328-110: Increased weight and range, enlarged dorsal fin
328-120: Improved short-field performance, enlarged dorsal and ventral fins
328-130: Further improvements in take-off performance; rudder enhanced deflection system (REDS)

FEATURES:
High/straight wing; twin wing-mounted P&WC PW119 turboprops with six-blade propellers; T-tail

Fokker F27 Friendship THE NETHERLANDS

Twin-turboprop short-haul airliner

First postwar Fokker design intended as a DC-3 replacement. Prototype first flew on November 24, 1955, but progressively stretched to eventually provide seating for 50 passengers. Aircraft also built under license by Fairchild (which see). First Fokker-built F27 went into service with Aer Lingus in December 1958. Total delivered: 579.

SPECIFICATION (Mk 500):

ACCOMMODATION: 2 + 60
CARGO/BAGGAGE: 8.4 m³ (297 cu.ft)
MAX SPEED: 259 kt (480 km/h)
RANGE: 935 nm (1741 km)

DIMENSIONS:
WINGSPAN: 29.0 m (95 ft 2 in)
LENGTH: 25.1 m (82 ft 3 in)
HEIGHT: 8.7 m (28 ft 7 in)

VARIANTS:
F27 Mk 100: Initial production model with Rolls-Royce Dart RDa6 engines
F27 Mk 200: Higher gross weight and uprated RDa7 engines
F27 Mk 300: Combi with forward side-loading cargo door, RDa6s
F27 Mk 400: Combined cargo door with RDa7s
F27 Mk 500: Large cargo door and lengthened fuselage
F27 Mk 600: Quick-change with roller tracks and palletized seats
Military versions include the F27 Mk 400M Troopship for 46 troops with enlarged parachute door on each side, and F27 Maritime and F27 Maritime Enforcer, respectively unarmed and armed

FEATURES:
High/straight wing; twin Rolls-Royce Dart turboprops with four-blade propellers; tailfin with large dorsal fin and low-set tailplane

Fokker 50/60

Twin-turboprop short-haul airliner

Follow-on development of the F27 announced on November 24, 1983. Substantial application of new technology structure and systems; more than 80% of components new or modified. Rolls-Royce Darts replaced by modern P&WC PW120 engines. Fokker 50 first flew on December 28, 1985, and entered service on August 7, 1987. Stretched Fokker 60 launched in February 1994. Total delivered: 212.

SPECIFICATION (Fokker 50):

ACCOMMODATION: 2 + 58
CARGO/BAGGAGE: 8.4 m³ (297 cu.ft)
MAX SPEED: 290 kt (537 km/h)
RANGE: 1216 nm (2252 km)

DIMENSIONS:
WINGSPAN: 29.0 m (95 ft 2 in)
LENGTH: 25.3 m (82 ft 10 in)
HEIGHT: 8.3 m (27 ft 3 in)

VARIANTS:
Fokker 50: Baseline model with PW125B turboprops, three or four doors
Fokker 50 High Performance: Uprated PW127B engines for improved hot-and-high performance
Fokker 50 Utility: Three-door model with additional multi-purpose door and heavy-duty floor
Fokker 60: Stretched baseline version; none ordered
Fokker 60 Utility: As Fokker 50 Utility, but additional upward-opening starboard front cargo door; ordered only by Royal Netherlands Air Force

FEATURES:
High/straight wing; twin PW120 turboprops with six-blade composite propellers; tailfin with large dorsal fin and low-set tailplane

HAI Y-12 CHINA

Twin-turboprop short-haul commuter

Developed from the Y-11 utility aircraft. Main changes in the Y-12 (Y for "Yunshuji" or Transport Aircraft) included the installation of P&WC PT6A turboprops, new aerofoil sections, bonded construction, and integral fuel tanks. First of three prototypes flew on July 14, 1982, and entered service with local airlines sometime in 1986. Total delivered: 130+.

SPECIFICATION (Y-12 (IV)):

ACCOMMODATION: 2 + 19
CARGO/BAGGAGE: 2.7 m³ (95 cu.ft)
MAX SPEED: 162 kt (300 km/h)
RANGE: 707 kt (1310 km)

DIMENSIONS:

WINGSPAN: 19.2 m (63 ft 0 in)
LENGTH: 14.9 m (48 ft 9 in)
HEIGHT: 5.6 m (18 ft 4 in)

VARIANTS:

Y-12 (I): Initial production version with PT6A-11s
Y-12 (II): Higher-rated engines, no leading-edge slats, and smaller ventral fin
Y-12 (III): Improved version with swept back wingtips, starboard rear baggage door, Western avionics, and cabin enhancements
Y-12E: More powerful engines, four-bladed propeller, and new avionics
Y-12F: Pressurized proposal
Y-12G: Proposed freighter with side cargo door
Twin Panda: Y-12 (IV) with uprated PT6A-34 engines for North American market; abandoned

FEATURES:

High, straight and braced wing with small stub wings at cabin-floor level; twin P&WC PT6A turboprops with three-blade propeller; upswept rear fuselage; large dorsal fin; ventral fin under tailcone

Ilyushin Il-18 "Coot" RUSSIA

Four-turboprop medium-haul airliner

New-generation turboprop airliner developed to meet the needs of Aeroflot. The prototype first flew in July 1957, then named "Moskva," and the new type entered Aeroflot service on April 20, 1959. It was first available with either Kuznetsov NK-4 or Ivchenko AI-20 turboprops, but the latter was adopted as standard from the 21st production aircraft. Total delivered: 800+.

SPECIFICATION (Il-18D):

ACCOMMODATION: 5 + 122
CARGO/BAGGAGE: 29.3 m³ (1035 cu.ft)
MAX SPEED: 364 kt (675 km/h)
RANGE: 1997 nm (3700 km)

DIMENSIONS:

WINGSPAN: 37.4 m (122 ft 9 in)
LENGTH: 35.9 m (117 ft 9 in)
HEIGHT: 10.2 m (33 ft 4 in)

VARIANTS:

Il-18: Initial version with either NK-4 or AI-20 engines
Il-18D: Additional fuel in center bag tanks for increased range
Il-18E: More powerful AI-20M engine and redesigned cabin for 110 passengers
Il-18V: Major production version with AI-20K engines
Also used as military and VIP transport. After retirement from frontline passenger service, many Il-18s were converted for cargo use with a large freight door in the rear fuselage

FEATURES:

Low/straight wing; four AI-20 turboprop engines with four-blade propellers; deeper inner engine nacelles; tailfin with large dorsal fin and low-set tailplane

Ilyushin Il-114 RUSSIA

Twin-turboprop short-haul regional airliner

Designed as successor to the An-24. Design finalized in 1986 and prototype made its first flight at Khodinka on March 29, 1990. Accidents and withdrawal of government funding delayed program, and first commercial service by Uzbekistan Airways not until August 27, 1998. Total delivered: 15+.

SPECIFICATION:

ACCOMMODATION: 2 + 64
CARGO/BAGGAGE: 76.0 m³ (2684 cu.ft, Il-114T)
MAX SPEED: 270 kt (500 km/h)
RANGE: 540 nm (1000 km)

DIMENSIONS:

WINGSPAN: 30.0 m (98 ft 5 in)
LENGTH: 26.9 m (88 ft 2 in)
HEIGHT: 9.2 m (30 ft 2 in)

VARIANTS:

Il-114: Baseline aircraft with Klimov TV7-117 engines
Il-114FK: Military reconnaissance; ELINT and cartographic version under development
Il-114M: Increased T-O weight; TV7M-117s
Il-114MA: As Il-114M, but proposed with P&WC engines
Il-114MP: Maritime Patrol with R-R AE2100
Il-114P: Maritime patrol version; large cargo door at portside rear; slightly reshaped nose for radar
Il-114PR: SIGINT model announced October 2000
Il-114T: Cargo version with portside rear cargo door and removable roller floor
Il-114-100: P&WC PW127H turboprops and six-blade propellers

FEATURES:

Low/straight wing; twin TV7-117 turboprops with six-blade propellers; swept fin and low-set tailplane

Lockheed L188 Electra USA

Four-turboprop short/medium-haul airliner

Designed to an American Airlines specification for a 100-seater with a range of some 2000 nm. First of four prototypes flew on December 6, 1957, and the Electra entered service with launch customers Eastern Air Lines on January 12, 1959, and with American Airlines on January 23. Electra later developed into the successful P-3 Orion (which see). Total delivered: 170 (civil).

SPECIFICATION (L188A):

ACCOMMODATION: 3 + 98
CARGO/BAGGAGE: 15.0m³ (530 cu.ft)
MAX SPEED: 352 kt (652 km/h)
RANGE: 1910 nm (3534 km)

DIMENSIONS:
WINGSPAN: 30.2 m (99 ft 0 in)
LENGTH: 31.8 m (104 ft 6 in)
HEIGHT: 10.0 m (32 ft 10 in)

VARIANTS:
L188A: Initial production model
L188C: Higher fuel capacity for longer range
L188AF: Freighter or combi conversion of L188A with large port cargo door forward of the wing and strengthened floor
L188CF: Freighter or combi conversion of L188C with large port cargo door forward of the wing and strengthened floor

FEATURES:
Low/straight wing; four Allison 501 turboprops with four-blade propellers; curved tail with dorsal fin and low-set dihedral tailplane

NAMC YS-11 JAPAN

Twin-turboprop short-haul regional airliner

Japan's first indigenous civil airliner built by Nihon Aircraft Manufacturing Co. (NAMC), a joint venture between six airframers, primarily for domestic airlines. The prototype first flew on August 30, 1962, with deliveries to airlines starting in March 1965. Total delivered: 182.

SPECIFICATION (YS-11A-200):

ACCOMMODATION: 2 + 60
CARGO/BAGGAGE: 10.7 m3 (378 cu.ft)
MAX SPEED: 253 kt (469 km/h)
RANGE: 590 nm (1092 km)

DIMENSIONS:
WINGSPAN: 32.0 m (105 ft 0 in)
LENGTH: 26.3 m (86 ft 4 in)
HEIGHT: 9.0 m (29 ft 6 in)

VARIANTS:
YS-11: Initial production version, later known as YS-11-100
YS-11A-200: Higher operating weights and increased payload
YS-11A-300: Mixed passenger/cargo model with forward side-loading cargo door
YS-11A-400: All-cargo aircraft; used mostly by military
YS-11A-500: As YS-11A-200 but increased T-O weight
YS-11A-600: As YS-11A-300 but increased T-O weight

FEATURES:
Low/straight wing; twin Rolls-Royce Dart turboprops; tailfin with large dorsal fin and low-set tailplane

Saab 340 SWEDEN

Twin-turboprop short-haul regional airliner

Jointly developed by Saab and Fairchild as a 34-seat regional aircraft,
initially known as the SF-340. The
SF designation was dropped when
Fairchild pulled out. First of three
test aircraft flew on January 25,
1983, and entered service with
launch customer Crossair on June
15, 1984. Total delivered: 459.

SPECIFICATION (340B):

ACCOMMODATION: 2 + 37
CARGO/BAGGAGE: 8.3 m³ (293 cu.ft)
MAX SPEED: 282 kt (522 km/h)
RANGE: 870 nm (1611 km)

DIMENSIONS:
WINGSPAN: 22.8 m (74 ft 8 in)
LENGTH: 19.7 m (64 ft 8 in)
HEIGHT: 7.0 m (22 ft 11 in)

VARIANTS:
340A: Initial production model with GE CT7-5A
engines
340B: Higher weights and increased tailspan,
CT7-9Bs
340BPlus: New interior, active noise control, and
wing extensions for improved performance; quick-
change and corporate versions have also been
produced
340AEW&C: Reconnaissance version for the
Swedish Air Force with dorsal-mounted Erieye
side-looking radar
SAR-200: 340B
Plus rescue version for the Japan Maritime Safety
Agency

FEATURES:
Low/straight wing; twin GE CT7 turboprops with
four-blade propellers; swept tailfin with large dorsal
fin and dihedral tailplane

Saab 2000 SWEDEN

Twin-turboprop short/medium-haul regional airliner

Design definition for a larger regional aircraft to complement the 340 began in 1988. Against the general trend, Saab persisted with a turboprop rather than jet configuration, but providing high-speed with low operating costs. It was the wrong decision, and the 2000 sold only in small numbers until production ended in 1998. First flown on March 26, 1992, it entered service with launch customer Crossair in September 1994. Total delivered: 63.

SPECIFICATION:

ACCOMMODATION: 2 + 58
CARGO/BAGGAGE: 10.2 m³ (360 cu.ft)
MAX SPEED: 368 kt (682 km/h)
RANGE: 1200 nm (2222 km)

DIMENSIONS:
WINGSPAN: 24.8 m (81 ft 3 in)
LENGTH: 27.3 m (89 ft 6 in)
HEIGHT: 7.7 m (25 ft 4 in)

VARIANTS:
2000: Only version built for airline and corporate customers, with stretched fuselage and greater wingspan than the 340

FEATURES:
Low/straight wing; twin Rolls-Royce (Allison) AE 2100A turboprops with six-blade propellers; swept tailfin with large dorsal fin; low-set straight, dihedral tailplane

Shorts 330 UK

Twin-turboprop short-haul regional airliner

Developed from the Skyvan to tackle the emerging market of the 30-seat commuter airliner, the Shorts 330, initially referred to as the SD3-30, received formal go-ahead on May 23, 1973. The first prototype flew on August 22, 1974, and entered revenue service with Time Air in Canada on August 24, 1976. Total delivered: 139.

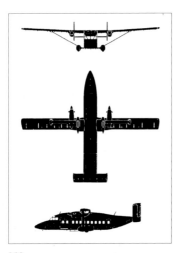

SPECIFICATION (330-200):

ACCOMMODATION: 2 + 30
CARGO/BAGGAGE: 4.1 m³ (145 cu.ft)
MAX SPEED: 190 kt (352 km/h0)
RANGE: 473 nm (876 km)

DIMENSIONS:
WINGSPAN: 22.8 m (74 ft 8 in)
LENGTH: 17.7 m (58 ft 0 in)
HEIGHT: 5.0 m (16 ft 3 in)

VARIANTS:
330-100: Initial production version continuously updated with various models of the PT6A turboprop
330-200: Increased fuel capacity for greater range
330-UTT: Utility tactical transport with strengthened floor, structural reinforcements and rear inward-opening cabin doors for paradropping
C-23A Sherpa: Military freighter for USAF with full-width rear ramp loading door, no cabin windows
C-23B: Utility version for U.S. Army National Guard; 11 cabin windows on each side

FEATURES:
High/straight braced wing; twin P&WC PT6A turboprops with five-blade propellers; square-section tapering fuselage; ramp in upswept rear fuselage in military versions; twin-tail unit

Shorts 360 UK
Twin-turboprop short-haul regional airliner

Developed from the 330 and stretched to take advantage of increased capacity allowed following deregulation in the U.S. Most notable difference from the 330 is the replacement of the twin tail with a conventional single fin. First flown on June 1, 1981, the 360 began revenue service with Suburban Airlines in the U.S. on December 1, 1982. Total delivered: 164.

SPECIFICATION (360-300):

ACCOMMODATION: 2 + 39
CARGO/BAGGAGE: 6.1 m³ (215 cu.ft)
MAX SPEED: 216 kt (400 km/h)
RANGE: 402 nm (745 km)

DIMENSIONS:
WINGSPAN: 22.8 m (74 ft 10 in)
LENGTH: 21.6 m (70 ft 10 in)
HEIGHT: 7.3 m (23 ft 11 in)

VARIANTS:
360-100: Initial production model, first known simply as 360
360-200: First referred to as 360 Advanced; introduced more powerful PT6A-65AR engines
360-300: New PT6A-67ARs, autopilot, and enhanced passenger appeal
360-300F: Freighter adaptation
C-23B+ Sherpa: Structural conversion for U.S. Army National Guard, basically to 330 configuration with twin-tail unit

FEATURES:
High, straight braced wing; twin P&WC PT6A turboprops with six-blade propellers; square-section, tapering fuselage; swept tailfin with dorsal fin and low-set straight tailplane

XAC Y7/MA60 CHINA

Twin-turboprop transport aircraft

Westernized version of Y7, which has been built in China since first flown on December 25, 1970, as a reverse-engineered model of the Antonov An-24. MA60 (Modern Ark 60) first flown as Y7-200A on December 26, 1993, and shown as MA60 for first time outside China at Asian Aerospace 2002 in Singapore. Total delivered: 100+ (Y7); 12 (MA60).

SPECIFICATION:

ACCOMMODATION: 2 + 60
CARGO/BAGGAGE: 11.2 m³ (395 cu.ft)
MAX SPEED: 248 kt (460 km/h)
RANGE: 1325 nm (2450 km)

DIMENSIONS:
WINGSPAN: 29.2 m (95 ft 10 in)
LENGTH: 24.7 m (81 ft 0 in)
HEIGHT: 8.9 m (29 ft 1 in)

VARIANTS:
Y7: Initial production version
Y7-100: Improved with winglets, new systems
Y7-200: New four-blade propellers, new avionics; winglets deleted
Y7H: Military cargo model with ramp/door; rough-field landing gear; derived from An-26
Y7H-500: Equivalent civil cargo version
MA40: Proposed shorter 40-seat variant of MA60
MA60: Development of Y7-200A, PW127 turboprops, Rockwell Collins avionics, APU, renovated cabin
MA60-100: Improved performance
MA60-500: Cargo version based on Y7H
MA60-MPA: Proposed military patrol aircraft, named Fearless Albatross

FEATURES:
High/straight wing with tapered leading edge; twin P&W PW127 turboprops with four-blade propellers; swept-back vertical tail with large dorsal fin; slight dihedral horizontal tailplane; retractable tricycle landing gear

Civil
Utility
Aircraft

Aeroprogress/ROKS-Aero T-101 Grach RUSSIA

Single-turbine utility aircraft

Designed as monoplane successor to Antonov An-2 and first flown on December 7, 1994. In limited-series production.

SPECIFICATION:

ACCOMMODATION: 1 + 9
CARGO/BAGGAGE: 1400 kg (3086 lb)
MAX SPEED: 162 kt (300 km/h)
RANGE: 685 nm (1270 km)

DIMENSIONS:
WINGSPAN: 18.2 m (59 ft 9 in)
LENGTH: 15.1 m (49 ft 5 in)
HEIGHT: 4.9 m (16 ft 0 in)

VARIANTS:
T-101: Basic passenger/cargo transport with Mars TVD-10B turboprop engine
T-101E: As T-101, but with P&WC PT6A turboprop
T-101L: Ski-landing gear
T-101P: Firefighting version; non-amphibious floats
T-101S: Military version with small stub wings with weapon pylons; two stores pylons under each wing
T-101SKh: Major redesign for agricultural work; strut-braced low wings and with spraybars under
T-501: Proposed twin-turboprop adaption

FEATURES:
Braced high/straight wing (low wing in T-101SKh); single Mars TVD-10 or P&WC PT6T turboshaft engine with three-blade propeller; nonretractable landing gear; swept-back fin with dorsal fin and low-set tailplane

Antonov An-2 "Colt" UKRAINE

Single-piston utility aircraft

Biplane designed to USSR Ministry specification for agricultural aircraft and first flown in 1947. Became all-round general-purpose aircraft; more than 5000 built before production moved to PZL-Mielec in Poland. Also license-built in China as the Shijiazhuang Y-5B. Total delivered: 17,000+.

SPECIFICATION:

ACCOMMODATION: 2 + 12
CARGO/BAGGAGE: 1500 kg (3307 lb)
MAX SPEED: 139 kt (258 km/h)
RANGE: 485 nm (897 km)

DIMENSIONS:

WINGSPAN (UPPER): 18.2 m (59 ft 8 in)
WINGSPAN (LOWER): 14.2 m (46 ft 8 in)
LENGTH: 13.0 m (42 ft 6 in)
HEIGHT: 4.2 m (13 ft 9 in)

VARIANTS:

An-2L: Water-bombing version
An-2M: Agricultural version
An-2P: Basic general-purpose aircraft with bulged side windows
An-2R: Polish designation of An-2S
An-2S: Agricultural version with long-stroke landing gear
An-2T: Polish-built mixed passenger/cargo version, equivalent to An-2P
An-2V: Floatplane version of An-2P
Plus many specialist variants for civil and military use
Antonov-3: TV-20 turboprop engine and other refinements

FEATURES:

Straight unequal-span biplane; single Shvetsov Ash-62 or PZL ASz-621 piston engine with four-blade propeller; nonretractable landing gear; round cabin windows; large rounded or squared-off tailfin with low-set tailplane

Antonov An-12 "Cub" UKRAINE

Four-turboprop cargo aircraft

Developed from the earlier passenger Antonov An-10, using the same airframe but with full-section rear doors. The An-12 flew for the first time in 1958 and entered service in 1959 with the Soviet armed forces, before also being used by Aeroflot and later sold to "friendly" airlines. Many now operated for commercial freight transport. Also built in China as the Y-8. Total delivered: 900+.

SPECIFICATION:

ACCOMMODATION: 5 + 100 (troops)
CARGO/BAGGAGE: 20,000 kg (44,090 lb)
MAX SPEED: 361 kt (670 km/h)
RANGE: 1940 nm (3600 km)

DIMENSIONS:
WINGSPAN: 38.0 m (124 ft 8 in)
LENGTH: 33.1 m (108 ft 7 in)
HEIGHT: 10.5 m (34 ft 6 in)

VARIANTS:
An-12BP: Original military version with twin gun turret at rear
An-12B: Dedicated civil version with turret removed
Plus other specialized military versions (which see)

FEATURES:
High/straight wing; four wing-mounted Ivchenko AI-20K turboprops with four-blade propellers; upswept rear fuselage with ramp/door for direct loading; large tailfin and dorsal fin with low-set tailplane; gun turret at rear of ex-military machines, otherwise faired over

Antonov An-38 UKRAINE

Twin-turboprop general-purpose aircraft

Details of high-wing light turboprop transport announced and model displayed at Paris Air Show in June 1991. Prototype made first flight on June 23, 1994, with Honeywell (Allied-Signal) TPE331 engines. Type entered service with Vostok Airlines following certification in April 1997. Produced in only small numbers to date.

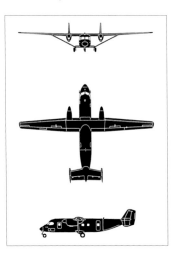

SPECIFICATION (An-38-100):

ACCOMMODATION: 2 + 27
CARGO/BAGGAGE: 2500 kg (5510 lb)
MAX SPEED: 219 kt (405 km/h)
RANGE: 486 nm (900 km)

DIMENSIONS:

WINGSPAN: 22.1 m (72 ft 5 in)
LENGTH: 15.7 m (51 ft 5 in)
HEIGHT: 5.0 m (16 ft 6 in)

VARIANTS:

An-38-100: Basic production model with Honeywell TPE331 turboprops
An-38-110: Reduced avionics fit
An-38-120: Enhanced avionics fit
An-38-200: With Omsk TVD-20 engines
An-38K: Convertible An-38-100 with large upward-hinged cargo door on portside at rear
Plus other options available, including forest patrol (An-38D), aerial photography (An-38F), survey (An-38GF), aerial ambulance (An-38S), and fishery/ice patrol (An-38LR)

FEATURES:

High/braced straight wing; twin wing-mounted Honeywell TPE-331 or Omsk TVD-20 turboprops with five-blade propellers; optional cargo door under upswept rear fuselage; twin tailfins

Beech 18 USA

Light utility transport

Development of this eight-seat commercial transport began in 1935. First flown on January 15, 1937, its production run was boosted by war requirements, with some 5000 built for the military. Production ceased in 1969. Total built: 9000+.

SPECIFICATION:

ACCOMMODATION: 2 + 6
MAX SPEED: 243 kt (450 km/h)
RANGE: 300 nm (555 km)

DIMENSIONS:
WINGSPAN: 15.1 m (49 ft 8 in)
LENGTH: 10.7 m (35 ft 3 in)
HEIGHT: 2.8 m (9 ft 4 in)

VARIANTS (MAJOR):
C18S: P&W Wasp Junior engines
D18S: Postwar civil model with streamlined nacelles
E18S: Roomier cabin with four enlarged windows, pointed nose; also known as Super 18
G18S: Panoramic center window, new cockpit
H18: Fully retracting mainwheels, optional tricycle undercarriage
Beech C-45: Major military designation, but many others used
Float and ski landing gear used frequently. Many later conversions undertaken, producing among others the Volpar Turboliner, Dumod, PAC Tradewind, and Hamilton Westwind

FEATURES:
Low/straight wing, tapered for most part; twin wing-mounted piston engines; cantilever tail unit with twin vertical fins; retractable tailwheel landing gear

Beech 65 Queen Air USA

Twin-piston light utility/commuter aircraft

Design of this large piston-twin started in April 1958, with first flight just four months later on August 28. The Queen Air combined the wing, tail, engines, and landing gear of the Twin Bonanza with a substantially larger fuselage. Total delivered (including military): 1001.

SPECIFICATION (65-B80):

ACCOMMODATION: 1 + 12
CARGO/BAGGAGE: 160 kg (350 lb)
MAX SPEED: 195 kt (362 km/h)
RANGE: 1055 nm (1950 km)

DIMENSIONS:
WINGSPAN: 15.3 m (50 ft 3 in)
LENGTH: 10.8 m (35 ft 6 in)
HEIGHT: 4.3 m (14 ft 3 in)

VARIANTS:
65 Queen Air: Initial production model with up to nine seats
A65 Queen Air: Fourth starboard cabin window; swept tail
A65-8200 Queen Air: A65 certificated at 8200 lb TOGW
70 Queen Air: Longer wingspan and seating for 11
65-80 Queen Air: Swept tail and more powerful engines
65-A80 Queen Air: Longer-span wing; increased weight; 11 seats
65-B80 Queen Air: Extra starboard window; higher weight; 13 seats
65-88 Queen Air: 10-seat pressurized cabin; porthole windows
65-A80-8800 Queen Airliner: Optimized for commuter operations
Also delivered to the U.S. Army as the U-8 Seminole, and to the JMSDF as navigation trainer

FEATURES:
Low/straight wing; twin Lycoming piston engines with three-blade propellers; three/four cabin windows; swept tailfin (except 65) and low-set tailplane; retractable tricycle landing gear

Beriev Be-103 RUSSIA

Six-seat twin-turboprop utility amphibian

Design of this light utility amphibian started in 1992, with first flight taking place at Taganrog on July 15, 1997. Prototype destroyed a month later, as was second prototype on April 29, 1999. Certificated to AP-23 Russian airworthiness standards in 2001, followed by U.S. FAR 23 in summer 2003. Production underway at KnAAPO at Komsomolsk-on-Amur. Total delivered: 10.

SPECIFICATION (Be-103):

ACCOMMODATION: 1+ 5
MAX SPEED: 130 kt (240 km/h)
RANGE: 600 nm (1110 km)

DIMENSIONS:
WINGSPAN: 12.7 m (41 ft 9 in)
LENGTH: 10.7 m (35 ft 0 in)
HEIGHT: 3.8 m (12 ft 4 in)

VARIANTS:
Be-103: Basic twin-engined production version for five passengers
SA-20P: Eight-seat single-engine derivative for local Russian market

FEATURES:
Low-mounted displacement wing of moderate sweep with large wingroot extensions; two-step boat hull but no stabilizing floats; horizontal strake each side of nose and vertical strake ahead of second hull step; Teledyne Continental engines mounted on horizontal pylons above and behind the wing; swept-back fin and rudder with mid-set tailplane

Beriev Be-200 Altair RUSSIA

Large twin-jet utility amphibian

Design of this multirole twin-jet amphibian initiated in 1989, but first flight from land not achieved until September 24, 1998; first water take-offs and landings on September 10, 1999. In small-scale production.

SPECIFICATION:

ACCOMMODATION: 2 + 72
CARGO/BAGGAGE: 84 m³ (2966 cu.ft)
MAX SPEED: 388 kt (720 km/h)
RANGE: 1000 nm (1850 km)

DIMENSIONS:
WINGSPAN: 32.8 m (107 ft 7 in)
LENGTH: 31.4 m (103 ft 1 in)
HEIGHT: 8.9 m (29 ft 2 in)

VARIANTS:
Be-200: Basic version available in passenger, cargo, ambulance, and patrol configurations
Be-200ChS: Firefighting version with tanks under cabin floor, retractable water scoops; jump door at rear of cabin on starboard side
Be-200P: Projected antisubmarine version
BE-200PS: SAR derivative with loudspeaker, searchlights, inflatable rafts, and motorboats
Be-210: Development for airline use with seating for 72 passengers; formerly known as Be-200M

FEATURES:
Swept wings with high-lift devices; single-step hull; all-swept T-tail; high-mounted ZMKB Progress D-436TP turbofan engines above the rear portion of center wing; strakes on each side of nose and by wings; large underwing pod each side of hull

Bombardier Canadair 415 CANADA

Twin-turboprop amphibian aircraft

Introduced as a follow-on to piston-engined CL-215 amphibious aircraft intended mainly for firefighting. Turboprop CL-415 officially launched on October 16, 1991. First flight on December 6, 1993, was followed by first deliveries in January 1995. Total delivered: 63.

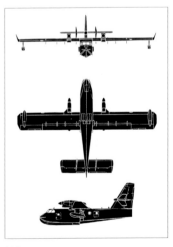

SPECIFICATION:

ACCOMMODATION: 2 + 14
CARGO/BAGGAGE: 6132 kg (13,500 lb)
MAX SPEED: 203 kt (376 km/h)
RANGE: 1310 nm (2426 km)

DIMENSIONS:

WINGSPAN: 28.6 m (93 ft 11 in)
LENGTH: 19.8 m (65 ft 0 in)
HEIGHT: 9.0 m (29 ft 6 in)

VARIANTS:

415: Standard production model in firefighting configuration
415GR: In service in Greece with boat-handling and cargo-hoist provisions
415M: Available for maritime, SAR, and special missions
415MP: Multipurpose verion with FLIR, SLAR, and nose-mounted search radar
215T: Turboprop retrofit of original piston-engined model; also some new-build aircraft

FEATURES:

High/straight wing with endplates; high-mounted twin P&WC PW123 turboprops with four-blade propeller; boat-hull fuselage; finlets and tailplane/fin bullet

Britten-Norman BN-2A Islander UK

Twin-piston or -turboprop light aircraft

Conceived by John Britten and Desmond Norman in early 1960s as rugged, low-cost general-purpose and commuter aircraft and first flown on June 13, 1965. First deliveries made to Glosair and Loganair in August 1967. Subsequently underwent several ownership changes. Total delivered: 1240.

SPECIFICATION (BN-2T):

ACCOMMODATION: 1 + 11
CARGO/BAGGAGE: 692 kg (1526 lb)
MAX SPEED: 170 kt (315 km/h)
RANGE: 1006 nm (1863 km)

DIMENSIONS:

WINGSPAN: 14.9 m (49 ft 0 in)
LENGTH: 10.9 m (35 ft 8 in)
HEIGHT: 4.2 m (13 ft 9 in)

VARIANTS:

BN-2 Islander: Initial production version
BN-2A Islander: Several product improvements
BN-2B Islander: Higher landing weight, extended span wingtips, improved interior, and various engine options
BN-2S: Islander: Long-nose variant with two more seats
BN-2T Turbine Islander: Allison 250 replacing Lycoming pistons
BN-2T-4R Defender: Military variant with four underwing hardpoints
BN-2T-4S Defender 4000: Enlarged wing and lengthened fuselage

FEATURES:

Straight/high wing with flared-up wingtips; twin Textron Lycoming piston or R-R (Allison) 250 turboprop engines with two-blade or three-blade propellers; swept tailfin with small dorsal fin and low-set tailplane; nonretractable tricycle landing gear with main leg mounted aft of rear wing spar

Britten-Norman BN-2A Mk III Trislander UK

Three-piston light aircraft

Design to "stretch" Islander began in 1968 and prototype flew on July 14, 1968. Additional power was needed and a third engine was then fitted at top of tailfin. It flew under the new configuration on September 11, 1970, and Aurigny Air Services took delivery of the first production aircraft on June 29, 1971. The Channel Islands–based airline remains the world's largest operator of the type. Total delivered: 85.

SPECIFICATION:

ACCOMMODATION: 2 + 16
CARGO/BAGGAGE: 1610 kg (3550 lb)
MAX SPEED: 156 kt (290 km/h)
RANGE: 868 nm (1610 km)

DIMENSIONS:

WINGSPAN: 16.2 m (53 ft 0 in)
LENGTH: 15.0 m (49 ft 3 in)
HEIGHT: 4.3 m (14 ft 2 in)

VARIANTS:

BN-2A Mk III Trislander: Initial production model
BN-2A Mk III-1 Trislander: Higher gross weight
BN-2A Mk III-2 Trislander: Long-nose version with additional baggage space
BN-2A Mk III-3 Trislander: Auto-feather system
Tri-Commutair: Trislander built under license by IAC in the U.S.; 12 completed

FEATURES:

High/straight wing with flared-up wingtips; three Textron Lycoming O-540 piston engines with two-blade propellers; third engine mounted high on tailfin together with tailplane; nonretractable tricycle landing gear

CASA C-212 Aviocar SPAIN

Twin-turboprop light aircraft

Developed in 1960s to meet Spanish Air Force requirement for tactical transport and first flown on March 26, 1971. Entered production for the Spanish Air Force, but CASA then designed 19-seat commuter aircraft for civil market. Also built under license by IPTN in Indonesia. Total delivered: 490.

SPECIFICATION (Series 200):

ACCOMMODATION: 2 + 24
CARGO/BAGGAGE: 2770 kg (6,107 lb)
MAX SPEED: 202 kt (374 km/h)
RANGE: 750 nm (1388 km)

DIMENSIONS:

WINGSPAN: 19.0 m (62 ft 4 in)
LENGTH: 15.2 m (49 ft 9 in)
HEIGHT: 6.3 m (20 ft 8 in)

VARIANTS:

C-212 CA: Initial civil variant with TPE331 turboprops
C-212 CB: Higher-gross-weight version
C-212 Series 100: TPE331-5 engines
C-212 Series 200: More powerful TPE331-10R and Dowty Rotol propellers; higher gross weight
C-212 Series 300: Updated engines; redesigned wingtips; more baggage space in nose
C-212-400: Improved model for hot-and-high conditions; higher payload
Plus military models for transport, ASW, maritime patrol, and ELINT/ECM (which see)

FEATURES:

High/straight wing; twin wing-mounted TPE331 turboprops with four-blade propellers; ramp/door in upswept rear fuselage; tailfin with large dorsal fin and low-set tailplane; nonretractable tricycle landing gear

Cessna 208 Caravan/Grand Caravan USA

Single-turboprop light aircraft

Launched in 1981 for passenger/cargo transport, but also aimed at a multitude of other roles. First flight of prototype was made on December 9, 1982, leading to full production from 1985, with early aircraft all delivered to Federal Express. Total delivered: 1591.

SPECIFICATION (Grand Caravan):

ACCOMMODATION: 1 + 13
CARGO/BAGGAGE: 1360 kg (3000 lb)
MAX SPEED: 175 kt (325 km/h)
RANGE: 960 nm (1776 km)

DIMENSIONS:
WINGSPAN: 15.9 m (52 ft 1 in)
LENGTH: 12.7 m (41 ft 8 in)
HEIGHT: 4.5 m (14 ft 10 in)

VARIANTS:
208 Caravan I: Basic utility version for passengers and cargo
208 Caravan Amphibian: Floats and tailplane finlets
208A Cargomaster: No windows and starboard door; underfuselage cargo pannier; extended tailfin
208B Super Cargomaster: Similar to 208A, but stretched fuselage and more powerful engine
Grand Caravan: 208B passenger version
Caravan 675: Combines 208 airframe with fully rated engine of 208B
Soloy Pathfinder 21: Dual-engine conversion
UC-27A: Military utility/special mission derivative of Model 208A

FEATURES:
Braced high/straight wing; single P&WC PT6A turboprop engine with three-blade propeller; swept tailfin with dorsal fillet; auxiliary fins on floatplane only; nonretractable tricycle landing gear or floats with or without retractable land wheels

de Havilland Canada DHC-2 Beaver/Turbo Beaver

CANADA

Single-piston/turboprop light STOL aircraft

First of a family of rugged STOL aircraft, the Beaver was designed for the Canadian wilderness. Work began in 1946 and the prototype first flew on August 16, 1947. Deliveries started to both civil and military customers following certification in March 1948. Turboprop development flew for the first time on December 30, 1963. Total built (including some 60 Turbo Beavers): 1692.

SPECIFICATION (Mk I):

ACCOMMODATION: 1 + 7
CARGO/BAGGAGE: 3.4 m³ (120 cu.ft)
MAX SPEED: 121 kt (225 km/h)
RANGE: 676 nm (1252 km)

DIMENSIONS:
WINGSPAN: 14.6 m (48 ft 0 in)
LENGTH: 9.2 m (30 ft 4 in); floatplane 10.0 m (32 ft 9 in)
HEIGHT: 2.8 m (9 ft 0 in); floatplane 3.2 m (10 ft 5 in)

VARIANTS:
Mk I Beaver: Standard production model available with wheeled, ski, and float landing gear
MK I Beaver Amphibian: Edo floats accommodating retractable main and nose wheels
Mk III Turbo Beaver: Turboprop version powered by the P&W PT6A
Plus military derivatives for U.S. Army as U-6A and British Army as AL.Mk I

FEATURES:
Braced high/straight wing; single P&W Wasp Junior piston or PT6A turboprop engine; rounded tail with large dorsal fin; nonretractable tailwheel type as standard, plus skis and floats (ventral strake under rear fuselage in amphibious version)

de Havilland Canada DHC-3 Otter CANADA

Single-piston light STOL aircraft

Larger development of successful Beaver with lengthened fuselage and greater wingspan. Design work on the Otter, originally known as the King Beaver, started in January 1951, culminating in the first flight on December 12 that year. The Otter went into commercial service a year later and was also used by the U.S. Army and other forces around the world. Total delivered: 460.

SPECIFICATION:

ACCOMMODATION: 1 + 11
CARGO/BAGGAGE: 3.8 m³ (134 cu.ft)
MAX SPEED: 140 kt (247 km/h)
RANGE: 760 nm (1410 km)

DIMENSIONS:
WINGSPAN: 17.7 m (58 ft 0 in)
LENGTH: 12.8 m (41 ft 10 in)
HEIGHT: 3.8 m (12 ft 7 in); floatplane 4.6 m (15 ft 0 in)

VARIANTS:
DHC-3 Otter: Standard production model available with wheeled, ski, and float landing gear
DHC-3 Otter Amphibian: Edo floats accommodating retractable main and nose wheels
Cox Turbo Single Otter: Small numbers of turboprop conversions by Cox Air Services with P&WC PT6A
Plus military derivatives for U.S. Army (as U-1A) and other customers simply with DHC-3 Otter designation

FEATURES:
Braced high/straight wing; single P&W piston engine; rounded tail with large dorsal fin; nonretractable tailwheel type as standard, plus skis and floats

de Havilland Canada DHC-6 Twin Otter CANADA

Twin-turboprop light aircraft

Design of this twin-engined development of the Otter began in January 1964, aimed specifically at the commercial operator requiring short take-off and landing (STOL) capabilities. First flight was on May 20, 1965 and first customer deliveries in July 1966. Total delivered: 842.

SPECIFICATION (Series 300):

ACCOMMODATION: 2 + 20
CARGO/BAGGAGE: 3.6 m³ (126 cu.ft)
MAX SPEED: 182 kt (338 km/h)
RANGE: 700 nm (1297 km)

DIMENSIONS:
WINGSPAN: 19.8 m (65 ft 0 in)
LENGTH: 15.8 m (51 ft 9 in)
HEIGHT: 5.9 m (19 ft 6 in)

VARIANTS:
Series 100: Initial production model
Series 200: Lengthened nose fairing with increased baggage space
Series 300: Uprated engines and improved payload/range
Series 300M: Basic military version available in transport and counterinsurgency roles
Series 300MR: Maritime reconnaissance model with chin-mounted radome and searchlight pod
Series 300S: Enhanced aerodynamics to operate from city-center STOLports
Series 400: New build with latest technologies, proposed by Viking Air, Canada

FEATURES:
Braced high/straight wing; twin wing-mounted P&WC PT6A turboprop engines with three-bladed propellers; swept tailfin with low-set tailplane; nonretractable tricycle landing gear

Dornier 228 GERMANY

Twin-turboprop light utility and commuter aircraft

Successor to the Do 28/128 with new-technology wing, turboprop engines, and generous use of composites in structure. Two versions with different lengths were developed in parallel and made their first flights on March 28 and May 9, 1981. Deliveries began in February 1982. Also built under license by Hindustan Aeronautics in India. Total delivered: 308.

SPECIFICATION (228-212):

ACCOMMODATION: 2 + 19
CARGO/BAGGAGE: 3.5 m³ (124 cu.ft)
MAX SPEED: 231 kt (428 km/h)
RANGE: 560 nm (1038 km)

DIMENSIONS:
WINGSPAN: 17.0 m (55 ft 8 in)
LENGTH: 16.6 m (54 ft 4 in)
HEIGHT: 4.9 m (16 ft 0 in)

VARIANTS:
228-100: Basic version for 15 passengers
228-101: Reinforced fuselage and new tyres to permit higher operating weights
228-200: Lengthened fuselage for 19 passengers
228-201: As -101, but lengthened fuselage
228-202: Further improvements in payload/range performance
228-212: Uprated engines, stronger landing gear, and new avionics
228 Maritime Patrol: Surveillance, SAR, and border and fisheries protection, with radar and bubble window for observer

FEATURES:
High/straight wing with tapered outer section and raked tips; twin wing-mounted Honeywell (AlliedSignal) TPE331 turboprops with four-blade propellers; long, pointed nose; swept tailfin with dorsal fin and low-set tailplane; retractable tricycle landing gear

GAF Nomad AUSTRALIA

Twin-turboprop light STOL aircraft

Development of small utility aircraft for civil and military roles began at the Government Aircraft Factories (GAF) in the mid-1960s. The high-wing monoplane flew for the first time on July 23, 1971, and went into service on December 18, 1975, with local commuter airline Aero Pelican. Total delivered: 170.

SPECIFICATION (N24A):

ACCOMMODATION: 2 + 17
CARGO/BAGGAGE: 1.13 m³ (40 cu.ft)
MAX SPEED: 169 kt (313 km/h)
RANGE: 580 nm (1074 km)

DIMENSIONS:
WINGSPAN: 16.5 m (54 ft 2 in)
LENGTH: 14.4 m (47 ft 2 in)
HEIGHT: 5.5 m (18 ft 2 in)

VARIANTS:
N22 Nomad: Initial production version
N22B Nomad: Standard short-fuselage version with higher gross weight
N24 Nomad: Lengthened for 17 passengers
N24A Nomad: Definitive version with increased gross weight
Floatmaster: Twin floats or amphibious gear
Medicmaster: Air-ambulance version
Missionmaster: Short-fuselage military version with four underwing pylons and drop doors in cabin floor
Searchmaster: Coastal patrol versions with search radar and scanner nose radome or undernose "guppy" radome
Surveymaster: Geological and geophysical research platform

FEATURES:
Braced high/straight wing; twin wing-mounted R-R (Allison) 250 turboprops with three-blade propellers; slab-sided fuselage upswept at rear; cranked tailfin with low-set tailplane

Gippsland GA8 Airvan AUSTRALIA

Single-piston light aircraft

Robust utility aircraft with short take-off and landing (STOL) capability. Prototype construction started in early 1994, with first flight on March 3, 1995, but aircraft destroyed during spinning trials on February 7, 1996. Two further prototypes completed leading to FAR Pt 23 certification on December 18, 2000. First delivery to Fraser Island Air four days later. Total deliveries: 84.

SPECIFICATION:

ACCOMMODATION: 1 + 7
CARGO/BAGGAGE: 90 kg (200 lb)
MAX SPEED: 130 kt (241 km/h)
RANGE: 730 nm (1350 km)

DIMENSIONS:
WINGSPAN: 12.4 m (40 ft 9 in)
LENGTH: 8.9 m (29 ft 3 in)
HEIGHT: 3.9 m (12 ft 9 in)

VARIANTS:
GA8 Airvan: Initial production model for passenger or freight use, or combination of the two

FEATURES:
Strut-braced high/straight wing; single Textron Lycoming IO-540 piston engine with two-blade propeller; swept-back vertical tailfin with dorsal fillet and straight rectangular tailplane; ventral finlet; nonretractable tricycle landing gear

Grob SPⁿ GERMANY

Twin-turbofan light utility and business aircraft

Twin-engined light business and utility jet of all-composite construction, capable of operating from all types of runways, including grass and gravel. It has a fully integrated all-glass cockpit and will be available with two standard luxury interiors designed by the Porsche Design Studio. First prototype flew in July 2005 and European EASA CS23 Commuter certification is expected in late 2007, followed by FAA FAR Pt 23 and first deliveries in early 2008. Total ordered: 30+.

SPECIFICATION:

ACCOMMODATION: 1 + 9 or 2 + 8
CARGO/BAGGAGE: 1.4 m³ (50.4 cu.ft)
MAX SPEED: 407 kt (754 km/h)
RANGE: 1170 nm (2167 km)

DIMENSIONS:
WINGSPAN: 14.9 m (48 ft 9 in)
LENGTH: 14.8 m (48 ft 7 in)
HEIGHT: 5.1 m (16 ft 10 in)

VARIANTS:
Grob SPⁿ: Initial production aircraft

FEATURES:
Slim fuselage with low/straight wing, prominent winglets, and conventional swept fin and low-set tailplane; twin rear-mounted Williams FJ44-3A turbofans; six cabin windows each side

Helio Courier USA

Single-piston light STOL aircraft

The Helio Courier, initially known as the Helioplane Four, first flew during 1953, with deliveries starting the following year. Continuous development resulted in many variants, all powered by Lycoming engines. Total delivered: 501.

SPECIFICATION (H-250):

ACCOMMODATION: 1 + 5
CARGO/BAGGAGE: 0.4 m³ (15 cu.ft)
MAX SPEED: 140 kt (257 km/h)
RANGE: 575 nm (1060 km/h)

DIMENSIONS:
WINGSPAN: 11.9 m (39 ft 0 in)
LENGTH: 9.5 m (31 ft 0 in)
HEIGHT: 2.7 m (18 ft 10 in)

VARIANTS:
H-391B Courier: Initial production model with GO-435 engine
H-392 Strato Courier: High-altitude version with GO-480 engine
H-395 Super Courier: Similar to H-391B, but more powerful engine
H-250 Courier II: Stretched fuselage with O-540
H-295 Super Courier: Similar to H-395
H-500 Helio Twin: Six-seat model, engines mounted on high wing
HST-550A Stallion: Turboprop version with PT6A
H-700 Courier: H-295 with new undercarriage and upturned wingtips
Plus various others built in small numbers and military derivatives under U-10 designation

FEATURES:
High/straight wing; single Lycoming piston engine with three-bladed propeller; swept tailfin with dorsal fin and low-set tailplane; nonretractable tailwheel-type landing gear

IAI Arava ISRAEL

Twin-turboprop light STOL aircraft

Design work began in 1966, with the objective to carry 25 troops into and out of short, unprepared airstrips. The result was a high-wing, short-fuselage aircraft with twin booms and tailfins. First flight was on November 27, 1969, and the type went into production in both civil and military versions. Total delivered: 90+.

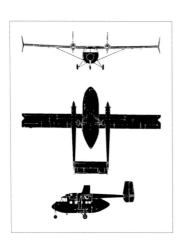

SPECIFICATION (Arava 102):

ACCOMMODATION: 2 + 20
CARGO/BAGGAGE: 5.8 m³ (205 cu.ft)
MAX SPEED: 176 kt (325 km/h)
RANGE: 540 nm (1000 km)

DIMENSIONS:
WINGSPAN: 21.0 m (68 ft 9 in)
LENGTH: 13.1 m (42 ft 9 in)
HEIGHT: 5.2 m (17 ft 1 in)

VARIANTS:
Arava 101B: Modified civil version with enhanced performance; marketed in the U.S. as the Cargo Commuterliner
Arava 102: Initial civil model with P&WC PT6A turboprops
Arava 201: Initial military transport, sold in greatest numbers
Arava 202: Upgraded and longer military derivative with "wet" wing and winglets; armed or unarmed; 24 troops

FEATURES:
Braced high/straight wing (endplate winglets on 202); twin wing-mounted P&WC PT6A turboprops with three-blade propellers; high-mounted twin booms with twin fins and rudders; nonretractable tricycle landing gear

Ibis Aerospace Ae 270 Spirit CZECH REPUBLIC/TAIWAN

Single-turboprop light transport

Announced by Aero Vodochody in Czechoslovakia in the early 1990s, initially designated L-270. Designed by Jan Mikula, the 9/10-passenger utility Ibis underwent several design changes prior to its first flight in July 2000. By that time, Ibis Aerospace had been set up as a joint venture between Aero Vodochody and AIDC of Taiwan. Certificated by EASA on December 12, 2005. Total ordered: 73.

SPECIFICATION (Ae 270P):

ACCOMMODATION: 2 + 8
CARGO/BAGGAGE: 1200 kg (2645 lb)
MAX SPEED: 206 kt (381 km/h)
RANGE: 1231 nm (2280 km)

DIMENSIONS:
WINGSPAN: 13.8 m (45 ft 3 in)
LENGTH: 12.2 m (40 ft 1 in)
HEIGHT: 4.8 m (15 ft 9 in)

VARIANTS:
Ae 270HP: High-performance production model with PT6A engine
Ae 270W: Walter M601F turboprop and Czech avionics; previously Ae 270U
Ae 270FP: Wheeled-float version of Ae 270P
Ae 270WP: Wheeled-float version of Ae 270W

FEATURES:
Low/straight dihedral wing with leading-edge taper; single P&WC PT6A turboprop engine with four-blade propeller; swept tailfin and low-set tailplane; retractable tricycle landing gear (wheeled floats optional)

Let L-410 Turbolet CZECH REPUBLIC

Twin-turboprop short-haul commuter and utility aircraft

After license production of Soviet types, the Let Kunovice works began design of a twin-engine transport to meet the needs of the Soviet Union and Eastern European satellite countries. The prototype first flew on April 16, 1969, initially powered by PT6A engines, replaced by Walter turboprops in production aircraft. The L-410 entered service with Slov-Air in late 1971. Total delivered: 1001.

SPECIFICATION (L-410UVP-E):

ACCOMMODATION: 2 +19
CARGO/BAGGAGE: 1.4 m³ (49 cu.ft)
MAX SPEED: 194 kt (360 km/h)
RANGE: 294 nm (546 km)

DIMENSIONS:
WINGSPAN: 20.0 m (65 ft 7 in)
LENGTH: 14.4 m (47 ft 4 in)
HEIGHT: 5.8 m (19 ft 1 in)

VARIANTS:
L-410A: Initial version with P&WC PT6A-27s
L-410AF: Aerial-survey model with glazed nose
L-410AS: Soviet avionics fit
L-410M: First production aircraft with the Walter M 601A
L-410MA: More powerful M 601B engines
L-410MU: Special equipment fit for Aeroflot
L-410UVP: Increased wingspan and aerodynamic changes
L-410UVP-E: Five-blade propellers, tip tanks, and more powerful engines
L-420: Upgraded version with more powerful Walter engines

FEATURES:
High/straight wing; twin wing-mounted P&WC/Walter PT6A or M 601 turboprops with three- or five-blade propellers; shallow dorsal fin and deeper ventral fin; tip tanks in UVP-E

Mitsubishi MU-2 JAPAN

Twin-turboprop STOL utility and business aircraft

Design of the twin-turboprop STOL aircraft was begun in 1960. It was first flown on September 14, 1963, with Turbomeca Astazou engines, but these were replaced by Garrett TPE331 engines, with which it was certificated on September 15 that year. Production ceased in 1986. Total delivered: 703.

SPECIFICATION (MU-2P):

ACCOMMODATION: 2 + 12
CARGO/BAGGAGE: 1.22 m³ (43 cu.ft)
MAX SPEED: 250 kt (465 km/h)
RANGE: 1460 nm (2700 km)

DIMENSIONS:
WINGSPAN: 11.9 m (39 ft 2 in)
LENGTH: 10.1 m (33 ft 3 in)
HEIGHT: 3.95 m (12 ft 11 in)

VARIANTS:
MU-2B: Initial production model
MU-2C: Reconnaissance variant for JGSDF
MU-2D: Additional fuel capacity; three with tip tanks as MU-2DP
MU-2E: SAR version for JASDF
MU-2F: Outer wing tanks for increased range
MU-2G: Stretched version
MU-2J: As MU-2G, but more powerful engine
MU-2K: Similar to MU-2J
MU-2L: Increased MTOW and more powerful engines
MU-2M: Short-body version of MU-2L
MU-2N: Long body; new engines and four-blade propellers
MU-2P: Short-body equivalent of MU-2N
Marquise: Long body with more powerful engines
Solitaire: Short body with more powerful engines
Various performance upgrades also available

FEATURES:
High/straight wing; several models with tip tanks; wing-mounted Garrett TPE331 turboprop engines; swept tailfin with low tailplane positioned on fuselage centerline; four large, square cabin windows

Lockheed L100 Hercules USA

Four-turboprop freight transport

The commercial Hercules originated as a civilianized version of the C-130 military tactical transport, which can be dated back to a USAF specification of 1951. A civil company demonstrator was first flown on April 21, 1964, and the L100 was put into production in 1965. It is used mostly for freight flights, although one customer used it in passenger configuration. Total built (civil only): 110.

SPECIFICATION (L100-30):

ACCOMMODATION: 3 + 128
CARGO/BAGGAGE: 23,158 kg (51,054 lb)
MAX SPEED: 315 kt (583 km/h)
RANGE: 1363 kg (2526 km)

DIMENSIONS:
WINGSPAN: 40.4 m (132 ft 7 in)
LENGTH: 34.4 m (112 ft 9 in)
HEIGHT: 11.7 m (38 ft 3 in)

VARIANTS:
L100-20: Similar to military C-130B, but uprated Allison D22A engines and lengthened fuselage
L100-30: Further fuselage stretch
Plus numerous military models (which see)

FEATURES:
High/straight wing; four wing-mounted Allison 501-D22A turboprops with four-blade propellers; upswept rear fuselage with loading ramp; tailfin with dorsal fillet and low-set tailplane; retractable tricycle landing gear

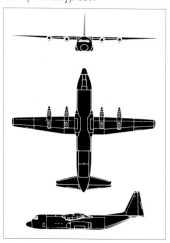

Pacific Aerospace 750XL NEW ZEALAND

Single-turboprop light utility aircraft

Developed from the Cresco agricultural and utility turboprop, work on this wide-body version with a single Pratt & Whitney Canada PT6A-34 engine began in January 2000. The prototype first flew September 5, 2001. Certification from the New Zealand CAA obtained August 20, 2003, and from the FAA March 2004, the 750XL becoming the first NZ-designed and -built aircraft to be accepted in the U.S. First customer delivery September 2003. Total delivered: 25+.

SPECIFICATION:

ACCOMMODATION: 2 + 9
CARGO/BAGGAGE: 3.8 m³ (134 cu.ft)
MAX SPEED: 155 kt (287 km/h)
RANGE: 595 nm (1100 km)

DIMENSIONS:
WINGSPAN: 12.8 m (42 ft 0 in)
LENGTH: 11.5 m (37 ft 7 in)
HEIGHT: 3.8 m (12 ft 7 in)

VARIANTS:
750XL: Initial production version

FEATURES:
Low/straight broad wing with outer dihedral; single P&WC PT6A turboprop engine with three-blade propeller; upright tapered tailfin with dorsal fillet; tailplane set low into rear fuselage; port freight door at rear; nonretractable tricycle landing gear

Pilatus PC-6 Porter/Turbo Porter SWITZERLAND

Single-piston/turboprop light STOL aircraft

Design of a single piston-engined general utility aircraft with STOL capability began in 1957. This resulted in the Porter braced high-wing taildragger, which first flew on May 4, 1959. Some 45 were built before being replaced by the Turbo Porter, which offered considerably improved performance. Some produced under license by Fairchild in the U.S. Total delivered: 534.

SPECIFICATION PC-6/B2-H4):

ACCOMMODATION: 1 + 10
CARGO/BAGGAGE: 945 kg (2083 lb)
MAX SPEED: 151 kt (280 km/h)
RANGE: 560 nm (1036 km)

DIMENSIONS:
WINGSPAN: 15.9 m (52 ft 1 in)
LENGTH: 11.0 m (35 ft 11 in)
HEIGHT: 3.2 m (10 ft 6 in)

VARIANTS:
PC-6: Basic Porter with Lycoming piston engine
PC-6/A-H1: Initial turboprop model with Turbomeca Astazou IIE
PC-6/A1-H2: More powerful Astazou XIIE engine
PC-6/B1-H2: First variant with P&WC PT6A turboprop
PC-6/B2-H2: Improved PT6A engine
PC-6/B2-H4: Strengthened airframe, enlarged dorsal fin, extended wingtips
PC-6/C1-H2: License-built with Garrett TPE331 turboprops
AU-23A2 Pacemaker and UV-20A Chiricahua are U.S. Army designations

FEATURES:
Braced high/straight wing; single P&WC PT6A turboprop with three-blade propeller; rectangular upright tailfin with dorsal fin and low-set tailplane; nonretractable tailwheel-type landing gear or floats with ground wheels

Pilatus PC-12 SWITZERLAND

Single-turbine light aircraft

Launched in October 1989 for executive use, its envelope was soon extended to cover the general utility market. The PC-12 (initially referred to as the PC-XII) made its maiden flight on May 31, 1991, and entered service in April 1994. Total delivered: 620.

SPECIFICATION:

ACCOMMODATION: 1 or 2 + 9
CARGO/BAGGAGE: 1.13 m³ (40 cu.ft)
MAX SPEED: 240 kt (444 km/h)
RANGE: 2261 nm (4187 km)

DIMENSIONS:
WINGSPAN: 16.2 m (53 ft 3 in)
LENGTH: 14.4 m (47 ft 3 in)
HEIGHT: 4.3 m (14 ft 0 in)

VARIANTS:
PC-12 Standard: Basic commuter or passenger/cargo combi
PC-12/45: Higher-gross-weight version
PC-12 Executive: Customized interior for up to six people
PC-12 Spectre: Surveillance and special-mission version with ventral pannier carrying E-O sensors (formerly Eagle)
PC-12M: Multimission development with enhanced equipment package
PC-12 Next Generation: More powerful PT6A-67P engines, integrated avionics and other advanced systems; available from end of 2007
U-28A: Designation for Special Operations Squadron of USAF

FEATURES:
Low/tapered wing with tiplets; single P&WC PT6A turboprop with four-blade propeller; T-tail with fin bullet fairing, enlarged dorsal fin, and ventral strakes; retractable tricycle landing gear

PZL (Antonov) An-28 POLAND

Twin-turboprop utility and commuter aircraft

Developed by Antonov in the former Soviet Union for Aeroflot and made its first flight as the An-28M in September 1969. A first pre-production aircraft did not fly until April 1978, after which sole production was assigned to PZL in Poland. The first Polish-built aircraft flew on July 22, 1984. Total delivered: 100+.

SPECIFICATION (Skytruck):

ACCOMMODATION: 2 + 18
CARGO/BAGGAGE: 2000 kg (4409 lb)
MAX SPEED: 178 kt (330 km/h)
RANGE: 736 nm (1365 km)

DIMENSIONS:
WINGSPAN: 22.1 m (72 ft 5 in)
LENGTH: 13.1 m (43 ft 0 in)
HEIGHT: 4.9 m (16 ft 1 in)

VARIANTS:
An-28: Basic commercial production version
An-28TD Bryza 1TD: Paradrop/transport version with rear clam-shell doors replaced by a single door sliding under fuselage
M-28B Bryza 1R: Maritime reconnaissance; formerly An-28RM
M-28M Bryza E: Twin rear doors and additional side door
M-28 Skytruck: Westernized development with P&WC PT6A turboprops and Honeywell avionics
M-28 Skytruck Plus: Stretched development with raised ceiling for both passenger and freight roles

FEATURES:
Braced high/straight wing with optional winglets; twin TVD-10 or P&WC PT6A turboprops with three-blade and five-blade propellers respectively; upswept rear fuselage incorporating clamshell doors; twin fins and rudder; short stub wing extending from lower fuselage to carry wing bracing and nonretractable tricycle landing gear

Quest Aircraft Kodiak USA

Single-turbine light STOL utility aircraft

High-wing utility aircraft optimized for operations from rough air strips, especially targeted at missionary and humanitarian work. First flight on October 16, 2004, and public debut at the Alaska State Aviation Trade Show in May 2005. Certification and first deliveries planned for late 2006/early 2007. Total ordered: 30+.

SPECIFICATION:

ACCOMMODATION: 1 + 9
CARGO/BAGGAGE: 1.8 m³ (63 cu.ft)
MAX SPEED: 190 kt (352 km/h)
RANGE: 1075 nm (1990 km)

DIMENSIONS:
WINGSPAN: 13.7 m (45 ft 0 in)
LENGTH: 16.9 m (55 ft 6 in)
HEIGHT: 4.7 m (15 ft 5 in)

VARIANTS:
Kodiak 100: Initial production version

FEATURES:
High-braced wing and wide-track landing gear; single P&WC PT6A-34 turboprop engine; tall swept-back fin with underfin, ventral fillet, and large rudder horn; underbelly pannier

Reims F406 Caravan II FRANCE

Twin-turboprop light multirole aircraft

Extrapolated from the Cessna Titan airframe and Conqest II wings and announced in mid-1982. Made its first flight in France on September 22, 1983, and entered service in 1985. Operated by a mix of commercial operators and government agencies. Total delivered: 96.

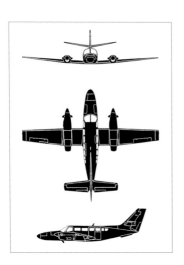

SPECIFICATION (Caravan II):

ACCOMMODATION: 2 + 12
CARGO/BAGGAGE: 1563 kg (3445 lb)
MAX SPEED: 229 kt (424 km/h)
RANGE: 1153 nm (2135 km)

DIMENSIONS:
WINGSPAN: 15.1 m (49 ft 6 in)
LENGTH: 11.9 m (39 ft 1 in)
HEIGHT: 4.0 m (13 ft 2 in)

VARIANTS:
F406 Caravan II: Basic passenger, freight, and utility version
F406 Mk II Caravan: New avionics and interior
Vigilant: Surveillance version with radar and FLIR
Vigilant Comint/Imint: Dedicated communication and imaging intelligence
Vigilant Frontier: Border patrol and anti-drug
Vigilant Polmar I, II, and III: Pollution surveillance with scanner and SLAR
Vigilant Surmar: Armed or unarmed maritime surveillance version
Vigilant Surpolmar: Maritime surveillance version for Hellenic Coast Guard

FEATURES:
Low/straight wing; twin wing-mounted P&WC PT6A turboprops with three- or four-blade (Mk II) propellers; swept tailfin with dorsal fin and dihedral tailplane; retractable tricycle landing gear

137

Rockwell (Aero Commander) Commander 500/560/580 USA

Twin-piston light corporate/utility aircraft

Prolific series of high-wing twin-piston aircraft originating from the L-3085 prototype, which first flew as long ago as April 23, 1948. The first production model was the 520, which led to many improved and more powerful models with both normally aspirated and turbo-charged engines. Total delivered: 710.

SPECIFICATION (680FL):

ACCOMMODATION: 1 + 10
CARGO/BAGGAGE: 1.7 m³ (60 cu.ft)
MAX SPEED: 212 kt (393 km/h)
RANGE: 1250 nm (2313 km)

DIMENSIONS:

WINGSPAN: 15.0 m (49 ft 1 in)
LENGTH: 12.6 m (41 ft 3 in)
HEIGHT: 4.4 m (14 ft 6 in)

VARIANTS:

500 Commander: As 560E, but with 250 hp engines
500U Shrike Commander: Pointed nose and squared-off fin
520 Commander: Initial model with two 290 hp engines
560 Commander: Swept tail, strengthened structure, seven seats
680F Commander: Fuel-injected engines, new landing gear
680FL Grand Commander: Stretched fuselage for 11 passengers, four square cabin windows
720 Alti Cruiser: 680 with pressurized cabin, extended wing
Plus many other variants and subvariants with suffixes E denoting extended wing, P for pressurized models, and L with long fuselage. Also used by U.S. Army and USAF with designation U-4

FEATURES:

High/straight wing with slight dihedral; twin Lycoming engines with two- or three-blade propellers; swept tailfin with dorsal fillet and low-set dihedral tailplane; retractable tricycle landing gear

Rockwell (Aero Commander) Turbo Commander/ Jetprop USA

Twin-turboprop corporate/utility aircraft

Based on the piston-engined pressurized 680FLP Grand Commander but substituting twin Garrett TPE331 turboprops, the Turbo Commander first flew on December 31, 1964, and entered production in 1965. This model spawned many variants, which were eventually built under different ownerships. Total delivered: 1290.

SPECIFICATION (Jetprop 1000):

ACCOMMODATION: 1 + 10
CARGO/BAGGAGE: 318 kg (700 lb)
MAX SPEED: 308 kt (571 km/h)
RANGE: 2080 nm (3855 km)

DIMENSIONS:
WINGSPAN: 15.9 m (52 ft 2 in)
LENGTH: 13.1 m (43 ft 0 in)
HEIGHT: 4.6 m (15 ft 0 in)

VARIANTS:
680T Turbo Commander: Initial production model
680W Turbo II Commander: Pointed nose, squared-off fin, one panoramic and two small cabin windows
681 Hawk Commander: Improved systems, redesigned nose
690 Commander: New wing center section, engines moved outwards
690C Jetprop 840: Increased wingspan and winglets
695A Jetprop 1000: More powerful engines, revised interior
Plus other variants differing mainly in fitted engines

FEATURES:
High/straight wing, with or without winglets; twin Garrett TPE331 turboprops with three-blade propellers; swept tailfin with long slim dorsal fillet and low-set dihedral tailplane; retractable tricycle landing gear

Socata TBM 700/850 FRANCE

Single-turbine light multirole aircraft

Originally developed in partnership with Mooney in the U.S. It first flew on July 14, 1988, with first delivery taking place on December 21, 1990. Although optimized for business flying, the TBM 700 has also found application in a variety of other roles. Total delivered: 341.

SPECIFICATION (TBM 700C2):

ACCOMMODATION: 1 + 5
CARGO/BAGGAGE: 150 kg (330 lb)
MAX SPEED: 300 kt (555 km/h)
RANGE: 1075 nm (1990 km)

DIMENSIONS:
WINGSPAN: 12.7 m (41 ft 8 in)
LENGTH: 10.6 m (34 ft 11 in)
HEIGHT: 4.4 m (14 ft 4 in)

VARIANTS:
TBM 700: Basic transport also offered in a variety of multimission versions, both civil and military
TBM 700B Freighter: Cargo version with reinforced floor, portside cargo door, and separate cockpit door
TBM 700C1: Improved version with strengthened airframe and other modifications
TBM 700C2: Increased payload/range capability
TBM 850: More powerful and faster variant, primarily for North American market

FEATURES:
Low/straight wing; single P&WC PT6A turboprop with four-blade propeller; conventional swept tailfin with extended dorsal fin and twin strakes under rear fuselage; retractable tricycle landing gear

Shorts SC.7 Skyvan UK

Twin-turboprop light STOL aircraft

Development for a small multirole transport with good STOL characteristics began in 1959, making use of the Miles high-aspect-ratio wing used on the Aerovan. The square-sided SC.7, later dubbed "Skyvan," flew on January 17, 1963, with Continental piston engines, but these were replaced by Turbomeca Astazou turboprops prior to the aircraft's entering service in 1966. Total built (including military versions): 150.

SPECIFICATION:

ACCOMMODATION: 2 + 19
CARGO/BAGGAGE: 2086 kg (4600 lb)
MAX SPEED: 175 kt (324 km/h)
RANGE: 162 nm (300 km)

DIMENSIONS:
WINGSPAN: 19.8 m (64 ft 11 in)
LENGTH: 12.2 m (40 ft 1 in)
HEIGHT: 4.6 m (15 ft 1 in)

VARIANTS:
Skyvan 2: Initial production version with Astazou engines
Skyvan 3: Switch to Garrett TPE331 turboprop engines
Skyliner: Higher-standard furnishings for airline use
Skyvan 3A: Increased take-off weight
Skyvan 3M: Designation of military transport
Skyvan 3M-200: Higher-gross-weight military version

FEATURES:
Braced high/straight wing; twin wing-mounted Garrett TPE331 turboprops with three-blade propellers; square-sided fuselage upswept at rear with loading ramp; twin square-sided tail units; fixed tricycle landing gear

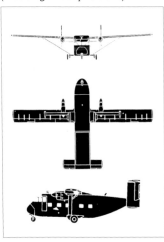

Smolensk (Technoavia) SM-92 Finist RUSSIAN FEDERATION

Single-piston light STOL aircraft

Design of this rugged STOL transport began started in July 1992 by Interavia. Initially known as the I-5, it was redesignated the SM-92 Finist by the time of the first flight on December 28, 1993. Total delivered: 26.

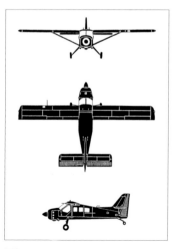

SPECIFICATION:

ACCOMMODATION: 1 + 6
CARGO/BAGGAGE: 600 kg (1323 lb)
MAX SPEED: 140 kt (260 km/h)
RANGE: 594 nm (1100 km)

DIMENSIONS:
WINGSPAN: 14.6 m (47 ft 11 in)
LENGTH: 9.3 m (30 ft 6 in)
HEIGHT: 3.1 m (10 ft 2 in)

VARIANTS:
SM-92: Basic production version available for passenger/freight transport and for other aerial work missions
SM-92P: Armed border patrol version with removable outrigger pylons for rockets and machine gun, and two underbelly hardpoints for 100 kg bombs or auxiliary tanks
SM-92T Turbo Finist: Tip tanks for increased range
SMG-92T Turbo Finist: Development with Walter M601D turboprop
Z 400 Rhino: License production by Zlin with Orenda OE-600A piston diesel engine

FEATURES:
Braced high/straight wing; single VOKBM M-14 piston engine with three-blade propeller; tapering fuselage ending in swept-back fin with small dorsal fin; tailplane with bracing strut each side; fixed tailwheel-type landing gear

Vulcanair (Partenavia) P68 Observer ITALY

Twin-piston light utility aircraft

Originally designed by Prof. Ing Luigi Pascale in 1968, the P68 Victor first flew on May 25, 1970. Various improved versions followed until 1994, when Partenavia assets were bought by Vulcanair. Total delivered (including license production in India): 420+.

SPECIFICATION:

ACCOMMODATION: 1 + 6
CARGO/BAGGAGE: 0.6 m³ (20 cu.ft)
MAX SPEED: 173 kt (320 km/h)
RANGE: 590 nm (1093 km)

DIMENSIONS:
WINGSPAN: 12.0 m (39 ft 5 in)
LENGTH: 9.4 m (30 ft 11 in)
HEIGHT: 3.4 m (11 ft 2 in)

VARIANTS:
P68 Victor: Original production model with Lycoming piston engine
P68B Victor: Enhanced development
P68C: Improved with lengthened nose and other refinements
P68C-TC: Turbocharged version for better hot-and-high performance
P68 Observer: Largely transparent nose section and underfloor hatch for various sensors
P68 Observer 2: Current model with further improvements
P68TC Observer: Turbocharged version for better hot-and-high performance
P68 Diesel: SMA SR305-230 diesel engine

FEATURES:
High/straight wing; twin wing-mounted Textron Lycoming piston engines with two-blade propellers; extensively glazed nose in Observer; swept tailfin and dorsal fin with low-seat tailplane; non-retractable landing gear; streamlined wheel fairings optional

Vulcanair (Partenavia) AP68TP Viator ITALY

Twin-turboprop light utility aircraft

Developed from the P68R, basically a P68B with retractable landing gear, but with Allison 250 turbo-props, lengthened fuselage, and larger fuel tanks. First flown on September 11, 1978. Produced by Partenavia until program taken over by Vulcanair. Total delivered: 23.

SPECIFICATION (Viator):

ACCOMMODATION: 1 + 10
CARGO/BAGGAGE: 0.55 m³ (20 cu.ft)
MAX SPEED: 200 kt (370 km/h)
RANGE: 777 nm (1440 km)

DIMENSIONS:
WINGSPAN: 12.0 m (39 ft 5 in)
LENGTH: 11.3 m (37 ft 0 in)
HEIGHT: 3.6 m (11 ft 11 in)

VARIANTS:
P68T: Initial version, but only four built
AP68TP-300 Spartacus: Improved version with fixed landing gear, better soundproofing, and upturned wingtips
AP68TP-600 Viator: Stretched and retractable landing gear
VA 300: New version with twin diesel engines was expected to enter service in 2005 but now abandoned

FEATURES:
High/straight wing; twin wing-mounted R-R (Allison) 250 turboprop engines with three-blade propellers; swept tailfin and dorsal fin with low-seat tailplane; retractable tricycle landing gear

Business Jets and Turbo-props

Adam A500 USA

Twin-turboprop light business aircraft

Designed by Burt Rutan, development of this lightweight centerline-thrust piston twin built of graphite–carbon composites started in September 1999, leading to first flight of proof-of-concept aircraft on March 21, 2000. Production-configuration A500 flew on July 11, 2002. VFR certification awarded by FAA on May 11, 2005, and first delivery made on November 7, 2005. Total delivered: 8 (ordered 85+).

SPECIFICATION:

ACCOMMODATION: 1 + 5
CARGO/BAGGAGE: 0.57 m³ (20 cu.ft)
MAX SPEED: 250 kt (460 km/h)
RANGE: 1050 nm (1940 km)

DIMENSIONS:
WINGSPAN: 13.4 m (44 ft 0 in)
LENGTH: 11.2 m (36 ft 8 in)
HEIGHT: 2.9 m (9 ft 6 in)

VARIANTS:
A500: Initial production version

FEATURES:
Straight/low wings with slight dihedral on outboard panels; two Teledyne Continental flat-six piston engines in centerline-thrust configuration; three cabin windows each side; twin-boom configuration with swept fins connected by high-set tailplane; retractable tricycle landing gear

Adam A700 AdamJet USA

Twin-turbofan light business jet

Jet development of A500 light piston business aircraft, powered by two Williams International FJ33 turbofans pylon-mounted on rear fuselage. Announced on October 21, 2002, and first flown on July 27, 2003. Certification was expected in late 2006/early 2007, with deliveries starting soon after. Total ordered: 300+.

SPECIFICATION:

ACCOMMODATION: 2 + 4
CARGO/BAGGAGE: 0.85 m³ (30 cu.ft)
MAX SPEED: 340 kt (630 km/h)
RANGE: 1100 nm (2040 km)

DIMENSIONS:
WINGSPAN: 13.4 m (44 ft 0 in)
LENGTH: 12.4 m (40 ft 9 in)
HEIGHT: 2.9 m (9 ft 6 in)

VARIANTS:
A700: Initial production version

FEATURES:
Straight/low wings with dihedral for full length; two Williams International FJ33 turbofan engines at rear fuselage; four cabin windows each side; twin-boom configuration with swept fins connected by high-set tailplane; retractable tricycle landing gear

Aerospatiale SN 601 Corvette FRANCE

Twin-turbofan light executive jet

Designed primarily as a corporate transport, it was also targeted at a variety of utility roles, including commuter, air taxi, aerial photography, trainer, ambulance, and others. First flown on July 16, 1970, the Corvette entered service in September 1974. Total delivered: 40.

SPECIFICATION:

ACCOMMODATION: 2 + 14
CARGO/BAGGAGE: 1000 kg (2205 lb)
MAX SPEED: M0.72 (410 kt; 759 km/h)
RANGE: 800 nm (1480 km)

DIMENSIONS:
WINGSPAN: 12.9 m (42 ft 3 in)
LENGTH: 13.8 m (45 ft 5 in)
HEIGHT: 4.2 m (13 ft 11 in)

VARIANTS:
Corvette 100: Standard production model
Corvette 200: Stretch proposal; never built

FEATURES:
Low/swept wing, with or without tip tanks; twin rear fuselage-mounted P&WC JT15D turbofans; highly swept tailfin with mid-mounted tailplane

British Aerospace (HS) BAe 125 UK

Twin-turbojet/turbofan light business jet

Developed as a private venture by de Havilland and first flew on August 13, 1962, by which time DH had become part of Hawker Siddeley. Early models, which entered service on October 10, 1964, were powered by the Viper turbojet. Total delivered: 572.

SPECIFICATION (Series 700):

ACCOMMODATION: 2 + 14
MAX SPEED: M0.76 (437 kt; 808 km/h)
RANGE: 2420 nm (4480 km)

DIMENSIONS:

WINGSPAN: 14.3 m (47 ft 0 in)
LENGTH: 15.4 m (15 ft 6 in)
HEIGHT: 5.3 m (17 ft 3 in)

VARIANTS:

125 Series 1: Initial production model
125 Series 1A: More powerful engines, for U.S. market
125 Series 1B: Similar, but for non-U.S. markets
125 Series 2: Dominie T.1 crew trainer for RAF
125 Series 3A: Higher gross weight, for U.S.
125 Series 3B: Similar, but for non-U.S. markets
125 Series 3A/RA: As 3A, but with ventral long-range fuel tank
125 Series 3B/RA: As 3B, but with ventral long-range fuel tank
125 Series 400A: Improved flight deck, for U.S.
125 Series 400B: Similar, for non-U.S. markets
125 Series 600A: Stretched, lengthened nose, sixth window
125 Series 600B: Similar, but for non-U.S. markets
125 Series 700A: Series 600A with Garrett TFE731 turbofans
125 Series 700B: Series 600B with TFE731s

FEATURES:

Low/swept wing; twin Rolls-Royce Viper turbojets or Garrett TFE731 turbofans; five or six cabin windows each side; highly swept tailfin with dorsal fin and high-mounted swept tailplane; small ventral strake below

Beech King Air 90/100 USA

Twin-turboprop business aircraft

Derived from the Queen Air, the pressurized King Air prototype first flew on January 20, 1964. Deliveries began later that year. The type has been continuously developed since and remains in production. Total built: 1996 (90); 394 (100).

SPECIFICATION (King Air C90B):

ACCOMMODATION: 2 + 6
CARGO/BAGGAGE: 1.5 m³ (54 cu.ft)
MAX SPEED: 247 kt (457 km/h)
RANGE: 1039 nm (1924 km)

DIMENSIONS:
WINGSPAN: 15.3 m (15 ft 3 in)
LENGTH: 10.8 m (35 ft 6 in)
HEIGHT: 4.3 m (14 ft 3 in)

VARIANTS:
King Air 90: Initial production model
King Air A90: Slight increase in engine power
King Air B90: Same engine as B90 with further enhancements
King Air C90: Improved engines and cabin refinements
King Air C90B: Current production model available since 1991
King Air C90GT: New P&WC PT6A-135A engines
King Air C90SE: Customized Special Edition
King Air E90: Combines airframe of C90 with PT6A-28 engines
King Air F90: Short-span wings of King Air 100 and T-tail of 200
King Air 100: Lengthened fuselage
King Air A100: Refined development
King Air B100: Garrett TPE331 turboprops

FEATURES:
Low/straight wing; twin wing-mounted P&WC PT6A turboprops with four-blade propellers; four cabin windows; swept tailfin and low-set tailplane

Beech King Air 200/300 USA

Twin-turboprop light business and multirole transport

Design of pressurized Super King Air 200 (the "Super" was deleted in 1996) began in October 1970. First flown on October 27, 1972, and entered service the following year. Higher-performance B200 sold from March 1981. Total delivered: 2423.

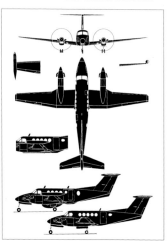

SPECIFICATION:

ACCOMMODATION: 2 + 9
CARGO/BAGGAGE: 1.5 m³ (54 cu.ft)
MAX SPEED: 292 kt (541 km/h)
RANGE: 1477 nm (2735 km)

DIMENSIONS:
WINGSPAN: 16.6 m (54 ft 6 in)
LENGTH: 13.4 m (43 ft 10 in)
HEIGHT: 4.5 m (14 ft 10 in)

VARIANTS:
King Air 200: Initial production version
King Air B200: Improved version from 1981
King Air B200C: As B200, but with cargo door
King Air B200CT: Combines tip tanks and cargo door; only nine built
King Air B200SE: Improved avionics and three-blade propellers
King Air B200T: Provision for removable tip tanks
200 HISAR: Radar surveillance platform
Plus various military models under C-12, RC-12, TC-12, and UC-12 designations
King Air 300: Improved model with more powerful engines
King Air 300LW: Lightweight model for European market
Blackhawk 200XP: PT6A-42 engine upgrade

FEATURES:
Low/straight wing; twin wing-mounted P&WC PT6A turboprops with four-blade propellers; five cabin windows; swept T-tail with dorsal fin and swept tailplane

Beech King Air 350 USA

Twin-turboprop business aircraft

Stretched development of King Air 300, first flown in September 1988 and introduced at the NBAA convention in 1989. Certified in commuter category, with initial delivery on March 6, 1990. Total delivered: 473.

SPECIFICATION:

ACCOMMODATION: 2 + 11
CARGO/BAGGAGE: 1.5 m³ (54 cu.ft)
MAX SPEED: 315 kt (584 km/h)
RANGE: 1358 nm (2515 km)

DIMENSIONS:
WINGSPAN: 17.7 m (57 ft 11 in)
LENGTH: 14.2 m (46 ft 8 in)
HEIGHT: 4.4 m (14 ft 4 in)

VARIANTS:
King Air 350: Baseline version
King Air 350C: Incorporates cargo door with built-in airstair passenger door
King Air 350ER: Special-missions variant with extended range
C-12S: Quick-change (QC) U.S. Army version
RC-350 Guardian: ELINT version with wingtip pods and underfuselage bulge
LR-2: JGSDF liaison and reconnaissance version

FEATURES:
Low/straight wing with winglets; twin wing-mounted P&WC PT6A turboprops with four-blade propellers; seven cabin windows; swept T-tail with dorsal fin and swept tailplane

Beech 390 Premier I USA

Twin-turbofan light business jet

Design started at Beechcraft in early 1994 under the designation PD374 (later PD390); details first revealed in June 1995, prior to launch at the NBAA convention the following September. The new type, the first to carry only the Raytheon name, first flew on December 22, 1998, and received FAA certification March 23, 2001. First deliveries followed later in 2001. Reverted to Beech name in 2002. Total delivered: 155.

SPECIFICATION:

ACCOMMODATION: 2 + 6
CARGO/BAGGAGE: 68 kg (150 lb)
MAX SPEED: M0.80 (461 kt; 854 km/h)
RANGE: 1500 nm (2778 km)

DIMENSIONS:
WINGSPAN: 13.6 m (44 ft 6 in)
LENGTH: 14.0 m (46 ft 0 in)
HEIGHT: 4.7 m (15 ft 4 in)

VARIANTS:
Premier I: Initial production version
Premier IA: More streamlined with luxurious interior and several options
Premier II: Proposed stretched development

FEATURES:
Low/swept wing mounted below fuselage; twin rear-mounted Williams FJ44 turbofans; three cabin windows; swept T-tail and swept tailplane

Bombardier BD-100 Challenger 300 CANADA

Twin-turbofan super mid-size business jet

Design study into super mid-size business jet with transcontinental range and high long-range cruise speed first revealed at Paris Air Show in June 1997 as the Model 70. Officially launched two years later. Maiden flight took place on August 14, 2001, designated BD-100 Continental. Renamed Challenger 300 on September 8, 2002. Transport Canada certification granted on May 31, 2003; first delivery to Flexjet December 23, 2003. Total delivered: 105.

SPECIFICATION:

ACCOMMODATION: 2 + 8
CARGO/BAGGAGE: 3.0 m³ (106 cu.ft)
MAX SPEED: M0.82 (470 kt; 870 km/h)
RANGE: 3100 nm (5741 km)

DIMENSIONS:
WINGSPAN: 19.5 m (63 ft 10 in)
LENGTH: 20.9 m (68 ft 8 in)
HEIGHT: 6.2 m (20 ft 3 in)

VARIANTS:
BD-100 Challenger 300: Initial production model

FEATURES:
Low/swept wing with winglets; rear fuselage-mounted twin Honeywell AS907 turbofans; swept T-tail with swept tailplane

Bombardier BD-700 Global Express CANADA

Twin-turbofan long-range business jet

Developed to meet perceived requirement for ultra-long-range business jet and announced at the NBAA convention in October 1991. Combines fuselage cross-section of Challenger with cabin length of CRJ, mated to a new supercritical wing. First flown on October 13, 1996, followed by initial delivery on July 8, 1999. Total delivered: 202.

SPECIFICATION (Global Express):

ACCOMMODATION: 2 + 19
CARGO/BAGGAGE: 4.95 m³ (175 cu.ft)
MAX SPEED: M0.88 (505 kt; 935 km/h)
RANGE: 5320 nm (9852 km)

DIMENSIONS:
WINGSPAN: 28.7 m (94 ft 0 in)
LENGTH: 30.3 m (99 ft 5 in)
HEIGHT: 7.6 m (24 ft 10 in)

VARIANTS:
Global Express: Basic corporate transport
Global Express XRS: Updated model with additional windows available from end of 2004
Global 5000: Shortened version launched in February 2002
Sentinel R.1 (ASTOR): Modified platform for UK airborne stand-off radar program
Sentinel AGS: Selected for NATO Alliance Ground Surveillance (AGS) System

FEATURES:
Low/swept wing with winglets; twin rear fuselage-mounted Rolls-Royce Deutschland BR710 turbofans; swept T-tail with swept anhedral tailplane

Bombardier Canadair CL-600 Challenger CANADA

Twin-turbofan mid-size business jet

Evolved from a design by Bill Lear for a fast 14-seat business jet dubbed the LearStar 600. Canadair acquired exclusive rights and launched the aircraft on October 29, 1976, leading to the first flight on November 8, 1978. By that time, the aircraft had been renamed the Challenger. First delivered on December 30, 1980. Total delivered: 697.

SPECIFICATION (604):

ACCOMMODATION: 2 + 19
CARGO/BAGGAGE: 3.25 m³ (115 cu.ft)
MAX SPEED: M0.82 (470 kt; 870 km/h)
RANGE: 3769 nm (6980 km)

DIMENSIONS:
WINGSPAN: 19.6 m (64 ft 4 in)
LENGTH: 20.9 m (68 ft 5 in)
HEIGHT: 6.3 m (20 ft 8 in)

VARIANTS:
Challenger 600: Initial production model with ALF502 turbofans
Challenger 601-1A: GE CF34 turbofans
Challenger 601-3A: Advanced "glass" cockpit and improved CF34s
Challenger 601-3R: Extended-range option with conformal tailcone fuel tank, which increased fuselage length
Challenger 604: Further range increase and other improvements
Challenger 605: New avionics, redesigned interior, and improved payload range
Plus military models for Canadian Department of National Defence designated CC-144

FEATURES:
Low/swept wing with winglets; twin rear fuselage-mounted GE CF34 turbofans (ALF502s in Model 600); swept T-tail with swept tailplane

Cessna 401/402/411 USA

Twin-piston business aircraft and commuterliner

Launched in the mid-1950s as a five/six-seat business transport, with both Model 401 and 402 developed simultaneously with identical airframe and engines. First flown on August 26, 1965. Total delivered: 546 (401); 1645 (402); 302 (411).

SPECIFICATION (402C):

ACCOMMODATION: 1 + 8
CARGO/BAGGAGE: 0.75 m³ (26 cu.ft)
MAX SPEED: 213 kt (394 km/h)
RANGE: 1273 nm (2379 km)

DIMENSIONS:

WINGSPAN: 13.5 m (44 ft 2 in)
LENGTH: 11.1 m (36 ft 5 in)
HEIGHT: 3.5 m (11 ft 6 in)

VARIANTS:

401: Baseline model, similar to 411 but broader tail
402: As 401, but with seating for nine passengers or utility interior
411: Retractable undercarriage, oval windows, airstair doors, and tip tanks
Suffix A on all three models denotes increased baggage space in lengthened nose
402B: Larger cabin and five square windows, available in Utiliner and Businessliner versions, the latter having additional deluxe cabin trim
402C: Increased T-O weight and longer span wing without tip tanks, also available in Utiliner and Businessliner versions

FEATURES:

Low/straight wing; twin wing-mounted Continental piston engines with three-blade propellers; swept tailfin with dorsal fin and low-set tailplane; four cabin portholes (five square windows in 402B/C); retractable tricycle landing gear

Cessna 404 Titan USA

Twin-piston business aircraft and commuterliner

Essentially a stretched 402B with enlarged vertical tail, dihedral tailplane, more powerful Continental engines, and higher gross weight. Made its first flight on February 26, 1975, followed by first deliveries in October 1976. Total delivered: 396.

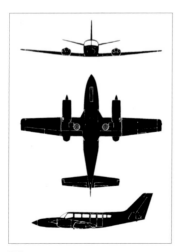

SPECIFICATION (404 Titan):

ACCOMMODATION: 2 + 10
CARGO/BAGGAGE: 680 kg (1500 lb)
MAX SPEED: 232 kt (430 km/h)
RANGE: 1843 nm (3410 km)

DIMENSIONS:
WINGSPAN: 14.2 m (46 ft 8 in)
LENGTH: 12.0 m (39 ft 5 in)
HEIGHT: 4.0 m (13 ft 2 in)

VARIANTS:
404 Titan: Baseline model
404 Titan Courier: Cargo interior
404 Titan Ambassador: Accommodation for 10 passengers
Suffixes II and III for each model denote improved versions with mainly equipment changes

FEATURES:
Low/straight wing; twin wing-mounted Continental piston engines with three-blade propellers; swept tailfin and low-set dihedral tailplane; six square cabin windows; retractable tricycle landing gear

Cessna 414 Chancellor USA

Twin-piston business aircraft

Introduced on December 10, 1969, as a "step-up" pressurized model, combining the basic fuselage and tail unit of the Model 421 with the wing of the Model 402, and powered by turbocharged Continental engines. It made its maiden flight on November 1, 1968. Total delivered: 1070.

SPECIFICATION:

ACCOMMODATION: 1 + 7
CARGO/BAGGAGE: 494 kg (1000 lb)
MAX SPEED: 235 kt (436 km/h)
RANGE: 1099 nm (2036 km)

DIMENSIONS:

WINGSPAN: 13.5 m (44 ft 2 in)
LENGTH: 11.1 m (36 ft 5 in)
HEIGHT: 3.5 m (11 ft 6 in)

VARIANTS:

414: Baseline model
414 Chancellor: Narrower tail, longer wingspan without tip tanks, lengthened nose
414 Chancellor II: Improved avionics as standard
414 Chancellor III: Air conditioning and all-weather avionics package

FEATURES:

Low/straight wing with or without tip tanks; twin wing-mounted Continental piston engines with three-blade propellers; swept tailfin with dorsal fin and low-set tailplane; five round cabin windows; retractable tricycle landing gear

Cessna 421 Golden Eagle USA

Twin-piston business aircraft

Similar to Model 411A with pressurized cabin, higher T-O weight, broader vertical tail, and smaller side windows. It first flew on October 14, 1965, and entered service the following year. Total built: 1916.

SPECIFICATION (421C):

ACCOMMODATION: 1 + 7
CARGO/BAGGAGE: 680 kg (1500 lb)
MAX SPEED: 258 kt (478 km/h)
RANGE: 1197 nm (2218 km)

DIMENSIONS:
WINGSPAN: 12.5 m (41 ft 1 in)
LENGTH: 11.1 m (36 ft 5 in)
HEIGHT: 3.5 m (11 ft 6 in)

VARIANTS:
421: Baseline model
421A: Minor improvements
421B Golden Eagle: Longer-span wings, longer cabin with toilet area, and lengthened nose for more baggage space
421C Golden Eagle: Narrower tailfin, longer-span wing without tip tanks, and new engines with larger propellers
Both models B and C were available in Executive Commuter versions with more luxurious interior, and with suffixes II and III denoting equipment and systems changes

FEATURES:
Low/straight wing; twin wing-mounted Continental GTSIO-520 piston engines with three-blade propellers; swept tailfin and low-set tailplane; five round cabin windows; retractable tricycle landing gear

Cessna 425 Corsair/Conquest I USA

Twin-turboprop business aircraft

Based on the Model 421C airframe, design of the Corsair began in November 1977, and a prototype flew for the first time on September 12, 1978. Customer deliveries started in November 1980. The name was changed to Conquest I in late 1982. Total delivered: 236.

SPECIFICATION:

ACCOMMODATION: 1 + 7
CARGO/BAGGAGE: 499 kg (1100 lb)
MAX SPEED: 264 kt (489 km/h)
RANGE: 1339 nm (2480 km)

DIMENSIONS:
WINGSPAN: 13.5 m (44 ft 2 in)
LENGTH: 10.9 m (35 ft 10 in)
HEIGHT: 3.8 m (12 ft 7 in)

VARIANTS:
425 Corsair/Conquest I: Only production model
Blackhawk 425XP: PT6A-135A engine upgrade

FEATURES:
Low/straight wing with slight dihedral; twin P&WC PT6A turboprops with three-blade propellers; five cabin windows; highly swept tailfin with dorsal fin and low-set dihedral tailplane; retractable tricycle landing gear

Cessna 441 Conquest II USA

Twin-turboprop business aircraft

Announced at the same time as the Model 404 Titan, the 441 was intended purely as a business aircraft, introducing for the first time turboprop engines in place of turbocharged piston engines. Flown on August 26, 1975. Total delivered: 362.

SPECIFICATION:

ACCOMMODATION: 1 + 10
CARGO/BAGGAGE: 680 kg (1500 lb)
MAX SPEED: 295 kt (547 km/h)
RANGE: 2063 nm (3820 km)

DIMENSIONS:
WINGSPAN: 15.0 m (49 ft 4 in)
LENGTH: 11.9 m (39 ft 1 in)
HEIGHT: 4.0 m (13 ft 2 in)

VARIANTS:
441 Conquest II: Only production model, available with a number of different options

FEATURES:
Low/straight wing; twin wing-mounted Garrett TPE331 turboprop engines with three-blade propellers; swept tailfin and low-set dihedral tailplane; six semi-square cabin windows; retractable tricycle landing gear

Cessna 500 Citation I USA

Twin-turbofan mid-size business jet

Pressurized executive Fanjet 500 turbofan aircraft, able to operate from most airfields, announced October 7, 1968. Name changed to Citation following first flight on September 15, 1969. Many subsequent changes and improvements incorporated and first delivery made on December 21, 1976. Total delivered: 691.

SPECIFICATION:

ACCOMMODATION: 2 + 7
CARGO/BAGGAGE: 454 kg (1000 lb)
MAX SPEED: M0.70 (402 kt; 745 km/h)
RANGE: 1328 nm (2459 km)

DIMENSIONS:
WINGSPAN: 14.4 m (47 ft 1 in)
LENGTH: 13.3 m (43 ft 6 in)
HEIGHT: 4.4 m (14 ft 4 in)

VARIANTS:
500 Citation I: Basic production version
501 Citation I/SP: Similar, but certificated for single-pilot operation

FEATURES:
Low/straight wing; twin P&WC JT15D turbofans mid-mounted on rear fuselage; four cabin windows each side; swept T-tail and large dorsal fin; low-set swept tailplane

Cessna 510 Mustang USA

Twin-turbofan very light business jet

Initial design studies for a new turbo-prop started in 1997, but twin-jet configuration chosen in early 2001 and announced at NBAA convention, Orlando, Florida, on September 10, 2002. Cessna's smallest business jet made its maiden flight on August 29, 2005. Certification to FAA FAR Pt 23 achieved on September 8, 2006. First deliveries in early 2007. Total ordered: 250.

SPECIFICATION:

ACCOMMODATION: 2 + 4
CARGO/BAGGAGE: 1.57 m³ (57 cu.ft)
MAX SPEED: 340 kt (630 km/h)
RANGE: 1150 nm (2130 km)

DIMENSIONS:
WINGSPAN: 13.15 m (43 ft 2 in)
LENGTH: 12.4 m (40 ft 7 in)
HEIGHT: 4.1 m (13 ft 5 in)

VARIANTS:
Mustang: Initial production version

FEATURES:
Low/straight wing; twin P&WC PW614F turbofans mid-mounted on rear fuselage; swept T-tail with high-set swept tailplane; distinctive extended underbelly; three cabin windows each side

Cessna 525 CitationJet USA

Twin-turbofan small business jet

Developed as a small, affordable entry-level jet to replace the earlier Citation I. Launched at the 1989 NBAA convention, the CitationJet made its first flight on April 29, 1991. First customer delivery took place on March 30, 1993. Replaced by improved CJ1 and CJ2 from 2000/2001. Total delivered: 963.

SPECIFICATION (CJ2):

ACCOMMODATION: 2 + 6
CARGO/BAGGAGE: 306 kg (675 lb)
MAX SPEED: M0.72 (413 kt; 764 km/h)
RANGE: 1475 nm (2731 km)

DIMENSIONS:
WINGSPAN: 15.1 m (49 ft 6 in)
LENGTH: 14.3 m (46 ft 11 in)
HEIGHT: 4.2 m (13 ft 10 in)

VARIANTS:
525 CitationJet: Initial production version
525 Citation CJ1: Increased T-O weight and new avionics suite
525 Citation CJ1+: New FJ44 engines, avionics upgrade, and performance improvements
525A Citation CJ2: Stretched CJ1 with more powerful engines and improved performance; more comfortable cabin
525A Citation CJ2+: New FJ44 engines, avionics upgrade, and performance improvements
525B Citation CJ3: Stretched development with uprated engines
525B Citation CJ4: New wing; first flight scheduled for 2008

FEATURES:
Low/straight wing; twin Williams FJ44 turbofans mounted high on rear fuselage; four cabin windows (six on CJ2, seven on CJ3); swept T-tail with straight tailplane

Cessna 550 Citation II/Bravo USA

Twin-turbofan mid-size business jet

Stretched version of the Citation I for up to 10 passengers, built in parallel. Announced on September 14, 1976, the Citation II made its first flight on January 31, 1977, and entered service in March 1978. Total built (including 15 T-47As for the U.S. Navy): 733. Replaced by Citation Bravo, which first flew on April 25, 1995. Total delivered: 329.

SPECIFICATION (Citation Bravo):

ACCOMMODATION: 2 + 8
CARGO/BAGGAGE: 522 kg (1150 lb)
MAX SPEED: 403 kt (746 km/h)
RANGE: 1780 nm (3295 km)

DIMENSIONS:
WINGSPAN: 15.9 m (52 ft 2 in)
LENGTH: 14.4 m (47 ft 3 in)
HEIGHT: 4.6 m (15 ft 0 in)

VARIANTS:
550 Citation II: Initial production version
551 Citation II/SP: Certificated for single-pilot operation
S550 Citation S/II: Improved model introduced in July 1984
550 Citation Bravo: More efficient wing, and new PW530 turbofans; substantial performance improvements
T-47A: Acquired by U.S. Navy for the radar training role

FEATURES:
Low/straight tapered wing; twin P&WC JT15D (or PW530 in Bravo) turbofans mid-mounted on rear fuselage; six cabin windows each side; swept tailfin with tapered mid-set tailplane

Cessna 560 Citation V/Ultra/Encore USA

Twin-turbofan mid-size business jet

Stretched and internally restyled development of the Citation II/SP announced at the 1987 NBAA convention. Most notable external feature was a seventh cabin window. Engineering prototype made its first flight in August 1987, and customer deliveries started in April 1989. Total delivered: 260. Replaced by Ultra and Encore. Total delivered: 524.

SPECIFICATION (Encore):

ACCOMMODATION: 2 + 7
CARGO/BAGGAGE: 272 kg (600 lb)
MAX SPEED: M0.75 (430 kt; 796 km/h)
RANGE: 2000 nm (3704 km)

DIMENSIONS:
WINGSPAN: 16.6 m (54 ft 6 in)
LENGTH: 14.9 m (48 ft 11 in)
HEIGHT: 4.6 m (15 ft 0 in)

VARIANTS:
560 Citation V: Initial production model with JT15Ds
560 Citation Ultra: Improved version with EFIS and increased payload/range performance
560 Citation Encore: More powerful PW535 turbofans
560 Citation Encore+: Enhanced avionics and increased MTOW
OT-47B: Radar-equipped tracker aircraft for USAF based on Ultra
UC-35A and UC-35B: Transport for U.S. Army and USMC
UC-35D: USMC model based on Ultra Encore

FEATURES:
Low/straight wing; twin P&WC JT15D or PW500 turbofans mid-mounted on rear fuselage; seven cabin windows; swept tailfin with large dorsal fin

Cessna 560XL Citation Excel/XLS USA

Twin-turbofan mid-size business jet

Announced at NBAA convention in October 1994 and made its first flight on February 29, 1996. Combines systems and wing and tail surfaces of the Citation Ultra (Encore) with shortened Citation X fuselage, providing 10-seat cabin with stand-up headroom. First delivery to Swift Transportation of Phoenix, Arizona, on July 2, 1998. Total delivered: 479.

SPECIFICATION (Citation Excel):

ACCOMMODATION: 2 + 9
CARGO/BAGGAGE: 317 kg (700 lb)
MAX SPEED: 429 kt (795 km/h)
RANGE: 2165 nm (4010 km)

DIMENSIONS:
WINGSPAN: 17.9 m (55 ft 9 in)
LENGTH: 15.8 m (51 ft 10 in)
HEIGHT: 5.2 m (17 ft 2 in)

VARIANTS:
Citation Excel: Initial production version
Citation XLS: Upgraded model available from 2004
Citation XLS+: PW535C engines with FADEC; more streamlined nose; new avionics

FEATURES:
Low/straight wing cranked at front and tapered at rear; rear fuselage-mounted P&WC PW545A turbofans; six cabin windows on right side and five on left; moderately swept tailfin with large dorsal fillet and low-set tailplane; dual ventral strakes

Cessna 650 Citation III/VI/VII USA

Twin-turbofan mid-size business jet

All-new high-performance aircraft designed to extend Cessna's portfolio to attract more prosperous customers. Notable features were a new supercritical wing, swept T-tail, and much longer fuselage. First flown May 30, 1979, the Citation III entered service in spring 1983. Total delivered: 187 (III), 37 (VI), 120 (VII).

SPECIFICATION (Citation VII):

ACCOMMODATION: 2 + 13
CARGO/BAGGAGE: 1.4 m³ (51 cu.ft)
MAX SPEED: M0.83 (476 kt; 881 km/h)
RANGE: 2180 nm (4037 km)

DIMENSIONS:
WINGSPAN: 16.3 m (53 ft 6 in)
LENGTH: 16.9 m (55 ft 6 in)
HEIGHT: 5.1 m (16 ft 9 in)

VARIANTS:
650 Citation III: Initial production model
650 Citation VI: Low-cost version with new avionics
650 Citation VII: More powerful engines for better hot-and-high performance
650 Citation Magnum: Choice of flight-management systems

FEATURES:
Low/swept wing; twin Honeywell TFE731 turbofans mounted on side of rear fuselage; six cabin windows; swept T-tail with swept tailplane

Cessna 680 Citation Sovereign USA

Twin-turbofan mid-size business jet

Design of this super midsize twin-jet with U.S. coast-to-coast range was initiated in 1998 and first announced at NBAA on October 18, that same year. Prototype first flew on February 27, 2002, and FAA certification was obtained on December 24, 2003. First delivered in early 2004. Total delivered: 85.

SPECIFICATION:

ACCOMMODATION: 2 + 9
CARGO/BAGGAGE: 2.83 m³ (100 cu.ft)
MAX SPEED: 429 kt (795 km/h)
RANGE: 2680 nm (4965 km)

DIMENSIONS:
WINGSPAN: 16.5 m (54 ft 1 in)
LENGTH: 14.9 m (48 ft 10 in)
HEIGHT: 4.6 m (15 ft 0 in)

VARIANTS:
Citation Sovereign: Initial production model

FEATURES:
Low/straight wing with swept-back leading edge; P&WC PW306C podded turbofans on rear fuselage shoulders; eight cabin windows on starboard side and seven on port; swept tailfin with mid-set swept tailplane

Cessna 750 Citation X USA

Twin-turbofan long-range mid-size business jet

Largest and fastest Cessna jet optimized for non-stop U.S. transcontinental and transatlantic operations. Announced at the NBAA convention in October 1990, the Citation X first flew on December 21, 1993. Golfer Arnold Palmer accepted the first aircraft in July 1996. Total delivered: 255.

SPECIFICATION:

ACCOMMODATION: 2 + 12
CARGO/BAGGAGE: 2.32 m³ (82 cu.ft)
MAX SPEED: M0.91 (521 kt; 965 km/h)
RANGE: 3430 nm (6352 km)

DIMENSIONS:
WINGSPAN: 19.4 m (63 ft 7 in)
LENGTH: 22.1 m (72 ft 4 in)
HEIGHT: 5.8 m (19 ft 2 in)

VARIANTS:
Citation X: Initial production model with Rolls-Royce AE 3007 turbofans

FEATURES:
Low/swept wing; twin Rolls-Royce (Allison) AE3007C turbofans mounted high on sides of rear fuselage; seven cabin windows; highly swept T-tail and tailplane

Dassault Falcon 10/100 FRANCE

Twin-turbofan small business jet

Smallest of Dassault's business jets, the Falcon 10 (originally called the Mini-Falcon) was a scaled-down version of the Falcon 20. Conceived in the late 1960s, it originally flew on December 1, 1970, with GE CJ610 turbojets. These were replaced by Garrett TFE731 turbofans, with which it flew for the first time on October 15, 1971. Customer deliveries started in November 1973. Total delivered: 195 (10), 31 (100).

SPECIFICATION:

ACCOMMODATION: 2 + 7
CARGO/BAGGAGE: 1305 kg (2414 lb)
MAX SPEED: M0.86 (492 kt; 912 km/h)
RANGE: 1880 nm (3480 km)

DIMENSIONS:
WINGSPAN: 13.1 m (40 ft 11 in)
LENGTH: 13. 9 m (45 ft 6 in)
HEIGHT: 4.6 m (15 ft 2 in)

VARIANTS:
Falcon 10: Initial production version
Falcon 100: Improved version with optional EFIS
Mystère 10 MER: Pilot trainer sold to French Navy

FEATURES:
Low/swept wings; twin Garrett TFE731 turbofans mounted on sides of rear fuselage; four cabin windows each side; highly swept tailfin with swept mid-mounted tailplane

Dassault Falcon 20/200 FRANCE
Twin-turbofan corporate and utility aircraft

Developed in a collaboration with Sud-Aviation in the late 1950s and first flew on May 4, 1963. The first prototype was fitted with the P&W JT12A turbojet, but production aircraft had GE CF700 turbofans, and first flew with these on January 1, 1965. First delivery, to Pan American, was made in June that year. Total delivered: 473 (20), 35 (200).

SPECIFICATION:

ACCOMMODATION: 2 + 12
CARGO/BAGGAGE: 1.45 m³ (52 cu.ft)
MAX SPEED: M0.82 (470 kt; 870 km/h)
RANGE: 2510 nm (4650 km)

DIMENSIONS:
WINGSPAN: 16.3 m (53 ft 6 in)
LENGTH: 17.2 m (56 ft 3 in)
HEIGHT: 5.3 m (17 ft 5 in)

VARIANTS:
Falcon 20C: Baseline aircraft
Falcon 20D: Uprated engines and more fuel
Falcon 20E: Higher T-O weight and revised rudder
Falcon 20F: Full leading-edge slats and further fuel increase
Falcon 20G: Maritime surveillance version
Falcon 200: New Garrett ATF3 turbofans and larger fuel tank; initially known as Falcon 20H
Falcon 20NA: French Air Force navigation-systems trainer
Falcon 20NR: French Air Force navigation/reconnaissance trainer
HU-25A/B/C Guardian: Three models for SAR, offshore surveillance, identification, and tracking, plus many other Falcon/Mystère 20s used for target towing, medevac, ECM, and remote sensing

FEATURES:
Low/swept wings; twin GE CF700 or Garrett ATF3 turbofans mounted on sides of rear fuselage; five cabin windows each side; highly swept tailfin with swept mid-mounted tailplane

173

Dassault Falcon 50 FRANCE

Three-turbofan long-range business jet

Developed to cover the emerging U.S. transcontinental and trans-atlantic business-jet market, the Falcon 50 used the fuselage cross-section of the Falcon 20/200 on a new super-critical wing, plus a third engine. First flown on November 7, 1976, the Falcon 50 entered service in early 1979. Total delivered: 346.

SPECIFICATION (50EX):

ACCOMMODATION: 2 + 19
CARGO/BAGGAGE: 3.97 m³ (140 cu.ft)
MAX SPEED: M0.86 (493 kt; 912 km/h)
RANGE: 3285 nm (6083 km)

DIMENSIONS:
WINGSPAN: 18.9 m (61 ft 11 in)
LENGTH: 18.5 m (60 ft 9 in)
HEIGHT: 7.0 m (22 ft 11 in)

VARIANTS:
Falcon 50: Initial production model
Falcon 50-4: Reconfigured with TFE731-4-1C for enhanced performance
Falcon 50-40: Retrofit with Honeywell TFE731-40 engine
Falcon 50EX: Uprated turbofans and increased range
Falcon 50M Surmar: Maritime surveillance version with search radar and FLIR
Falcon 50 Sigint: Proprosed signal intelligence version

FEATURES:
Low/swept and tapered wing; three Honeywell TFE731 turbofans, two mounted on sides of rear fuselage, the third atop and at base of tail at centerline; seven cabin windows each side; tall swept tailfin and low-mounted tailplane

Dassault Falcon 900 FRANCE

Three-turbofan long-range business jet

Development of intercontinental business jet announced at Paris Air Show on May 27, 1983. Derived from the Falcon 50, but substantially revised, the prototype Falcon 900 powered by Garrett TFE731 turbofan engines first flew on September 21, 1984. First customer deliveries took place in December 1986. Total delivered: 378.

SPECIFICATION (900EX):

ACCOMMODATION: 2 + 19
CARGO/BAGGAGE: 3.6 m³ (127 cu.ft)
MAX SPEED: M0.84 (481 kt; 891 km/h)
RANGE: 3810 nm (7056 km)

DIMENSIONS:
WINGSPAN: 19.3 m (63 ft 5 in)
LENGTH: 20.2 m (66 ft 3 in)
HEIGHT: 7.6 m (24 ft 10 in)

VARIANTS:
Falcon 900: Initial production model
Falcon 900B: Increased power and range; able to operate from unprepared airstrips
Falcon 900C: Enhanced avionics from 900EX
Falcon 900DX: Honeywell TFE731-60 engines from 900EX; EASy flight deck
Falcon 900EX: Longer range; further increase in engine thrust
Falcon 900MPA: Proposed maritime patrol aircraft
JMSA: Long-range surveillance aircraft with U.S. search radar; in service in Japan

FEATURES:
Low/swept and tapered wing; three Honeywell TFE731 turbofans, two mounted on sides of rear fuselage, the third atop and at base of tail; 12 cabin windows; tall swept tailfin and mid-mounted swept tailplane

Dassault Falcon 2000 FRANCE

Twin-turbofan long-range wide-body business jet

Direct descendant from the Falcon 900, with a two-engine configuration and area-ruled rear fuselage the obvious external changes. Announced at the Paris Air Show in 1989 as the Falcon X, it was launched as the Falcon 2000 on October 4, 1990, and first flew on March 4, 1993. First delivery on February 16, 1995. Total delivered: 264.

SPECIFICATION (2000EX):

ACCOMMODATION: 2 + 19
CARGO/BAGGAGE: 3.8 m³ (134 cu.ft)
MAX SPEED: M0.84 (481 kt; 891 km/h)
RANGE: 3800 nm (7030 km)

DIMENSIONS:
WINGSPAN: 19.3 m (63 ft 5 in)
LENGTH: 20.2 m (66 ft 4 in)
HEIGHT: 7.1 m (23 ft 2 in)

VARIANTS:
Falcon 2000: Basic production version
Falcon 2000DX: Reduced fuel capacity for shorter range
Falcon 2000EX: Increased range, new PW308C turbofans, and new avionics

FEATURES:
Low/swept wing; two Honeywell TFE731 or PW308C (2000EX) turbofans mounted on sides of rear fuselage; 10 cabin windows; tall swept tailfin and mid-mounted swept tailplane

Dassault Falcon 7X FRANCE

Three-turbofan large-cabin business jet

Announced under the designation of Falcon Next at Paris Air Show in June 2001. Then became Falcon FNX, followed by formal designation Falcon 7X on October 29, 2001. First flight on May 5, 2005; public debut at the Paris Air Show in June that same year. Certification due in first quarter of 2007, with first deliveries soon after. Total ordered: 80+.

SPECIFICATION:

ACCOMMODATION: 3 + 19
CARGO/BAGGAGE: 4.0 m³ (141 cu.ft)
MAX SPEED: 370 kt (685 km/h)
RANGE: 5950 nm (11,020 km)

DIMENSIONS:
WINGSPAN: 25.2 m (82 ft 8 in)
LENGTH: 23.2 m (76 ft 1 in)
HEIGHT: 7.8 m (25 ft 7 in)

VARIANTS:
Falcon 7X: Initial production version

FEATURES:
Swept wing with winglets; three P&WC PW307A turbofans, two pod-mounted each side of rear fuselage and third in center at the back with air intake above the fuselage ahead of the tailfin; swept mid-mounted tailplane

Eclipse Aviation Eclipse 500 USA

Twin-turbofan very light business jet

Development of world's first very light jet (VLJ) began in June 1999, followed by maiden flight of Williams-powered aircraft on August 26, 2002. That engine was abandoned for Pratt & Whitney Canada PW610F in 2003, with which the aircraft first flew on December 31, 2004. Full FAA Type Certification was obtained on September 30, 2006, with first deliveries at the end of October 2006. Total ordered: 2500.

SPECIFICATION:

ACCOMMODATION: 1 + 5
CARGO/BAGGAGE: 0.74 m³ (26 cu.ft)
MAX SPEED: 375 kt (695 km/h)
RANGE: 1280 nm (2370 km)

DIMENSIONS:

WINGSPAN: 11.55 m (37 ft 11 in)
LENGTH: 10.3 m (33 ft 9 in)
HEIGHT: 3.35 m (11 ft 0 in)

VARIANTS:

Eclipse 500: Initial production version

FEATURES:

Conventional metal airframe with straight wings and distinctive wingtip fuel tanks; T-tail with dorsal fin and swept tailplane; twin rear fuselage-mounted PW610F turbofan engines; three cabin windows each side, the first set into the door

Embraer EMB-121 Xingu BRAZIL

Twin-turboprop corporate transport

Combining the wing and engines of the Bandeirante with an all-new fuselage, the 10-seat Xingu made its maiden flight on October 10, 1976, and entered service the following year with both civil and military customers. An improved version flew on September 4, 1981. Total delivered: 105.

SPECIFICATION (Xingu II):

ACCOMMODATION: 2 + 9
CARGO/BAGGAGE: 1.0 m³ (35.3 cu.ft)
MAX SPEED: 251 kt (465 km/h)
RANGE: 1230 nm (2278 km)

DIMENSIONS:
WINGSPAN: 14.1 m (46 ft 2 in)
LENGTH: 12.3 m (40 ft 3 in)
HEIGHT: 4.8 m (15 ft 10 in)

VARIANTS:
Xingu I: Initial production model
Xingu II: More powerful PT6A engine, increased seating and fuel
Plus military derivatives for France, used for training and liaison, and to the Brazilian Air Force under designation VU-9

FEATURES:
Low/straight wing; twin wing-mounted P&WC PT6A turboprops with three- or four-blade propellers; swept T-tail with large dorsal fin and tapered tailplane

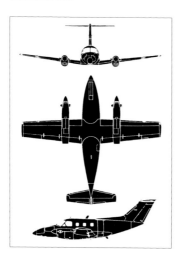

Grumman G-159 Gulfstream I USA

Twin-turboprop executive transport

Work started in 1956 on a new design to replace war-surplus piston twins then used for executive transport, incorporating a generous cabin cross-section and Rolls-Royce Dart turboprops for a high-speed cruise. The first Gulfstream I flew on August 14, 1958, and customer deliveries followed from June 1959. Total delivered: 200 (including five G-IC conversions).

SPECIFICATION (G-1):

ACCOMMODATION: 2 + 24
CARGO/BAGGAGE: 3.62 m³ (128 cu.ft)
MAX SPEED: 302 kt (560 km/h)
RANGE: 2206 nm (4087 km)

DIMENSIONS:
WINGSPAN: 23.9 m (78 ft 6 in)
LENGTH: 19.4 m (63 ft 9 in)
HEIGHT: 6.9 m (22 ft 9 in)

VARIANTS:
Gulfstream I: Basic production version
Gulfstream I-C: Stretched airliner conversion seating 38 passengers
TC-4C: Navigator trainer for U.S. Navy with A-6A radome nose
VC-4A: VIP transport for U.S. Coast Guard

FEATURES:
Low/straight wing with front and rear taper; twin wing-mounted Rolls-Royce Dart turboprops with four-blade propeller; five cabin windows; swept tailfin with low-set tailplane

Grumman G-1159 Gulfstream II/III USA

Twin-turbofan large long-range business jet

Jet-powered development of the Gulfstream I announced on May 17, 1965. Apart from the engines, other significant differences were a new swept wing and T-tail. It first flew on October 2, 1966, and entered service in December 1967. The improved G-III followed the purchase of Grumman's GA aircraft line by Gulfstream American in 1978. The G-III flew on December 2, 1979. Total delivered: 258 (G-II), 206 (G-III).

SPECIFICATION (G-III):

ACCOMMODATION: 2 + 21
CARGO/BAGGAGE: 907 kg (2000 lb)
MAX SPEED: M0.85 (501 kt; 928 km/h)
RANGE: 3650 nm (6760 km)

DIMENSIONS:
WINGSPAN: 23.7 m (77 ft 10 in)
LENGTH: 25.3 m (83 ft 1 in)
HEIGHT: 7.4 m (24 ft 4 in)

VARIANTS:
Gulfstream II: Initial jet-powered model
Gulfstream IIB: Retrofit with G-III wing
Gulfstream IISP: With Aviation Partners winglets (as pictured)
Gulfstream III: Stretched version; redesigned wing with winglets and increased fuel capacity
Gulfstream Maritime: Used on fishery patrols by Royal Danish Air Force
Gulfstream SRA-1: Special-missions variant
C-20A: Modified for USAF airlift under C-SAM

FEATURES:
Low/swept wing with winglets; twin Rolls-Royce157 Spey turbofans mounted on sides of rear fuselage; five cabin windows; swept T-tail with swept tailplane

Gulfstream Aerospace Gulfstream IV/G300/G350/G400/G450 USA

Twin-turbofan large long-range business jet

Significantly improved and advanced development of G-III with new Rolls-Royce Tay engines, stretched fuselage, revised wing, and "glass" cockpit. Design was initiated in April 1982 and the G-IV flew for the first time on September 19, 1985. Customer deliveries commenced in spring 1987. Total delivered: 550+.

SPECIFICATION (IV-SP):

ACCOMMODATION: 2 + 19
CARGO/BAGGAGE: 907 kg (2000 lb)
MAX SPEED: M0.88 (505 kt; 936 km/h)
RANGE: 4220 nm (7805 km)

DIMENSIONS:
WINGSPAN: 23.7 m (77 ft 11 in)
LENGTH: 26.9 m (88 ft 4 in)
HEIGHT: 7.4 m (24 ft 5 in)

VARIANTS:
Gulfstream IV: Initial production model
Gulfstream IV-SP: Higher weight and improved payload/range
Gulfstream IV-MPA: Quick-change multipurpose version
G300: Mid-range version of IV-SP
G350: Shorter range G450
G400: New; similar to IV-SP
G450: Upgraded, with G550 avionics
Gulfstream SRA-4: Special-missions versions, including ASW, electronic surveillance, maritime patrol, medevac, and others. Designations C-20F/G/H applied to U.S. Army, Navy, and USAF aircraft respectively; electronic intelligence gathering as S 102B Korpen and military transport as Tp 102 for Swedish Air Force; and multimission aircraft for JASDF as UC-4

FEATURES:
Low/swept wing with winglets; twin Rolls-Royce157 Tay turbofans mounted on sides of rear fuselage; six cabin windows; swept T-tail with swept tailplane

Gulfstream Aerospace Gulfstream V/G500/G550 USA

Twin-turbofan large ultra long-range business jet

Study into very-long-range business jet was announced at the NBAA convention in October 1991. Based on a lengthened and re-engineered G-IV fuselage, but with more efficient wing and new Rolls-Royce157 Deutschland BR710 turbofans, the G-V made its first flight on November 28, 1995, and subsequently set many world records. First customer delivery on July 1, 1997. Total delivered: 334.

SPECIFICATION:

ACCOMMODATION: 2 + 19
CARGO/BAGGAGE: 6.4 m³ (226 cu.ft)
MAX SPEED: M0.85 (488 kt; 903 km/h)
RANGE: 6500 nm (12,038 km)

DIMENSIONS:
WINGSPAN: 28.5 m (93 ft 6 in)
LENGTH: 29.4 m (96 ft 5 in)
HEIGHT: 7.9 m (25 ft 10 in)

VARIANTS:
Gulfstream V: Standard production version
Gulfstream V-SP: Enhanced performance, more usable cabin space
G500: Reduced-range version of V
G550: New; similar to V-SP
C-37A: Military transport version of G500 operated by the USAF
C-37B: Military transport version of G550 operated by U.S. Army and U.S. Navy

FEATURES:
Low/swept wing with winglets; twin Rolls-Royce157 Deutschland BR710 turbofans mounted on sides of rear fuselage; six cabin windows each side (seven in V-SP); swept T-tail with swept tailplane

Gulfstream Aerospace (IAI) Astra G100/G150 USA

Twin-turbofan mid-size business jet

Descendant of Aero Commander 1121 Jet Commander, acquired by Israel Aircraft Industries in 1968 and developed successively as the Commodore Jet and Westwind. The Model 1125 was launched at NBAA in October 1979 and named Astra in 1981. First flown on March 19, 1984, deliveries of the Astra started on 30 June 1986. Astra line sold to Gulfstream Aerospace in June 2001 and redesignated. Total delivered: 170.

SPECIFICATION (G100):

ACCOMMODATION: 2 + 9
CARGO/BAGGAGE: 1.4 m³ (51 cu.ft)
MAX SPEED: M0.85 (501 kt; 928 km/h)
RANGE: 2949 nm (5461 km)

DIMENSIONS:

WINGSPAN: 16.6 m (54 ft 7 in)
LENGTH: 16.9 m (55 ft 7 in)
HEIGHT: 5.5 m (18 ft 2 in)

VARIANTS:

Astra: Initial production version
Astra SP: Improved with new avionics and revised cabin interior
Astra SPX: More powerful engine, winglets, and advanced avionics
C-38A: Transport and medevac aircraft operated by U.S. Air National Guard
G100: Current production model
G150: Wide-cabin version of G100; shorter nose, small fuselage stretch

FEATURES:

Low/swept wing with winglets (SPX only); twin Honeywell TFE731 turbofans; six cabin windows; swept tailfin with low-mounted swept tailplane

Gulfstream Aerospace (IAI) Galaxy G200 USA

Twin-turbofan super mid-size business jet

Initiated by Israel Aircraft Industries as a derivative of the Astra SP with a new wide-body fuselage and more headroom, new engines, and transatlantic range. Formally announced on September 20, 1993, and first flown on December 25, 1997. First customer delivery made in January 2000. Astra/Galaxy line sold to Gulfstream Aerospace in June 2001 and redesignated. Total delivered: 144.

SPECIFICATION:

ACCOMMODATION: 2 + 18
CARGO/BAGGAGE: 3.7 m³ (130 cu.ft)
MAX SPEED: M0.82 (470 kt; 870 km/h)
RANGE: 3620 nm (6704 km)

DIMENSIONS:
WINGSPAN: 17.7 m (58 ft 1 in)
LENGTH: 19.0 m (62 ft 3 in)
HEIGHT: 6.5 m (21 ft 5 in)

VARIANTS:
Galaxy: Original production model of Israel Aircraft Industries
G200: Current production version

FEATURES:
Low/swept wing with winglets; twin P&WC PW306 turbofans; eight cabin windows; swept tailfin with mid-mounted swept tailplane

Hawker 400 USA

Twin-turbofan business jet and military trainer

Started life as the Mitsubishi MU-300 Diamond, which first flew on August 29, 1978. Beech acquired rights from Mitsubishi in December 1985 and renamed the improved aircraft the Beechjet 400. Deliveries of the Beechjet began in June 1986. Transferred to Hawker marque in May 2003. Total delivered (including military): 718.

SPECIFICATION (400A):

ACCOMMODATION: 2 + 8
CARGO/BAGGAGE: 0.75 m³ (26.4 cu.ft)
MAX SPEED: M0.82 (470 kt; 870 km/h)
RANGE: 1673 nm (1925 km)

DIMENSIONS:
WINGSPAN: 13.3 m (43 ft 6 in)
LENGTH: 14.8 m (48 ft 5 in)
HEIGHT: 4.2 m (13 ft 11 in)

VARIANTS:
Beechjet 400: Initial production version
Beechjet 400A: Enhanced performance model with new EFIS
Beechjet 400T: Military trainer for JASDF designated T-400
Beechjet T-1A Jayhawk: U.S. Air Force tanker and transport trainer
Hawker 400XP: Current version with payload increase, thrust reverser, and equipment enhancements

FEATURES:
Low/swept wing; twin rear fuselage-mounted P&WC JT15D turbofans; six cabin windows; swept T-tail and tailplane with small ventral fin

Hawker 800/900 UK/USA

Twin-turbofan mid-size business jet

Derived from the BAe 125 built in the UK, with a number of improvements, including the introduction of an EFIS cockpit, the first in a business jet. First Series 800 flew on May 26, 1983, and entered service in spring 1984. Adopted the Hawker 800 name when program purchased by Raytheon in 1993. Total delivered: 774.

SPECIFICATION (XP):

ACCOMMODATION: 2 + 14
CARGO/BAGGAGE: 1.67 m³ (59 cu.ft)
MAX SPEED: M0.80 (461 kt; 854 km/h)
RANGE: 2955 nm (5472 km)

DIMENSIONS:

WINGSPAN: 15.7 m (51 ft 5 in)
LENGTH: 15.6 m (51 ft 2 in)
HEIGHT: 5.4 m (17 ft 7 in)

VARIANTS:

125-800/Hawker 800: Initial production model
Hawker 750: As 850XP, without winglets
Hawker 800SP: Modification with winglets
Hawker 800XP: Extended-range version
Hawker 800XPi: Upgraded avionics and cabin interior
Hawker 800FI: Flight-calibration model sold to USAF as C-29A, Brazilian Air Force as EU-93, and JASDF as U-125
Hawker 800RA: Surveillance version of XP
Hawker 800SIG: Signals-intelligence version of XP
Hawker 800SM: SAR version operated by JASDF as U-125A
Hawker 850XP: Winglets and improved climb and range
Hawker 900X: New TFE731-50R engines

FEATURES:

Low/swept wing; twin Honeywell TFE731 turbofans mounted on sides of rear fuselage; six cabin windows; highly swept tailfin with high-mounted swept tailplane

Hawker 1000 UK/USA

Twin-turbofan long-range mid-size business jet

Based on the Hawker 800, but with a stretched fuselage and new P&WC PW305 turbofans replacing the TFE731s. Launched by British Aerospace in October 1989, the BAe 1000 made its maiden flight on June 16, 1990, and entered service in December 1991. Redesignated Hawker 1000 when program purchased by Raytheon in 1993. Total delivered: 51.

SPECIFICATION:

ACCOMMODATION: 2 + 15
CARGO/BAGGAGE: 1043 kg (2300 lb)
MAX SPEED: M0.82 (470 kt; 870 km/h)
RANGE: 3635 nm (6736 km)

DIMENSIONS:
WINGSPAN: 15.7 m (51 ft 4 in)
LENGTH: 16.4 m (53 ft 10 in)
HEIGHT: 5.2 m (17 ft 1 in)

VARIANTS:
125-1000/Hawker 1000: Basic production model

FEATURES:
Low/swept wing; twin P&WC PW305 turbofans mounted on sides of rear fuselage; seven cabin windows; highly swept tailfin with high-mounted swept tailplane

Hawker 4000 USA

Twin-turbofan mid-size business jet

All-new design under PD376 started by Raytheon Aircraft in 1993, but not announced until NBAA convention in November 1996, as the Hawker Horizon. Generally conventional layout, but with flat-floor stand-up cabin. First flown on August 11, 2001, the Hawker Horizon entered service in summer 2004. New model number applied in October 2005. Total delivered: 5 (ordered 74).

SPECIFICATION:

ACCOMMODATION: 2 + 12
CARGO/BAGGAGE: 2.83 m³ (100 cu.ft)
MAX SPEED: M0.84 (481 kt; 890 km/h)
RANGE: 3340 nm (6180 km)

DIMENSIONS:
WINGSPAN: 18.8 m (61 ft 9 in)
LENGTH: 21.1 m (69 ft 2 in)
HEIGHT: 6.0 m (19 ft 7 in)

VARIANTS:
Hawker 4000: Initial production model

FEATURES:
Low/swept wing; twin P&WC PW308A turbofans mounted on sides of rear fuselage; swept T-tail with swept tailplane

IAI Westwind ISRAEL

Twin-turbojet/turbofan mid-size business jet

Origins in Jet Commander first flown in USA on January 27, 1963. Production transferred in 1968 to IAI in Israel, which later developed the Commodore Jet and Westwind derivatives. The first stretched 1123 Westwind, powered by GE CJ610 turbojets, flew in September 1970. Production transferred to the new 1124 model with Garrett TFE731 turbofans, introduced in 1975. Total delivered: 36 (1123), 256 (1124).

SPECIFICATION:

ACCOMMODATION: 2 + 10
CARGO/BAGGAGE: 476 kg (1050 lb)
MAX SPEED: M0.82 (470 kt; 870 km/h)
RANGE: 2905 nm (5385 km)

DIMENSIONS:
WINGSPAN: 13.7 m (44 ft 10 in)
LENGTH: 15.9 m (52 ft 3 in)
HEIGHT: 4.8 m (15 ft 9 in)

VARIANTS:
1123 Westwind: Initial production model with GE turbojets
1124 Westwind: Initial turbofan-powered production model
1124 Westwind I: Increased fuel and various enhancements
1124A Westwind 2: New wing and improved hot-and-high performance
1124N Sea Scan: Maritime version with search radar and bubble windows delivered to the Israeli Navy

FEATURES:
Mid/straight wing with front and rear taper and tip-mounted fuel tanks (winglets on Westwind 2); twin GE CJ610 turbojets or Garrett TFE731 turbofans mounted on sides of rear fuselage; swept tailfin and low-mounted tailplane

Learjet 23/24/25/28/29 USA

Twin-turbojet light business jet

Designed by Bill Lear in Switzerland as the SAAC-23, but production moved to the USA, where the Learjet 23, powered by a pair of GE CF610 turbojets, made its first flight on October 7, 1963. Replaced by a number of improved models. Total delivered: 105 (23), 258 (24), 368 (25), 5 (28), 2 (29).

SPECIFICATION (25D):

ACCOMMODATION: 2 + 8
CARGO/BAGGAGE: 1.13 m³ (40 cu.ft)
MAX SPEED: 464 kt (859 km/h)
RANGE: 1437 nm (2660 km)

DIMENSIONS:
WINGSPAN: 10.8 m (35 ft 7 in)
LENGTH: 14.5 m (47 ft 4 in)
HEIGHT: 3.7 m (12 ft 3 in)

VARIANTS:
Learjet 23: Initial production version
Learjet 24: Improved cruise performance
Learjet 24B: Increased thrust
Learjet 24D: Longer range and square windows
Learjet 24E: Refined interiors and enhanced aerodynamics
Learjet 24F: Increased weight and range
Learjet 25: Stretched for up to eight passengers
Learjet 25B: No bullet fin fairing and four rectangular windows
Learjet 25C: Long-range model
Learjet 25D: Improved engines and new wing
Learjet 25F: Further increases in fuel and range
Learjet 25G: 25D with increased weight and wing modifications
Learjet 28: Supercritical wing with winglets, no tip tanks
Learjet 29 Longhorn: Long-range variant of Model 28

FEATURES:
Low/straight wing with tapered leading edge and tip tanks (tip tanks replaced by wingtips on 28/29); twin rear fuselage-mounted GE CJ610 turbojets; T-tail (bullet fin fairing on earlier models); three or four round or square windows

Learjet 31 USA

Twin-turbofan light business jet

Combines the fuselage and power-plant of the Model 35/36 with the more modern wing of the Learjet 55. Delta fins were added to the rear to stabilize the aircraft at high speeds. An aerodynamic prototype first flew on May 11, 1987, and the new type was officially introduced the follow-ing September. Deliveries started in summer 1988. Total delivered: 246.

SPECIFICATION (31A):

ACCOMMODATION: 2 + 7
CARGO/BAGGAGE: 1.76 m³ (62 cu.ft)
MAX SPEED: M0.81 (465 kt; 860 km/h)
RANGE: 1455 nm (2691 km)

DIMENSIONS:
WINGSPAN: 13.36 m (43 ft 10 in)
LENGTH: 14.83 m (48 ft 8 in)
HEIGHT: 3.75 m (12 ft 4 in)

VARIANTS:
Learjet 31: Initial production model
Learjet 31A: New integrated avionics and increase in speed
Learjet 31A/ER: Optional extended range with more fuel

FEATURES:
Low/straight wing with tapered leading edge and winglets; twin rear fuselage-mounted Honeywell TFE731 turbofans; swept T-tail and tailplane; delta fin (strake) each side below tail; six cabin windows on right side

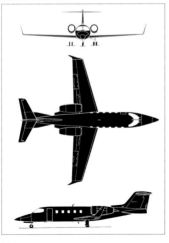

Learjet 35/36 USA

Twin-turbofan light business jet and special-missions aircraft

Larger and turbofan-powered development of Learjet 25, featuring Garrett TFE731 engines, a slightly bigger wing, and additional window on right side of fuselage. Prototype (originally known as the Learjet 26) flew on January 4, 1973, and customer deliveries started in summer 1974. Total delivered: 710.

SPECIFICATION (35A):

ACCOMMODATION: 2 + 8
CARGO/BAGGAGE: 1.13 m³ (40 cu.ft)
MAX SPEED: M0.82 (470 kt; 870 km/h)
RANGE: 2289 nm (4239 km)

DIMENSIONS:
WINGSPAN: 12.0 m (39 ft 6 in)
LENGTH: 14.8 m (48 ft 8 in)
HEIGHT: 3.7 m (12 ft 3 in)

VARIANTS:
Learjet 35: Initial production version
Learjet 35A: Redesigned wing for better short-field performance
Learjet 36: Long-range variant with increased fuel
Learjet 36A: Same wing modifications as Model 35A
C-21A: Operational support aircraft of USAF (Model 35A)
U-36A: Liaison/training aircraft operated by the JASDF plus many special-missions 35A/36A variants operated by a number of other military forces

FEATURES:
Low/straight wing with tapered leading edge and tip tanks; twin rear fuselage-mounted Garrett TFE731 turbofans; swept T-tail and tailplane; five cabin windows on right side, four on left

Learjet 40/45 USA

Twin-turbofan mid-size business jet

All-new design unveiled at the NBAA convention in September 1992. Although generally similar to the Model 31, the Learjet 45 is marked by a larger fuselage, wing, and tail unit, and increased head and shoulder room. First flown on October 7, 1995, first customer delivery on July 28, 1998. Deliveries of Learjet 40 started in January 2004. Total delivered: 299.

SPECIFICATION (Learjet 45):

ACCOMMODATION: 2 + 9
CARGO/BAGGAGE: 1.45 m³ (51 cu.ft)
MAX SPEED: M0.81 (465 kt; 860 km/h)
RANGE: 2120 nm (3922 km)

DIMENSIONS:
WINGSPAN: 14.5 m (47 ft 9 in)
LENGTH: 17.6 m (57 ft 9 in)
HEIGHT: 4.3 m (14 ft 2 in)

VARIANTS:
Learjet 45: Initial production version
Learjet 45XR: Longer range and improved hot-and-high performance
Learjet 40: Slightly shorter, high-performance derivative
Learjet 40XR: Enhanced engines delivering better hot-and-high performance and shorter take-off run

FEATURES:
Low/straight wing with tapered leading edge and winglets; twin Honeywell TFE731 turbofans, mounted high on rear fuselage; eight cabin windows; swept T-tail and tailplane; delta fin (strake) each side under tail

Learjet 55/60 USA

Twin-turbofan mid-size business jet (Learjet 60 pictured)

New series of business jets announced at Paris Air Show in June 1977, known as the Longhorn 50 series, with a stand-up "wide-body" cabin and accommodation for 10 passengers. The name "Longhorn" was subsequently dropped. The prototype Model 55 made its first flight on November 15, 1979, and deliveries started on April 30, 1981. Replaced by the stretched Learjet 60 in January 1993. Total delivered: 147 (55), 285 (60).

SPECIFICATION (Learjet 60):

ACCOMMODATION: 2 + 9
CARGO/BAGGAGE: 1.39 m³ (49 cu.ft)
MAX SPEED: M0.81 (465 kt; 860 km/h)
RANGE: 2735 nm (5065 km)

DIMENSIONS:
WINGSPAN: 13.35 m (43 ft 9 in)
LENGTH: 17.9 m (58 ft 8 in)
HEIGHT: 4.45 m (14 ft 7 in)

VARIANTS:
Learjet 55: Initial production model
Learjet 55B: Improved performance and digital flight deck
Learjet 55C: Delta fins and redesigned pylons
Learjet 55C/ER: Additional fuel tank in tailcone
Learjet 55C/LR: Further increase in range with optional fuel tank
Learjet 55LR: Seven-seat cabin and more fuel
Learjet 55XLR: Six-passenger cabin and further fuel increase
Learjet 60: Stretched fuselage and new PW305As
Learjet 60XR: New flight deck and redesigned interior

FEATURES:
Low/straight wing with tapered leading edge and winglets; twin Honeywell TFE731 or P&WC PW305A turbofans, mounted high on rear fuselage; six cabin windows on right, five on left; swept T-tail and tailplane; delta fin (strake) each side under tail

Lockheed L.1329 JetStar USA

Four-turbojet/turbofan mid-size corporate transport

Designed initially to fulfill a USAF requirement for a multiengined light transport, and first announced in March 1957. The four-engined JetStar first flew on September 4, that year and entered service with the USAF in 1960. The first civil customer took delivery in early 1961. Total delivered: 204.

SPECIFICATION:

ACCOMMODATION: 2 + 10
CARGO/BAGGAGE: 1280 kg (2822 lb)
MAX SPEED: M0.86 (493 kt; 912 km/h)
RANGE: 2220 nm (3573 km)

DIMENSIONS:
WINGSPAN: 16.6 m (54 ft 5 in)
LENGTH: 18.4 m (60 ft 5 in)
HEIGHT: 6.2 m (20 ft 5 in)

VARIANTS:
JetStar: Initial production version with P&W JT12A turbojets
JetStar II: Enhanced turbofan-powered development
C-140A: Navaid calibration aircraft operated by USAF
VC-140B: VIP transport operated by USAF

FEATURES:
Low/swept wings with fuel tanks set into mid-wing; four P&W JT12A turbojets or Garrett TFE731 turbofans in pairs on sides of rear fuselage; five cabin windows; swept tailfin and mid-mounted swept tailplane

Piaggio P.180 Avanti ITALY

Twin-turboprop high-speed corporate transport

Designed to provide jet speed with turboprop economics and launched in 1982. Gates Learjet became a partner in the program, but withdrew in January 1986 and Piaggio continued development on its own. First flight was made on September 23, 1986, followed by first customer delivery on September 30, 1990. Avanti II received EASA certification on October 24, 2005. Total delivered: 120.

SPECIFICATION:

ACCOMMODATION: 2 + 9
CARGO/BAGGAGE: 1.25 m³ (44 cu.ft)
MAX SPEED: 395 kt (732 km/h)
RANGE: 1850 nm (3426 km)

DIMENSIONS:
WINGSPAN: 14.0 m (46 ft 0 in)
LENGTH: 14.4 m (47 ft 4 in)
HEIGHT: 4.0 m (13 ft 1 in)

VARIANTS:
P.180 Avanti: Standard production model for corporate market
P.180 Avanti II: New integrated digital avionics and uprated engines
P.180 AM Avanti: Italian Air Force variant
P.180 E/ACTL-2 Avanti: Italian Army variant

FEATURES:
Mid/straight wing towards rear of fuselage; nose-mounted canard foreplane; twin wing-mounted P&WC PT6A turboprops with five-blade pusher propeller; swept T-tail and swept tailplane; two delta fin strakes under tail

Piper PA-31 Navajo/Mojave USA

Twin-piston business aircraft and commuterliner

Series of light six/eight-seat business twins with Lycoming piston engines, first flown as the original Navajo on September 30, 1964. Progressively improved and also targeted at the air-taxi and commuter market. Total built: 4318.

SPECIFICATION (Chieftain):

ACCOMMODATION: 1 + 9
CARGO/BAGGAGE: 318 kg (700 lb)
MAX SPEED: 231 kt (428 km/h)
RANGE: 1210 nm (2240 km)

DIMENSIONS:
WINGSPAN: 12.4 m (40 ft 8 in)
LENGTH: 10.6 m (34 ft 8 in)
HEIGHT: 4.0 m (13 ft 2 in)

VARIANTS:
PA-31 Navajo: Baseline model with Lycoming IO-470 engines
PA-31 Navajo B: Turbocharged TIO-540 engines
PA-31 Navajo C: Minor improvements
PA-31-325 Navajo C/R: Counterrotating propellers
PA-31-350 Chieftain: Stretched fuselage and 10-seat interior
PA-31-350 T-1020: Chieftain for commuter use with special interior
PA-31P-425 Pressurized Navajo: Pressurized fuselage, one less window on port side
PA-31P-350 Mojave: Combines Cheyenne I fuselage and Chieftain wings and tail
GM-17 Viper: Russian modification with single Walter M601E turboprop

FEATURES:
Low/straight and cranked wing with slight dihedral; twin wing-mounted Lycoming TIO-540 piston engines with three-blade propellers; three or four cabin windows; swept tailfin with low-set tailplane

Piper PA-31T Cheyenne USA

Twin-piston business aircraft and commuterliner

Essentially a P-31P pressurized Navajo fitted with P&WC PT6A turboprop engines, wingtip fuel tanks, and new flight-control system. It first flew on October 22, 1969, and was superseded by several improved models in subsequent years. Total delivered: 819.

SPECIFICATION (T-1040):

ACCOMMODATION: 1 + 9
CARGO/BAGGAGE: 227 kg (500 lb)
MAX SPEED: 236 kt (437 km/h)
RANGE: 1400 nm (2592 km)

DIMENSIONS:
WINGSPAN: 12.5 m (41 ft 1 in)
LENGTH: 11.2 m (36 ft 8 in)
HEIGHT: 4.0 m (13 ft 2 in)

VARIANTS:
PA-31T Cheyenne: Baseline model with PT6A-28 engines, later designated Cheyenne II
PA-31T1 Cheyenne I: Lighter and less powerful PT6A-11 engines
PA-31T1 Cheyenne IA: More powerful engines and improved interior and cockpit layout
PA-31T2 Cheyenne IIXL: Stretched fuselage and extra cabin window
PA-31T3 T-1040: Combines Chieftain fuselage with wings and landing gear of Cheyenne IIXL and engines of Cheyenne I
Blackhawk Cheyenne XP: PT6A-135A engine upgrade

FEATURES:
Low/straight and cranked wing with slight dihedral; twin wing-mounted P&WC PT6A turboprops with three-blade propellers; three or four rectangular cabin windows; swept tailfin with low-set tailplane

Piper PA-42 Cheyenne III USA

Twin-turboprop business aircraft

Announced on September 26, 1977, the Cheyenne III differed from earlier Cheyenne models primarily in having increased wingspan, a lengthened fuselage, T-tail, and more powerful engines. The production prototype first flew on May 18, 1979, and deliveries began June 30, 1980. Total delivered: 178.

SPECIFICATION (400LS):

ACCOMMODATION: 2 + 6
CARGO/BAGGAGE: 136 kg (300 lb)
MAX SPEED: 246 kt (455 km/h)
RANGE: 1400 nm (2592 km)

DIMENSIONS:
WINGSPAN: 14.5 m (47 ft 8 in)
LENGTH: 13.2 m (43 ft 4 in)
HEIGHT: 5.0 m (16 ft 5 in)

VARIANTS:
PA-42 Cheyenne III: Initial production model
PA-42-720 Cheyenne IIIA: Improved engines, increased weight, and extra cabin window on each side
PA-42-1000 Cheyenne 400LS: More powerful Garrett TPE331 turboprops, increased T-O weight, and updated systems

FEATURES:
Low/straight wing with slight dihedral and wingtip tanks; twin wing-mounted P&WC PT6A or Garrett TPE331 turboprops with three-blade and four-blade propellers respectively; four cabin windows; swept T-tail

Piper PA-46 Malibu Mirage/Meridian USA

Twin-piston/turboprop light business and private aircraft

Light six-seat business aircraft, which made its first flight on November 30, 1979. Replaced by improved Mirage from October 1988. New Meridian launched at 1997 NBAA convention, made its first flight on August 21, 1998, and entered service in mid-2000. Malibu Mirage and Meridian remain in production. Total delivered: 404 (Malibu), 564 (Mirage), 241 (Meridian).

SPECIFICATION (Meridian):

ACCOMMODATION: 1 + 6
CARGO/BAGGAGE: 0.94 m³ (33 cu.ft)
MAX SPEED: 262 kt (485 km/h)
RANGE: 1070 nm (1981 km)

DIMENSIONS:
WINGSPAN: 13.1 m (43 ft 0 in)
LENGTH: 9.0 m (29 ft 7 in)
HEIGHT: 3.5 m (11 ft 4 in)

VARIANTS:
PA-46-310P Malibu: Initial production model
PA-46-350P Malibu Mirage: New Lycoming engine replacing the Continental piston engine, increased gross weight
PA-46-500TP Malibu Meridian: New PT6A turboprop engine, strengthened wing, and enlarged and strengthened tail
JetPROP DLX: STC for conversion with PT6A-35 turboprops and Hartzell four-blade propeller

FEATURES:
Low/straight wing with dihedral (cranked leading edge on Meridian); twin wing-mounted Continental or Lycoming piston engine, or P&WC turboprop with three-blade propellers; three cabin windows; swept tailfin and low-set tailplane

Piper (Ted Smith) 600 Aerostar USA

Twin-piston light business aircraft

Mid-wing six-seat cabin monoplane with circular fuselage and swept tailfin designed by Ted Smith and first flown in production form on December 20, 1967. The Aerostar line was purchased by Piper Aircraft in March 1978 and continued in production until 1984. Total delivered: 1076.

SPECIFICATION (700P):

ACCOMMODATION: 1 + 5
CARGO/BAGGAGE: 109 kg (240 lb)
MAX SPEED: 266 kt (492 km/h)
RANGE: 890 nm (1648 km)

DIMENSIONS:

WINGSPAN: 11.2 m (36 ft 8 in)
LENGTH: 10.6 m (34 ft 10 in)
HEIGHT: 3.7 m (12 ft 1 in)

VARIANTS:

Model 600: Initial production model with Lycoming IO-540 engines
Model 600A: Minor changes
Model 601: Addition of turbocharged TIO-540 engines
Model 601B: Increased wingspan and higher gross weight
Model 601P: Pressurized version
Model 602P: Piper development of 601P, initially named Sequoia
Suffix E applied to various models for the European market
PA-60-700P: Model 602P with counterrotating Lycoming engines

FEATURES:

Mid/straight wing; twin wing-mounted Lycoming IO-540 piston engines with three-blade propellers; three cabin windows; swept tailfin and low-set tailplane

Rockwell Sabreliner USA

Twin-turbojet/turbofan executive jet

Started life in 1952 with North American Aviation (NAA) as the NA.286 Sabreliner, which first flew on September 16, 1958, and entered service with the USAF. The first civil model was certificated in April 1963. NAA later became part of Rockwell International, which itself sold the line to a new company, Sabreliner. Total delivered (including military T-39s): 631.

SPECIFICATION (75A):

ACCOMMODATION: 2 + 10
CARGO/BAGGAGE: 1135 kg (2500 lb)
MAX SPEED: M0.85 (487 kt; 901 km/h)
RANGE: 1713 nm (3174 km)

DIMENSIONS:
WINGSPAN: 13.6 m (44 ft 8 in)
LENGTH: 14.4 m (47 ft 2 in)
HEIGHT: 5.3 m (17 ft 3 in)

VARIANTS:
Sabreliner 40: First civil model similar to the T-39 and powered by P&W JT12A turbojets
Sabreliner 60: Lengthened fuselage for 10 passengers
Sabreliner 60A: Aerodynamic improvements
Sabreliner 65A: More efficient Garrett TFE731s
Sabreliner 75: Stand-up cabin and square windows, JT12As
Sabreliner 75A: JT12As replaced by GE CF700s
T-39 Sabre: Trainer and utility aircraft for U.S. forces, including the T-39A support aircraft; T-39B and T-39D radar and radar-interception trainers; CT-39E rapid-response airlifter; CT-39G tactical support aircraft; and T-39N navigation trainer

FEATURES:
Low/swept wing; twin rear-mounted P&W JT12A turbojets or Garrett TFE731 or GE CF700 turbofans; squat fuselage with rounded triangular windows (square in 75A); swept tail with low-mounted tailplane

203

Sino Swearingen SJ30 USA/TAIWAN

Twin-turbofan light business jet

Announced on October 30, 1986, as SA-30 Fanjet. Underwent several ownership changes prior to first flight on February 13, 1991. Aircraft continuously revised with stretched fuselage, more powerful engines, and aerodynamic improvements, which made for long development program. Crash of first conforming prototype on April 26, 2003, further delayed certification, but this was finally achieved October 27, 2005. First customer deliveries February 2007. Total ordered 295.

SPECIFICATION:

ACCOMMODATION: 2 + 6
CARGO/BAGGAGE: 1.7 m³ (60 cu.ft)
MAX SPEED: M 0.80 (459 kt; 849 km/h)
RANGE: 2500 nm (4630 km)

DIMENSIONS:
WINGSPAN: 12.9 m (42 ft 4 in)
LENGTH: 14.3 m (46 ft 11 in)
HEIGHT: 4.3 m (14 ft 3 in)

VARIANTS:
SJ30-2: Initial production version powered by Williams FJ44-2A fanjets

FEATURES:
Low/swept wing; twin rear fuselage-mounted Williams FJ44 turbofans; five cabin windows; highly swept tailfin and high tailplane

Private

Light

Aircraft

Aero Boero AB.95/115/180 ARGENTINA

Single-piston light aircraft

Design of conventional braced high-wing monoplane series began in the late 1950s, and the AB.95 was first flown on March 12, 1959, and entered service in 1961. Subsequent models were distinguished by increases in power and specialist applications. Total delivered: 600+.

SPECIFICATION (AB.180):

ACCOMMODATION: 1 + 3
CARGO/BAGGAGE: 100 kg (220 lb)
MAX SPEED: 108 kt (201 km/h)
RANGE: 635 nm (1175 km)

DIMENSIONS:
WINGSPAN: 10.8 m (35 ft 5 in)
LENGTH: 7.1 m (23 ft 3 in)
HEIGHT: 2.1 m (6 ft 9 in)

VARIANTS:
AB.95: Initial version with 95 hp Continental C-90 engine
AB.95A: More powerful 100 hp Continental O-200 engine
AB.95-115: 115 hp Lycoming O-235 engine
AB.115: Refined version with metal ailerons and modified landing gear; later fitted with larger wing and swept tail
AB.115/150RV: Rear-vision window for training; 150 hp Lycoming
AB.180 Condor: Enlarged version with four seats; more powerful engine
Several models were produced in ambulance configuration with suffix BS, agricultural (AG), with rear-view window (RV), and glider tug (RVR)

FEATURES:
High/braced straight wing with rounded tips; single Continental or Lycoming piston engine with two-blade propeller; swept tailfin (AB.115/180) and low-set tailplane; tailwheel-type landing gear and wheel fairings on some models

Beech 23/24 Musketeer/Sierra/Sundowner USA

Single-piston light aircraft

Developed as lower-cost, lower-performance complement to the Debonair/Bonanza range. First flown on October 23, 1961, the all-metal Musketeer differed in having less powerful engines and a fixed tricycle landing gear. Continual product upgrades resulted in a number of variants very different from the original. The Musketeer name was dropped in 1971, when existing production models were renamed Sundowner and Sierra. Total delivered: 4455.

SPECIFICATION (C23):

ACCOMMODATION: 1 + 3
CARGO/BAGGAGE: 122 kg (270 lb)
MAX SPEED: 123 kt (228 km/h)
RANGE: 641 nm (1187 km)

DIMENSIONS:
WINGSPAN: 10.0 m (32 ft 9 in)
LENGTH: 7.9 m (25 ft 11 in)
HEIGHT: 2.5 m (8 ft 3 in)

VARIANTS:
23 Musketeer: Initial production model
A23 Musketeer II: Fuel-injected engine; third window each side
A23A Musketeer Custom III: Higher TOGW and minor system changes
A23-19 Musketeer Sport III: Trainer version with two windows
A23-24 Musketeer Super III: Fuel injection; higher payload
C23 Sundowner 180: Standard port and starboard doors; deeper side windows
B24R Sierra 200: Retractable landing gear; extra portside door
C24R Sierra: Increased fuel capacity; larger propeller
Minor detail changes produced several other subvariants

FEATURES:
Low/straight wing; single Continental or Lycoming piston engine with two-blade propeller; two or three windows; swept tailfin with dorsal fillet and low-set tailplane; fixed or retractable landing gear

Beech 33 Debonair/Bonanza USA

Single-piston light aircraft

Similar in configuration to the Model 35 Bonanza but distinguished by a conventional tail unit and swept vertical tail surfaces. The prototype first flew on September 14, 1959, and production models were known as Debonairs until 1967. Total delivered: 3210+.

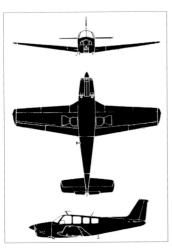

SPECIFICATION (F33A):

ACCOMMODATION: 1 + 4
CARGO/BAGGAGE: 122 kg (270 lb)
MAX SPEED: 182 kt (338 km/h)
RANGE: 838 nm (1553 km)

DIMENSIONS:
WINGSPAN: 10.2 m (33 ft 6 in)
LENGTH: 8.1 m (26 ft 7 in)
HEIGHT: 2.5 m (8 ft 3 in)

VARIANTS:
33 Debonair: Initial production model with utility interior
A33 Debonair: Rear side windows
C33 Debonair: Teardrop rear side windows, enlarged dorsal fillet
C33A Debonair: Optional fifth seat
E33 Bonanza: Less powerful engine, but improved trim
F33 Bonanza: Minor improvements, deeper rear side windows
Plus a number of other models and subtypes with minor detail changes and various engine models, including the B33, D33, E33A, E33B, E33C, F33A, F33C, and G33

FEATURES:
Low/straight wing; single Continental piston engine with two-blade propeller; three windows each side; swept tailfin with small dorsal fillet and low tailplane; retractable tricycle landing gear

Beech V35 Bonanza USA

Single-piston light aircraft

The prototype all-metal, high-performance Bonanza flew for the first time on December 22, 1945, and the type went into production in 1947. It featured a distinctive V-tail and retractable landing gear, and was powered by a 165 hp Continental piston engine. Total delivered: 10,404.

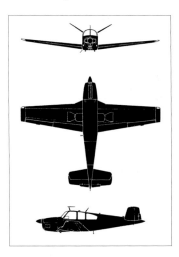

SPECIFICATION (V35B):

ACCOMMODATION: 1 + 4
CARGO/BAGGAGE: 122 kg (270 lb)
MAX SPEED: 182 kt (338 km/h)
RANGE: 838 nm (1553 km)

DIMENSIONS:
WINGSPAN: 10.2 m (33 ft 6 in)
LENGTH: 8.1 m (26 ft 7 in)
HEIGHT: 2.3 m (7 ft 6 in)

VARIANTS:
35: Initial production version
C35: Metal propeller and larger tail surfaces
F35: Additional rear window each side, auxiliary fuel tanks
H35: New propeller and structural strengthening
M35: Optional fifth seat
N35: Teardrop rear side windows, increased fuel capacity
S35: Longer cabin with optional fifth and sixth seats
V35: Single-piece and streamlined windshield
V35-TC: Turbocharged engine
Plus many other models and subtypes with progressive increase in power and weight, but minimal external changes, including B35, D35, E35, G35, J35, K35, P35, V35A, and V35B

FEATURES:
Low/straight wing, with or without tip tanks; single Continental piston engine with two-blade propeller; three windows each side; V-tail; retractable tricycle landing gear

Beech 36 Bonanza/T36 Turbo Bonanza USA

Single-piston light aircraft

Developed from the V35B Bonanza, the A36 differs in having a fuselage stretch for a full six-seat capacity, swept tailfin, large double doors on the starboard side, and increased baggage capacity. It first flew on January 4, 1968, and remains in production: Total delivered: 4350.

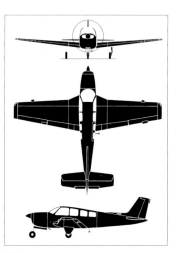

SPECIFICATION (B36TC):

ACCOMMODATION: 1 + 5
CARGO/BAGGAGE: 181 kg (400 lb)
MAX SPEED: 213 kt (394 km/h)
RANGE: 1022 nm (1893 km)

DIMENSIONS:
WINGSPAN: 11.5 m (37 ft 10 in)
LENGTH: 8.4 m (27 ft 6 in)
HEIGHT: 2.6 m (8 ft 6 in)

VARIANTS:
36 Bonanza: Initial production model with 285 hp engine
A36 Bonanza: Deluxe interior
A36AT Bonanza: Dedicated airline trainer, three-blade propeller
A36TC Bonanza: 300 hp turbocharged Continental engine
B36TC Bonanza: Longer span, increased range
G36 Bonanza: New Garmin G1000 avionics
T36TC Bonanza: T-tail version

FEATURES:
Low/straight tapered wings; single Continental piston engine with two- or three-blade propeller; four windows each side; swept tailfin and low-set swept tailplane (T-tail on T36TC); retractable tricycle landing gear

Beech 55/56/58 Baron/Turbo Baron USA

Twin-piston light aircraft

Essentially a reengineered and re-engined B95 Travel Air with swept-back tailfin and longer side windows, the 95-55 Baron made its first flight on February 29, 1960, with deliveries starting during 1961. Several model improvements led to the 58 Baron, which remains in production. Total delivered: 3728 (55), 94 (56), 2790 (58).

SPECIFICATION (58):

ACCOMMODATION: 1 + 5
CARGO/BAGGAGE: 181 kg (400 lb)
MAX SPEED: 203 kt (376 km/h)
RANGE: 860 nm (1593 km)

DIMENSIONS:
WINGSPAN: 11.5 m (37 ft 9 in)
LENGTH: 9.1 m (29 ft 9 in)
HEIGHT: 3.0 m (9 ft 11 in)

VARIANTS:
95-55 Baron: Initial production model
A55 Baron: Optional sixth seat, narrower fin/rudder
B55 Baron: Full six-seat cabin
B55B Cochise: B55 for U.S. Army as T-42A
C55/D55/E55 Baron: Minor changes
56TC Turbo Baron: Turbocharged Lycoming
A56TC Turbo Baron: Minor system changes
58 Baron: Longer cabin, dual starboard rear doors
58P Pressurized Baron: Pressurized cabin, turbocharged Continental engines; three-blade propellers
58TC Baron: Unpressurized version of 58P
G58 Baron: Upgraded with Garmin G1000 avionics

FEATURES:
Low/straight tapered wing with leading-edge gloves; twin Lycoming or Continental piston engines with two-blade or three-blade propellers; four windows each side; swept tailfin with dorsal fillet and low-set tailplane; retractable tricycle landing gear

Beech 60 Duke USA

Twin-piston light touring aircraft

Designed in early 1965 to slot in between the Queen Air and Baron in size, the pressurized, turbo-charged, and high-performance six-seat Duke first flew on December 29 that year. Initial deliveries followed in July 1968. Total delivered: 596.

SPECIFICATION (B60):

ACCOMMODATION: 1 + 4
MAX SPEED: 239 kt (433 km/h)
RANGE: 1020 nm (1887 km)

DIMENSIONS:
WINGSPAN: 12.0 m (39 ft 3 in)
LENGTH: 10.3 m (33 ft 10 in)
HEIGHT: 3.8 m (12 ft 5 in)

VARIANTS:
60 Duke: Initial production model with turbocharged Lycoming engines and rear portside entry door
A60 Duke: Increased T-O weight and improved turbocharger
B60 Duke: Larger cabin and enhanced pressurization system

FEATURES:
Low/straight wing; twin Lycoming piston engines with three-blade propeller; three cabin windows; swept tailfin with dorsal fillet and low-set tailplane; retractable tricycle landing gear

Beech 76 Duchess USA

Twin-piston light aircraft

Developed in the mid-1970s, the Duchess featured a T-tail, entry doors on each side of the cabin, and electric trim and flap controls. A prototype, designated PD289, flew in September 1974, but the definitive aircraft did not take to the skies until May 24, 1977. Deliveries commenced in May 1978. Total delivered: 437.

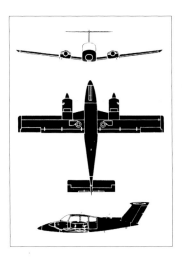

SPECIFICATION:

ACCOMMODATION: 1 + 3
CARGO/BAGGAGE: 91 kg (200 lb)
MAX SPEED: 166 kt (308 km/h)
RANGE: 711 nm (1317 km)

DIMENSIONS:
WINGSPAN: 11.6 m (38 ft 1 in)
LENGTH: 8.9 m (29 ft 2 in)
HEIGHT: 2.9 m (9 ft 6 in)

VARIANTS:
76 Duchess: Only version built, but several factory-installed optional equipment packages were available, including "Weekender" incorporating sun visor and tinted windscreen, cabin boarding steps and more; "Holiday" with coat hook and garment hanger and enhanced avionics; and "Professional," with two-seat headrests, true airspeed indicator, and wing-mounted taxi lights

FEATURES:
Low/straight wing with leading-edge wing gloves; twin wing-mounted Lycoming piston engines with two-blade propeller; three windows each side; swept T-tail; retractable tricycle landing gear

Bellanca 17 Viking USA

Single-piston light touring aircraft

Developed from the Bellanca 260 series with improved engines and minor airframe changes, replacing the former in 1967. The Viking proved a capable and successful aircraft, but production was halted in April 1980. Total delivered (including the Aries): 1383.

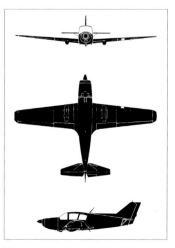

SPECIFICATION:

ACCOMMODATION: 1 + 3
CARGO/BAGGAGE: 84 kg (186 lb)
MAX SPEED: 181 kt (335 km/h)
RANGE: 929 nm (1722 km)

DIMENSIONS:
WINGSPAN: 10.4 m (34 ft 2 in)
LENGTH: 8.0 m (26 ft 3 in)
HEIGHT: 2.2 m (7 ft 3 in)

VARIANTS:
17-30 Viking 300: Initial production model with 300 hp engine
17-30A Super Viking: New airframe and enlarged wing tanks
17-30B Super Viking: Minor internal changes
17-31 Viking 300: 290 hp engine
17-31A Super Viking: Improved Lycoming engine
17-31TC Turbo Viking: Rayjay-supercharged engine
17-31ATC Turbo Super Viking: Improved supercharged engine
T-250 Aries 250: Improved performance, retractable landing gear

FEATURES:
Low/straight tapered wing; single Continental or Lycoming engine with two-blade propeller; swept tailfin with dorsal fillet and low-set tailplane; fixed tricycle landing gear (retractable in Aries)

Cessna 172 Skyhawk/Cutlass/175 Skylark USA

Single-piston light aircraft

Started initially as a tricycle development of the Model 170 and went on to become the most successful general-aviation aircraft. The high-wing Model 172 first flew on June 12, 1955, and remained in production for 30 years. Total built (all models): 41,091 (172), 2118 (175).

SPECIFICATION (172RG):

ACCOMMODATION: 1 + 3
CARGO/BAGGAGE: 54 kg (120 lb)
MAX SPEED: 140 kt (259 km/h)
RANGE: 840 nm (1554 km)

DIMENSIONS:
WINGSPAN: 10.9 m (35 ft 10 in)
LENGTH: 8.2 m (26 ft 11 in)
HEIGHT: 2.6 m (8 ft 6 in)

VARIANTS:
172: Initial production model
172A: Swept-back fin and rudder
172B Skyhawk: External streamlining and new avionics, spats optional
172RG Cutlass: Retractable landing gear and three-blade prop
172S Skyhawk SP: Special-performance version
FR172E Reims Rocket: Built in France by Reims Aviation
R172E: More powerful engines; also used by USAF as T-41 Mescalero
R172K Hawk XP: Luxury interior
175 Skylark: Uprated engine and redesigned engine cowlings
Plus many other variants within the Skyhawk, Cutlass, and Skylark series

FEATURES:
High/braced straight wing; single Continental or Lycoming piston engine with two-blade propeller; swept tailfin with dorsal fillet and low-set tailplane; fixed or retractable tricycle landing gear (wheel fairing on some models)

Cessna 177 Cardinal USA

Single-piston light aircraft

All-new replacement for the Model 172 family, featuring more spacious cabin and other external and internal refinements. First flown on July 15, 1966. Total delivered: 4240.

SPECIFICATION (177RG):

ACCOMMODATION: 1 + 3
MAX SPEED: 156 kt (289 km/h)
RANGE: 895 nm (1656 km)

DIMENSIONS:
WINGSPAN: 10.8 m (35 ft 6 in)
LENGTH: 8.3 m (27 ft 3 in)
HEIGHT: 2.6 m (8 ft 6 in)

VARIANTS:
177: Basic production version with fixed landing gear
177A: More powerful engine and new tailcone
177B: Redesigned wing with cambered wingtips. Deluxe models of 177 and 177A with main wheel fairings, overall paint scheme, and refined interior are named Cardinal, with deluxe 177B named Cardinal Classic
177RG Cardinal RG: Uprated engine and retractable landing gear
F177RG: Reims-built model

FEATURES:
High/braced straight wing; single Lycoming engine with two-blade propeller; swept tailfin with dorsal fillet and swept low-set tailplane; fixed or retractable tricycle landing gear

Cessna 180/185 Skywagon USA

Single-piston light utility aircraft

More powerful development of the Model 170B with rectangular tailfin with dorsal fairing and reshaped side windows. It first flew on May 26, 1952, and spawned numerous variants with engine upgrades and minor detail changes. The larger, six-seat Model 185 was first flown in July 1960. Total delivered: 6210 (180); 4339 (185), including military.

SPECIFICATION (A185F):

ACCOMMODATION: 1 + 5
CARGO/BAGGAGE: 160 kg (350 lb)
MAX SPEED: 147 kt (272 km/h)
RANGE: 850 nm (1573 km)

DIMENSIONS:
WINGSPAN: 11.0 m (36 ft 1 in)
LENGTH: 7.9 m (25 ft 9 in)
HEIGHT: 2.4 m (7 ft 10 in)

VARIANTS:
180: Initial production version
180G: Six-seat capacity and extra side windows
180H Skywagon: Detail changes
185 Skywagon: Strengthened airframe, enlarged dorsal fin, optional utility interior, cargo pod, skis, and floats
A185E Skywagon: Increased weight and more powerful engine
A185F Skywagon: Three-blade propeller and minor improvements
Plus many other models with minor changes in engine power and external and internal details, including the 180A, 180B, 180C, 180E, 180F, 180J, 180K, 185A, 185B. 185C, 185D, 185E, and special AgCarryall agricultural model. Also used by USAF as U-17A, U-17B, and U-17C

FEATURES:
Low/straight wing; single Continental piston engine with two- or three-blade propeller; tailfin with large dorsal fillet and low-set tailplane; tailwheel-type landing gear

Cessna 182 Skylane USA

Single-piston light aircraft

Essentially a Model 180 with a fixed tricycle landing gear, the Model 182 first flew in 1956 and went into service in January 1958. Final versions had retractable landing gear. Total delivered: 22,000+.

SPECIFICATION (182R):

ACCOMMODATION: 1 + 3
CARGO/BAGGAGE: 91 kg (200 lb)
MAX SPEED: 150 kt (278 km/h)
RANGE: 1025 nm (1896 km)

DIMENSIONS:
WINGSPAN: 10.9 m (35 ft 10 in)
LENGTH: 8.5 m (27 ft 11 in)
HEIGHT: 2.8 m (9 ft 3 in)

VARIANTS:
182: Initial basic production version
182C: Swept tailfin and third cabin window
182E: Cut-down rear fuselage and omni-vision rear windows
182P: Tubular steel landing-gear legs, larger dorsal fin
182R: Optional turbocharged engine
182S Skylane: New production from 1995
182T Skylane: Improved model from 2001
T182T Turbo Skylane: Turbocharged model
182R Skylane: Optional turbocharged engine
R182 Skylane RG: Retractable landing gear and optional turbocharger
FR182 Skylane RG: Reims-built Model R182
Plus many other variants with minor changes, including 182A, 182B, 182D, 182F, 182G, 182H, 182J, 182K, 182L, 182M, 182N, and 182Q. DINFIA-built models have prefix A
Deluxe versions with overall paint scheme and wheel fairings named Skylane

FEATURES:
High/braced straight wing; single Continental or Lycoming piston engine with two-blade propeller; swept tailfin with dorsal fillet and low-set tailplane; fixed or retractable landing-gear (wheel fairings on some models)

Cessna 205/206/207 Super Skywagon/Stationair USA

Single-piston light utility aircraft

Fixed undercarriage derivative of the Model 210 Centurion optimized for cargo/utility roles, featuring an additional small cargo door on the portside of the fuselage. Deliveries began in August 1962, leading to a multitude of developments until production ceased in 1985. Total built: 574 (205), 8400+ (206), 790 (207).

SPECIFICATION (U206G):

ACCOMMODATION: 1 + 5
CARGO/BAGGAGE: 109 kg (240 lb)
MAX SPEED: 147 kt (272 km/h)
RANGE: 680 nm (1259 km)

DIMENSIONS:
WINGSPAN: 10.9 m (35 ft 10 in)
LENGTH: 8.6 m (28 ft 3 in)
HEIGHT: 2.8 m (9 ft 3 in)

VARIANTS:
205: Initial production model
206 Super Skywagon: Uprated engine, starboard double cargo door
P206 Super Skylane: Deluxe interior, wheel fairings, two main doors
U206A Super Skywagon: Optional belly cargo pod and turbocharger
U206F Stationair: Cambered wing, new instrument panel, three-blade propeller
U206G Stationair 6: Turbocharged engine
206H Stationair 6: Redesigned wingtips, fuel-injected engine
207 Skywagon: Stretched 206D with seven seats
207A Stationair 8: Fitted with eight seats
Plus many other variants with minor changes, including 205A, U206, and 206A, 206B, 206C, 206D, 206E, each model with U, P, and TU (turbocharged) prefixes

FEATURES:
High/braced straight wing; single Continental or Lycoming piston engine with two- or three-blade propeller; swept tailfin with dorsal fillet and low-set tailplane; fixed tricycle landing gear with optional wheel fairings; optional floats

Cessna 210 Centurion USA

Single-piston light utility aircraft

First Cessna model to have retractable tricycle landing gear, but otherwise followed the usual braced high-wing and swept-tailfin formula. First flown in January 1957, the Model 210 entered service in late 1959. Total delivered: 9240.

SPECIFICATION (T210M):

ACCOMMODATION: 1 + 5
CARGO/BAGGAGE: 109 kg (240 lb)
MAX SPEED: 193 kt (357 km/h)
RANGE: 900 nm (1667 km)

DIMENSIONS:
WINGSPAN: 11.2 m (36 ft 9 in)
LENGTH: 8.6 m (28 ft 3 in)
HEIGHT: 2.9 m (9 ft 6 in)

VARIANTS:
210: Initial production model
210A: Third window on each side, higher rear roof
210B: Cut-down rear fuselage, rear-vision window
210D Centurion: Increased weight and more powerful engine
210G Centurion: Cantilever wing and wraparound rear window
210K Centurion: Enlarged cabin with six seats
P210N Pressurized Centurion: 210N with pressurized cabin and four windows each side
P210R Centurion: Cambered wingtips, more powerful engine
Plus other versions with minor changes, including 210C, 210E, 210F, 210H, 210J, 210L, 210M, 210N, and 210R. Models with turbocharged engines are prefixed T and are known as Turbo Centurion

FEATURES:
High/braced or cantilever straight wing; single Continental piston engine with two- or three-blade propeller; swept tailfin with dorsal fillet and low-set tailplane; retractable tricycle landing gear

Cessna T303 Crusader USA

Twin-piston light corporate aircraft

Originally developed as a four-seat aircraft, but redesigned for six seats and with turbocharged engines and counterrotating propellers, with which it first flew on October 17, 1979. First deliveries were made in October 1981, but production ceased four years later. Total delivered: 297.

SPECIFICATION:

ACCOMMODATION: 1 + 5
CARGO/BAGGAGE: 267 kg (590 lb)
MAX SPEED: 196 kt (363 km/h)
RANGE: 895 nm (1658 km)

DIMENSIONS:
WINGSPAN: 11.9 m (39 ft 0 in)
LENGTH: 9.3 m (30 ft 5 in)
HEIGHT: 4.1 m (13 ft 4 in)

VARIANTS:
T303 Crusader: Only production model; initially named Clipper

FEATURES:
Low/straight dihedral wing; twin turbocharged Continental piston engine with three-blade counterrotating propellers; swept tailfin with dorsal fillet and mid-mounted tailplane; retractable tricycle landing gear

Cessna 310/320 Skyknight USA

Twin-piston light aircraft

First twin-engined Cessna design to enter production after the war, including fuel storage in tip tanks and thrust augmentation from engine exhausts. The Model 310 first flew on January 3, 1953, and went into production in 1954. The enlarged turbocharged 320 Skyknight followed. Total delivered: 5438, including military models (310), 575 (320).

SPECIFICATION (310L):

ACCOMMODATION: 1 + 5
CARGO/BAGGAGE: 163 kg (360 lb)
MAX SPEED: 193 kt (357 km/h)
RANGE: 676 nm (1250 km)

DIMENSIONS:

WINGSPAN: 11.3 m (37 ft 1 in)
LENGTH: 9.0 m (29 ft 6 in)
HEIGHT: 3.0 m (9 ft 10 in)

VARIANTS:

310: Initial production version
310F: Extra cabin window, pointed nose, reshaped tip tanks
310K: Higher weight, "vista view" side windows
310Q: Bulged rear roof and rear-view windows in later models
310R: Lengthened nose with baggage compartment, three-blade propellers
320 Skyknight: Enlarged 310F with six seats and extra window
320E Executive Skyknight: Pointed nose, single-piece windscreen
Plus many other variants with minor changes, including 310B, 310C, 310D, 310E, 310G, 310H, 310I, 310J, 310L, 310M, 310N, 310P, 320A, 320B, 320C, and 320D. USAF acquired the 310A Blue Canoe designated U-3A, and the 310E Blue Canoe as the U-3B

FEATURES:

Low/straight wing with tip tanks; twin Continental piston engines with two- or three-blade propellers; swept tailfin with small dorsal fillet and low-set tailplane; retractable tricycle landing gear

Cessna 336 Skymaster/337 Super Skymaster USA

Twin-piston light corporate/utility aircraft

A major departure for Cessna, the Skymaster used a push-pull engine configuration to eliminate asymetric handling characteristics in one-engine-out situations, combined with a twin-boom tail layout. The Model 336 first flew on February 18, 1961, and entered service in mid-1963, but was quickly replaced by the improved 337 Super Skymaster. Total delivered: 195 (336), 2798 (337).

SPECIFICATION (T337G):

ACCOMMODATION: 1 + 5
CARGO/BAGGAGE: 165 kg (364 lb)
MAX SPEED: 205 kt (380 km/h)
RANGE: 1308 nm (2422 km)

DIMENSIONS:

WINGSPAN: 11.6 m (38 ft 1 in)
LENGTH: 9.1 m (29 ft 9 in)
HEIGHT: 2.8 m (9 ft 3 in)

VARIANTS:

336 Skymaster: Initial production model
337 Super Skymaster: Redesigned nose, retractable landing gear, revised rear engine intake
337B Super Skymaster: Optional belly cargo pack and optional turbocharged engines
337G Super Skymaster: Split airstair door, smaller rear windows, larger propeller
T337G Pressurized Skymaster: Pressurized cabin, dual front-seat windows, turbocharged engines
Plus many other variants with minor changes, including 337A, 337C, 337D, 337E, 337F, and 337H. Reims-built models are prefixed F, pressurized models P. Also M337 operated by USAF as O-2A, and MC337 operated as O-2B

FEATURES:

High/braced straight wing; twin Continental piston engines with two-blade push-pull propellers; twin slim metal tailbooms with swept tailfins and connecting tailplanes; retractable tricycle landing gear

Cessna 335/340 USA

Twin-piston corporate aircraft

Development of the pressurized Model 340 with retractable under-carriage, tip tanks, turbocharged engines, and portside rear entry door began in 1969, leading to service entry on December 8, 1971. Total delivered: 64 (335), 1287 (340).

SPECIFICATION (340A):

ACCOMMODATION: 1 + 5
CARGO/BAGGAGE: 422 kg (930 lb)
MAX SPEED: 229 kt (425 km/h)
RANGE: 1106 nm (2049 km)

DIMENSIONS:
WINGSPAN: 11.6 m (38 ft 1 in)
LENGTH: 10.5 m (34 ft 4 in)
HEIGHT: 3.8 m (12 ft 5 in)

VARIANTS:
335: Low-cost, non-pressurized version of Model 340
340: Initial pressurized production version
340A: More powerful engines, improved air conditioning, prop synchrophasers, new seats
340A II: Enhanced avionics package
340A III: Higher level of avionics

FEATURES:
Low/straight wing with tip tanks; twin Continental turbocharged piston engines with three-blade propellers; four round porthole-type cabin windows; swept tailfin and low-set tailplane; retractable tricycle landing gear

Cirrus Design SR20/SR22 USA

Single-piston light personal/business aircraft

Development of this low-wing composites aircraft began in 1990, with mock-up first revealed at Oshkosh in 1994. First flight was made on March 31, 1995, but deliveries did not start until March 22, 1999. Total delivered: 601 (SR20), 1705 (SR22).

SPECIFICATION:

ACCOMMODATION: 1 + 3
MAX SPEED: 160 kt (296 km/h)
RANGE: 800 nm (1481 km)

DIMENSIONS:
WINGSPAN: 10.8 m (35 ft 6 in)
LENGTH: 7.9 m (25 ft 11 in)
HEIGHT: 2.8 m (9 ft 3 in)

VARIANTS:
SR20: Initial production model
SR20A: Increased T-O weight and higher-specification avionics; further upgrades in versions 2.0, 2.1, and 2.2
SR20-G2: New, lighter fuselage and general improvements
SR20-GTS: Customized special edition
SRV: VFR-only version
SR21tdi: SR22 airframe with SMA SR-305 turbocharged diesel engine
SR22: Modified wing and more powerful engine; also available in -G2, -GTS, -SE, and Centennial Edition

FEATURES:
Low/straight wing with slight dihedral and upturned wingtips; single Teledyne Continental piston engine with two-blade propeller; swept and curved tailfin with dorsal fillet and low-set tailplane; fixed tricycle landing gear

Diamond DA40 Diamond Star AUSTRIA/CANADA

Four-seat turbo-diesel light touring/utility aircraft

Four-seat development of DA 20-C1, launched on April 23, 1997, at Aero 97 in Friedrichshafen, initially named Katana. Proof-of-concept prototype first flown November 5, 1997, with JAR certification October 25, 2000. First deliveries to U.S. customers during EAA Air-Venture, July 2001. Turbo-diesel prototype first flew 22 November 2001. Total delivered: 554.

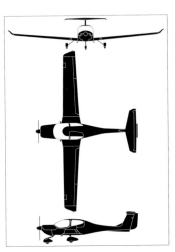

SPECIFICATION (DA40-TDI):

ACCOMMODATION: 1 + 3
CARGO/BAGGAGE: 30 kg (66 lb)
MAX SPEED: 154 kt (285 km/h)
RANGE: 750 nm (1390 km)

DIMENSIONS:
WINGSPAN: 11.9 m (39 ft 2 in)
LENGTH: 8.0 m (26 ft 3 in)
HEIGHT: 2.0 m (6 ft 7 in)

VARIANTS:
DA40-180: Original version with Lycoming IO-360 engines; now produced in Canada
DA40-FP: Fixed-pitch propeller
DA40-TDI: Thielert TAE 125 turbo-diesel variant; built in Austria
DA40XL: Uprated engine, higher gross weight, digital autopilot

FEATURES:
Low/straight wing; single turbo-diesel with three-blade propeller; streamlined fuselage with integral T-tail with dorsal fillet and downturned tips; single strake/tail bumper; fixed tricycle landing gear; speed fairings on all three wheels

Diamond DA42 Twin Star AUSTRIA

Four-seat twin turbo-diesel light touring/utility aircraft

Twin-engined version of DA40 Diamond Star. Decision to build was taken in November 2001 and the aircraft was formally launched on May 7, 2002, with letter of intent from Lufthansa training school for 40 aircraft. Prototype first flew on December 9, 2002. First deliveries were made on March 24, 2005. Total delivered: 125.

SPECIFICATION:

ACCOMMODATION: 1 + 3
CARGO/BAGGAGE: 93 kg (205 lb)
MAX SPEED: 203 kt (376 km/h)
RANGE: 1060 nm (1965 km)

DIMENSIONS:
WINGSPAN: 13.2 m (44 ft 0 in)
LENGTH: 8.5 m (27 ft 11 in)
HEIGHT: 2.6 m (8 ft 6 in)

VARIANTS:
DA42-TDI Twin Star: Initial production version with Thielert TAE 125 turbocharged diesel engines
DA42-360 Twin Star: Conversion with Lycoming engines
DA42 OPALE: Multipurpose aerial sensor surveillance platform

FEATURES:
Low/straight wing with large winglets; twin turbo-diesel engines with three-blade propeller; streamlined fuselage with integral T-tail with dorsal fillet and downturned tips; single strake/tail bumper; retractable tricycle landing gear

Extra EA-400/EA-500 GERMANY

Single-piston light touring/business aircraft

Announced in February 1993 and designed in collaboration with Delft University, the high-wing, high-performance, composites Extra 400 first flew on April 4, 1996. Turboprop EA-500 first flew on April 26, 2002. First customer delivery followed on August 21, 1998. Total delivered: 28.

SPECIFICATION:

ACCOMMODATION: 1 + 5
CARGO/BAGGAGE: 90 kg (198 lb)
MAX SPEED: 243 kt (450 km/h)
RANGE: 1403 nm (2600 km)

DIMENSIONS:
WINGSPAN: 11.5 m (37 ft 9 in)
LENGTH: 9.6 m (31 ft 5 in)
HEIGHT: 3.1 m (10 ft 2 in)

VARIANTS:
Extra EA-400: Initial production model with Teledyne Continental Voyager TSIOL engine
EA-500: Turboprop version powered by a single R-R 250-B17F/2 with five-bladed propeller

FEATURES:
High/cantilever straight wing with dihedral; single Teledyne Continental Voyager engine with four-blade propeller (three-blade optional); highly swept T-tail; retractable tricycle landing gear; R-R Model 250 in turboprop variant

Fuji FA-200 Aero Subaru JAPAN

Single-piston light touring aircraft

First indigenous light aircraft to enter series production in Japan. Design of this conventional low-wing aircraft started in 1964, followed by the first flight on August 12, 1965, with deliveries starting a year later. Total delivered: 299.

SPECIFICATION (FA-200-180):

ACCOMMODATION: 1 + 3
CARGO/BAGGAGE: 20 kg (44 lb)
MAX SPEED: 126 kt (233 km/h)
RANGE: 755 nm (1400 km)

DIMENSIONS:
WINGSPAN: 9.4 m (30 ft 11 in)
LENGTH: 8.0 m (26 ft 3 in)
HEIGHT: 2.0 m (6 ft 8 in)

VARIANTS:
FA-200-160: Basic production aircraft with a 160 hp engine
FA-200-180: More powerful 180 hp fuel-injected engine
FA-200-180AO: Low-cost reduced-specification model

FEATURES:
Low/straight dihedral wing; single Lycoming piston engine with two-blade propeller; swept tailfin and straight horizontal tailplane; fixed tricycle landing gear

Grumman American AA-5 Traveler/Cheetah/Tiger USA

Single-piston light touring aircraft

Larger four-seat development of the two-seat American Aviation AA-1, with which it shares some 60% commonality. It first flew on August 21, 1970, followed by initial customer deliveries in December 1971. Total delivered: 3225+.

SPECIFICATION (AA-5B):

ACCOMMODATION: 1 + 3
CARGO/BAGGAGE: 54 kg (120 lb)
MAX SPEED: 143 kt (265 km/h)
RANGE: 550 nm (1018 km)

DIMENSIONS:
WINGSPAN: 9.6 m (31 ft 5 in)
LENGTH: 6.7 m (22 ft 0 in)
HEIGHT: 2.4 m (7 ft 10 in)

VARIANTS:
AA-5 Traveler: Initial four-seat model with 150 hp engine
AA-5A Cheetah: Aerodynamic changes, longer rear windows
AA-5B Tiger: More powerful 180 hp engine, increased weight
AG-5B Tiger: Refined Tiger built by American General

FEATURES:
Low/straight wing; single Lycoming engine with two-blade propeller; tailfin with dorsal fillet and low-set tailplane; fixed tricycle landing gear with optional wheel fairings

Gulfstream Aerospace (Grumman American)
GA-7 Cougar USA

Twin-piston light touring aircraft

Grumman American design, first flown December 20, 1974. Over subsequent years, many design changes were made, including replacing the sliding canopy and adding a third window on each side. Deliveries started February 1978, by which time Grumman's light aircraft division had been bought by Gulfstream. The production run was short-lived as Gulfstream opted out of light aircraft manufacture the following year. Total delivered: 115.

SPECIFICATION:

ACCOMMODATION: 1 + 3
MAX SPEED: 160 kt (9296 km/h)
RANGE: 1170 nm (2165 km)

DIMENSIONS:
WINGSPAN: 11.2 m (36 ft 9 in)
LENGTH: 9.1 m (29 ft 9 in)
HEIGHT: 3.2 m (10 ft 4 in)

VARIANTS:
GA-7 Cougar: Only production model with twin 160hp Lycoming engines.; a higher-specification model was also available, but with same model number

FEATURES:
Low/straight wing with leading edge wing gloves; twin Lycoming engines with two-blade propeller; swept tailfin and low-set tailplane; retractable tricycle landing gear

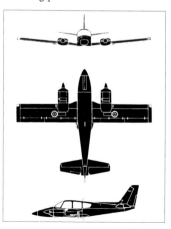

Ilyushin Il-103 RUSSIA

Four-seat single-piston-engine light aircraft

Exhibited in model form in Moscow in 1990 and made its first flight on May 17, 1994. Definitive Russian certification not achieved until December 4, 1997, followed a year later by FAR Pt 23 certification. Local deliveries believed to have begun in 1998. Total delivered: 50+.

SPECIFICATION:

ACCOMMODATION: 1 + 3
CARGO/BAGGAGE: 60 kg (132 lb)
MAX SPEED: 119 kt (220 km/h)
RANGE: 432 nm (800 km)

DIMENSIONS:
WINGSPAN: 10.6 m (34 ft 8 in)
LENGTH: 8.0 m (26 ft 3 in)
HEIGHT: 3.1 m (10 ft 3 in)

VARIANTS:
Il-103-01: Baseline version for Russian market
Il-103-10: Export version with upgraded avionics
Il-103-11: Export version with partly upgraded avionics for local navigation
Il-103P: Surveillance version with sensors and possible armament
Il-103SKh: Crop-sprayer, first flown on March 29, 2000

FEATURES:
Low/straight dihedral wing tapered front and rear; single Teledyne Continental or Lycoming piston engine; PT6A turboprop engine with two-blade propeller; moderately swept tailfin with low-set tailplane port freight door at rear; nonretractable tricycle landing gear

Lake LA-4 Buccaneer/Renegade/SeaFury/SeaWolf USA

Single-piston light amphibious aircraft

Development of the Colonial C-2 Skimmer IV with greater wingspan, strengthened structure, and higher weights, the LA-4 made its first flight in November 1959 and entered production in August 1960. Several more and improved variants built for both civil and military markets. Total delivered: 1100+.

SPECIFICATION (Renegade):

ACCOMMODATION: 1 + 5
CARGO/BAGGAGE: 90 kg (200 lb)
MAX SPEED: 139 kt (258 km/h)
RANGE: 900 nm (1668 km)

DIMENSIONS:
WINGSPAN: 11.6 m (38 ft 1 in)
LENGTH: 8.6 m (28 ft 3 in)
HEIGHT: 2.8 m (9 ft 3 in)

VARIANTS:
LA-4-180: Initial model with 180 hp engine
LA-4-200 Buccaneer: More powerful 200 hp engine, extra fuel
LA-4-200EP: Extended prop shaft, redesigned cowling
LA-4-200EPR: Reversible propeller
LA-250 Renegade/Renegade 2: Six-seat stretched fuselage, swept tail, 250 hp engine,starboard hatch
LA-250 Turbo/Renegade 2T: Renegade with turbocharged 250 hp engine
LA-270 Turbo: Turbo Renegade with uprated 270 hp engine
LA-250 SeaWolf: Military derivative with four hardpoints, nacelle-mounted radar, 290 hp engine
LA-270 SeaFury: Improved corrosion proofing for saltwater operations

FEATURES:
Mid/straight dihedral wing with balancer floats; single Lycoming engine mounted on pylon above hull with two-blade propeller; swept tailfin with high-mounted tailplane; retractable tricycle landing gear

Lancair/Columbia Aircraft Columbia USA

Single-piston light touring aircraft and trainer

Announced in 1996 by Lancair (now Columbia Aircraft) as the LC-40, this low-wing monoplane made its first flight in July 1996 and made its public debut at Oshkosh in August 1997. First production aircraft was delivered on February 24, 2000. Total delivered: 366.

SPECIFICATION (Columbia 350):

ACCOMMODATION: 1 + 3
CARGO/BAGGAGE: 54 kg (120 lb)
MAX SPEED: 235 kt (435 km/h)
RANGE: 1315 nm (2435 km)

DIMENSIONS:
WINGSPAN: 11.0 m (36 ft 1 in)
LENGTH: 7.7 m (25 ft 3 in)
HEIGHT: 2.7 m (9 ft 0 in)

VARIANTS:
Columbia 300: Basic production aircraft with 300 hp engine
Columbia 350: All-electric systems, more powerful engine
Columbia 350i: Enhanced avionics
Columbia 350SL: Further systems and equipment improvements
Columbia 350SLX: Anti-icing and climate control
Columbia 400: Turbocharged version; also available in SL and SLX configuration

FEATURES:
Low/straight wing; single Teledyne Continental engine with three-blade propeller; swept tailfin with curved leading edge and low-set tailplane; fixed tricycle landing gear

Let L-200 Morava CZECHOSLOVAKIA

Twin-piston light touring/business aircraft

Designed by Ladislav Smrcek, the all-metal L-200 was first flown on April 8, 1957. It was distinguised by its clean lines, twin tail, retractable landing gear, and wingtip tanks. Production was undertaken both by the National Aircraft Works in Kunovice, and by LIBIS in the then Yugoslavia. Total delivered: 1000+.

SPECIFICATION (L-200D):

ACCOMMODATION: 1 + 4
CARGO/BAGGAGE: 135 kg (297 lb)
MAX SPEED: 157 kt (290 km/h)
RANGE: 923 nm (1710 km)

DIMENSIONS:
WINGSPAN: 12.3 (40 ft 5 in)
LENGTH: 8.6 (28 ft 3 in)
HEIGHT: 2.3 m (7 ft 6 in)

VARIANTS:
L-200 Morava: Initial version with two 160 hp Walter engines
L-200A Morava: Higher powered 210 hp M337 fuel-injected engines driving electrically operated propellers, reprofiled cabin, hydraulically operated landing gear
L-200D Morava: Three-blade propeller, strengthened landing gear, improved electronics and equipment

FEATURES:
Low/straight wing with wingtip fuel tanks; twin wing-mounted Walter engines; twin rounded triangular tailfins; retractable tricycle landing gear

Maule M-4/M-7/M9 Rocket/Comet/Orion USA

Single-piston light STOL aircraft

Originally intended as a kitbuilt aircraft, the M-4, first flown on September 8, 1960, spawned a prolific series of rugged high-wing STOL taildragger aircraft, which remains in production. Total delivered of all series: 2450+.

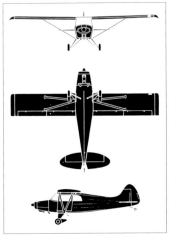

SPECIFICATION:

ACCOMMODATION: 1 + 4
CARGO/BAGGAGE: 349 kg (770 lb)
MAX SPEED: 130 kt (241 km/h)
RANGE: 829 nm (1537 km)

DIMENSIONS:
WINGSPAN: 10.3 m (33 ft 10 in)
LENGTH: 7.2 m (23 ft 6 in)
HEIGHT: 1.9 m (6 ft 4 in)

VARIANTS:
M-4 Jetasen/Rocket/Astro Rocket/Strata Rocket/ M-4-180V: Seven other variants and subvariants differing primarily in engine make and power, with or without cargo door
M-5 Strata Rocket/Lunar Rocket: Six variants with enlarged swept tail, drooped wingtips, four cabin doors, different engines
M-6 Super Rocket: Longer wingspan, increased T-O weight, optional seats and windows
M-7/MT-7/MX-7/MXT-7 Super Rocket/Star Rocket/Comet/Orion: Enlarged cabin, various engine and landing-gear combinations; current production models
M-9-230: M-7 with SMA SR305-230 diesel engine

FEATURES:
High/braced straight dihedral wing; single Continental, Franklin, or Lycoming engine; swept tailfin and low-set tailplane; tailwheel-type or fixed tricycle landing gear

Mooney M.20A/G Ranger/Chaparral/ Executive/Master/Statesman USA

Single-piston light touring aircraft

Based on a single-seat design by Al Mooney, the new improved and high-performance four-seater M.20 with a distinctive forward-swept tail flew on August 10, 1953, and went into production in 1955. Several variants were produced and in early 1970s were known as Aerostar when bought by Aerostar Aircraft Corporation. Production ceased in 1972. Total delivered: 6235.

SPECIFICATION (M.20F):

ACCOMMODATION: 1 + 3
CARGO/BAGGAGE: 54 kg (120 lb)
MAX SPEED: 152 kt (283 km/h)
RANGE: 997 nm (1845 km)

DIMENSIONS:
WINGSPAN: 10.7 m (35 ft 1 in)
LENGTH: 7.4 m (24 ft 3 in)
HEIGHT: 2.5 m (8 ft 3 in)

VARIANTS:
M.20: Initial production model with 150 hp engine
M.20A: More powerful 180 hp engine
M.20B Mk.21: Reengineered to all-metal construction
M.20C Ranger: Squared-off windows and new windshield
M.20D Master: Low-specification model with fixed landing gear
M.20E Super 21: Increased T-O weight and 200 hp engine
M.20E Chaparral: Squared-off windows and new windshield
M.20F Executive: Longer fuselage with three windows each side
M.20G Statesman: Reduced power

FEATURES:
Low/straight dihedral wing with wing glove; single continental or Lycoming engine with two-blade propeller; forward swept tailfin and low-set tailplane; two or three cabin windows each side; retractable landing gear (fixed in M.20D)

Mooney M.20J/S Allegro/Encore/Bravo/Eagle/Ovation

USA

Single-piston light touring aircraft

Improved Mooney range put into production following the acquisition of Mooney by the Republic Steel Company in late 1973. Initially, the Ranger, Chaparral, and Executive were produced before a new line emerged in 1976 with a more stream-lined exterior, new windscreen, and rounded-off window. Several models remain in production. Total delivered: 4145.

SPECIFICATION (M.20M):

ACCOMMODATION: 1 + 3
CARGO/BAGGAGE: 54 kg (120 lb)
MAX SPEED: 220 kt (407 km/h)
RANGE: 1070 nm (1982 km)

DIMENSIONS:
WINGSPAN: 11.0 m (36 ft 1 in)
LENGTH: 8.2 m (26 ft 11 in)
HEIGHT: 2.5 m (8 ft 3 in)

VARIANTS:
M.20J 201: Cleaned-up exterior, two windows each side, produced in LM (Lean Machine), SE (Special Edition), 205 with rounded side windows, ATS reduced specification, and MSE modified IFR versions; MSE named Allegro from 1990
M.20K 231: Turbocharged 210 hp engine, increased fuel; also in SE and 252TSE turbocharged SE variants, named Encore from 1997
M.20L PFM: Longer fuselage and 217 hp Porsche
M.20M TLS: Turbocharged 270 hp engine, three-blade propeller; named Bravo from 1996
M.20R Ovation: Luxury interior and 280 hp Continental engine
M.20S Eagle: Lower-cost entry-level version, derated engine
Ovation 2 and Eagle 2 are latest models. Also available in DX, GX, and GX 60th Anniversary Edition with enhanced avionics and systems

FEATURES:
Low/straight dihedral wing with wing glove; single Continental, Lycoming, or Porsche engine with two-or three-blade propeller; two cabin windows each side; forward swept tailfin with dorsal fillet and low-set tailplane; retractable tricycle landing gear

Piper PA-23 Apache/Aztec USA

Twin-piston light aircraft

Based on a Stinson design for a four-seat light twin, the PA-23 Apache, an all-metal monoplane with retractable landing gear, first took to the skies on March 2, 1952, and entered production in March 1954. Enlarged and more powerful Aztec was available from the end of 1959. Total delivered: 2047 (Apache), 4929 (Aztec).

SPECIFICATION (Aztec C):

ACCOMMODATION: 1 + 5
CARGO/BAGGAGE: 136 kg (300 lb)
MAX SPEED: 179 kt (331 km/h)
RANGE: 970 nm (1779 km)

DIMENSIONS:
WINGSPAN: 11.3 m (37 ft 1 in)
LENGTH: 9.2 m (30 ft 2 in)
HEIGHT: 3.1 m (10 ft 2 in)

VARIANTS:
PA-23-150 Apache: Initial production model with 150 hp engine
PA-23-160 Apache G: Longer internal cabin and extra rear window
PA-23-250 Aztec: Enlarged and more powerful 250 hp engine, swept tailfin
PA-23-250 Aztec B: Longer nose with baggage compartment
PA-23-250 Aztec C: Improved engine, optional turbocharger
PA-23-250 Aztec E: More pointed nose, single-piece windscreen
PA-23-250 Aztec F: System improvements, cambered wingtips
Plus other variants, including the PA-23-160 Apache E and H, and the PA-23-235 Apache. Also Aztec operated by U.S. Navy with designation U-11A

FEATURES:
Low/straight wing; twin Lycoming piston engines with two-blade propellers; three or four cabin windows; swept tailfin and low-set tailplane; retractable tricycle landing gear

Piper PA-24 Comanche USA

Single-piston light aircraft

High-performance all-metal design with retractable landing gear, swept fin, and laminar flow wing. First flown on May 24, 1956, with deliveries starting in late 1957. Total delivered: 4856.

SPECIFICATION (Comanche B):

ACCOMMODATION: 1 + 3
CARGO/BAGGAGE: 113 kg (250 lb)
MAX SPEED: 158 kt (293 km/h)
RANGE: 964 nm (1783 km)

DIMENSIONS:

WINGSPAN: 11.0 m (36 ft 1 in)
LENGTH: 7.7 m (25 ft 3 in)
HEIGHT: 2.3 m (7 ft 6 in)

VARIANTS:

PA-24-180 Comanche: Initial production version
PA-24-250 Comanche: More powerful 250 hp engine
PA-24-260 Comanche B: Increased weight and engine power
PA-24-260 Comanche C: Various improvements including "Tiger Shark" cowling, optional turbocharged engine
PA-24-400 Comanche 400: 400 hp engine, three-blade propeller, modified engine cowling, enlarged tailplane

FEATURES:

Low/straight wing; single Lycoming piston engine with two- or three-blade propeller; swept tailfin and low-set tailplane; retractable tricycle landing gear

Piper PA-28 Cherokee USA

Single-piston light touring aircraft and trainer

A low-wing metal replacement for Piper's PA-22 series, the Cherokee made its first flight on January 14, 1960 and was the forerunner of numerous variants with more powerful engines and performance improvements. Deliveries started in 1961. Total delivered: 30,000+.

SPECIFICATION (PA-28-181 Archer III):

ACCOMMODATION: 1 + 3
CARGO/BAGGAGE: 91 kg (200 lb)
MAX SPEED: 133 kt (246 km/h)
RANGE: 444 nm (822 km)

DIMENSIONS:
WINGSPAN: 10.8 m (35 ft 6 in)
LENGTH: 7.3 m (24 ft 0 in)
HEIGHT: 2.2 m (7 ft 4 in)

VARIANTS:
PA-28-140 Cherokee: Basic two-seat model with 150 hp engine
PA-28-150 Cherokee: Four-seater
PA-28-151 Warrior: New wing, tapered outer panels
PA-28-161 Warrior II: Uprated 160 hp engine
PA-28-161 Warrior III: Refined development with new wing
PA-28-161 Cadet: 2+2-seat trainer
PA-28-180 Challenger: Fuselage stretch and increase in wingspan
PA-28-180 Archer: Minor changes
PA-28-181 Archer II: Tapered wings of Warrior II
PA-28-181 Archer III: Exterior and interior restyling
PA-28-235 Cherokee: Longer wings and 235 hp engine, extra fuel
PA-28-235 Charger: Enlarged windows and door
PA-28-235 Pathfinder: Minor changes
PA-28-236 Dakota: Pathfinder with semitapered Warrior wing
PA-28-201T Turbo Dakota: Turbocharged 200 hp engine
Plus numerous other variants suffixed B, C, D, E, and F denoting minor changes

FEATURES:
Low/straight wing, some with semitapers; single Lycoming engine with two-blade propeller; swept tailfin with low-set tailplane; nonretractable landing gear (optional wheel fairings)

Piper PA-28R Cherokee Arrow USA

Single-piston light tourer

Derived from the Cherokee Archer II, but with more powerful engine, retractable landing gear with automatic extension, and untapered wings. First flown on February 1, 1967. Total delivered: 7000+.

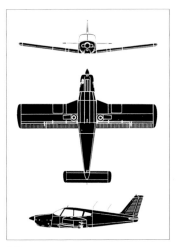

SPECIFICATION (Arrow III):

ACCOMMODATION: 1 + 3
CARGO/BAGGAGE: 90 kg (200 lb)
MAX SPEED: 145 kt (268 km/h)
RANGE: 880 nm (1630 km)

DIMENSIONS:
WINGSPAN: 10.8 m (35 ft 6 in)
LENGTH: 7.5 m (24 ft 8 in)
HEIGHT: 2.4 m (7 ft 10 in)

VARIANTS:
PA-28R-180 Cherokee Arrow: Initial production model
PA-28R-200 Cherokee Arrow: 200 hp engine
PA-28R-200 Cherokee Arrow B: New fuel system
PA-28R-200 Cherokee Arrow II: Small fuselage stretch, larger door
PA-28R-201 Arrow III: Longer semitapered wing
PA-28R-201 Arrow IV: Redesigned rear fuselage and new T-tail; Arrow III and IV also built as PA-28RT-201T with turbocharged engine

FEATURES:
Low/straight tapered wing with leading-edge wing gloves; single Lycoming engine with two-blade propeller; swept tailfin with dorsal fillet and low-set tailplane (T-tail in Arrow IV); retractable landing gear

Piper PA-30/39 Twin Comanche USA

Twin-piston light aircraft

A twin-engined development of the PA-24 Comanche, the PA-30 made its maiden flight on November 7, 1962, and was first delivered in summer 1963. The PA-39 introduced counterrotating propellers. Total delivered: 2001 (PA-30), 155 (PA-39).

SPECIFICATION (Twin Comanche B):

ACCOMMODATION: 1 + 3
CARGO/BAGGAGE: 113 kg (250 lb)
MAX SPEED: 167 kt (312 km/h)
RANGE: 892 nm (1650 km)

DIMENSIONS:

WINGSPAN: 11.0 m (36 ft 1 in)
LENGTH: 7.7 m (25 ft 3 in)
HEIGHT: 2.5 m (8 ft 3 in)

VARIANTS:

PA-30 Twin Comanche: Initial production version
PA-30 Twin Comanche B: Third cabin window each side and optional turbocharged engines
PA-30 Twin Comanche C: Improved engine, new instrument panel, optional tip tanks and turbocharged engine
PA-39 Twin Comanche C/R: Counterrotating propellers and optional turbocharged engine

FEATURES:

Low/straight wing with optional tip tanks; twin Lycoming piston engines with two-blade propellers; two or three windows each side; swept tailfin and low-set tailplane; retractable tricycle landing gear

Piper PA-32 Cherokee Six/Lance/Saratoga USA

Single-piston light tourer/business aircraft

Higher-capacity six-seat stretched model developed from the PA-28-235 and incorporating strengthened landing gear and larger tail unit. The Cherokee Six was first flown on December 6, 1963, with deliveries from mid-1965. Also built in Brazil as EMB-720 Minuano. A new wing and fuel-injected engine produced the Saratoga, while the Lance was fitted with a T-tail. Total delivered: 7200+.

SPECIFICATION (Saratoga II HP):

ACCOMMODATION: 1 + 5
CARGO/BAGGAGE: 90 kg (200 lb)
MAX SPEED: 175 kt (324 km/h)
RANGE: 859 nm (1590 km)

DIMENSIONS:
WINGSPAN: 11.0 m (36 ft 1 in)
LENGTH: 8.5 m (27 ft 11 in)
HEIGHT: 2.6 m (8 ft 6 in)

VARIANTS:
PA-32 Cherokee Six: Initial production model with 250 hp engine
PA-32-260 Cherokee Six: 260 hp engine
PA-32-300 Cherokee Six: 300 hp engine
PA-32-301 Saratoga: New semitapered wing
PA-32-301T Turbo Saratoga: Turbocharged
PA-32R-300 Cherokee Lance: PA-32-300 with retractable landing gear
PA-32RT-300 Lance II: Fitted with T-tail
PA-32R-301 Saratoga SP: Lance retractable landing gear, no T-tail
PA-32R-301 Saratoga II HP: High-performance model, reduced-depth side windows
PA-32R-301T Saratoga II TC: New interior
Some models also built with turbocharged engines; Cherokee Six also with B, C, D, and E suffixes denoting minor changes
PA-32-301FT 6X: Fixed-gear version of Saratoga II; rear cabin window removed
PA-32-301XTC 6XT: Turbocharged

FEATURES:
Low/straight wing with leading-edge wing gloves; single Lycoming piston engine with two-blade propeller; swept tailfin with small dorsal fillet and low-set tailplane (T-tail in Lance II)

Piper PA-34 Seneca USA

Twin-piston light aircraft

Twin-engined development of the Cherokee Six, first flown in definitive form in October 1969. Production deliveries began on September 23, 1971, and latest model remains in service. Also built in Poland under license by PZL-Mielec as the M-20 Mewa and in Brazil as the EMB-810. Total delivered: 4700+.

SPECIFICATION (Seneca IV):

ACCOMMODATION: 1 + 5
CARGO/BAGGAGE: 84 kg (185 lb)
MAX SPEED: 193 kt (358 km/h)
RANGE: 826 nm (1529 km)

DIMENSIONS:

WINGSPAN: 11.9 m (38 ft 11 in)
LENGTH: 8.7 m (28 ft 7 in)
HEIGHT: 3.0 m (9 ft 10 in)

VARIANTS:

PA-34-200 Seneca: Initial production model with 200 hp engines
PA-34-200T Seneca II: Turbocharged engines
PA-34-220T Seneca III: 220 hp turbocharged engine, single-piece windshield, increased MGTOW, new instrument panel
PA-34-220T Seneca IV: Upgraded interior, reduced-depth side windows
PA-34-220T Seneca V: Upgraded interior, new turbocharged Teledyne Continental engine

FEATURES:

Low/straight wing with leading-edge wing gloves; twin Continental or Lycoming piston engines with three- or two-blade propellers respectively; swept tailfin and low-set tailplane; retractable tricycle landing gear

Piper PA-44 Seminole USA

Twin-piston light aircraft

Conceived in 1970s as a Twin Comanche replacement and as a twin-engined trainer. Developed from the PA-28R Archer, it featured a T-tail and swept fin, and first flew in May 1976. FAA certification received on March 10, 1978. Turbocharged model introduced from 1980. Seminole remains in production. Total delivered: 720.

SPECIFICATION (PA-44-180T):

ACCOMMODATION: 1 + 3
CARGO/BAGGAGE: 91 kg (200 lb)
MAX SPEED: 168 kt (311 km/h)
RANGE: 820 nm (1517 km)

DIMENSIONS:
WINGSPAN: 11.8 m (38 ft 7 in)
LENGTH: 8.4 m (27 ft 7 in)
HEIGHT: 2.6 m (8 ft 6 in)

VARIANTS:
PA-44-180 Seminole: Production model with 180 hp engine
PA-44-180T Turbo Seminole: Turbocharged engine; production discontinued in 1982

FEATURES:
Low/straight tapered wing with leading-edge wing gloves; twin Lycoming piston engine with three- or two-blade (turbocharged model) propellers; swept T-tail; retractable tricycle landing gear

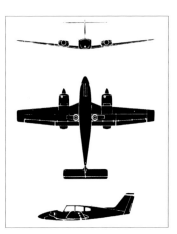

PZL Warszawa PZL-104 Wilga POLAND

Single-piston light general-purpose aircraft

Development of this rugged high-wing aircraft began in the early 1960s, with the prototype Wilga 1 making its maiden flight on April 24, 1962. Substantial redesign followed and the Wilga 2 flew in August 1963. Some early models also built in Indonesia by Lipnur Gelatik. The latest Wilga 2000 remains in production: Total delivered: 1150+.

SPECIFICATION (Wilga 2000):

ACCOMMODATION: 1 + 3
CARGO/BAGGAGE: 35 kg (77 lb)
MAX SPEED: 112 kt (208 km/h)
RANGE: 750 nm (1390 km)

DIMENSIONS:
WINGSPAN: 11.3 m (37 ft 1 in)
LENGTH: 8.1 m (26 ft 7 in)
HEIGHT: 3.0 m (9 ft 11 in)

VARIANTS:
PZL-104 Wilga 3: Initial production model in 3A utility and 3S ambulance versions
PZL-104 Wilga 32: Indonesian-built and modified Wilga 35
PZL-104 Wilga 35: Reconfigured cabin and landing gear
PZL-104 Wilga 80: Minor changes to air intake
PZL-104M Wilga 2000: Westernized version flown on August 21, 1996; improved PZL-100MA Wilga 2000 from 2005
PZL-104MF Wilga 2000: Polish Border Guard version
PZL-104MW Wilga 2000 Hydro: Floatplane
Plus several subvariants of Wilga 35 and 80 models suffixed A for flying-club use with glider-towing hook; H for floatplane, P for ambulance, with two stretchers; and R for agricultural, with underfuselage hooper and spraybars

FEATURES:
High/straight wing; single PZL AI-14 or Textron Lycoming IO-540 engine with two- or three-blade propeller respectively; swept wing with dorsal fillet and low-set tailplane; nonretractable tailwheel-type landing gear

Robin DR 400 Petit Prince/Dauphin/Major/Regent

FRANCE

Single-piston light touring and training aircraft

Evolved from the Jodel taildraggers, combining the wing with a four-seat cabin and tricycle landing gear, the DR 400 Petit Prince first flew on May 15, 1972. It was subsequently developed into a number of improved models and for different roles, and remains in production as a tourer and gliding tug. Total delivered: 1700+.

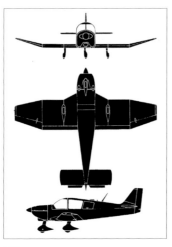

SPECIFICATION (Regent):

ACCOMMODATION: 1 + 3
CARGO/BAGGAGE: 60 kg (132 lb)
MAX SPEED: 140 kt (260 km/h)
RANGE: 785 nm (1453 km)

DIMENSIONS:
WINGSPAN: 8.7 m (28 ft 7 in)
LENGTH: 7.0 m (22 ft 10 in)
HEIGHT: 2.2 m (7 ft 3 in)

VARIANTS:
DR 400-120 Petit Prince: 120 hp engine, forward-sliding canopy
DR 400/120 Dauphin 2+2: Extra cabin windows and 2+2 seating
DR 400/140B Dauphin 4: Full four-seater, previously known as Major 80
DR 400/160 Major: Additional rear cabin window on each side, external baggage-compartment door on portside
DR 400/180 Regent: 180 hp engine
DR 400/180R Remo 180: Glider tug, formerly named Remorqueur
DR 400/200R Remo 200: 200 hp engine
Plus several other earlier models distinguished largely through engine power

FEATURES:
Low/straight tapered wing with upturned outer section; single Textron Lycoming engine with two-blade propeller; swept tailfin with low-set tailplane; fixed tricycle landing gear with wheel fairings; tail skid

Robin HR.100 Royal/Safari/R.1180 Aiglon FRANCE

Single-piston light aircraft

Low-wing all-metal design with spatted fixed tricycle landing gear and enclosed cabin for four people, the HR.100 first flew on April 3, 1969, and entered production in 1971. Unlike previous Robin Jodel designs, the HR.100 abandoned the traditional cranked wing shape. Total delivered: 174.

SPECIFICATION:

ACCOMMODATION: 1 + 4
MAX SPEED: 135 kt (251 km/h)
RANGE: 878 nm (1624 km)

DIMENSIONS:
WINGSPAN: 9.1 m (29 ft 9 in)
LENGTH: 7.6 m (24 ft 11 in)
HEIGHT: 2.7 m (8 ft 10 in)

VARIANTS:
HR.100-200B Royal: Initial production model with 200 hp engine
HR.100-210 Safari: 210 hp Continental engine, increased TOGW
HR.100-210D: Special designation German version
HR.100-250TR Tiara: 250 hp Continental Tiara engine, increased HGTOW
HR.100-285TR Tiara: More powerful 285 hp Continental Tiara
R.1180 Aiglon: Modified HR.100 with lighter airframe
R.1180T Aiglon: Longer cabin windows, more fuel
R.1180TD Aiglon II: New interior

FEATURES:
Low/straight wing; single Continental or Lycoming engine with two-blade propeller; swept tailfin and low-set tailplane; fixed tricycle landing gear

Rockwell (Aero Commander) Commander 112/114 USA

Single-piston light touring aircraft

Designed by Rockwell's Aero Commander division, the low-wing four-seater with a retractable tricycle landing gear made its first flight on December 4, 1970. The first production aircraft was delivered in August 1972. More powerful versions followed, but production ceased in 1979. Total delivered: 1310.

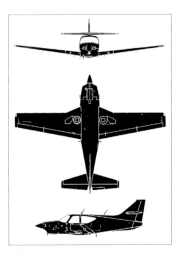

SPECIFICATION (114):

ACCOMMODATION: 1 + 3
MAX SPEED: 157 kt (290 km/h)
RANGE: 730 nm (1350 km)

DIMENSIONS:
WINGSPAN: 10.0 m (32 ft 9 in)
LENGTH: 7.6 m (24 ft 11 in)
HEIGHT: 2.6 m (8 ft 6 in)

VARIANTS:
112: Basic production model with 200 hp engine
112A: Strengthened airframe, metal cabin doors
112B: Increased wingspan, higher payload, new propeller, and larger wheels
112TC: Turbocharged engine
112TC-A Alpine Commander: Similar improvements to 112B
114: More powerful 260 hp fuel-injected engine
114A Grand Turismo Commander: Similar airframe modifications as 112B
114B: New propeller and external detail changes, interior restyling

FEATURES:
Low/straight dihedral wing; single Lycoming engine with two- or three-blade propeller; swept tailfin with dorsal fillet and mid-mounted tailplane; retractable tricycle landing gear

SIAI-Marchetti S.205/S.208 ITALY

Single-piston light touring aircraft

Work on a four-seat, all-metal aircraft was started in March 1964, designed to form the basis of several models with different engine options and either fixed or retractable landing gear. The S.205 made its first flight in 1965, with the larger S.208 following in 1968. Total delivered: 620.

SPECIFICATION (S208):

ACCOMMODATION: 1 + 4
MAX SPEED: 162 kt (300 km/h)
RANGE: 973 nm (1800 km)

DIMENSIONS:
WINGSPAN: 11.2 m (36 ft 9 in)
LENGTH: 8.1 m (26 ft 7 in)
HEIGHT: 2.9 m (9 ft 6 in)

VARIANTS:
S.205/18F: Initial production model with 180 hp engine and fixed landing gear
S.205/18R: Similar but retractable landing gear
S.205/20F: 200 hp engine
S.205/20R: 20F with retractable landing gear
S.205/22R: 220 hp Franklin engine, known as Sirius or Vela in the U.S.
S.208: Five-seat versions, 260 hp engine
S.208M: Military derivative sold to Italian Air Force

FEATURES:
Low/straight wing; single Lycoming or Franklin engine with two-blade propeller; tailfin with large dorsal fin and low-set tailplane; fixed or retractable tricycle landing gear

Socata GY Horizon/ST Diplomate FRANCE

Single-piston light aircraft

The original low-wing Horizon began life as a private design by Yves Gardan, who flew a prototype on July 21, 1960. Sud-Aviation acquired the manufacturing rights on July 10, 1962, and put the type into production in 1963. Transferred in 1966 to the new Socata works at Tarbes-Ossun. An improved version, the Super Horizon 200, flew on November 7, 1967. It later became the Provence and then Diplomate. Total delivered: 267 (Horizon), 55 (Diplomate).

SPECIFICATION (Horizon):

ACCOMMODATION: 1 + 3
CARGO/BAGGAGE: 40 kg (88 lb)
MAX SPEED: 126 kt (234 km/h)
RANGE: 515 nm (953 km)

DIMENSIONS:
WINGSPAN: 9.7 m (31 ft 10 in)
LENGTH: 6.6 m (21 ft 9 in)
HEIGHT: 2.6 m (8 ft 6 in)

VARIANTS:
GY-80-150 Horizon: Basic production version with 150 hp engine
GY-80-160 Horizon: Alternative higher-powered 160 hp model
GY-80-180 Horizon: More powerful 180 hp engine
ST-10 Diplomate: Stretched cabin and 200 hp fuel-injected engine

FEATURES:
Low/straight wing with outer dihedral; single Lycoming piston engine with two-bladed propeller; swept tailfin with small dorsal fillet and low-set tailplane; semiretractable tricycle landing gear

Socata MS Rallye Club/Commodore FRANCE

Single-piston light touring and training aircraft

Originally designed by Moraine Saulnier, the first three-seater Rallye with tricycle landing gear and various aerodynamic innovations flew on June 10, 1959. Deliveries started at the end of 1961, leading to the production of a prolific family of light three/four-seat aircraft. Also built in Poland as the Koliber. Total delivered: 3500+.

SPECIFICATION (MS.880B):

ACCOMMODATION: 1 + 3
CARGO/BAGGAGE: 40 kg (88 lb)
MAX SPEED: 105 kt (194 km/h)
RANGE: 460 nm (853 km)

DIMENSIONS:
WINGSPAN: 9.6 m (31 ft 5 in)
LENGTH: 7.0 m (22 ft 11 in)
HEIGHT: 2.7 m (8 ft 10 in)

VARIANTS:
MS.880B Rallye Club: Initial production version with 100 hp engine
MS.883 Rallye 115: Large dorsal fin and 115 hp engine
MS.885 Super Rallye: More powerful engine and increased weight
MS.892A Commodore: 145 hp engine, heavier airframe, enlarged tail unit, enhanced equipment fit
MS.893A Commodore 180: 180 hp engine and streamlined body
MS.894A Minerva 220: 220 hp Franklin engine
Rallye 235GT Gabier: 235 hp engine
Plus many other variants and subvariants

FEATURES:
Low/straight wing; single Continental, Lycoming, or Franklin engine with two- or three-blade propeller; swept tailfin and low-set tailplane; fixed tricycle landing gear (skis or floats also used)

Socata TB Tampico/Tobago/Trinidad FRANCE

Single-piston light touring aircraft

Design work began in 1975 on a new aircraft intended to replace the successful Rallye series. Of conventional low-wing configuration, the prototype first flew on February 23, 1977, with initial deliveries commencing in September 1979. Similar but more powerful additions to the line followed in quick succession. Total delivered: 2248.

SPECIFICATION (TB 200 Tobago GT):

ACCOMMODATION: 1 + 4
CARGO/BAGGAGE: 45 kg (100 lb)
MAX SPEED: 130 kt (241 km/h)
RANGE: 637 nm (1180 km)

DIMENSIONS:
WINGSPAN: 10.0 m (32 ft 9 in)
LENGTH: 7.7 m (25 ft 3 in)
HEIGHT: 3.0 m (9 ft 11 in)

VARIANTS:
TB 9 Tampico: Initial production model with 160 hp engine
TB 10 Tobago: More powerful 180 hp engine, faired undercarriage, higher gross weight
TB 200 Tobago XL: Fuel-injected engine
TB 20 Trinidad: More powerful 250 hp engine, retractable gear
TB 20 Trinidad GT Premium: Limited-edition deluxe version
TB 21 Trinidad TC: Turbocharged variant of TB 20 Tobago, also built with fixed-pitch propeller (suffixed *FP*), and with constant speed propeller (suffixed *CS*); various improvements produced the Tampico Club and Tampico Sprint models. New, improved models from 2000 carry suffix *GT* (Generation Two)

FEATURES:
Low/straight dihedral wing with upturned wingtips; single Textron Lycoming engine with two-blade propeller; swept tailfin and low-set tailplane; fixed tricycle landing gear (retractable in Trinidad models)

Civil
Helicopters

Aerospatiale SA 315B Lama FRANCE

Single-turboshaft utility helicopter

Design of the Lama began in late 1968, initially to meet a requirement of the Indian armed forces. It combined the airframe of the Alouette II and the dynamic systems and engine of the Alouette III. A prototype was first flown on March 17, 1969, and the type went into service the following year. Total delivered: 418 (in France and Brazil); 245 in India, where production continues.

SPECIFICATION:

ACCOMMODATION: 1 + 4
CARGO/BAGGAGE: 450 kg (992 lb)
MAX SPEED: 113 kt (210 km/h)
RANGE: 296 nm (550 km)

DIMENSIONS:
MAIN ROTOR DIAMETER: 11.0 m (36 ft 1 in)
LENGTH: rotors turning, 12.9 m (42 ft 4 in)
HEIGHT: 3.1 m (10 ft 2 in)

VARIANTS:
SA 315B Lama: French-built production model
SA 315B Gaviao: Small number built under licence by Helibras
HAL Cheetah: License-built by Hindustan Aeronautics in India

FEATURES:
Three-blade main rotor/single exposed Turbomeca Artouste turboshaft; glazed bubble canopy; lattice tailboom; fixed-skid landing gear with removable ground-handling wheels

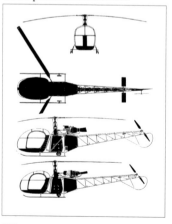

Aerospatiale SA 316B/319B Alouette III FRANCE

Single-turboshaft utility helicopter

Developed from the Alouette II, with larger cabin, greater power, improved equipment, and higher performance. The prototype flew for the first time on February 28, 1958, and the type entered service in 1960. Total delivered: 1523 (346 civil, 1097 military). Hindustan Aeronautics continues to build small numbers under the name of Chetak.

SPECIFICATION (SA 316B):

ACCOMMODATION: 1 + 6
CARGO/BAGGAGE: 750 kg (1653 lb)
MAX SPEED: 113 kt (210 km/h)
RANGE: 257 nm (477 km)

DIMENSIONS:
MAIN ROTOR DIAMETER: 11.0 m (36 ft 1 in)
LENGTH: rotors turning, 12.8 m (42 ft 1 in)
HEIGHT: 3.0 m (9 ft 9 in)

VARIANTS:
SE 3160: Initial production model
SA 316B: Artouste-powered version with strengthened transmission, higher gross weight, and increased payload
IAR-316B: Built under license by IAR in Romania
SA 319B: Similar to 316B, but with Astazou XIV turboshaft
HAL Chetak: SA 316B built under license in India
HAL Chetan: Artouste replaced with Turbomeca TM 333-2M2

FEATURES:
Three-blade rotor; single exposed Turbomeca Artouste or Astazou turboshaft; tricycle landing gear; enclosed cabin and tailboom; tricycle landing gear or fixed skids

AgustaWestland A 109 ITALY

Twin-turbine light utility helicopter

Feasibility studies for medium-capacity twin-turbine model, began in 1969, led to the start of construction in summer 1970. Five prototypes were used in certification work, the first of which flew on August 4, 1971. Deliveries commenced in early 1976. Latest A 109 Power first flew in October 1994. Total delivered: 750.

SPECIFICATION (A 109 Power):

ACCOMMODATION: 1 + 7
CARGO/BAGGAGE: 1000 kg (2204 lb)
MAX SPEED: 154 kt (285 km/h)
RANGE: 528 nm (977 km)

DIMENSIONS:
MAIN ROTOR DIAMETER: 11.0 m (36 ft 1 in)
LENGTH: rotors turning, 13.0 m (42 ft 9 in)
HEIGHT: 3.5 m (11 ft 6 in)

VARIANTS:
A 109A: Initial production model with Allison 250
A 109A MkII: Extensive improvements in equipment and systems fit
A 109A MkII Plus: Law-enforcement model
A 109C: More powerful engines and "wide-body" interior
A 109K2: SAR and police version with special equipment
A 109MAX: Medevac model with upward-opening "bulged" doors
A 109E Power: Extensively upgraded version based on K2 airframe, but wider, new FADEC-equipped P&WC engines, and new landing gear
A 109S Grand: Stretched cabin; P&WC PW207C engines; scimitar-shaped tail rotor

FEATURES:
Four-blade main rotor and two-blade tail rotor; twin Rolls-Royce 250 or P&WC PW206C turboshafts; swept upper and lower vertical fin; retractable tricycle landing gear

AgustaWestland A 119 Koala ITALY

Single-turbine light helicopter

Go-ahead for single-engine version based on the A 109 given in August 1994, with first flight early in 1995. Initially flown with Turbomeca Arriel, but Pratt & Whitney Canada PT6B adopted for production model. First delivered in summer 1999. Total delivered: 61.

SPECIFICATION:

ACCOMMODATION: 1 + 7
CARGO/BAGGAGE: 1420 kg (3130 lb)
MAX SPEED: 150 kt (278 km/h)
RANGE: 479 nm (886 km)

DIMENSIONS:
MAIN ROTOR DIAMETER: 10.8 m (36 ft 6 in)
LENGTH: rotors turning, 13.0 m (42 ft 9 in)
HEIGHT: 3.8 m (12 ft 5 in)

VARIANTS:
A 119 Koala: Only production model to date

FEATURES:
Four-blade main rotor and two-blade tail rotor; twin P&WC PT6B turboshafts; swept upper vertical fin and horizontal stabilizers at rear of tailboom; fixed-skid landing gear; large tail skid

AgustaWestland AW139 ITALY/UK

Twin-turboshaft intermediate helicopter

Joint development with Bell for multirole helicopter announced at the Farnborough Air Show in September 1998, then known as AB 139. Bell has since pulled out. First flight on February 3, 2001, Italian IFR certification obtained on June 20, 2003. First delivery to Elilano December 2003. Total delivered: 27.

SPECIFICATION (AW139):

ACCOMMODATION: 1 + 15
CARGO/BAGGAGE: 2700 kg (5952 lb)
MAX SPEED: 157 kt (290 km/h)
RANGE: 400 nm (740 km)

DIMENSIONS:
MAIN ROTOR DIAMETER: 13.8 m (45 ft 3 in)
LENGTH: rotors turning, 16.7 m (54 ft 8 in)
HEIGHT: 5.0 m (16 ft 3 in)

VARIANTS:
AW139: Initial civil version

FEATURES:
Five-blade main rotor and four-blade tail rotor mounted atop swept tailfin on right; twin P&WC PT6C turboshafts; tricycle landing gear retracting into side sponsons

Bell 47 USA

Single-piston general utility helicopter

Made its first flight on December 8, 1945, and granted first helicopter type certificate in the USA on March 8, 1946. Produced in many versions, and also under license by Agusta as the AB-47; Kawasaki as the KH-4; and Westland in the UK for the army. Total delivered: 5048.

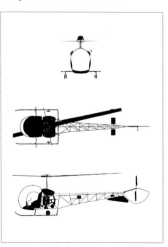

SPECIFICATION (47G-4A):

ACCOMMODATION: 1 + 2
CARGO/BAGGAGE: 454 kg (1000 lb)
MAX SPEED: 91 kt (9169 km/h)
RANGE: 225 nm (416 km)

DIMENSIONS:

MAIN ROTOR DIAMETER: 11.3 m (37 ft 1 in)
LENGTH: rotors turning, 13.2 m (43 ft 3 in)
HEIGHT: 2.8 m (9 ft 3 in)

VARIANTS:

47G-2: Initial production version with Lycoming engine
47G-3: More powerful and later turbocharged engine
47G-4A: Basic three-seat utility version available from December 1965
47G-5: Low-cost models with nonessentials removed
47H-1: Deluxe version with enclosed and soundproofed cabin
47J Ranger: Redesigned with fully enclosed cabin and bench seat
H-13: U.S. military designation (which see)

FEATURES:

Twin-blade main rotor; single Franklin or Lycoming piston engine; bubble canopy; lattice tailboom with twin-blade tail rotor; fixed-skid landing gear with small ground-handling wheels

Bell 206 JetRanger USA

Single-turbine light helicopter

Developed from a losing design for a Light Observation Helicopter (LOH) for the U.S. Army and targeted at civil market. First flight was made on January 10, 1966, and first deliveries in January 1967. Also built under license by Agusta as the AB 206. Total delivered: 7870 (including military OH-58).

SPECIFICATION (206B JetRanger III):

ACCOMMODATION: 1 + 5
CARGO/BAGGAGE: 680 kg (1500 lb)
MAX SPEED: 115 kt (214 km/h)
RANGE: 365 nm (676 km)

DIMENSIONS:

MAIN ROTOR DIAMETER: 10.2 m (33 ft 4 in)
LENGTH: rotors turning, 11.8 m (38 ft 9 in)
HEIGHT: 3.2 m (10 ft 5 in)

VARIANTS:

206A JetRanger: Initial production model with Allison 250-C18
206B JetRanger II: More powerful 250-C20 engine
206B JetRanger III: Current model with greater power
TH-57 SeaRanger: US Navy primary trainer
TH-67 Creek: U.S. Army pilot trainer
OH-58 Kiowa: Military version (which see)

FEATURES:

Twin-blade main and tail rotor; single Rolls-Royce 250 turboshaft; swept upper and lower vertical fins; horizontal stabilizers at mid-section tailboom; fixed-skid landing gear; two side windows

Bell 206L LongRanger USA

Single-turbine light helicopter

Stretched derivative of JetRanger to increase seating capacity from five to seven, announced on September 25, 1973. Made its first flight on September 11, 1974, with first deliveries in early 1976. Total delivered to date: 1733.

SPECIFICATION (206L-4 Long-Ranger IV):

ACCOMMODATION: 1 + 7
CARGO/BAGGAGE: 907 kg (2000 lb)
MAX SPEED: 112 kt (207 km/h)
RANGE: 321 nm (595 km)

DIMENSIONS:

MAIN ROTOR DIAMETER: 11.3 m (37 ft 0 in)
LENGTH: rotors turning, 13. 0 m (42 ft 7 in)
HEIGHT: 3.1 m (10 ft 3 in)

VARIANTS:

206L LongRanger: Initial model powered by 250-C20B
206L-1 LongRanger II: Higher-powered version from 1978
206L-3 LongRanger III: Improved performance from 1982
206L-4 LongRanger IV: Improved current standard version available from December 1992
206LT TwinRanger: Small number of twin-engine versions built from new, others converted from L-3 and L-4 models by Tridair as the Gemini ST

FEATURES:

Twin-blade main and tail rotor; single Rolls-Royce 250 turboshaft (two in 206LT); swept upper and lower vertical fins; horizontal stabilizers at mid-section tailboom; fixed-skid landing gear; three side windows

Bell 214 USA

Twin-turboshaft intermediate helicopter

Developed from the Huey and first delivered as military models to Iran from April 26, 1975. Commercial variant announced on January 4, 1974, as 214B, and later stretched as the 214ST, which first flew in February 1977. Total delivered (civil): 65 (214B), 96 (214ST).

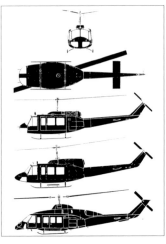

SPECIFICATION (214ST):

ACCOMMODATION: 2 + 18
CARGO/BAGGAGE: 3628 kg (8000 lb)
MAX SPEED: 140 kt (259 km/h)
RANGE: 463 nm (858 km)

DIMENSIONS:

MAIN ROTOR DIAMETER: 15.9 m (52 ft 0 in)
LENGTH: rotors turning, 19.0 m (62 ft 3 in)
HEIGHT: 4.8 m (15 ft 10 in)

VARIANTS:

214A: Initial model delivered to the Iranian Imperial Forces
214B BigLifter: Commercial version with Lycoming T5508Ds
214B-1: As 214B, but with restricted internal gross weight
214ST: Stretched derivative, also known as a Super Transporter

FEATURES:

Two-blade main rotor; twin Lycoming T5508D (214B) or GE CT7 (214ST) turboshafts; large swept vertical tailfin with top-mounted two-blade tail rotor; large horizontal stabilzer at rear; nonretractable skid or wheeled landing gear

Bell 222 USA

Twin-turboshaft intermediate helicopter

First commercial light twin helicopter in the USA, making its maiden flight on August 13, 1976. First delivery, to Petroleum Helicopters, made on January 16, 1980. Production ceased in 1989. Total delivered: 188.

SPECIFICATION (222B):

ACCOMMODATION: 1 + 7
CARGO/BAGGAGE: 1134 kg (2500 lb)
MAX SPEED: 150 kt (278 km/h)
RANGE: 255 nm (472 km)

DIMENSIONS:

MAIN ROTOR DIAMETER: 12.8 m (42 ft 0 in)
LENGTH: rotors turning, 15.4 m (50 ft 5 in)
HEIGHT: 3.5 m (11 ft 6 in)

VARIANTS:

222A: Initial production model with Lycoming LTS 101 turboshafts
222B: More powerful LTS 101 engines and larger main rotor
222B Executive: Improved systems and luxury interior
222UT: Utility version; skid gear with lock-on ground-handling wheels

FEATURES:

Two-blade main rotor; twin LTS 101 turboshafts; swept upper and lower vertical fins with two-blade tail rotor; mid-section horizontal stabilizers with swept endplate fins; retractable tricycle or skid-type gear with ground wheels

Bell 230 USA

Twin-turbine intermediate helicopter

Modernized version of Bell 222, announced at 1989 NBAA convention. Two Bell 222s converted as prototypes for new model, which first flew on August 12, 1991. Deliveries started on November 16, 1992. Production ceased in 1996; replaced by Model 430. Total delivered: 37.

SPECIFICATION:

ACCOMMODATION: 2 + 7
CARGO/BAGGAGE: 1270 kg (2800 lb)
MAX SPEED: 141 kt (261 km/h)
RANGE: 385 nm (713 km)

DIMENSIONS:
MAIN ROTOR DIAMETER: 12.8 m (42 ft 0 in)
LENGTH: rotors turning, 15.3 m (50 ft 2 in)
HEIGHT: 3.7 m (12 ft 2 in)

VARIANTS:
230 Executive: Basic production aircraft for corporate use
230 Utility: Model for general transport applications
230 EMS: Air-ambulance version with one or two stretchers and three or four medical attendants

FEATURES:
Two-blade main rotor; twin Rolls-Royce 250-C30 turboshafts; swept upper and lower vertical fins with two-blade tail rotor and tail skid; mid-section horizontal stabilizer with swept endplate fins; retractable tricycle or skid-type landing gear; short-span sponsons on fuselage sides

Bell 407 USA/CANADA

Single-turbine light helicopter

Design definition launched in 1993 and concept demonstrator (modified 206L-4) first flown on April 21, 1994. Officially launched at Heli-Expo in Las Vegas in January 1995, leading to first flight of prototype on June 1, that same year. First delivery in February 1996. Total delivered: 654.

SPECIFICATION:

ACCOMMODATION: 2 + 5
CARGO/BAGGAGE: 1200 kg (2646 lb)
MAX SPEED: 128 kt (237 km/h)
RANGE: 312 nm (577 km)

DIMENSIONS:

MAIN ROTOR DIAMETER: 10.7 m (35 ft 0 in)
LENGTH: rotors turning, 12.7 m (41 ft 9 in)
HEIGHT: 3.6 m (11 ft 10 in)

VARIANTS:

407: Initial production model
407 ARH: Armed reconnaissance helicopter for U.S. Army
417: More powerful and new Honeywell HTS900 engine

FEATURES:

Four-blade main rotor; single Rolls-Royce209 250-C47B turboshaft; swept upper and lower vertical fins with two-blade tail rotor and tail skid; mid-section horizontal stabilizer with swept endplate fins; fixed-skid landing gear; tail skid

Bell 412 USA/CANADA

Twin-turboshaft intermediate helicopter

Development of Bell Model 212 announced on September 8, 1978, featuring an advanced four-blade rotor design. Two new 212s were modified for certification program, with flight trials starting on August 4, 1979. First delivery made on January 18, 1981. Also license-built in Indonesia by ITPN as NBell-412 and in Italy by Agusta as AB412EP. Total delivered to date (civil only): 570.

SPECIFICATION (412EP):

ACCOMMODATION: 2 + 14
CARGO/BAGGAGE: 2041 kg (4800 lb)
MAX SPEED: 122 kt (226 km/h)
RANGE: 402 nm (745 km)

DIMENSIONS:
MAIN ROTOR DIAMETER: 14.0 m (46 ft 0 in)
LENGTH: rotors turning, 17.1 m (56 ft 2 in)
HEIGHT: 4.6 m (15 ft 0 in)

VARIANTS:
412: Initial model powered by P&WC PT6T-3b turboshafts
412EP: Enhanced Performance version
412HP: Improved transmission
412SP: Special Performance version with increased T-O weight and better seating
Griffon: Military variants (which see)

FEATURES:
Four-blade main rotor; twin P&WC PT6T turboshafts; swept vertical fin with top-mounted two-blade tail rotor; horizontal stabilizers at rear; high skid, emergency pop-out float, or non-retractable tricycle landing gear; fixed stabilizers

Bell 427/429 USA

Twin-turboshaft light helicopter

Collaborative program between Bell and Samsung announced at Heli-Expo 96. Based on Bell 407 but slightly longer, the Model 427 made its first flight on December 11, 1997, and entered service in early 2000. Final assembly by Bell at Mirabel, Canada, and by Samsung at Sachon plant for China and Korea. Total delivered: 48.

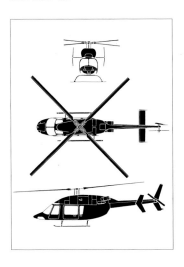

SPECIFICATION:

ACCOMMODATION: 1 + 6
CARGO/BAGGAGE: 1361 kg (3000 lb)
MAX SPEED: 140 kt (259 km/h)
RANGE: 390 nm (722 km)

DIMENSIONS:
MAIN ROTOR DIAMETER: 11.3 m (37 ft 0 in)
LENGTH: rotors turning, 13.1 m (42 ft 11 in)
HEIGHT: 3.5 m (11 ft 6 in)

VARIANTS:
427: Initial production model
427i: IFR version with "glass" cockpit; superseded by Model 429
SB427: Korean-assembled version
429 Global Ranger: Improved version with "glass" cockpit and new main and tail rotors

FEATURES:
Four-blade main rotor; twin P&WC PW207 turboshafts; fixed high or low skids or emergency floats; swept upper and lower vertical fins; mid-mounted horizontal stabilizers with endplate fins

Bell 430 USA/CANADA

Twin-turboshaft intermediate helicopter

Higher-powered variant of Bell 230 with stretched, four-blade rotor. Prototype modified from Bell 230 first flew on October 25, 1994. Deliveries began on June 25, 1996. Total delivered: 108.

SPECIFICATION:

ACCOMMODATION: 2 + 9
CARGO/BAGGAGE: 1587 kg (3500 lb)
MAX SPEED: 138 kt (256 km/h)
RANGE: 272 nm (503 km)

DIMENSIONS:
MAIN ROTOR DIAMETER: 12.8 m (42 ft 0 in)
LENGTH: rotors turning, 15.3 m (50 ft 3 in)
HEIGHT: 4.0 m (13 ft 2 in)

VARIANTS:
430: Initial production model with Rolls-Royce209 250-C40B turboshafts

FEATURES:
Four-blade main rotor; twin Rolls-Royce209 250 turboshafts; fixed-skid or retractable tricycle landing gear; swept upper and lower vertical fins; small tail skid; mid-mounted horizontal stabilizers with endplate fins; short-span sponsons on fuselage side

Brantly B-2B USA

Single-piston light utility helicopter

Developed from the B-1 by N. O. Brantly and made its maiden flight as long ago as 1953. First deliveries made in 1960. Underwent several ownership changes since, as well as some breaks in production. Presently in production by Brantly International. Total delivered: 338.

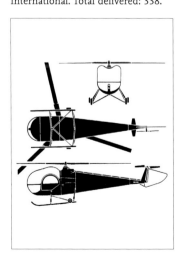

SPECIFICATION (B-2B):

ACCOMMODATION: 1 + 1
CARGO/BAGGAGE: 113 kg (250 lb)
MAX SPEED: 87 kt (161 km/h)
RANGE: 217 nm (402 km)

DIMENSIONS:

MAIN ROTOR DIAMETER: 7.2 m (23 ft 9 in)
LENGTH: rotors turning, 8.5 m (28 ft 0 in)
HEIGHT: 2.1 m (6 ft 9 in)

VARIANTS:

B-2A: Initial production version
B-2B: Improved model with new metal rotor blades and fuel-injected Lycoming piston engine
H-2: Designation of B-2B when produced by Brantly-Hynes between 1976 and 1979

FEATURES:

Three-blade main rotor; single Textron Lycoming IVO-360 air-cooled engine; slightly swept vertical fin with top-mounted two-blade tail rotor and tail skid; fixed skid or float gear and fixed tail skid; bubble canopy

Enstrom F28/280 USA
Single-piston light utility helicopter

Development of this three-seater helicopter started in 1960, leading to the first flight of the F-28 on May 27, 1962. Continuously updated and built side-by-side with the aerodynamically refined 280 Shark. Total delivered: 985.

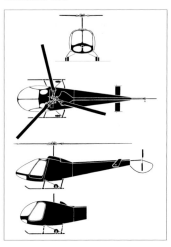

SPECIFICATION (280FX):

ACCOMMODATION: 1 + 2
CARGO/BAGGAGE: 49 kg (108 lb)
MAX SPEED: 102 kt (189 km/h)
RANGE: 260 nm (483 km)

DIMENSIONS:
MAIN ROTOR DIAMETER: 9.8 m (32 ft 0 in)
LENGTH: 8.9 m (29 ft 3 in)
HEIGHT: 2.7 m (9 ft 0 in)

VARIANTS:
F28A: Initial production version
F28C: Turbocharged with two-piece windscreen
F28C-2: Similar but single-piece windscreen and new console
F28F Falcon: Present much-improved model
F28F-P Sentinel: Dedicated police patrol version with searchlight, FLIR, and PA systems
280 Shark: Aerodynamic restyling for corporate market
280C Shark: Aerodynamically refined version of F28C-2
280FX Shark: New seats, new tailplane and faired landing gear

FEATURES:
Three-blade main rotor; single Textron Lycoming HIO-360 turbocharged piston engine; fixed skids or floats; tailboom with horizontal stabilizers and swept endplate fins to rear; large tail-skid protection for two-blade tail rotor

Enstrom 480 USA

Single-turboshaft light helicopter

Developed to meet U.S. Army training requirement, but lost out to Bell. Definitive wide-cabin 480/TH-28 flown for first time in October 1989, first delivery following FAA certification in 1994. Total delivered: 98.

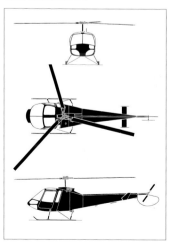

SPECIFICATION (480B):

ACCOMMODATION: 1 + 4
CARGO/BAGGAGE: 592 kg (1305 lb)
MAX SPEED: 125 kt (231 km/h)
RANGE: 435 nm (806 km)

DIMENSIONS:
MAIN ROTOR DIAMETER: 9.8 m (32 ft 0 in)
LENGTH: 9.1 m (29 ft 10 in)
HEIGHT: 3.0 m (9 ft 10 in)

VARIANTS:
480: Initial civil version with four staggered seats or convertible to three-seat training/executive layout
480B: Enhanced and more powerful version available since early 2001
480B Guardian: Law enforcement variant with searchlight, FLIR, and siren/PA system
TH-28: Military training/light patrol version with crashworthy seats and fuel tanks

FEATURES:
Three-blade main rotor; single Rolls-Royce 250 turboshaft; fixed skids or pop-out floats; tailboom with horizontal stabilizers and swept endplate fins to rear; large tail-skid protection for two-blade tail rotor

Eurocopter EC 120 Colibri FRANCE/GERMANY/CHINA/SINGAPORE

Single-turboshaft light helicopter

Multinational partnership program launched by Eurocopter, CATIC, and Singapore Technologies Aerospace on February 15, 1990. Like EC 135, but new single Turbomeca Arrius 2F turboshaft and new-generation Fenestron tail rotor. First flight on June 9, 1995, first delivery on January 23, 1998. Total delivered: 420.

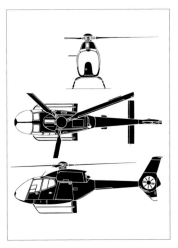

SPECIFICATION:

ACCOMMODATION: 1 + 4
CARGO/BAGGAGE: 700 kg (1543 lb)
MAX SPEED: 150 kt (278 km/h)
RANGE: 395 nm (732 km)

DIMENSIONS:

MAIN ROTOR DIAMETER: 10.0 m (32 ft 10 in)
LENGTH: blades folded, 11.5 m 937 ft 9 in)
HEIGHT: 3.4 m (11 ft 2 in)

VARIANTS:

EC 120B: Initial production version, available with mission-specific kits for passenger, corporate, police, training, and EMS work
HC 120: Model to be assembled by Hafei Aviation Industry in China

FEATURES:

Three-blade main rotor and eight-blade shrouded Fenestron tail rotor; single Turbomeca Arrius turboshaft; fixed-skid landing gear; horizontal stabilizer at rear

Eurocopter EC 130 FRANCE/GERMANY

Single-turboshaft light helicopter

Derived from the AS 350 B3 Ecureuil, but with Fenestron tail rotor and wider cabin. First flown in June 1999, with deliveries starting after the model was revealed at Heli-Expo 01 in Las Vegas in February. Total delivered: 140.

SPECIFICATION:

ACCOMMODATION: 1 + 7
CARGO/BAGGAGE: 400 kg (882 lb)
MAX SPEED: 155 kt (287 km/h)
RANGE: 345 nm (640 km/h)

DIMENSIONS:
MAIN ROTOR DIAMETER: 10.7 m (35 ft 1 in)
LENGTH: rotors turning, 12.6 m (41 ft 4 in)
HEIGHT: 3.6 m (11 ft 10 in)

VARIANTS:
EC 130 B4: Initial production version

FEATURES:
Three-blade main rotor and 10-blade shrouded Fenestron tail rotor; horizontal stabilizers at rear; single Turbomeca Arriel turboshaft; fixed-skid landing gear; tail skid

Eurocopter EC 135 FRANCE/GERMANY

Twin-turbine light helicopter

Designed to succeed the BO 105, a technology prototype designated BO 108 made its first flight on October 15, 1988. Design progressively improved and preproduction model with advanced Fenestron tail rotor flown on February 15, 1994. Deliveries began on July 31, 1996. Total delivered: 449.

SPECIFICATION:

ACCOMMODATION: 1 + 7
CARGO/BAGGAGE: 1361 kg (3000 lb)
MAX SPEED: 150 kt (278 km/h)
RANGE: 402 nm (745 km)

DIMENSIONS:
MAIN ROTOR DIAMETER: 10.2 m (33 ft 6 in)
LENGTH: rotors turning, 12.2 m (39 ft 11 in)
HEIGHT: 3.6 m (11 ft 10 in)

VARIANTS:
EC 135 P1: P&W-powered model
EC 135 P2: PW206B, increased T-O weight
EC 135 P2i: Improved, FADEC
EC 135 T1: Turbomeca-powered alternative
EC 135 T2: Arrius 2B2
EC 135 T2i: Increased T-O weight; FADEC
EC 635 P1: Multimission armed or unarmed, with P&WC engines
EC 635 T1: Turbomeca engines

FEATURES:
Four-blade main rotor and 11-blade shrouded Fenestron tail rotor; twin P&WC PW206 or Turbomeca Arrius turboshafts; fixed-skid landing gear, horizontal stabilizer with swept endplate fins

Eurocopter EC 155 FRANCE/GERMANY

Twin-turboshaft intermediate helicopter

Higher-performance development of successful Dauphin 2 series, first unveiled at Paris Air Show in June 1997; initially designated AS 365 N4. Main differences are new five-blade main rotor and redesigned wide-body cabin. First flight on June 17, 1997, with first deliveries in March 1999. Total delivered: 67.

SPECIFICATION:

ACCOMMODATION: 2 + 12
CARGO/BAGGAGE: 2000 kg (4409 lb)
MAX SPEED: 170 kt (315 km/h)
RANGE: 448 nm (830 km)

DIMENSIONS:

MAIN ROTOR DIAMETER: 12.6 m (41 ft 4 in)
LENGTH: rotors turning, 14.4 m (47 ft 4 in)
HEIGHT: 4.4 m (14 ft 4 in)

VARIANTS:

EC 155B: Initial production model
EC 155B1: More powerful Arriel 2C2 engines
EC 155 HTT: Helicoptère Tous Temps (all-weather) technology demonstrator

FEATURES:

Five-blade main rotor and 10-blade shrouded Fenestron tail rotor; tailboom stabilizers with swept downward endplate fins at rear; retractable tricycle landing gear

Eurocopter (Aerospatiale) AS 332 Super Puma

FRANCE/GERMANY

Twin-turbine intermediate helicopter

Extensively improved derivative of SA 330 Puma, receiving formal go-ahead from the French government in June 1975. Prototype flew for the first time on September 13, 1978. First civil model delivered in 1981. Total built to date (civil/paramilitary only): 185.

SPECIFICATION (AS 332 L2):

ACCOMMODATION: 2 + 24
CARGO/BAGGAGE: 5000 kg (11,023 lb)
MAX SPEED: 177 kt 9327 km/h)
RANGE: 460 nm (851 km)

DIMENSIONS:
MAIN ROTOR DIAMETER: 16.2 m (53 ft 2 in)
LENGTH: rotors turning, 19.5 m (63 ft 11 in)
HEIGHT: 4.9 m (16 ft 2 in)

VARIANTS:
AS 332 C: Initial civil version
AS 332 C1: SAR version with search radar and six stretchers
AS 332 L: As 332 C, but lengthened fuselage and increased fuel
AS 332 L1: Long fuselage and airline interior
AS 332 L2: Mk II Super Puma with Spheriflex rotor head and EFIS
EC 225: New five-bladed main rotor, new engines, increased gross weight
AS 532 and EC 725 Cougar: Military versions (which see)

FEATURES:
Four- or five-blade main rotor and five-blade tail rotor on side of tailboom; twin Turbomeca Makila turboshafts; retractable tricycle landing gear; lateral sponsons

Eurocopter (Aerospatiale) AS 350 Ecureuil/AStar

FRANCE/GERMANY

Single-turboshaft light helicopter

Developed as successor to Alouette, the Ecureuil (Squirrel) embodies Aerospatiale's Starflex-type rotor head. It first flew on June 27, 1974, and entered service early in 1978. Built in France and by Helibras in Brazil. Total delivered: 2936.

SPECIFICATION (AS 350 B3):

ACCOMMODATION: 1 + 5
CARGO/BAGGAGE: 550 kg (1213 lb)
MAX SPEED: 155 kt (287 km/h)
RANGE: 360 nm (666 km)

DIMENSIONS:

MAIN ROTOR DIAMETER: 10.7 m (35 ft 1 in)
LENGTH: rotors turning, 12.9 m (42 ft 5 in)
HEIGHT: 3.1 m (10 ft 3 in)

VARIANTS:

AS 350 B: Initial production model with Turbomeca Arriel 1
AS 350 B1: More powerful, higher weight replacement from 1987
AS 350 B2: Further increase in engine power, new rotor blades
AS 350 B3: Improved with Arriel 2 with FADEC
AS 350C AStar: Original Lycoming-powered version for U.S. market
AS 350D AStar: Improved for U.S. market
AS 550 Fennec: Military versions (which see)
Various civil upgrades available

FEATURES:

Three-blade main rotor and two-blade tail rotor on right; single Turbomeca Arriel or Honeywell (AlliedSignal) LTS101 turboshaft; fixed-skid landing gear; swept fins above and below tail; horizontal stabilizers at rear

Eurocopter (Aerospatiale) AS 355 Ecureuil II

FRANCE/GERMANY

Twin-turboshaft light helicopter

Development of this twin-engined version of the AS 350 began in mid-1978. Largely similar, but major changes to rotor blades, power plant, transmission, fuel system, and fuselage structure. First flew on September 28, 1979, followed by customer deliveries in January 1981. Total delivered: 719.

SPECIFICATION (AS 355 N):

ACCOMMODATION: 1 + 5
CARGO/BAGGAGE: 1134 kg (2500 lb)
MAX SPEED: 150 kt (278 km/h)
RANGE: 389 nm (722 km)

DIMENSIONS:

MAIN ROTOR DIAMETER: 10.7 m (35 ft 1 in)
LENGTH: rotors turning, 12.9 m (42 ft 5 in)
HEIGHT: 3.1 m (10 ft 3 in)

VARIANTS:

AS 355 E: Initial production model with Allison 250 turboshafts
AS 355 F: Improved rotor blades and systems
AS 355 F1: Increased power, weight, and payload
AS 355 F2: Upgraded transmission and higher gross weight
AS 355 N: Current improved civil production version; known as TwinStar in the U.S.
AS 555 Fennec: Military versions (which see)

FEATURES:

Three-blade main rotor and two-blade tail rotor on right; twin Turbomeca Arrius turboshafts; fixed-skid landing gear; swept fins above and below tail; horizontal stabilizers at rear

Eurocopter (Aerospatiale) AS 365 Dauphin

FRANCE/GERMANY

Twin-turboshaft intermediate helicopter

Developed initially as a single-engined replacement for Alouette III under designation SA 360 Dauphin, but with limited success. First twin-engined SA 365 Dauphin 2 flew on January 24, 1975, with Astazou engines and characteristic Fenestron tail rotor. Prefix *SA* (Sud-Aviation) later changed to *AS* (Aerospatiale). Total delivered: 721.

SPECIFICATION (AS 365 N2):

ACCOMMODATION: 1 + 12
CARGO/BAGGAGE: 1600 kg (3527 lb)
MAX SPEED: 155 kt (287 km/h)
RANGE: 464 nm (859 km)

DIMENSIONS:
MAIN ROTOR DIAMETER: 11.9 m (39 ft 2 in)
LENGTH: rotors turning, 13.7 m (44 ft 11 in)
HEIGHT: 4.0 m (13 ft 1 in)

VARIANTS:
SA 360: Initial single-engined model
AS 365 C: Twin-turboshaft production version
AS 365 N: Improved model with 90 new components
AS 365 N1: Power reserve-margin increase through Turbomeca Arriel 1s
AS 365 N2: Further improvements
AS 365 N3: Improved hot-and-high performance with FADEC-equipped Arriel 2s
AS 565 Panther: Military versions (which see)

FEATURES:
Four-blade main rotor and 11-blade shrouded Fenestron tail rotor; twin Turbomeca Arriel turboshafts; retractable tricycle landing gear; horizontal stabilizer with endplate fins at rear

Eurocopter (MBB) BO 105 GERMANY

Twin-turboshaft light helicopter

Development began in July 1962 and first flying prototype took to the air in Germany on February 16, 1967. Many design changes undertaken. Full-scale production commenced in 1972, now completed. Total delivered: 1404.

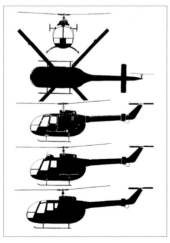

SPECIFICATION (CBS-4):

ACCOMMODATION: 1 + 5
CARGO/BAGGAGE: 800 kg (1764 lb)
MAX SPEED: 131 kt (242 km/h)
RANGE: 305 nm (565 km)

DIMENSIONS:
MAIN ROTOR DIAMETER: 9.8 m (32 ft 3 in)
LENGTH: rotors turning, 11.9 m (38 ft 11 in)
HEIGHT: 3.0 m (9 ft 11 in)

VARIANTS:
BO 105 C: Initial version with choice of Allison 250 engines
BO 105 CB: Improved engines and better hot-and-high performance
BO 105 CBS-4: Small cabin extension for more leg room. Named Twin Jet II in US
BO 105 D: UK certified offshore version
BO 105 LS: Increased power, built in Canada
BO 105 LSA-3: Hot-and-high version, solely built in Canada
BO 105 LSA-3 Super Lifter: Optimised for external load missions, built in Canada
EC Super Five: High performance version of CBS-4
Plus several armed/unarmed military derivatives (which see)

FEATURES:
Four-blade main rotor; twin Rolls-Royce 250 turboshafts; fixed-skid landing gear; horizontal stabilizer with small endplate fins at rear of high tailboom; swept tailfin with top-mounted two-blade tail rotor

Eurocopter/Kawasaki BK 117/EC 145 FRANCE/GERMANY/JAPAN

Twin-turboshaft intermediate helicopter

Developed under joint agreement signed on February 25, 1977, between MBB and Kawasaki. First of four prototypes flew on June 13, 1979, and deliveries began in early 1983. Built in Germany and Japan. Total delivered: 555.

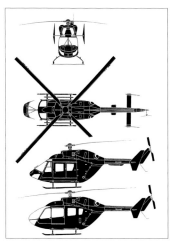

SPECIFICATION (BK 117 C-2):

ACCOMMODATION: 1 + 9
CARGO/BAGGAGE: 1700 kg (3748 lb)
MAX SPEED: 145 kt (268 km/h)
RANGE: 378 nm (700 km)

DIMENSIONS:
MAIN ROTOR DIAMETER: 11.0 m (36 ft 1 in)
LENGTH: rotors turning, 13.0 m (42 ft 8 in)
HEIGHT: 3.8 m (12 ft 7 in)

VARIANTS:
BK 117 A: Initial production version with Lycoming LTS101s
BK 117 A-1: Increased T-O weight
BK 117 A-3: Further growth in T-O weight and enlarged tail rotor
BK 117 A-4: Uprated transmission and improved tail-rotor head
BK 117 B-1: Further improvements
BK 117 B-1C: UK certified with reduced range and endurance
BK 117 B-2: Production model from 1992, increased T-O weight
BK 117 C-1: New cockpit and Arriel engines
BK 117 C-2: Larger cabin, increased payload
EC 145: European-built version of BK 117 C-2
UH 145: Variant for U.S. LUH programme

FEATURES:
Four-blade main rotor; twin Honeywell (AlliedSignal) LTS101 or Turbomeca Arriel turboshafts; fixed-skid landing gear with ground-handling wheels; detachable tailcone with tail rotor and horizontal stabilizer with large offset endplate fins; EC 145 has more rounded nose

Hiller UH-12 USA

Single-piston light utility helicopter

Designed by Stanley Hiller and derived from the Model 360 of 1948. Initially produced for U.S. military as H-23 Raven. Production ceased in 1983, but a few were subsequently built, first by Rogerson-Hiller, then by a newly constituted Hiller Aircraft. Total delivered: 2595.

SPECIFICATION (UH-12E3):

ACCOMMODATION: 1 + 2
CARGO/BAGGAGE: 600 kg (1323 lb)
MAX SPEED: 83 kt (154 km/h)
RANGE: 202 nm 9373 km)

DIMENSIONS:
MAIN ROTOR DIAMETER: 10.8 m (35 ft 5 in)
LENGTH: rotors turning, 12.4 m (40 ft 8 in)
HEIGHT: 3.1 m (10 ft 2 in)

VARIANTS:
UH-12A: Original model powered by Franklin piston engine
UH-12B: Improved trainer used by U.S. Navy
UH-12C: All-metal rotor blades and "goldfish bowl" canopy
UH-12D: U.S. Army version; Lycoming V-540
UH-12E: Increased Lycoming power
UH-12ET: Allison 250-powered turbine version
UH-12E3: New three-seat production version
UH-12E3T: Turbine-powered new production version
UH-12E4: Four-seat configuration, anhedral stabilizer
UH-12E4T: Turbine-powered version of four-seat configuration
UH-12L-4: Lengthened and wider cabin doors

FEATURES:
Two-blade main rotor; single Franklin or Lycoming piston engine, or Allison 250 turbine; bubble canopy; thin sloped tailboom with two-blade tail rotor and tail skid

Kaman K-MAX USA

Single-turbine external lift helicopter

Developed for external-lift operations and first flown on December 23, 1991. Made public debut in March 1992. First deliveries followed certification in August 1994, but production run was small. Total delivered: 31.

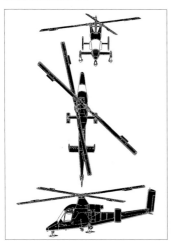

SPECIFICATION:

ACCOMMODATION: Pilot only
CARGO/BAGGAGE: 2721 kg (6000 lb)
MAX SPEED: 100 kt (185 km/h)
RANGE: 300 nm (555 km)

DIMENSIONS:
MAIN ROTOR DIAMETER: 14.7 m (48 ft 4 in)
LENGTH: rotors turning, 15.9 m (52 ft 1 in)
HEIGHT: 4.1 m (13 ft 7 in)

VARIANTS:
K-1200 K-MAX: Basic production version
FIREMAX: Firefighting modification with 2650-liter tank system

FEATURES:
Twin two-blade intermeshing main rotors; no tail rotor; single Lycoming turboshaft; tricycle landing gear; single tailfin and mid-mounted tailplane with endplate fins

Kamov Ka-26/126 "Hoodlum" RUSSIA

Twin-piston light helicopter

Versatile machine developed for agricultural and other aerial work, and first flown in 1965. Notable for the interchangeable modules aft of the flight deck for passenger/freight transport, aerial ambulance, firefighting, and more. Entered service in the Soviet Union in 1970. Total delivered: 850+.

SPECIFICATION:

ACCOMMODATION: 1 + 6
CARGO/BAGGAGE: 1100 kg (2425 lb)
MAX SPEED: 91 kt (170 km/h)
RANGE: 215 nm (400 km)

DIMENSIONS:

MAIN ROTOR DIAMETER: 13.0 m (42 ft 8 in)
LENGTH: of fuselage, 7.8 m (25 ft 7 in)
HEIGHT: 4.1 m (13 ft 4 in)

VARIANTS:

Ka-26: Basic production model
Ka-126: Turbine-powered development

FEATURES:

Twin four-blade coaxial contrarotating main rotors; twin Vedeneyev air-cooled piston engines mounted in pods on short stub wings at top of fuselage; twin tailboom with horizontal stabilizer and large downward-oriented endplate fins

Kamov Ka-32 "Helix-C" RUSSIA

Twin-turbine medium helicopter

Developed jointly with KA-27 naval model and features typical Kamov contrarotating rotors. First Ka-32 flew on January 11, 1980, and exhibited at Minsk in late 1981. Total delivered: 170+.

SPECIFICATION (Ka-32T):

ACCOMMODATION: 2 + 16
CARGO/BAGGAGE: 5000 kg (11,023 lb)
MAX SPEED: 135 kt (250 km/h)
RANGE: 432 nm (800 km/h)

DIMENSIONS:
MAIN ROTOR DIAMETER: 15.9 m (52 ft 2 in)
LENGTH: rotors folded, 12.3 m (40 ft 3 in)
HEIGHT: 5.4 m (17 ft 9 in)

VARIANTS:
Ka-32A: Initial production version
Ka-32A1: Firefighting version equipped with Bambi bucket
Ka-32A2: Police version with two searchlights and loudspeaker
Ka-32A3: Special version for rescue, salvage, and evacuation
Ka-32A7: Armed version developed from military Ka-27PS
Ka-32A11BC: Transport Canada–certified version
Ka-32A12: Swiss-registered and -approved version
Ka-32K: Flying crane with retractable gondola for second pilot
Ka-32M: Under development with TV3-117VHA-SB3 engines
Ka-32S: Maritime version with undernose radar
Ka-32T: Utility transport

FEATURES:
Three-blade coaxial contrarotating rotors; no tail rotor; twin Klimov TV3 turboshaft engines; short tailboom with large twin endplate fins; four-wheel landing gear (skis optional)

Kamov Ka-226 Sergei RUSSIA

Twin-turbine light helicopter

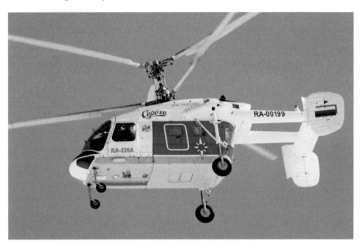

Refined development of the Ka-126 with changes to shape of nose and tailfins, rudder, and passenger pod. Announced at Heli-Expo in Dallas in 1990, but not flown until September 4, 1997.

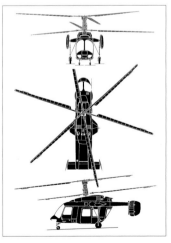

SPECIFICATION:

ACCOMMODATION: 1 or 2 + 6
CARGO/BAGGAGE: 1300 kg (2865 lb)
MAX SPEED: 115 kt (214 km/h)
RANGE: 324 nm (600 km)

DIMENSIONS:

MAIN ROTOR DIAMETER: 13.0 m (42 ft 8 in)
LENGTH: of fuselage, 8.1 m (26 ft 7 in)
HEIGHT: 4.2 m (13 ft 8 in)

VARIANTS:

Ka-226A: Basic civil production version
Ka-226A-50: Improved model
Ka-226AG: Cargo winch and medical equipment for Gazprom
Ka-226T: Turbomeca Arrius 2G2 turboshafts
Ka-226U: Military training version

FEATURES:

Three-blade coaxial contrarotating rotors; no tail rotor; twin Rolls-Royce 250 turboshaft engines; interchangeable accommodation pods; short twin tailboom with large downward endplate fins; four-wheel landing gear

Kazan Ansat RUSSIA

Twin-turboshaft light utility helicopter

Design started in 1993 and fuselage mock-up first displayed at Paris Air Show in June 1995. First hover of prototype made on August 17, 1999, followed by initial forward flight on October 6. Russian AP-29 type certificate awarded December 29, 2004. Total orders (unconfirmed): 312.

SPECIFICATION:

ACCOMMODATION: 2 + 9
CARGO/BAGGAGE: 1000 kg (2204 lb)
MAX SPEED: 148 kt (275 km/h)
RANGE: 342 nm (635 km)

DIMENSIONS:

MAIN ROTOR DIAMETER: 11.5 m (37 ft 9 in)
LENGTH: rotors turning, 13.5 m (44 ft 5 in)
HEIGHT: 3.4 m (11 ft 2 in)

VARIANTS:

Ansat: Initial production model with PW207K engines
Ansat-AG: Version for Gazprom pipeline inspection
Ansat-UT: Proposed variant optimized for training with dual controls and wheeled landing gear.
Ansat 2RT: Proposed military scout version with much-modified nose section and tandem seating

FEATURES:

Four-blade main rotor and two-blade tail rotor; horizontal stabilizers with endplate fins at rear tailboom; two P&W Rus PW207K turboshaft engines; fixed skid-type landing gear

MD Helicopters MD 500/530 USA

Single-turbine light helicopter

Civilian development of the Hughes OH-6A Cayuse military helicopter announced on April 21, 1965. First Model 500 (engineering designation 369) flew early 1967, with full-scale production commencing November 1968. In January 1984, Hughes sold out to McDonnell Douglas, which became a subsidiary of Boeing in August 1997. Light-helicopter line sold to RDM Holdings in January 1999. Total delivered: 4570.

SPECIFICATION:

ACCOMMODATION: 1 + 4
CARGO/BAGGAGE: 907 kg (2000 lb)
MAX SPEED: 152 kt (282 km/h)
RANGE: 233 nm (431 km)

DIMENSIONS:
MAIN ROTOR DIAMETER: 8.1m (26 ft 5 in)
LENGTH: rotors turning, 8.6 m (28 ft 3 in)
HEIGHT: 2.7 m (8 ft 9 in)

VARIANTS:
500: Initial model with Allison 250-C18 turboshaft engine
500C: Improved hot-and-high performance with more powerful engine
500D: New five-blade main rotor, small T-tail
500E/MD 500E: Many cabin improvements and external changes
530F/MD 530F: Increased main rotor and transmission rating
Plus military models (which see)

FEATURES:
Five-blade main rotor two-blade tail rotor; single Rolls-Royce 250 turboshaft engine; narrow-chord fin with high-set tailplane and endplate fins (500D and 500E only); fixed-skid landing gear

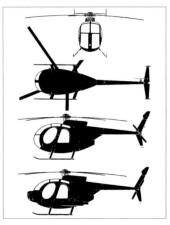

MD Helicopters MD 520N USA

Single-turboshaft light helicopter

Developed from the Model 500, but with new NOTAR (no tail rotor) system. Commercial version announced in February 1988 and officially launched in January 1999. First flight of MD 530N on December 29, 1989, but none built to date. First flight of MD 520N on May 1, 1990, and delivered to Phoenix Police on October 31, 1991. Total delivered: 86.

SPECIFICATION:

ACCOMMODATION: 1 + 4
CARGO/BAGGAGE: 1004 kg (2214 lb)
MAX SPEED: 152 kt (281 km/h)
RANGE: 202 nm (375 km)

DIMENSIONS:
MAIN ROTOR DIAMETER: 8.3 m (27 ft 4 in)
LENGTH: rotors turning, 9.8 m (32 ft 2 in)
HEIGHT: 2.7 m (9ft 0 in)

VARIANTS:
MD 520N: Basic production version

FEATURES:
Five-blade main rotor; single Rolls-Royce 250 turboshaft engine; high tailboom with NOTAR and top-mounted stabilizer with endplate fins; fixed-skid landing gear

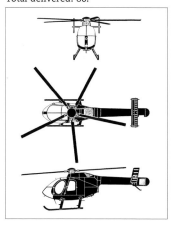

MD Helicopters MD 600N USA

Single-turbine light helicopter

Stretched development of MD 520N with new six-blade main rotor, more powerful engine, and uprated transmission. First flight of prototype MD 630N (converted from MD 630F) on November 22, 1994. Public debut at Heli-Expo in Las Vegas in January 1995. First flight with definitive Allison 250-C47 engine on November 6, 1995. First delivery to launch customer AirStar Helicopters on June 6, 1997. Total delivered: 59.

SPECIFICATION:

ACCOMMODATION: 1 + 7
CARGO/BAGGAGE: 1361 kg (3000 lb)
MAX SPEED: 135 kt (250 km/h)
RANGE: 342 nm (633 km)

DIMENSIONS:
MAIN ROTOR DIAMETER: 8.4 m (27 ft 7 in)
LENGTH: rotors turning, 11.3 m (36 ft 11 in)
HEIGHT: 2.7 m (8 ft 9 in)

VARIANTS:
MD 600N: Basic production model

FEATURES:
Six-blade main rotor; single Rolls-Royce 250 turboshaft engine; high tailboom with NOTAR and top-mounted stabilizer with endplate fins; fixed-skid landing gear

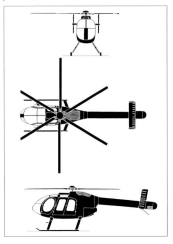

MD Helicopters MD Explorer USA

Twin-turbine light helicopter

Twin-engined NOTAR model, formerly known as MDX, announced in February 1988 and launched in January 1989. First flight on December 18, 1992, and first delivery December 16, 1994. Total delivered: 98.

SPECIFICATION:

ACCOMMODATION: 2 + 6
CARGO/BAGGAGE: 1361 kg (3000 lb)
MAX SPEED: 160 kt (296 km/h)
RANGE: 293 nm (542 km)

DIMENSIONS:
MAIN ROTOR DIAMETER: 10.3 m (33 ft 10 in)
LENGTH: rotors turning, 11.8 m (38 ft 10 in)
HEIGHT: 3.7 m (12 ft 1 in)

VARIANTS:
MD 900 Explorer: Initial utility model powered by P&WC PW206A engines
MD 901 Explorer: Civil utility model with alternative Turbomeca Arrius engines; none ordered
MD 902 Explorer: Higher-performance replacement from November 1997
MH-90 Enforcer: Armed variant operated by U.S. Coast Guard
Combat Explorer: Demonstrator displayed at Paris Air Show in June 1995
Plus specially equipped Police and EMS versions

FEATURES:
Five-blade main rotor; twin P&WC PW200 turboshaft engines; high tailboom with NOTAR and top-mounted stabilizer with endplate fins; fixed-skid landing gear

Mil Mi-2 "Hoplite" RUSSIA/POLAND

Twin-turbine light helicopter

Designed in the USSR and first flown September 22, 1961. Agreement signed for further development, exclusive production, and marketing with Polish industry; first Polish-built example flew November 4, 1965. Total delivered (including military): 5450.

SPECIFICATION:

ACCOMMODATION: 1 + 8
CARGO/BAGGAGE: 800 kg (1763 lb)
MAX SPEED: 113 kt (210 km/h)
RANGE: 237 nm (440 km)

DIMENSIONS:

MAIN ROTOR DIAMETER: 14.5 m (47 ft 7 in)
LENGTH: rotors turning, 17.4 m (57 ft 2 in)
HEIGHT: 3.8 m (12 ft 4 in)

VARIANTS:

Mi-2: Basic civil version
Mi-2B: Improved systems and navigational aids
Mi-2P: Standard passenger/cargo convertible with external sling and electric hoist
Mi-2S: Medevac equipped for up to four litters plus attendant
Kania: Substantially improved model with Rolls-Royce 250-C20B turboshafts
PZL Mi2plus: Improved version with more powerful GTD-350W2 engines, all-composite main rotor blades, new avionics
Plus many specialized military versions

FEATURES:

Three-blade main rotor and two-blade tail rotor; twin Isotov GTD-350 turboshaft engines; square cabin windows; fixed-skid landing gear, plus tail skid

Mil Mi-8 "Hip" RUSSIA

Twin-turbine medium helicopter

Development started in May 1962 to replace piston-engined Mi-4. First prototype with single AI-24V turboshaft and four-blade rotor flew in June 1961, but replaced by second prototype with twin TV2 engines and five-blade rotor adopted for production. Total delivered (military and civil): 10,000+.

SPECIFICATION (Mi-8T):

ACCOMMODATION: 2 + 32
CARGO/BAGGAGE: 3000 kg (6614 lb)
MAX SPEED: 140 kt (260 km/h)
RANGE: 229 nm (425 km)

DIMENSIONS:
MAIN ROTOR DIAMETER: 21.3 m (69 ft 11 in)
LENGTH: rotors turning, 25.2 m (82 ft 9 in)
HEIGHT: 5.7 m (18 ft 7 in)

VARIANTS:
Mi-8AT: Basic civil transport version built at Ulan-Ude
Mi-8ATS: Agricultural helicopter with hoppers and spray bars
Mi-8P: Standard passenger model with square windows
Mi-8S: VIP configuration for 9–11 passengers
Mi-8T: Civil utility version and circular cabin windows
Mi-8TM: Upgraded transport with weather radar
Mi-8 VIP: Current deluxe version by Kazan, 7–9 passengers
Plus many military models (which see)

FEATURES:
Five-blade main rotor and three-blade starboard tail rotor; twin Klimov TV2-117 turboshaft engines; horizontal stabilizer near rear of tailboom; rear clamshell doors; rectangular or round cabin windows; tricycle landing gear

Mil Mi-17 "Hip" RUSSIA

Twin-turbine medium helicopter

Improved successor to Mi-8 for civil use and export. Prototype built with basic Mi-8 airframe and powerplant and dynamics of Mi-14, and first displayed at Paris Air Show in 1981. First exported in 1983. Production continues at Kazan and Ulan-Ude. Total delivered: 1100+.

SPECIFICATION:

ACCOMMODATION: 2 + 32
CARGO/BAGGAGE: 3000 kg (6614 lb)
MAX SPEED: 135 kt (250 km/h)
RANGE: 267 nm (495 km)

DIMENSIONS:
MAIN ROTOR DIAMETER: 21.3 m (69 ft 11 in)
LENGTH: rotors turning, 25.4 m (83 ft 3 in)
HEIGHT: 5.7 m (18 ft 7 in)

VARIANTS:
Mi-17: Basic production model
Mi-17KF: Updated to meet U.S. and Canadian certification
Mi-17-1V: Improved hot-and-high version for export; designated Mi-8MTV-1 for local use
Mi-17V-5: Enlarged portside door and new starboard sliding door, rear ramp
Mi-171: More powerful turboshafts, improved rates of climb
Mi-17-1VA: Flying hospital
Mi-172: Equipment changes and performance improvements
Plus military models under Mi-17 and Mi-8 designations (which see)

FEATURES:
Five-blade main rotor and three-blade portside tail rotor; twin Klimov TV3-117 turboshafts with shorter engine nacelles; horizontal stabilizer near rear of tailboom; rear clam-shell doors; rectangular or round cabin windows

Mil Mi-26 "Halo" RUSSIA

Twin-turbine heavy helicopter

World's largest helicopter, first displayed in the West at the 1981 Paris Air Show. Development started in early 1970s and prototype first flew December 14, 1977. Operational in 1983, with export deliveries starting in June 1986. Total delivered: 300+.

SPECIFICATION:

ACCOMMODATION: 4 + 80
CARGO/BAGGAGE: 22,000 kg (48,500 lb)
MAX SPEED: 159 kt (295 km/h)
RANGE: 270 nm (500 km)

DIMENSIONS:

MAIN ROTOR DIAMETER: 32.0 m (105 ft 0 in)
LENGTH: rotors turning, 40.0 m (131 ft 3 in)
HEIGHT: 8.2 m (26 ft 9 in)

VARIANTS:

Mi-26MS: Medevac with fully equipped medical section
Mi-26P: Civil transport configuration for 63 passengers
Mi-26PK: Flying-crane derivative with operator's gondola on port fuselage side
Mi-26T: Basic civil utility transport
Mi-26TC: Cargo version with 6-tonne hoist and electric winches
Mi-26TM: Flying-crane derivative with gondola under fuselage, either aft of nose or under rear-loading ramp
Mi-26TP: Firefighting version with belly-mounted water or retardant dump
Mi-26TZ: Flying tanker plus several military transport versions

FEATURES:

Eight-blade main rotor and five-blade starboard tail rotor; twin ZMKB Progress D-136 turboshafts; clamshell rear doors; swept tail rotor/stabilizer support; tricycle landing gear

Mil Mi-34 "Hermit" RUSSIA

Single-piston or -turbine light helicopter

Multi-purpose light helicopter first flown November 17, 1986, and exhibited at Paris Air Show in mid-1987. Series production started at Progress Plant in Arsenyev in 1993. Total delivered 30+.

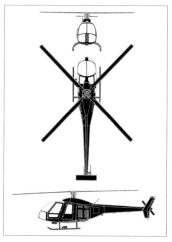

SPECIFICATION:

ACCOMMODATION: 1 + 3
CARGO/BAGGAGE: 550 kg (1213 lb)
MAX SPEED: 122 kt (225 km/h)
RANGE: 194 nm (360 km)

DIMENSIONS:

MAIN ROTOR DIAMETER: 10.0 m (32 ft 10 in)
LENGTH: rotors turning, 11.4 m (37 ft 5 in)
HEIGHT: 2.8 m (9 ft 1 in)

VARIANTS:

Mi-34: Basic production version
Mi-34A: Proposal to replace piston engine with Rolls-Royce 250-C20R turboshaft
Mi-34L: Projected version with Lycoming engine
Mi-34M: Projected twin-turbine six-seat version
Mi-34P: Police variant in service with Moscow City Police
Mi-34S: As basic Mi-34, but upgraded to meet FAR Pt 27; also marketed as Mi-34C
Mi-34UT: Dual-control trainer
Mi-234: Proposal with rotary engines; formerly Mi-34VAZ

FEATURES:

Four-blade main rotor and two-blade starboard tail rotor; single VOKBM M-14V piston engine; bubble canopy; swept-back tailfin with small unswept T-tailplane; fixed-skid landing gear

PZL Šwidnik SW-4 Maluch POLAND

Single-turbine light helicopter

Development began in 1985, but major redesigns initiated by the time of the first flight on October 29, 1996. Series production started in July 2002 and first aircraft were delivered to Polish Air Force on November 15, 2004. Delivered: 10+.

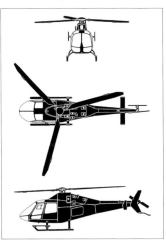

SPECIFICATION:

ACCOMMODATION: 1 + 4
CARGO/BAGGAGE: 750 kg (1653 lb)
MAX SPEED: 155 kt (88 km/h)
RANGE: 468 nm (860 km)

DIMENSIONS:

MAIN ROTOR DIAMETER: 9.0 m (29 ft 6 in)
LENGTH: rotors turning, 10.6 m (34 ft 8 in)
HEIGHT: 3.1 m (10 ft 3 in)

VARIANTS:

SW-4: Initial production version

FEATURES:

Three-blade main rotor and two-blade starboard tail rotor; single Rolls-Royce 250 turboshaft; arrowhead tailfin; narrow tailplane with small endplate fins; fixed-skid landing gear

Robinson R22 USA

Single-piston light helicopter

Design began in 1973, leading to the first flight on August 28, 1975. Deliveries started in October 1979. Total delivered: 4025.

SPECIFICATION:

ACCOMMODATION: 1 + 1
CARGO/BAGGAGE: 181 kg (400 lb)
MAX SPEED: 102 kt (190 km/h)
RANGE: 174 nm (322 km)

DIMENSIONS:
MAIN ROTOR DIAMETER: 7.7 m (25 ft 2 in)
LENGTH: rotors turning, 8.8 m (28 ft 9 in)
HEIGHT: 2.7 m (8 ft 9 in)

VARIANTS:
R22: Initial production model
R22HP: Higher-powered version introduced in 1981
R22 Alpha: Improved and increased gross weight from 1983
R22 Beta: More powerful engines
R22 Mariner: Floats and ground wheels, corrosion-proofed
R22 Beta II: Current production model with significant improvements
R22 Mariner II: Current improved production model
R22 Beta II Police: Equipped with searchlight, loudspeaker, and more
Plus other specialist versions available for training and agricultural work

FEATURES:
Two-blade main rotor and two-blade tail rotor on port side; high-mounted rotorhead; single Textron Lycoming O-360 piston engine; upper and lower tailfin; fixed-skid landing gear or floats and ground wheels

Robinson R44 USA

Single-piston light helicopter

Four-seat development of the R22 began in 1986. First flight of the R44 took place on March 31, 1990, and first deliveries in early 1993. Total delivered: 2628.

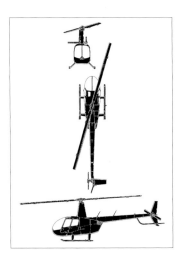

SPECIFICATION:

ACCOMMODATION: 1 + 3
CARGO/BAGGAGE: 445 kg (981 lb)
MAX SPEED: 113 kt (209 km/h)
RANGE: 347 nm (643 km)

DIMENSIONS:
MAIN ROTOR DIAMETER: 10.1 m (33 ft 0 in)
LENGTH: rotors turning, 11.7 m (38 ft 3 in)
HEIGHT: 3.3 m (10 ft 9 in)

VARIANTS:
R44 Astro: Initial production model with fixed skids
R44 Clipper: Float-equipped and lights for night flying
R44 Police: Law-enforcement model with specialized equipment
R44 IFR Trainer: Specialized equipment for pilot training
R44 Newscopter: Production-line ENG model with cameras and audio system
R44 Raven I: Enhanced version available from April 2000
R44 Raven II: Further enhancements from 2002; fuel-injected engine, redesigned main and tail rotors

FEATURES:
Two-blade main rotor and two-blade tail rotor on port side; high-mounted rotorhead; single Textron Lycoming O-540 piston engine; upper and lower tailfin; fixed-skid landing gear or floats and ground wheels

Schweizer (Hughes) 300 USA

Single-piston light helicopter

Design and development of original two-seat Hughes Model 269 began in September 1955, and the first prototype flew in October 1956. Several improved models followed, and in July 1983, production was transferred from Hughes to Schweizer. Total delivered (including military): 3657.

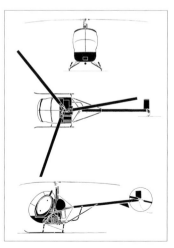

SPECIFICATION (300C):

ACCOMMODATION: 1 + 2
CARGO/BAGGAGE: 975 kg (2150 lb)
MAX SPEED: 91 kt (169 km/h)
RANGE: 194 nm (360 km)

DIMENSIONS:
MAIN ROTOR DIAMETER: 8.2 m (26 ft 10 in)
LENGTH: rotors turning, 9.4 m (30 ft 10 in)
HEIGHT: 2.7 m (8 ft 9 in)

VARIANTS:
269A: Original production model
269A-1: Re-engined with fuel injection and larger main rotor
300 (269B): Three-seat follow-up with quiet tail rotor (QTR)
300C (269C): Standard civil production version
300C Sky Knight: Special police version
300CB: "Bare" version of 300C for training role
300CBi: Improved with fuel-injected engine
Shen2B: Chinese-built 300CBi
Shen3A: Chinese-built 300C
TH-55A: Light primary trainer bought by U.S. Army in 1960s
TH-300C: Current military training version

FEATURES:
Three-blade main rotor and two-blade tail rotor; single Textron Lycoming HIO-360 piston engine; braced tubular tailboom with separate dihedral tailplane and fin; bubble canopy; fixed-skid landing gear with ground wheels

Schweizer 330 USA

Single-turbine light helicopter

Developed initially for the U.S. Army training-helicopter requirement won by Bell. Announced in 1987 and made its first flight in public June 14, 1988. Deliveries started in mid-1993. Total delivered: 57.

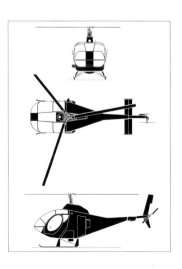

SPECIFICATION (333):

ACCOMMODATION: 1 + 3
CARGO/BAGGAGE: 608 kg (1340 lb)
MAX SPEED: 105 kt (195 km/h)
RANGE: 319 nm (590 km)

DIMENSIONS:

MAIN ROTOR DIAMETER: 8.4 m (27 ft 6 in)
LENGTH: rotors turning, 9.5 m (31 ft 1 in)
HEIGHT: 3.4 m (11 ft 10 in)

VARIANTS:

330 (269D): Initial production version
330SP: Improved performance, available as retrofit to earlier aircraft
333: Enhanced derivative of 330SP with better operating performance and 30% more payload
Shen4T: Chinese-assembled 333

FEATURES:

Three-blade main rotor and two-blade tail rotor on port side; single Rolls-Royce Model 250 turboshaft engine; upper and lower fin; large tailplane with endplate fins at rear of tailboom; fixed-skid landing gear

Sikorsky S-58 USA

Single-piston or twin-turbine intermediate helicopter

Developed to a U.S. Navy specification for antisubmarine helicopter and first flown March 8, 1954. Also built under license by Sud-Aviation in France, and by Westland in the UK as the Wessex. First commercial deliveries made in 1956. First flight of turbine-powered conversion on August 19, 1970. Total built (including military): 1821.

SPECIFICATION (S-58T):

ACCOMMODATION: 2 + 12
CARGO/BAGGAGE: 2460 kg (5423 lb)
MAX SPEED: 120 kt (222 km/h)
RANGE: 260 nm (481 km)

DIMENSIONS:
MAIN ROTOR DIAMETER: 17.1 m (56 ft 0 in)
LENGTH: rotors turning, 17.3 m (56 ft 8 in)
HEIGHT: 4.9 m (15 ft 11 in)

VARIANTS:
S-58B: Initial civil passenger/freight version
S-58C: Similar, but with two doors on starboard side
S-58D: Improved model
S-58T: Turbine conversion with P&W PT6T Twin-Pac providing improved performance
Wessex: License-produced UK version
H-34: U.S. Army/Navy designation

FEATURES:
Four-blade main rotor and four-blade portside tail rotor atop swept fin; single Wright R-1820 piston engine or P&W PT6T Twin-Pac turboshaft engines; high-mounted cockpit; three-wheel undercarriage

Sikorsky S-61 USA

Twin-turbine medium helicopter

Developed to meet U.S. Navy requirement for ASW helicopter with boat-type hull and retractable landing gear. Prototype first flew March 11, 1959. First commercial version flew December 6, 1960. Also built under license by Agusta, Mitsubishi, and Westland. Total delivered: 794.

SPECIFICATION (S-61N):

ACCOMMODATION: 2 + 30
CARGO/BAGGAGE: 3630 kg (8000 lb)
MAX SPEED: 144 kt (267 km/h)
RANGE: 450 nm (833 km)

DIMENSIONS:

MAIN ROTOR DIAMETER: 18.9 m (62 ft 0 in)
LENGTH: overall, 22.2 m (72 ft 8 in)
HEIGHT: 5.6 m (18 ft 5 in)

VARIANTS:

S-61L: Nonamphibious civil model with modified landing gear
S-61L Mk II: Improved version with more powerful CT58 turboshaft engines and individual cargo bins
S-61N: Similar to S-61L, but sealed hull and stabilizing floats
S-61N Mk II: Similar to S-61L Mk II, but with sealed hull and stabilizing floats
S-61R: Many design changes including rear loading ramp and new landing gear
Plus many military versions under H-3, AS-61, and Sea King/Commando designations (which see)

FEATURES:

Five-blade main rotor and five-blade portside tail rotor; twin GE CT58 turboshaft engines; boat hull; twin-wheel undercarriage retracting into stabilizing floats with fixed tailwheel (nonretractable on S-61L)

Sikorsky S-64 Skycrane/Aircrane USA

Twin-turbine heavylift helicopter

Designed initially for military transport duties and flew for the first time on May 9, 1962. Received civil certification in 1969 as the S-64E for the carriage of external cargo. In 1992, Erickson Air-Crane acquired the type certificate and is now marketing improved versions worldwide for various specialist applications. Total delivered: 100.

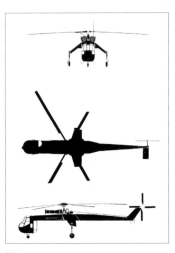

SPECIFICATION (S-64E):

ACCOMMODATION: 3 flight crew
CARGO/BAGGAGE: 9072 kg (20,000 lb)
MAX SPEED: 115 kt (213 km/h)
RANGE: 200 nm (370 km)

DIMENSIONS:
MAIN ROTOR DIAMETER: 22.0 m (72 ft 0 in)
LENGTH: overall, 27.0 m (88 ft 6 in)
HEIGHT: 7.8 m (25 ft 5 in)

VARIANTS:
CH-54A: Original model delivered to U.S. Army
CH-54B: Improved U.S. Army version with increased payload, new rotor system with high-lift rotor blades, increased weight
S-64E: New-built civil version, or improved modification of military CH-54A
S-64F: Civil upgrade of military CH-54B
Helitanker: Specialist firefighting version with 10,000-liter water tank
Plus military versions under CH-54 designation (which see)

FEATURES:
Six-blade main rotor and four-blade portside tailrotor; twin P&W JFTD-12 turboshaft engines; nonretractable tricycle landing gear; cockpit pod and beam-type fuselage; starboard stabilizer on top of tail unit

Sikorsky S-76 USA

Twin-turbine intermediate helicopter

Development of executive transport helicopter announced on January 19, 1975, and first flown March 13, 1977. Deliveries started in early 1979. Two military models also offered, but these proved unsuccessful. Total delivered: 594.

SPECIFICATION (S-76C+):

ACCOMMODATION: 2 + 13
CARGO/BAGGAGE: 1497 kg (3300 lb)
MAX SPEED: 155 kt (287 km/h)
RANGE: 453 nm (839 km)

DIMENSIONS:

MAIN ROTOR DIAMETER: 13.4 m (44 ft 0 in)
LENGTH: rotors turning, 16.0 m (52 ft 6 in)
HEIGHT: 4.4 m (14 ft 5 in)

VARIANTS:

S-76A: Original transport version with P&WC PT6Bs
S-76A Mk II: Standard production version from March 1982
S-76A Utility: Basic version with sliding doors and strengthened floor
S-76A+: Retrofit with Turbomeca Arriel 1S
S-76A++: Retrofit with Turbomeca Arriel 1S1
S-76B: Powered by P&WC PT6B-36A turboshafts
S-76C: Essentially as S-76B, but with Arriel 1S1s
S-76C+: Uprated Arriel 1S1s with FADEC
S-76D: New P&WC PW210S engines and other improvements; to be available from 2008
S-76N: Naval version operated by Royal Thai Navy

FEATURES:

Four-blade main rotor and four-blade portside tail rotor; twin P&WC PT6B or Turbomeca Arriel turboshafts; retractable tricycle-type landing gear; two large doors on each side; horizontal stabilizers at base of tail unit

Sikorsky S-92 USA

Twin-turbine medium helicopter

First announced as growth development of Black Hawk in March 1992 and launched as international risk-sharing partnership with Mitsubishi Heavy Industries, Jingdezhen Helicopter, and Gamesa at Paris Air Show in June 1995. Made first flight on December 23, 1998, and achieved FAA FAR Pt 29 Category A certification on December 17, 2002. First delivery made in March 2004. Total delivered: 22.

SPECIFICATION:

ACCOMMODATION: 2 + 22
CARGO/BAGGAGE: 4536 kg (10,000 lb)
MAX SPEED: 165 kt (305 km/h)
RANGE: 475 nm (879 km)

DIMENSIONS:

MAIN ROTOR DIAMETER: 17.2 m (56 ft 4 in)
LENGTH: rotors turning, 20.9 m (68 ft 6 in)
HEIGHT: 5.4 m (17 ft 9 in)

VARIANTS:

S-92A: Transport version for civil market
S-92IU: International civil/military utility version
H-92 Superhawk: Military transport derivative with uprated CT7-8C engines and folding main and tail rotors
H-92 Cyclone: Canadian military version
HV-92: Proposed military VIP version

FEATURES:

Four-blade main rotor and four-blade tail rotor on starboard side; large horizontal stabilizer on port side; rear loading ramp; tricycle landing gear retractable into large side sponsons

Whisper Jet (Sikorsky) S-55QT USA

Single-turbine light helicopter conversion

Project initiated in 1992 by Papillon
Grand Canyon Helicopters and
Vertical Aviation Technologies (VAT)
to produce ultra-quiet helicopter for
sightseeing flights. Main changes
from basic S-55 include new five-
blade main rotor and turboshaft
engine with acoustically modified
engine inlet plenum. Total of 100
S-55 airframes available for
conversion. Total converted: 5.

SPECIFICATION:

ACCOMMODATION: 1 + 9
CARGO/BAGGAGE: 1134 kg (2500 lb)
MAX SPEED: 99 kt (183 km/h)
RANGE: 215 nm (398 km)

DIMENSIONS:
MAIN ROTOR DIAMETER: 15.3 m (50 ft 2 in)
LENGTH: rotors turning, 19.0 m (62 ft 4 in)
HEIGHT: 4.7 m (15 ft 3 in)

VARIANTS:
S-55QT: Initial version with glass-bottom floor and
large viewing windows for sightseeing flights

FEATURES:
Five-blade main rotor and two-blade tail rotor
on port side; single Garrett TSE331 turboshaft
engine; quadricycle landing gear; large viewing
windows and glass-bottom floor

Combat
Aircraft

AIDC F-CK-1 Ching-Kuo TAIWAN

Air superiority fighter

First flight of prototype, aka Indigenous Fighter Aircraft (IDF), on May 28, 1989, with production deliveries (of 120 IDFs) from 1994 to January 2000. Upgrade prototype of C-model flown November 2006.

SPECIFICATION:

ACCOMMODATION: F-CK-1A, pilot; F-CK-1B, student and instructor
MAX SPEED: 700 kt (1296 km/h)
RANGE: n/a

ARMAMENT:
INTERNAL GUNS: one 20 mm M61 cannon
HARDPOINTS: six (plus wingtips)
MAX WEAPON LOAD: 3901 kg (8600 lb)
REPRESENTATIVE WEAPONS: AAMs; ASMs; AGMs; PGMs; bombs; FFAR pods

DIMENSIONS:
WINGSPAN: 8.5 m (28 ft 0 in) over missile rails
LENGTH: 13.3 m (43 ft 6 in)
HEIGHT: 4.7 m (15 ft 3 in)

VARIANTS & OPERATORS:
F-CK-1A: RoCAF
F-CK-1B: RoCAF

FEATURES:
Like F-16, but with two underwing air intakes; mid-swept wing; twin ITEC TFE1042-70 turbofans; tallfin
Not to be confused with F-16, T-50, F-2

AMX International AMX ITALY/BRAZIL

Strike/attack fighter

The AMX International consortium (Alenia and Aermacchi of Italy and EMBRAER of Brazil) was created in 1980 to replace the G91R/Y and F-104G/S in Italy and the MB-326 Xavante in Brazil. First flown on May 15, 1984; 198 delivered.

SPECIFICATION:

ACCOMMODATION: AMX, pilot; AMX-T, student and instructor
MAX SPEED: M0.86
RADIUS OF ACTION: 480 nm (889 km)

ARMAMENT:
INTERNAL GUNS: one 20 mm M61 (Italy) or two 30 mm DEFA cannon (Brazil)
HARDPOINTS: five (plus wingtips)
MAX WEAPON LOAD: 3800 kg (8377 lb)
REPRESENTATIVE WEAPONS: wingtip AAMs; Paveway II LGBs; AM-39 Exocet or Marte ASMs; bombs; FFAR pods

DIMENSIONS:
WINGSPAN: 10.0 m (32 ft 8 in)
LENGTH: 13.2 m (43 ft 5 in)
HEIGHT: 4.5 m (14 ft 11 in)

VARIANTS & OPERATORS:
AMX: Brazil (A-1), Italy
AMX-T: Brazil (AT-1), Italy
AMX-ATA: (Super AMX-T)

FEATURES:
Shoulder/swept wing; single Rolls-Royce Spey Mk.807 turbofan; shoulder intakes; wingtip missiles

BAE Systems (British Aerospace) Hawk 200 UK

Light multirole fighter

Derived from the Hawk 100 series advanced jet trainer, the single-seat Hawk 200 series has the APG-66 radar of the F-16A/B. First flown on May 19, 1986; 62 have been built.

SPECIFICATION:

ACCOMMODATION: Pilot only
MAX SPEED: 540 kt (1000 km/h)
RADIUS OF ACTION: 345 nm (638 km)

ARMAMENT:
INTERNAL GUNS: none
HARDPOINTS: five (plus wingtips)
MAX WEAPON LOAD: 3000 kg (6614 lb)
REPRESENTATIVE WEAPONS: centerline 30 mm gun pod; AIM-9 AAM; AGM-65 Maverick AGM; bombs; FFAR pods; CBLS; external fuel tanks

DIMENSIONS:
LENGTH: 11.3 m (37 ft 2 in)
WINGSPAN: 9.4 m (30 ft 9 in)
HEIGHT: 4.1 m (13 ft 7 in)

VARIANTS & OPERATORS:
Mk.203: Oman (12)
Mk.208: Malaysia (18)
Mk.209: Indonesia (32)

FEATURES:
Low/swept wing; single Rolls-Royce/Turbomeca Adour Mk.871 turbofan; blown canopy

BAE Systems (British Aerospace) Sea Harrier FRS.51 UK

STOVL fighter, recce and strike aircraft

Sea Harrier FRS.51 is export version of RN FRS.1 (first flown August 20, 1978) for India. Deliveries from December 1983 to April 1992. RN Sea Harrier FA.2 withdrawn in March 2006.

SPECIFICATION:

ACCOMMODATION: pilot
MAX SPEED: FRS.51, 618 kt (1144 km/h)
RADIUS OF ACTION: FRS.51, 200 nm (370 km)

ARMAMENT:
INTERNAL GUNS: none, but two 30 mm Aden cannon fuselage pods
HARDPOINTS: five
MAX WEAPON LOAD: 3630 kg (8000 lb)
REPRESENTATIVE WEAPONS: AAMs; ASMs; bombs or PGMs; Lepus flares; CBLS; external fuel tanks

DIMENSIONS:
LENGTH: 14.5 m (47 ft 7 in)
WINGSPAN: 7.7 m (25 ft 3 in)
HEIGHT: 3.7 m (12 ft 2 in)

VARIANTS & OPERATORS:
Sea Harrier FRS.51: Indian Navy (23)

FEATURES:
Shoulder/swept wing; single Rolls-Royce Pegasus vectored-thrust turbofan; four nozzles; blown canopy
Not to be confused with AV-8B or Harrier GR.7/9

Boeing B-52H Stratofortress USA

Long-range bomber

First flown on April 15, 1952, and entered USAF service in 1955. Only the B-52H (102 built 1960-61) remains in service. All aircraft now capable of conventional as well as nuclear role. Many system upgrades in place with more pending.

SPECIFICATION:

ACCOMMODATION: Pilot, co-pilot, three WSOs
MAX SPEED: 516 kt (957 km/h)
RANGE: 8685+ nm (16,093+ km)

ARMAMENT:
Original tail-mounted 20 mm M61 cannon now deleted
Bomb bays and two underwing hardpoints
MAX WEAPON LOAD: 24,750 kg (60,000 lb)
REPRESENTATIVE WEAPONS: 20 AGM-86C CALCM (12 internal, 8 external); nuclear weapons; PGMs; bombs and mines; JDAM, JSOW, and JASSM weapons

DIMENSIONS:
LENGTH: 49.0 m (160 ft 11 in)
WINGSPAN: 56.4 m (185 ft 0 in)
HEIGHT: 12.4 m (40 ft 8 in)

VARIANTS & OPERATORS:
B-52H: USAF (60)

FEATURES:
Shoulder/swept wing; four engine pylons each with two P&W TF33-P-3 turbofans; outboard underwing tanks; tall fin

Boeing (McDonnell Douglas) F-15 Eagle USA

Air superiority fighter

First flown on July 27, 1972, and entered USAF service in 1974. Sold to Israel, Saudi Arabia, and Japan (built under license by Mitsubishi). Last of 894 USAF versions delivered in 1989.

SPECIFICATION:

ACCOMMODATION: F-15A/C, pilot; F-15B/D/DJ, student and instructor
MAX SPEED: M2.5 (800 kt, 1 482 km/h)
FERRY RANGE: 2500+ nm (4631+ km)

ARMAMENT:
INTERNAL GUNS: one 20 mm M61 cannon
HARDPOINTS: nine
MAX WEAPON LOAD: 10,705 kg (23,600 lb) plus four fuselage AAMs
REPRESENTATIVE WEAPONS: AIM-7, AIM-9, AIM-120 AAMs; Mk.80 bombs; Paveway LGBs; ECM pods; CFT and external fuel tanks

DIMENSIONS:
LENGTH: 19.4 m (63 ft 9 in)
WINGSPAN: 13.5 m (42 ft 9 in)
HEIGHT: 5.6 m (18 ft 5 in)

VARIANTS & OPERATORS:
F-15A/B: USAF, Israel
F-15C: USAF, Israel, Saudi Arabia
F-15D: USAF, Israel, Saudi Arabia
F-15DJ: Japan
F-15J: Japan

FEATURES:
Twin fins; shoulder/swept wings; two P&W F100 turbofans; blown canopy
Not to be confused with MiG-25 and MiG-31

Boeing (McDonnell Douglas) F-15E Strike Eagle USA

Dual-role attack fighter

Derived from the F-15B, the industry-funded Strike Eagle flew in 1982. First production F-15E flew December 11, 1986, and entered USAF service in 1988. Reduced internal fuel capacity but can use F-15 CFT.

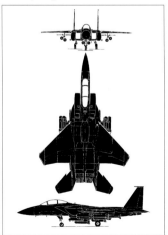

SPECIFICATION:

ACCOMMODATION: All versions, pilot and WSO
MAX SPEED: M2.5 (800 kt, 1482 km/h)
RADIUS OF ACTION: 685 nm (1270 km)

ARMAMENT:
INTERNAL GUNS: one 20 mm M61 cannon
HARDPOINTS: nine
MAX WEAPON LOAD: 11,113 kg (24,500 lb)
REPRESENTATIVE WEAPONS: AIM-7, AIM-9, AIM-120 AAMs; nuclear weapons; JDAM bombs; Paveway LGBs; AGM-84 Harpoon; AGM-88 HARM; GBU-15; ECM pods; LANTIRN pods; CFT and external fuel tanks

DIMENSIONS:
LENGTH: 19.4 m (63 ft 9 in)
WINGSPAN: 13.5 m (42 ft 9 in)
HEIGHT: 5.6 m (18 ft 5 in)

VARIANTS & OPERATORS:
F-15E: USAF (235+)
F-15I: Israel (25)
F-15K: South Korea (40)
F-15S: Saudi Arabia (72)
F-15T: Singapore (12)

FEATURES:
Twin fins; shoulder/swept wings; two P&W F100 (GE F110 in F-15K) turbofans; blown canopy
Not to be confused with MiG-25 and MiG-31

Boeing (McDonnell Douglas) F/A-18 Hornet USA

Carrier-based attack fighter

Derived from Northrop YF-17 with McDD, first prototype F-18 flew on November 18, 1978. The Hornet entered USN/USMC service from 1980. The last of 1479 first-generation Hornets delivered in September 2000. Upgrades for Australia, Canada, and Spain.

SPECIFICATION:

ACCOMMODATION: F/A-18A/C, pilot; F/A-18B/D, student and instructor
MAX SPEED: M1.8+
RADIUS OF ACTION: 290 nm (537 km)

ARMAMENT:
INTERNAL GUNS: one 20 mm M61 cannon
HARDPOINTS: seven (plus wingtips)
MAX WEAPON LOAD: 7031 kg (15,500 lb)
REPRESENTATIVE WEAPONS: AIM-7, AIM-9, AIM-120 AAMs; bombs; Paveway LGBs; AGMs; ECM pods; designator pods and external fuel tanks

DIMENSIONS:
LENGTH: 17.1 m (56 ft 0 in)
WINGSPAN: 11.4 m (37 ft 6 in)
HEIGHT: 4.7 m (15 ft 3 in)

VARIANTS & OPERATORS:
F/A-18A: USN/USMC, Australia, Canada, Spain
F/A-18B: USN/USMC, Australia, Canada, Spain
F/A-18C: USN/USMC, Finland, Kuwait, Switzerland
F/A-18D: USN/USMC, Finland, Kuwait, Malaysia, Switzerland

FEATURES:
Twin fins; shoulder/swept wings; long LERX; two GE F404-GE-400 turbofans; blown canopy
Not to be confused with F/A-18E/F/G, which have square engine air intakes

Boeing (McDonnell Douglas) F/A-18E/F/G Super Hornet USA

Carrier-based attack fighter (EA-18G pictured)

A "stretched" F/A-18C, the first proto-type F-18E flew on November 29, 1995. Super Hornet entered service with the USN in 1999, with combat debut (VFA-115) in November 2002. At present, some 314 Super Hornets are planned (not all funded), plus 90 F/A-18G Growlers, as replacement for EA-6B Prowler SEAD/EW aircraft.

F/A-18E

SPECIFICATION:

ACCOMMODATION: F/A-18E, pilot; F/A-18F, student and instructor; F/A-18G, pilot and EWO
MAX SPEED: M1.8+
RADIUS OF ACTION: interdiction, 945 nm (1750 km)
RADIUS OF ACTION: fighter escort, 795 nm (1472 km)

ARMAMENT:

INTERNAL GUNS: one 20 mm M61A2 cannon
HARDPOINTS: nine (plus wingtips)
MAX WEAPON LOAD: 8051 kg (17,750 lb)
REPRESENTATIVE WEAPONS: AIM-9, AIM-120 AAMs; bombs; Paveway LGBs; AGMs; SLAM-ER; HARM; JSOW; JDAM; ECM pods; designator pods and external fuel tanks

DIMENSIONS:

LENGTH: 18.4 m (60 ft 3 in)
WINGSPAN: 13.6 m (44 ft 8 in)
HEIGHT: 4.9 m (16 ft 0 in)

VARIANTS & OPERATORS:

F/A-18E: USN/USMC
F/A-18F: USN/USMC
F/A-18G: USN/USMC

FEATURES:

Twin fins; shoulder/swept wings; long LERX; two GE F414-GE-400 turbofans; blown canopy
Not to be confused with F/A-18A/B/C/D, which have round engine air intakes

CAC J-7 (F-7) CHINA

Fighter and ground-attack aircraft

Chinese variant of MiG-21, in PLAAF service from 1967. Several thousand in various variants produced for China. Current export model is the F-7MG, with a double-delta wingplan, Western avionics, and uprated engine. About 400 of all types exported.

SPECIFICATION:

ACCOMMODATION: J-7/F-7 variants, pilot; JJ-7 (FT-7), student and instructor
MAX SPEED: (J-7C) M2.1
RADIUS OF ACTION: interdiction, (F-7M) 324 nm (600 km)

ARMAMENT (F-7MG):
INTERNAL GUNS: one 30 mm Type 30-1 cannon
HARDPOINTS: five
MAX WEAPON LOAD: about 1500 kg (3300 lb)
REPRESENTATIVE WEAPONS: PL-7, AIM-9, Magic AAMs; bombs; FFAR pods; external fuel tanks

DIMENSIONS:
LENGTH: 12.2 m (39 ft 11 in)
WINGSPAN: 8.3 m (27 ft 3 in)
HEIGHT: 4.1 m (13 ft 5 in)

VARIANTS & OPERATORS:
China J-7 II/III/IV, J-7E/EB, JJ-7 (two-seater built by GAIC); Albania (F-7A); Bangladesh (F-7M); Egypt (F-7B); Iran (F-7M); Myanmar (F-7M); Pakistan (F-7P/MP/PG); Sri Lanka (F-7BS); Sudan (F-7B); Tanzania (F-7A); Zimbabwe (F-7B/IIN)

FEATURES:
Low double-delta wing; swept tailplanes; single LMC (Liyang) WP13F turbojet; nose intake with central radome
Not to be confused with MiG-21; CAC/PAC FC-1/JF-17 Xiaolong/Thunder; Dassault Mirage F1

CAC J 10 (F-10) CHINA

Multirole fighter

Similar in weight and performance to the Eurofighter Typhoon and Dassault Rafale, the J-10 bears a close external resemblance to the cancelled IAI Lavi of the late 1980s. Believed to have made its maiden flight by mid-1996, up to eight prototype/development aircraft flown. In February 2003, ten aircraft reported to be undergoing evaluation. The two-seat J-10B reported to have made first flight on December 26, 2003.

SPECIFICATION:

ACCOMMODATION: J-10A, pilot; J-10B, student and instructor
MAX SPEED: M1.85
COMBAT RADIUS: 250–300 nm (463–555 km)

ARMAMENT:
INTERNAL GUNS: 23 mm cannon
HARDPOINTS: 11
MAX WEAPON LOAD: 4500 kg (9921 lb)
REPRESENTATIVE WEAPONS: PL-8/-11/-12 AAMs; C-801/802 ASMs; YJ-9 ARMs

DIMENSIONS:
LENGTH: 8.78 m (28 ft 10 in)
WINGSPAN: 14.57 m (47 ft 9 in)
HEIGHT: 4.78 m (15 ft 8 in)

VARIANTS & OPERATORS:
China

FEATURES:
Rear delta wing with canard foreplanes; single Saturn/Lyulka AL-31FN afterburning turbofan engine with undernose engine intake; twin ventral mini-fins below rear fuselage
Not to be confused with Rafale, Typhoon, or Su-27-series "Flanker"

CAC/PAC FC-1/JF-17 Xiaolong/Thunder CHINA/PAKISTAN

Multirole attack aircraft

Joint venture between China and Pakistan launched in 1991. First flight on August 25, 2003, with second prototype flying on April 9, 2004. Chinese avionics with Western radar. China plans for 1000 aircraft, Pakistan for 150.

SPECIFICATION:

ACCOMMODATION: pilot
MAX SPEED: M1.6
RADIUS OF ACTION: fighter, 648 nm (1200 km)

ARMAMENT:
INTERNAL GUNS: one 23 mm GSh-23-2 cannon pod on centerline
HARDPOINTS: seven
MAX WEAPON LOAD: about 3800 kg (8380 lb)
REPRESENTATIVE WEAPONS: PL-12, AIM-9, Magic AAMs; bombs; LGBs; designator pod; external fuel tanks

DIMENSIONS:
LENGTH: 14.7 m (48 ft 3 in)
WINGSPAN: 9.5 m (31 ft 2 in)
HEIGHT: 4.8 m (15 ft 9 in)

VARIANTS & OPERATORS:
China: FC-1
Pakistan: JF-17

FEATURES:
Low delta wing; swept tailplanes; single Klimov RD-93 turbofan; side intakes with central radome

Dassault Mirage III/5/50 FRANCE

Interceptor and multirole fighter

Designed as all-weather interceptor (C/O/S), first flown on November 17, 1956. Developed into a two-seat trainer (B/D), long-range fighter bomber (E), and recce (R) aircraft. A total of 1420 Mirage III/5/50 were built.

SPECIFICATION:

ACCOMMODATION: all except those B/D models, pilot; all B/D models, student and instructor
MAX SPEED: M2.2 (1268 kt, 2350 km/h)
RADIUS OF ACTION: 700 nm (1300 km)

ARMAMENT (MIRAGE 5):
INTERNAL GUNS: two 30 mm DEFA cannon
HARDPOINTS: seven
MAX WEAPON LOAD: 3800 kg (8370 lb)
REPRESENTATIVE WEAPONS: Magic, AIM-9 AAMs; AS-30 AGM on centerline; PGMs; bombs; FFAR pods or external fuel tanks

DIMENSIONS:
LENGTH: Mirage IIIE, 15 m (49 ft 3 in); Mirage 5/50, 15.5 m (51 ft 0 in)
WINGSPAN: Mirage IIIE/5/50, 8.2 m (26 ft 11 in)
HEIGHT: 4.5 m (14 ft 9 in)

VARIANTS & OPERATORS:
Mirage IIIB/C/D/E/O/R/S: Argentina, Pakistan
Mirage 5A/C/D/E/F/G/M/P/R: Argentina, Chile (aka Elkan), Colombia, Egypt, Gabon, Pakistan
Mirage 50C/D/E/FC: Chile (aka Pantera) and Venezuela

FEATURES:
Low/swept delta wing; single SNECMA Atar 9C/9K-50 turbojet
Not to be confused with Mirage 2000 and Rafale

Dassault Mirage F1 FRANCE

Air defense/multirole fighter

Prototype flew on December 23, 1966, and Mirage F-1C entered French service in 1973. Developed into an attack aircraft (A/J), two-seater trainer (B/D), long-range fighter bomber (E), and recce (R) aircraft. A total of 731 were built by 1992.

SPECIFICATION:

ACCOMMODATION: all except those B/D models, pilot; all B/D models, student and instructor
MAX SPEED: M1.2 (800 kt, 1480 km/h)
RADIUS OF ACTION: 378 nm (700 km)

ARMAMENT:
INTERNAL GUNS: two 30 mm DEFA cannon
HARDPOINTS: seven
MAX WEAPON LOAD: 6300 kg (13,890 lb)
REPRESENTATIVE WEAPONS: Magic, AIM-9, Super 530 AAMs; AS 30L AGM; PGMs; ASMs; bombs; FFAR pods; designator, EW, and/or recce pods, plus external fuel tanks

DIMENSIONS:
LENGTH: 15.2 m (49 ft 11 in)
WINGSPAN: 8.4 m (27 ft 7 in)
HEIGHT: 4.5 m (14 ft 9 in)

VARIANTS & OPERATORS:
F1-A: Libya (AD)
F1-B: France (B), Jordan (BJ), Libya (BD), and Spain (B/BE)
F1-C: France (C/CR/CT), Jordan (CJ), Morocco (CH), and Spain (CE)
F1-D: Spain (DDA)
F1-E: Iran (EQ), Jordan (EJ), Libya (ED), Morocco (EH/EH-2000), and Spain (EDA/EE)
F1-J: Ecuador (JA/JE)

FEATURES:
Shoulder/swept wing; single SNECMA Atar 9K-50 turbojet; wingtip missiles; sharp pointed nose

Dassault Mirage 2000 FRANCE

Air defense/multirole fighter

Successor to Mirage III/F1, prototype flown on March 10, 1979, and entered French service in 1984. Developed into a two-seater trainer (2000B), multirole fighter (2000E and 2000-5/-9), and strike/attack aircraft (2000D/N, which see). Over 600 are in service or on order.

SPECIFICATION (Mirage 2000-5):

ACCOMMODATION: all except those B/D models, pilot; all B/D models, student and instructor
MAX SPEED: M2.2
RADIUS OF ACTION: 800 nm (1480 km)

ARMAMENT (MIRAGE 2000-5):
INTERNAL GUNS: two 30 mm DEFA cannon
HARDPOINTS: nine
MAX WEAPON LOAD: 7260 kg (16,005 lb)
REPRESENTATIVE WEAPONS: Magic, Super 530, Mica AAMs; BAP 100 anti-runway bomb; bombs; Paveway LGBs; FFAR pods; external fuel tanks; designator, EW, and/or recce pods

DIMENSIONS:
LENGTH: 14.6 m (48 ft 0 in)
WINGSPAN: 9.1 m (29 ft 11 in)
HEIGHT: 5.2 m (17 ft 1 in)

VARIANTS & OPERATORS:
France: 2000B and 2000C (37 converted to 2000-5F)
Abu Dhabi (UAE): 2000DAD/RAD/EAD (33 converted to 2000-9 DAD and 9RAD)
Brazil: 2000B/C
Egypt: 2000EM/BM
Greece: 2000C/2000EG (10 converted to 2000-5 Mk.2), 2000BG and 2000-5 Mk.2
India: 2000H/TH
Peru: 2000P/DP
Qatar: 2000-5EDA/DDA
Taiwan: 2000-5Ei/Di

FEATURES:
Low delta wing; single SNECMA M53 turbofan; sharp pointed nose
Not to be confused with Mirage III/5/50

Dassault Mirage 2000D/N

Strike/attack aircraft

Derived from Mirage 2000B, prototype 2000N nuclear-attack version flew on February 3, 1983, and entered service in 1988. Developed into a conventional attack version, the 2000D, first flown on February 19, 1991, and entered service in 1993. In all, 86 2000Ds and 75 2000Ns were delivered.

SPECIFICATION:

ACCOMMODATION: pilot and WSO
MAX SPEED: M2.2
RADIUS OF ACTION: 2000-N, 1800 nm (3333 km)

ARMAMENT:
INTERNAL GUNS: none
HARDPOINTS: nine
MAX WEAPON LOAD: 7260 kg (16,005 lb)
REPRESENTATIVE WEAPONS: Magic 2 AAMs; ASMP; APACHE; AGMs; bombs; Paveway LGBs; FFAR pods; designator, EW, and/or recce pods; external fuel tanks

DIMENSIONS:
LENGTH: 14.5 m (47 ft 5 in)
WINGSPAN: 9.1 m (29 ft 11 in)
HEIGHT: 5.1 m (16 ft 10 in)

VARIANTS & OPERATORS:
2000D: France
2000N: France

FEATURES:
Low delta wing; single SNECMA M53 turbofan; sharp pointed nose (2000D lacks nose pitot tube)
Not to be confused with Mirage III/5/50

Dassault Rafale FRANCE

Multirole fighter

Prototype Rafale A flew on July 4, 1986, and first production Rafale B flown November 24, 1998. Two-seater strike D version preferred to single-seater C model. Carrier-borne M model entered service in 2001 and first Armée de l'Air aircraft in 2006. With a requirement of 294, 120 Rafales are on firm order.

SPECIFICATION:

ACCOMMODATION: Rafale B, student and instructor; Rafale C/M, pilot; Rafale D, pilot and WSO
MAX SPEED: M1.8 (750 kt, 1390 km/h)
RADIUS OF ACTION: 570 nm (1055 km)

ARMAMENT:

INTERNAL GUNS: one 30 mm DEFA cannon
HARDPOINTS: 12 (plus wingtips)
MAX WEAPON LOAD: 9500 kg (20,944 lb)
REPRESENTATIVE WEAPONS: Magic, Mica AAMs; APACHE/SCALP; AGMs; ASMs; PGMs; bombs; Paveway LGBs; designator, EW, and/or recce pods; external fuel tanks

DIMENSIONS:

LENGTH: 15.3 m (50 ft 1 in)
WINGSPAN: 10.8 m (35 ft 5 in)
HEIGHT: 5.3 m (17 ft 6 in)

VARIANTS & OPERATORS:

Rafale B: trainer, France (both services)
Rafale C: French Air Force
Rafale D: French Air Force
Rafale M: French Navy

FEATURES:

Swept nose canards; mid-delta wing; twin SNECMA M88-2 turbofans; chin intakes beneath canards
Not to be confused with Typhoon and Gripen

Dassault Super Etendard FRANCE

Carrier-based strike fighter and recce aircraft

Super Etendard prototype flew on July 28, 1974, with deliveries to Aeronavale from May 1982. Upgrade with SLEP and new avionics from 1990, as Super Etendard Modernisé. Sold to Argentina in 1979. Deliveries completed in 1983.

SPECIFICATION:

ACCOMMODATION: Super Etendard/Super Etendard Modernisé, pilot
MAX SPEED: M1.0 (637 kt, 1180 km/h)
RADIUS OF ACTION: 460 nm (850 km)

ARMAMENT:
INTERNAL GUNS: two 30 mm DEFA cannon
HARDPOINTS: six
MAX WEAPON LOAD: 2100 kg (4630 lb)
REPRESENTATIVE WEAPONS: Magic AAMs; AM 39 Exocet ASM; 250 kg and 400 kg bombs; external fuel tanks; EW and/or recce pods

DIMENSIONS:
LENGTH: 14.3 m (46 ft 11 in)
WINGSPAN: 9.6 m (31 ft 6 in)
HEIGHT: 3.86 m (12 ft 8 in)

VARIANTS & OPERATORS:
Super Etendard/Super Etendard Modernisé:
French Navy (51)
Super Etendard: Argentine Navy (11)

FEATURES:
Chubby nose; low/swept wing; swept tailplanes; one SNECMA 8K-50 turbojet; fuselage intakes by cockpit

Embraer EMB-314M (A-29) Super Tucano BRAZIL

Patrol attack fighter

Derived from EMB-312 trainer, the EMB-314M (Brazilian designation is A-29) features a more powerful PT6A turboprop engine, reprofiled wing, and two fuselage extensions. YA-29 single-seat prototype was rolled-out on May 28, 1999. A trainer version, AT-29, is also being procured. First A-29 for Brazil delivered December 18, 2003; first Colombian aircraft delivered December 7, 2006.

SPECIFICATION:

ACCOMODATION: A-29, pilot; AT-29, student and instructor
MAX SPEED: 301 kt (557 km/h)
RADIUS OF ACTION: 847 nm (1568 km)

ARMAMENT:

INTERNAL GUNS: two 12.7 mm (0.5 in) machine guns
HARDPOINTS: four
MAX WEAPON LOAD: n/a
REPRESENTATIVE WEAPONS: MAA-1 Piranha AAM; Mk.81 250 lb bombs; Mk.82 500 lb bombs; BLG-252 cluster weapons and LGBs

DIMENSIONS:

LENGTH: 11.4 m (37 ft 5 in)
WINGSPAN: 11.1 m (36 ft 6 in)
HEIGHT: 3.9 m (12 ft 9 in)

VARIANTS & OPERATORS:

A-29: Brazilian Air Force (49 on order)
AT-29: Brazilian Air Force (50 on order)
EMB-314M: Colombia (25 on order)

FEATURES:

Low tapered wing; blown canopy; one P&WC PT6A-68C turboprop

English Electric (British Aerospace) Canberra UK

Bomber, intruder, and recce aircraft

First flown on May 13, 1949, the Canberra entered RAF service in 1951. Built in 20 different versions (plus seven in the U.S.) and widely exported. Total UK production was 924, 48 in Australia, and 403 in the U.S.

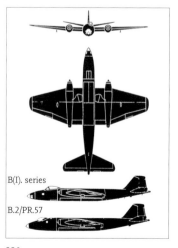

B(I). series

B.2/PR.57

SPECIFICATION:

ACCOMMODATION: PR.57, pilot and two navigators; T.4/T.54, student and instructor (plus one); B(I) versions, pilot and navigator
MAX SPEED: 470 kt (871 km/h)
RADIUS OF ACTION: 700 nm (1296 km)

ARMAMENT (B(1)TT.58):
INTERNAL GUNS: four 20 mm Hispano cannon (optional)
HARDPOINTS: four in bomb bay, two underwing
MAX WEAPON LOAD: 3630 kg (8000 lb)
REPRESENTATIVE WEAPONS: 500 lb, 1000 lb, and 4000 lb bombs; wingtip fuel tanks and underwing target-towing stores

DIMENSIONS:
LENGTH: B(I).58, 19.9 m (65 ft 6 in)
WINGSPAN: B(I).58, 19.5 m (64 ft 0 in)
HEIGHT: 4.8 m (15 ft 8 in)

VARIANTS & OPERATORS:
India: Canberra B(TT).2/PR.57 (3); B(I)TT.58 (10)

FEATURES:
Mid-tapered wing; hemispherical canopy; two mid-wing-mounted Rolls-Royce Avon 206 turbojets

Eurofighter EF2000 Typhoon INTERNATIONAL

Swing-role fighter (Typhoon F.2 pictured)

Collaborative venture between Germany (EADS/DASA), Italy (Alenia Aerospazio), Spain (EADS/CASA), and the UK (BAE Systems). The first of seven development aircraft was flown on March 27, 1994. Deliveries began from 2003. Austria confirmed order in 2003; Saudi Arabia selected Typhoon in 2005.

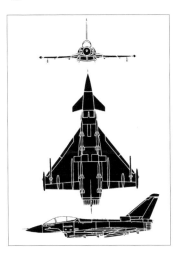

SPECIFICATION:

ACCOMMODATION: single-seater, pilot; trainer, student and instructor
MAX SPEED: M2.0
RADIUS OF ACTION: ground attack 750 nm (1389 km)

ARMAMENT:
INTERNAL GUNS: one 27 mm Mauser cannon
HARDPOINTS: nine
MAX WEAPON LOAD: 23,000 kg (50,706 lb)
REPRESENTATIVE WEAPONS: AIM-120, AIM-9, ASRAAM, IRIS-T AAMs; various bombs, LGBs, and PGMs; Storm Shadow AGM (UK); Brimstone ATGW (UK); designator and recce pods plus external fuel tanks

DIMENSIONS:
LENGTH: 15.9 m (52 ft 4 in)
WINGSPAN: 10.9 m (35 ft 11 in)
HEIGHT: 5.3 m (17 ft 4 in)

VARIANTS & OPERATORS:
Austria: 18 aircraft
Germany: 147 single-seaters, 33 two-seaters
Italy: 106 single-seaters, 15 two-seaters
Saudi Arabia: 72 aircraft
Spain: 72 C.16 single-seaters, 15 CE.16 two-seaters
UK: 195 F.2 single-seaters, 37 T.1 two-seaters

FEATURES:
Tall fin; canard; cranked-delta wings; twin Eurojet EJ200 turbojets; underfuselage inlets
Not to be confused with Rafale and Gripen

Fairchild Republic (Lockheed Martin) A-10A USA

Close-support aircraft

Prototype YA-10A flew on May 10, 1972, and 713 production A-10As were built for the USAF between 1975 and 1983, plus one two-seater. Many converted to forward-observation role as 0A-10A. Lockheed Martin to conduct SLEP for service to 2028; many being upgraded to C-model configuration.

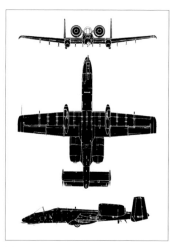

SPECIFICATION:

ACCOMMODATION: pilot
MAX SPEED: 390 kt (722 km/h)
RADIUS OF ACTION: 540 nm (1000 km)

ARMAMENT:
INTERNAL GUNS: one 30 mm GAU-8/A cannon
HARDPOINTS: 11
MAX WEAPON LOAD: 9450 kg (21,000 lb)
REPRESENTATIVE WEAPONS: AIM-9 AAMs;
Mk.80-series bombs; BLU-27/B Rockeye cluster
bombs; Paveway II LGBs; AGM-65 Maverick
AGMs; designator and EW/ECM pods; external
fuel tanks

DIMENSIONS:
LENGTH: 16.3 m (53 ft 4 in)
WINGSPAN: 17.5 m (57 ft 6 in)
HEIGHT: 4.5 m (14 ft 8 in)

VARIANTS & OPERATORS:
A/OA-10A: USAF (362 remain in service)

FEATURES:
Twin fins; low plank wings; twin GE TF34 turbofans
on rear-fuselage pods

FMA (LMAA) IA 58 Pucara ARGENTINA

Close-support and recce aircraft

Designed by Argentina's Military Aircraft Factory (FMA)—privatized and renamed Lockheed Martin Aircraft Argentina (LMAA) since 1995. Deliveries of 105 Pucaras to the Argentine Air Force in 1976–86. Developed to IA 58B/C and IA 66, but these only reached prototype stage.

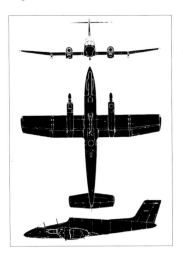

SPECIFICATION:

ACCOMMODATION: IA 58A, pilot and navigator/WSO; IA 58C, pilot
MAX SPEED: 405 kt (750 km/h)
RADIUS OF ACTION: 350 nm (650 km)

ARMAMENT:
INTERNAL GUNS: two 20 mm Hispano cannon and four 7.62 mm machine guns
HARDPOINTS: three
MAX WEAPON LOAD: 2000 kg (4410 lb)
REPRESENTATIVE WEAPONS: 125 kg or 500 kg bombs; 2.75 in FFAR pods; gun or EW/ECM pods, or external fuel tanks

DIMENSIONS:
LENGTH: 14.3 m (46 ft 9in)
WINGSPAN: 14.5 m (47 ft 6 in)
HEIGHT: 5.4 m (17 ft 1 in)

VARIANTS & OPERATORS:
IA 58A: Argentina (35 in service) and Uruguay (5)

FEATURES:
T-tail; low plank wings; twin Turbomeca Astazou XVIG turboprops on wings

General Dynamics (Lockheed Martin) F-111 USA

Bomber and recce aircraft

Prototype F-111A V-G strike fighter for the USAF flew on December 21, 1964; 538 F-111s were built for USAF and 24 for RAAF, with last deliveries in 1976. USAF EF-111A were withdrawn in 1996. The RAAF bought four F-111As in 1982 and 25 ex-USAF F-111Gs in 1993–98, 10 of which were for spares. RAAF F-111s being upgraded for service to 2020.

F-111C

F-111G

SPECIFICATION:

ACCOMMODATION: All versions, pilot and navigator/WSO in a jettisonable escape capsule
MAX SPEED: M2.2
RANGE: 2750+ nm (5093 km)

ARMAMENT:
INTERNAL GUNS: one 20 mm M61 cannon (optional)
HARDPOINTS: eight
MAX WEAPON LOAD: about 14,228 kg (31,500 lb)
REPRESENTATIVE WEAPONS: AIM-9 AAM;
Mk.80-series bombs; Paveway II LGB; AGM-84 Harpoon; EW/ECM or desigator pods; plus external fuel tanks

DIMENSIONS:
LENGTH: 22.4 m (73 ft 6 in)
WINGSPAN: spread 21.3 m (70 ft 0 in); fully swept 10.3 m (33 ft 11 in)
HEIGHT: 5.2 m (17 ft 1 in)

VARIANTS & OPERATORS:
F-111A(C): RAAF (4)
F-111C: RAAF (13)
F-111G: RAAF (14)
RF-111C: RAAF (4)

FEATURES:
Shoulder-mounted V-G wings; twin P&W TF30-P-3 turbofans; side-by-side cockpit; wide sleek nose
Not to be confused with Su-24

Grumman (Northrop Grumman) EA-6B Prowler USA

Electronic-combat aircraft

Derived from the A-6 Intruder, prototype EA-6B Prowler flown on May 25, 1968, and entered USN service in 1971. Its ALQ-99 tactical jamming system progressively upgraded to ICAP III level. In all, 170 Prowlers were built. Now flown by mixed USN/USAF crews.

SPECIFICATION:

ACCOMMODATION: two pilots and two EWOs
MAX SPEED: 530 kt (982 km/h)
RADIUS OF ACTION: 878 nm (1627 km)

ARMAMENT:

INTERNAL GUNS: none
HARDPOINTS: one centerline, four under each wing
MAX WEAPON LOAD: about 4547 kg (10,025 lb)
REPRESENTATIVE WEAPONS: AGM-88 HARM plus external fuel tanks

DIMENSIONS:

LENGTH: 18.2 m (59 ft 10 in)
WINGSPAN: 16.1 m (53 ft 0 in)
HEIGHT: 4.9 m (16 ft 3 in)

VARIANTS & OPERATORS:

EA-6B: USN (91 in service)

FEATURES:

Bulbous fin fairing; swept mid-mounted wings; twin P&W J52 turbojets; lower fuselage intakes; double side-by-side cockpits

Israel Aerospace Industries Kfir (Lion Cub) ISRAEL

Fighter/attack aircraft

Derived from the Nesher (Mirage 5J). Powered by a US J79 turbojet in place of the Atar 9K-50, with an auxiliary air intake forward of the fin root, canard foreplanes, and lengthened nose. Prototype Kfir flown in 1973 and revealed in April 1975. A total of 27 Kfir C1s and 185 C2/TC2s were built, many upgraded to C7/TC7 configuration.

SPECIFICATION:

ACCOMMODATION: Kfir C2/C7, pilot; Kfir TC2/TC7, student and instructor
MAX SPEED: 750 kt (1389 km/h)
RADIUS OF ACTION: 640 nm (1186 km)

ARMAMENT:
INTERNAL GUNS: two 30 mm DEFA cannon
HARDPOINTS: seven
MAX WEAPON LOAD: about 6085 kg (13,415 lb)
REPRESENTATIVE WEAPONS: AIM-9 or Python-3/-4 AAMs; Mk.80-series bombs; AGM-45 Shrike; AGM-65 Maverick; GBU-15 PGM; FFAR pods; EW/ECM or designator pods; plus external fuel tanks

DIMENSIONS:
LENGTH: 15.7 m (51 ft 4 in)
WINGSPAN: 8.2 m (26 ft 11 in)
HEIGHT: 4.5 m (14 ft 11 in)

VARIANTS & OPERATORS:
Kfir C2: single-seater, Ecuador and Sri Lanka
Kfir TC2: two-seat operational trainer, Ecuador and Sri Lanka
Kfir C7: single-seater, Colombia and Sri Lanka
Kfir TC7: two-seat operational trainer, Colombia

FEATURES:
Low delta wing; intake-mounted canards; single GE J79-J1E turbojet, with fin-root intake

KFIR C2

KFIR TC2

Lockheed Martin AC-130H/U USA

Special-operations gunship

The Hercules gunship concept goes back to the AC-47 of the Vietnam War era. The first C-130H Spectre, fitted with various sensors and a heavy armament, flew in September 1989. The improved AC-130U Spooky, modified by Rockwell North American (now Boeing), flew in December 1990.

SPECIFICATION:

ACCOMMODATION: three flight crew plus mission crew of 10 (AC-130U) or 11 (AC-130H)
MAX SPEED: 325 kt (602 km/h)
RANGE: 2046 nm (3791 km)

ARMAMENT (AC-130U):
INTERNAL GUNS: one 25 mm GAU-12/U cannon; one 40 mm M2A1 Bofors gun; one 105 mm M137A1 howitzer, on w of fuselage
HARDPOINTS: four
REPRESENTATIVE WEAPONS: use of AGM-114 Hellfire AGM studied; external fuel tanks under wing

DIMENSIONS:
LENGTH: 29.8 m (97 ft 9 in)
WINGSPAN: 40.4 m (132 ft 7 in)
HEIGHT: 11.7 m (38 ft 3 in)

VARIANTS & OPERATORS:
AC-130H Spectre: USAF (8)
AC-130U Spooky: USAF (13 + 10 more conversions in hand)

FEATURES:
High/straight wings; four Allison (Rolls-Royce) T56 turboprops

Lockheed Martin F-16 Fighting Falcon USA

Multirole fighter

Prototype YF-16A flew on February 2, 1974, and F-16A/B entered USAF from 1979. Progressively developed with Block improvements to current model F-16C/D Block 50/52. The B and D models are two-seat trainers. Over 4,450 ordered and 4144 delivered, the F-16 has sold to 23 nations, plus USAF and USN.

SPECIFICATION:

ACCOMMODATION: F-16A/C/N, pilot; F-16B/D, student and instructor
MAX SPEED: M2.0+
RADIUS OF ACTION: 500+ nm (925+ km)

ARMAMENT:

INTERNAL GUNS: one 20 mm M61 cannon
HARDPOINTS: nine (plus wingtips)
MAX EXTERNAL LOAD: about 7226+ kg (15,930 lb)
REPRESENTATIVE WEAPONS: AIM-9, AIM-120 AAMs; Mk.80-series and cluster bombs; Paveway-series LGBs; AGM-65F Maverick; Penguin ASM; ECM pods; designator pods and external fuel tanks

DIMENSIONS:

LENGTH: 15.0 m (49 ft 4 in)
WINGSPAN: 10.0 m (32 ft 9 in)
HEIGHT: 5.1 m (16 ft 8 in)

VARIANTS: & OPERATORS

F-16A/B: USAF, Belgium, Denmark, Egypt, Indonesia, Israel, Italy*, Jordan*, Netherlands, Norway, Pakistan, Portugal, Singapore, Taiwan, Thailand, Venezuela
F-16C/D: USAF, Bahrain, Chile, Egypt, Greece, Israel, Korea (South), Oman, Poland, Singapore, Turkey
F-16E/F: UAE
F-16I: Israel
* receiving used F-16s

FEATURES:

Swept fin; mid-swept wings; one P&W F100 or GE F110 turbofan; chin intake
Not to be confused with Mitsubishi F-1, T-50/A-50 Golden Eagle or F-CK-1 Ching-Kuo

Lockheed Martin F/A-22 Raptor USA

Air superiority fighter

Prototype YF-22 flew September 29, 1990 (with GE YF120 engines), in competiton with Northrop YF-23 for ATF program. USAF selected YF-22 with P&W YF119 engines on April 23, 1991. Nine EMD F-22As in test, first LRIP batch (ten aircraft) in 2001, against the USAF's reduced requirement of 276. IOC in December 2005. As of FY06 budget, 123 Raptors funded.

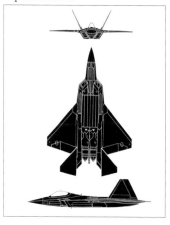

SPECIFICATION:

ACCOMMODATION: pilot
MAX SPEED SUPERCRUISE: M1.58; with reheat, M1.7+ at 30,000 ft
RADIUS OF ACTION: n/a

ARMAMENT:
INTERNAL GUNS: one 20 mm M61A2 cannon
HARDPOINTS: four underwing + three internal bays
MAX WEAPON LOAD: external, 2268 kg (5000 lb); internal, n/a
REPRESENTATIVE WEAPONS: AIM-9, AIM-120 AAMs; SDB and JDAM-series bombs; WCMDs; AGM-88 HARM; Paveway III LGB; external fuel tanks

DIMENSIONS:
LENGTH: 18.9 m (62 ft 1 in)
WINGSPAN: 13.6 m (44 ft 6 in)
HEIGHT: 5.1 m (16 ft 8 in)

VARIANTS & OPERATORS
F/A-22A: USAF

FEATURES:
Twin fins; shoulder/swept wings; two P&W F119 turbofans; intake under LERX

Lockheed Martin F-35 Lightning II JSF USA

Fighter and attack aircraft

Prototype X-35 flew on October 24, 2000 (with JSF119-PW-611 engine—now F135), USN/USMC/USAF/RN/RAF program. Flown in three versions: X-35A (CTOL), X-35B (STOVL) and X-35C (CV). X-35 with P&W F135 engines selected on October 26, 2001. LRIP expected in 2007 for 459 aircraft in six batches. Overall requirement is 2593. Named Lightning II in 2006 with first flight of F-35 SDD aircraft (AA-1) on December 15, 2006.

SPECIFICATION:

ACCOMMODATION: pilot
MAX SPEED: M1.6
RADIUS OF ACTION: F-35A, 600+ nm (1111 km); F-35B, 450+ nm (833 km); F-35C, 700+ nm (1296 km)

ARMAMENT:
INTERNAL GUNS: one 25 mm GAU-12 cannon (USAF F-35A)
HARDPOINTS: four/six underwing plus two internal bays
MAX WEAPON LOAD: about 9072+ kg (20,000+ lb)
REPRESENTATIVE WEAPONS: ASRAAM, AIM-9, AIM-120C AAMs; AGM-154 JSOW, JDAM-series bombs; Paveway-series LGBs; external fuel tanks

DIMENSIONS (F-35A/B):
LENGTH: 15.6 m (51 ft 1 in)
WINGSPAN: 10.7 m (35 ft 0 in)
HEIGHT: 4.6 m (15 ft 0 in)

DIMENSIONS (F-35C):
LENGTH: 15.7 m (51 ft 5 in)
WINGSPAN: 13.1 m (43 ft 0 in)
HEIGHT: 4.7 m (15 ft 6 in)

VARIANTS: & OPERATORS
USAF: 1763 F-35As required
USN/USMC: 680 F-35B/Cs required
Royal Navy: 60 F-35Bs required
RAF: 90 F-35Bs required
Orders possible from Australia (100), Canada, Denmark, Israel, Italy, the Netherlands, Norway, Singapore, and Turkey

FEATURES:
Twin fins; shoulder swept/tapered wings; "shark"-bevelled nose; one P&W F135 turbofan; side intakes

Lockheed Martin F-117A Nighthawk USA

Stealth attack fighter

Prototype Have Blue demonstrator flew in December 1977, with pre-series F-117A flying on June 18, 1981. Entered USAF service on August 23, 1982, and was publicly revealed on November 10, 1988. Of a planned 100 aircraft, 59 were built and periodically upgraded.

SPECIFICATION:

ACCOMMODATION: pilot
MAX SPEED: M1.0+
RADIUS OF ACTION: n/a

ARMAMENT:

INTERNAL GUNS: none
HARDPOINTS: weapons bays but no external hardpoints
REPRESENTATIVE WEAPONS: Mk.84 bomb; BLU-109B, GBU-10, GBU-27 LGBs; AGM-65 Maverick; AGM-88 HARM

DIMENSIONS:

LENGTH: 20.1 m (65 ft 11 in)
WINGSPAN: 13.2 m (43 ft 4 in)
HEIGHT: 3.8 m (12 ft 5 in)

VARIANTS & OPERATORS:

F-117A: USAF

FEATURES:

Swept butterfly fins; low/swept wings blended to angular fuselage; two GE F404 turbofans

McDonnell Douglas (Boeing)/BAE Systems AV-8B Harrier GR.7/9 USA

STOVL attack fighter

First YAV-8B demonstrator flown November 9, 1978, with first FSD AV-8B flying November 5, 1981. Entered USMC service September 1982; some upgraded to Night Attack and Harrier II Plus. First RAF Harrier GR.5 flown April 30, 1985, and entered RAF service on July 1, 1987. Three upgrades followed to GR.5A/7/9s. A total of 391 AV-8B/Harrier GR.5/7/9s and 37 TAV-8B/Harrier T.10/12 trainers built by October 1995.

Harrier GR.7/9

Harrier T.10/12

SPECIFICATION:

ACCOMMODATION: AV-8B/Harrier GR.7/9, pilot; TAV-8B/Harrier T.10/12, student and instructor
MAX SPEED: 575 kt (1065 km/h)
RADIUS OF ACTION: 594 nm (1101 km)

ARMAMENT:
INTERNAL GUNS: one 25 mm GAU-12/U cannon (USMC), two 25 mm Aden cannon (now abandoned by RAF)
HARDPOINTS: seven (nine on RAF and Harrier II Plus)
REPRESENTATIVE WEAPONS: AIM-9; Mk.80-series bombs; AGM-65 Maverick; Paveway LGBs; FFAR pods; Brimstone AAAW; external fuel tanks

DIMENSIONS:
LENGTH: AV-8B, 14.1 m (46 ft 4 in); Harrier GR.5/7/9, 14.4 m (47 ft 1 in)
WINGSPAN: 9.2 m (30 ft 4 in)
HEIGHT: 3.5 m (11 ft 7 in)

VARIANTS & OPERATORS:
AV-8B: USMC, Italy, Spain
Harrier GR.7/9: RAF
TAV-8B: USMC, Italy, Spain
Harrier T.10/12: RAF

FEATURES:
Shoulder/swept wings; LERX; one Rolls-Royce Pegasus 11-61 vectored-thrust turbofan

McDonnell Douglas (Douglas) A-4 Skyhawk USA

Attack bomber

XA4D-1 Skyhawk prototype flown on June 22, 1954, with production reaching 2960 (mostly for the USN/ USMC). Sold to nine nations and many upgraded, including Singapore's Skyhawks, re-engined with GE F404 turbofans. Deliveries completed in 1979.

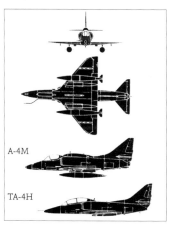

A-4M

TA-4H

SPECIFICATION:

ACCOMMODATION: A-4AR/E/H/MB/N/SU, pilot; TA-4AR/H/J/SU, student and instructor
MAX SPEED: 561 kt (1040 km/h)
RADIUS OF ACTION: 800 nm (1480 km)

ARMAMENT:
INTERNAL GUNS: two 20 mm Mk.12 cannon
HARDPOINTS: five
MAX WEAPON LOAD: 4528 kg (10,000 lb)
REPRESENTATIVE WEAPONS: AIM-9 AAMs; AGM-65 Maverick; Paveway LGBs; Mk.80-series bombs; FFAR pods; external fuel tanks and recce pods

DIMENSIONS:
LENGTH: 12.3 m (40 ft 4 in)
WINGSPAN: 8.4 m (27 ft 6 in)
HEIGHT: 4.6 m (15 ft 0 in)

VARIANTS & OPERATORS:
Argentina: A-4AR (converted OA/A-4Ms), TA-4AR
Brazil: A-4MB, TA-4MB (ex-Kuwait TA/A-4KUs)
Israel: A-4N, TA-4H/J
Singapore: A-4SU, TA-SU (converted A-4Bs)

FEATURES:
Low delta wing; delta tailplanes; one P&W J52-P-408 turbojet; fuselage intakes by cockpit

McDonnell Douglas (Boeing) F-4 Phantom II USA

Multirole fighter

XF4H-1 Phantom prototype flown on May 27, 1958, with production reaching 5195 of all versions (including Japanese-built examples). Still in service with seven nations and many upgraded. Deliveries completed in 1981.

SPECIFICATION:

ACCOMMODATION: pilot and WSO
MAX SPEED: M2.0+
RADIUS OF ACTION: 618 nm (1145 km)

ARMAMENT (F-4E/F):
INTERNAL GUNS: one 20 mm M61 cannon
HARDPOINTS: nine
MAX WEAPON LOAD: 7250 kg (16,000 lb)
REPRESENTATIVE WEAPONS: AIM-7, AIM-9, AIM-120 AAMs; AGM-65 Maverick; Paveway LGBs; Mk.80-series bombs; FFAR pods; ECM, recce, and designator pods; external fuel tanks

DIMENSIONS:
LENGTH: 19.2 m (63 ft 0 in)
WINGSPAN: 11.8 m (38 ft 7 in)
HEIGHT: 5.0 m (16 ft 5 in)

VARIANTS & OPERATORS:
RF-4C: South Korea
F-4D: Iran, South Korea
F-4E: Egypt, Greece, Iran, South Korea, Turkey
RF-4E: Greece, Iran, Turkey
RF-4EJkai: Japan
F-4F: Germany

FEATURES:
Anhedral tailplane; low/swept wing with dihedral outer panels; two P&W J79 turbojets; fuselage intakes by cockpit

Mikoyan-Guryevich (RAC-MiG) MiG-21 (J-7) "Fishbed"

RUSSIA

Fighter-bomber

Ye-6 prototype first flown in late 1957 and the MiG-21 entered Soviet service in 1958. Progressively developed and several thousand sold worldwide. India and Romania (among others) are having major upgrades. Also built in China as J-7 (exported as F-7), where it was further developed and is still in production.

SPECIFICATION:

ACCOMMODATION: MiG-21 fighter series, pilot; MiG-21U-series ("Mongol"), student and instructor
MAX SPEED: M2.2 (1159 kt, 2150 km/h)
RADIUS OF ACTION: 400 nm (740 km)

ARMAMENT (MIG-21MF FISHBED-J):
INTERNAL GUNS: one twin-barrel 23 mm GSh-23 cannon
HARDPOINTS: five
MAX WEAPON LOAD: about 1500 kg (3307 lb) plus centerline tank
REPRESENTATIVE WEAPONS: K-13 Atoll AAMs; FFAR pods; bombs; external fuel tanks

DIMENSIONS:
LENGTH: 15.8 m (51 ft 8 in)
WINGSPAN: 7.1 m (23 ft 5 in)
HEIGHT: 4.1 m (13 ft 5 in)

VARIANTS & OPERATORS:
MiG-21: Angola (21bis/UM), Azerbaijan (21), Bulgaria (21/bis/UM), Cambodia (21bis/UM), Croatia (21bis/UM), Cuba (21bis/UM), Egypt (21R/MF/UM), Ethiopia (21MF/UM), Guinea Republic (21PFM), India (21FL/M/MF/bis/I/U/UM/US), Libya (21bis/UM), Madagascar (21FL/U), Mali (21MF/UM), Mozambique (21bis), Namibia (21bis/UM), Nigeria (21MF/UM), North Korea (21bis/PF/PFM/U), Romania (21MF/UM), Serbia (21M/bis/UM), Syria (21bis/U), Turkmenistan (21), Uganda (21bis/UM), Ukraine (21UM), Vietnam (21bis/UM), Yemen (21bis/U), Zambia (21MF/UM)
J-7/F-7: Albania, Bangladesh, China, Egypt, Iran, Myanmar, Pakistan, Sudan, Sri Lanka, Tanzania, Zimbabwe

FEATURES:
Swept tailplane; delta wing; one Tumansky R-13 turbojet; nose intake

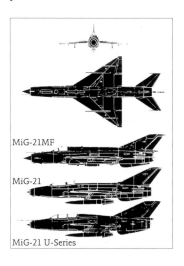

MiG-21MF

MiG-21

MiG-21 U-Series

Mikoyan-Guryevich (RAC-MiG) MiG-23/27 "Flogger"

RUSSIA

Air combat fighter (MiG-27 pictured)

Prototype first flown in June 1967. MiG-23 V-G interceptor entered Soviet service in 1973. Progressively developed; 4000+ sold worldwide. MiG-27 ground-attack version also developed.

MiG-27

SPECIFICATION:

ACCOMMODATION: MiG-23/27 fighter series, pilot; MiG-23UB, student and instructor
MAX SPEED: M2.35 (1350 kt, 2500 km/h)
RADIUS OF ACTION: 620 nm (1150 km)

ARMAMENT (MIG-23):
INTERNAL GUNS: one twin-barrel 23 mm GSh-23L
HARDPOINTS: six
MAX WEAPON LOAD: 3000 kg (6615 lb)
REPRESENTATIVE WEAPONS: R-23 Apex, R-60 Aphid AAMs; FFAR pods; external fuel tanks

DIMENSIONS:
LENGTH: 16.7 m (54 ft 10 in)
WINGSPAN: spread, 13.9 m (45 ft 10 in); swept, 7.8 m (25 ft 6 in)
HEIGHT: 4.8 m (15 ft 9 in)

VARIANTS & OPERATORS:
MiG-23: Algeria (23MS/UB), Angola (23B/ML/UB), Cuba (23MF/ML/UB), Ethiopia (23BN/UB), India (23BN/MF/UB), Kazakhstan (23/MLD/UB), Libya (23B/MS/UB), Namibia (23), North Korea (23ML/UB), Russia (23M/UB), Sri Lanka (23B), Sudan (23B), Syria (23BN/UB), Turkmenistan (23M/UB), Yemen (23ML/UB), Zimbabwe (23)
MiG-27: India (27M), Kazakhstan (27M), Sri Lanka (27M)

FEATURES:
Swept tailplane; shoulder-mounted V-G wing; one Soyuz/Khachaturov R-35 turbofan; rear ventral fin

Mikoyan-Guryevich (RAC-MiG) MiG-25 "Foxbat" RUSSIA

Interceptor fighter and recce aircraft

Developed as Ye-155P interceptor, first flown in 1964, the MiG-25BM high-altitude recce version entered Soviet service in 1971. Progressively developed as an interceptor (MiG-25P/PD/PDS), with more specialized recce versions (MiG-25R/RB) and two-seat conversion trainer (MiG-25PU/RU). Some 1186 MiG-25s of all versions built from 1970 to 1985.

MiG-25 "Foxbat-C"

MiG-25PU/UB

SPECIFICATION:

ACCOMMODATION: MiG-25BM/P/PD/R/RB, pilot; MiG-25PU/UB, student and instructor
MAX SPEED: M2.83
RADIUS OF ACTION: 933 nm (1730 km)

ARMAMENT (MIG-25 P/PD):
INTERNAL GUNS: none
HARDPOINTS: four
MAX WEAPON LOAD: 1800 kg (3968 lb)
REPRESENTATIVE WEAPONS: R-23 Apex, R-40R/R-40T Acrid, R-60T Aphid, R-73T Archer AAMs; external fuel tanks

DIMENSIONS:
LENGTH: 23.8 m (78 ft 1 in)
WINGSPAN: 14.0 m (45 ft 11 in)
HEIGHT: 6.1 m (20 ft 0 in)

VARIANTS & OPERATORS:
Algeria (25PD/PU/RB), Azerbaijan (25PD/PU/RB/RU), Kazakhstan (25PU/RB/RU), Russia (25BM/R/RU), Syria (25PD/PU/RB/RU), Turkmenistan (25/PU)

FEATURES:
Twin fins; shoulder/swept wing; two Soyuz/ Tumansky R-15B turbojets; angular swept intakes
Not to be confused with F-15 Eagle and MiG-31

Mikoyan-Guryevich (RAC-MiG) MiG-29 "Fulcrum"

RUSSIA

Air combat fighter

First flown on October 6, 1977, the MiG-29 entered Soviet service in 1983. Progressively developed as MiG-29S-series Fulcrum-C multi-mission fighter, MiG-29UB Fulcrum-B two-seat conversion trainer, and MiG-29K, carrier-borne version, plus other upgrade developments. Over 1100 MiG-29s of all versions built.

SPECIFICATION:

ACCOMMODATION: MiG-29/29S, pilot; MiG-29UB, student and instructor
MAX SPEED: M2.3 (1320 kt, 2445 km/h)
RADIUS OF ACTION: about 380 nm (704 km)

ARMAMENT:
INTERNAL GUNS: one 30 mm GSh-30-1 cannon
HARDPOINTS: seven
MAX WEAPON LOAD: about 4000 kg (8816 lb)
REPRESENTATIVE WEAPONS: R-27 Alamo, R-60T Aphid, R-73T Archer AAMs; bombs; FFAR pods; external fuel tanks

DIMENSIONS:
LENGTH: 17.3 m (56 ft 10 in)
WINGSPAN: 11.4 m (37 ft 3 in)
HEIGHT: 4.7 m (15 ft 6 in)

VARIANTS & OPERATORS:
Algeria (29S/UB), Bangladesh (29/UB), Belarus (29S/UB), Bulgaria (29/UB), Cuba (29/UB), Eritrea (29), Hungary (29/UB), India (29/UB/K), Iran (29/UB), Kazakhstan (29/UB), Libya (29), Malaysia (29/UB), Myanmar (29/UB), North Korea (29/UB), Peru (29S/UB), Poland (29/UB), Russia (29/S/UB/K), Serbia (29/UB), Slovak Republic (29/UB), Sudan (SE/UB), Syria (29/UB), Turkmenistan (29/UB), Ukraine (29/S/UB), Uzbekistan (29/UB), Yemen (29/UB)

FEATURES:
Twin fins; mid/swept wing; two Klimov/Sarkisov RD-33 turbofans; intakes under LERX
Not to be confused with F-15 and F-18

Mikoyan-Guryevich (RAC-MiG) MiG-31 "Foxhound"

RUSSIA

All-weather, all-altitude interceptor fighter

First flown as Ye-155MP interceptor on September 16, 1975, the two-seat MiG-31 entered Soviet service in 1982. Progressively evolved as interceptor with more missiles and improved radar (MiG-31M). Russia is now upgrading further.

SPECIFICATION:

ACCOMMODATION: pilot and WSO
MAX SPEED: M2.83
RADIUS OF ACTION: 647 nm (1200 km)

ARMAMENT:
INTERNAL GUNS: provision for one 23 mm GSh-6-23M six-barrel cannon
HARDPOINTS: ten
MAX WEAPON LOAD: about 2700 kg (5951 lb)
REPRESENTATIVE WEAPONS: R-33 Amos, R-37 (AA-X-13), R-40R/R-40T Acrid, R-60T Aphid, R-77 Adder AAMs; external fuel tanks

DIMENSIONS:
LENGTH: 22.3 m (74 ft 5 in)
WINGSPAN: 13.5 m (44 ft 2 in)
HEIGHT: 6.1 m (20 ft 2i n)

VARIANTS & OPERATORS:
Kazakhstan (34) and Russia (315)

FEATURES:
Twin fins; shoulder/swept wing; two Aviadvigatel D-30F6 turbojets; angular swept intakes
Not to be confused with F-15 and MiG-25

Mitsubishi F-1 JAPAN

Close-air-support fighter

Derived from the Mitsubishi T-2 trainer, the first F-1 flew on June 3, 1975, and entered JASDF service in 1976. The last of 177 aircraft delivered in 1987.

SPECIFICATION:

ACCOMMODATION: pilot
MAX SPEED: M1.6
RADIUS OF ACTION: N/A

ARMAMENT:
INTERNAL GUNS: one 20 mm JM61 cannon
HARDPOINTS: five
MAX WEAPON LOAD: 2721 kg (5997 lb)
REPRESENTATIVE WEAPONS: ASM-1 ASM; bombs, FFAR pods; external fuel tanks

DIMENSIONS:
LENGTH: 17.8 m (58 ft 6 in)
WINGSPAN: 7.9 m (25 ft 10 in)
HEIGHT: 4.5 m (14 ft 8 in)

VARIANTS & OPERATORS:
Japan

FEATURES:
Shoulder/swept wing; two Rolls-Royce/Turbomeca Adour 108 turbofans; rear ventral fins
Not to be confused with Jaguar and Mitsubishi T-2

Mitsubishi F-2 JAPAN

Close-air-support fighter

Based on F-16C and codeveloped with Lockheed Martin, the first F-2A flew on October 7, 1995. A combat-capable two-seater (F-2B) is planned. First deliveries to JASDF in September 2000. As of March 2005, 57 delivered of 75 on order.

SPECIFICATION:

ACCOMMODATION: F-2A, pilot; F-2B, student and instructor
MAX SPEED: M2.0
RADIUS OF ACTION: N/A

ARMAMENT:
INTERNAL GUNS: one 20 mm M61 cannon
HARDPOINTS: 13
MAX WEAPON LOAD: 6498 kg (14,320 lb)
REPRESENTATIVE WEAPONS: AAM-3, AIM-7, AIM-9 AAMs; ASM-1/-2 ASMs; bombs; FFAR pods; external fuel tanks

DIMENSIONS:
LENGTH: 15.5 m (58 ft 6 in)
WINGSPAN: 11.1 m (36 ft 6 in)
HEIGHT: 4.9 m (16 ft 3 in)

VARIANTS & OPERATORS:
Japan

FEATURES:
Mid/swept wing; GE F110 turbofan; chin intake
Not to be confused with F-CK-1, F-16, and T-50

NAMC Q-5/A-5 "Fantan" CHINA

Close-air-support fighter

The twin-jet attack Q-5, derived
from the J-6/MiG-19, first flew on
June 4, 1965, and entered service in
1970. Sold to four countries as the
A-5; improved Q-5 II (A-5M)
developed but not sold. About 1000
have been built.

SPECIFICATION:

ACCOMMODATION: pilot
MAX SPEED: M1.12 (643 kt, 1190 km/h)
RADIUS OF ACTION: 324 nm (600 km)

ARMAMENT:
INTERNAL GUNS: one 23 mm cannon
HARDPOINTS: 10
MAX WEAPON LOAD: 2000 kg (4410 lb)
REPRESENTATIVE WEAPONS: PL-2, PL-7, AIM-9,
Magic AAMs; bombs; FFAR pods; external fuel
tanks

DIMENSIONS:
LENGTH: 16.2 m (53 ft 4 in)
WINGSPAN: 9.7 m (31 ft 10 in)
HEIGHT: 4.5 m (14 ft 9 in)

VARIANTS & OPERATORS:
China (Q-5), Bangladesh (A-5), Myanmar (A-5),
North Korea (A-5, Q-5IA), Pakistan (A-5)

FEATURES:
Swept wing; two Shenyang WP6 turbojets; intakes
by cockpit; pointed nose

Northrop (N-G) B-2A Spirit USA

Long-range bomber

With a low-observable (stealth) configuration built as a flying wing, the first B-2A flew on July 17, 1989, and entered USAF service in 1996. Only 21 built, but these are having capability upgrades.

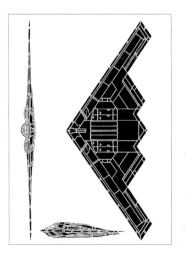

SPECIFICATION:

ACCOMMODATION: two pilots (plus third seat)
MAX SPEED: N/A
RANGE: internal fuel, 4500 nm (8334 km)

ARMAMENT:

INTERNAL GUNS: none
WEAPONS BAYS: two, each with eight-store rotary launcher, no external hardpoints
MAX WEAPON LOAD: 18,144 kg (40,000 lb)
REPRESENTATIVE WEAPONS: AGM-129 ACM; JDAM, JSOW, and JASSM weapons; nuclear and conventional bombs

DIMENSIONS:

LENGTH: 21.0 m (69 ft 0 in)
WINGSPAN: 52.4 m (172 ft 0 in)
HEIGHT: 5.2 m (17 ft 0 in)

VARIANTS & OPERATORS:
USAF

FEATURES:
No fin; flying wing with blended fuselage (tadpole-like); serrated trailing edge; four GE F118 turbofans

Northrop (N-G) F-5A/B Freedom Fighter USA

Lightweight fighter-bomber

The N-156C prototype first flew on July 30, 1959, and was widely exported from 1963. Two-seat F-5B flown February 24, 1964. Built under license in Canada and Spain. Many upgraded. Last of 1199 F-5A/B delivered in 1976.

SPECIFICATION:

ACCOMMODATION: F-5A, EF-5A, RF-5A, pilot; F-5B, F-5M, student and instructor
MAX SPEED: 710 kt (1315 km/h)
RANGE: internal fuel, 485 nm (898 km)

ARMAMENT:

INTERNAL GUNS: two 20 mm cannon
HARDPOINTS: five (plus wingtips)
MAX WEAPON LOAD: 2812 kg (6200 lb)
REPRESENTATIVE WEAPONS: AIM-9 AAMs; bombs; FFAR pods; external fuel tanks (sometimes on wingtips)

DIMENSIONS:

LENGTH: 14.4 m (47 ft 2 in)
WINGSPAN: 7.7 m (25 ft 3 in)
HEIGHT: 4.0 m (13 ft 2 in)

VARIANTS & OPERATORS:

Botswana (CF-5A/D), Morocco (F-5A/B, RF-5A), Norway (F-5B), Philippines (F-5A/B), South Korea (F-5A/B, EF-5A, RF-5A), Spain (F-5M), Thailand (F-5B), Turkey (NF/F-5A/B,RF-5A), Venezuela (VF-5A/D, NF-5B), Yemen (F-5B)

FEATURES:

Low tailplane; low/swept wing; two GE J85 turbojets

Northrop (N-G) F-5E/F Tiger II USA

Lightweight fighter-bomber (RF-5S pictured)

An improved version of the F-5A/B, the first F-5E flew on August 11, 1972, and was widely exported. Two-seat F-5F flown September 25, 1974. Built under license in Switzerland and Taiwan. Many upgraded. Last of 1418 F-5E/F delivered in 1989.

SPECIFICATION:

ACCOMMODATION: F-5E/S, RF-5E/S Tigereye, pilot; F-5F/T, student and instructor
MAX SPEED: 710 kt (1315 km/h)
RANGE: internal fuel, 570 nm (1056 km)

ARMAMENT:
INTERNAL GUNS: two 20 mm cannon (one on F-5F)
HARDPOINTS: five (plus wingtips)
MAX WEAPON LOAD: 3175 kg (7000 lb)
REPRESENTATIVE WEAPONS: AIM-9 AAMs; bombs; FFAR pods; external fuel tanks

DIMENSIONS:
LENGTH: 14.5 m (47 ft 5 in)
WINGSPAN: 8.1 m (26 ft 8 in)
HEIGHT: 4.1 m (13 ft 4 in)

VARIANTS & OPERATORS:
Austria (F-5E/F, leased), Bahrain (F-5E/F), Brazil (F-5E/F), Chile (F-5E/F), Honduras (F-5E/F), Indonesia (F-5E/F), Iran (F-5E/F), Jordan (F-4E/F), Kenya (F-5E/F), Malaysia (RF/F-5E/F), Mexico (F-5E/F), Morocco (F-5E/F), Saudi Arabia (RF/F-5E/F), Singapore (RF/F-5S/T), South Korea (F-5E/F), Switzerland (F-5E/F), Taiwan (RF/F-5E/F), Thailand (F-5E/F), Tunisia (F-5E/F), USA (F-5E/F), Yemen (F-5E)

FEATURES:
Low tailplane; low/swept wing; two GE J85 turbojets; some aircraft have dorsal-fin extension

F-5E

Panavia Tornado IDS/ECR GERMANY/ITALY/UK

Interdictor strike and recce aircraft

First prototype Tornado IDS (aka MRCA) flew on August 14, 1974, and deliveries began in 1980. Built in Germany, Italy, and UK and sold to Saudi Arabia. IDS designated GR.1 by RAF, now upgraded to GR.4. ECR (converted from IDS) developed by Germany and flown August 18, 1988. Last of 795 Tornado IDS/ECRs delivered in 1992. German and Italian Tornados also being upgraded.

SPECIFICATION:

ACCOMMODATION: pilot and navigator/WSO
MAX SPEED: M2.2
RANGE: internal fuel, 750 nm (1390 km)

ARMAMENT:
INTERNAL GUNS: two 27 mm BK27 cannon
HARDPOINTS: seven
MAX WEAPON LOAD: about 7530 kg (16,600 lb)
REPRESENTATIVE WEAPONS: AIM-9 AAM; AGM-65 Maverick; AGM-88 HARM; ALARM; Kormoran ASM; Storm Shadow AGM; bombs; rockets; CBLS; ECM, designator and recce pods; external fuel tanks

DIMENSIONS:
LENGTH: 16.7 m (54 ft 10 in)
WINGSPAN: spread, 13.9 m (45f t 7 in); swept, 8.6 m (28 ft 2 in)
HEIGHT: 5.9 m (19 ft 6 in)

VARIANTS & OPERATORS:
German Air Force/Navy (IDS/ECR), Italian Air Force (IDS/ECR), RAF (IDS), Saudi Arabia (IDS)

FEATURES:
Large fin; V-G wing; two Turbo-Union RB199 turbofans

Panavia Tornado F.3 ADV GERMANY/ITALY/UK

Air defence fighter

First prototype Tornado ADV flew on October 27, 1979. Tornado F.2 (18 only) now out of service; Tornado F.3 (with RB199 104 engines) deliveries began in 1986. Sold to Saudi Arabia (24), and 24 RAF F.3s leased by Italy (now returned). RAF aircraft being upgraded, including six to EF.3. Total of 197 ADVs built.

SPECIFICATION:

ACCOMMODATION: pilot and navigator/WSO
MAX SPEED: M2.2
RANGE: internal fuel, 1000+ nm (1853 km)

ARMAMENT:
INTERNAL GUNS: one 27 mm BK27 cannon
HARDPOINTS: eight
MAX WEAPON LOAD: 8500 kg (18,740 lb)
REPRESENTATIVE WEAPONS: AIM-9, AIM-120, ASRAAM, Skyflash AAMs; ALARM (EF.3); Ariel towed radar decoy; ECM pods; external fuel tanks

DIMENSIONS:
LENGTH: 18.7 m (61 ft 3 in)
WINGSPAN: spread, 13.9 m (45 ft 7 in); swept, 8.6 m (28 ft 2 in)
HEIGHT: 5.9 m (19 ft 6 in)

VARIANTS & OPERATORS:
RAF (EF/F.3), Saudi Arabia (F.53)

FEATURES:
Large fin; V-G wing; two Turbo-Union RB199 turbofans

Rockwell (Boeing) B-1B Lancer USA

Long-range bomber

Original B-1A first flew on December 23, 1974, and four prototypes flown. Resurrected in 1981, 100 improved B-1Bs were ordered, the first flying on October 18, 1984. Entered USAF service in May 1985. Deliveries completed in April 1988. Capability upgrades underway.

SPECIFICATION:

ACCOMMODATION: two pilots, two WSOs
MAX SPEED: M1.25
RANGE: unrefuelled, 6475 nm (12,000 km)

ARMAMENT:
INTERNAL GUNS: none
WEAPONS BAYS: three internal plus six external hardpoints
MAX WEAPON LOAD: internal, 34,019 kg (75,000 lb); external, 26,762 kg (59,000 lb)
REPRESENTATIVE WEAPONS: AGM-86 ALCM; AGM-69 SRAM; nuclear weapons; bombs; JDAM, JSOW, WCMD weapons; mines

DIMENSIONS:
LENGTH: 44.8 m (147 ft 0 in)
WINGSPAN: spread, 41.7 m (136 ft 8 in); swept, 23.8 m (78 ft 2 in)
HEIGHT: 10.4 m (34 ft 0 in)

VARIANTS & OPERATORS:
USAF

FEATURES:
V-G wing blended to fuselage; four GE F101 turbofans in underfuselage pods; small canards
Not to be confused with Tu-22M '"Backfire" and Tu-160 "Blackjack"

Rockwell (Boeing) OV-10 Bronco USA

Mulltipurpose COIN aircraft

YOV-10A prototype flown on July 16, 1965, and 271 Broncos entered USMC and USAF service, though they have now been withdrawn. Some export sales, some ex-U.S. transfers with 360 built.

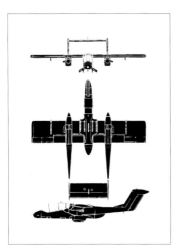

SPECIFICATION:

ACCOMMODATION: two pilots
MAX SPEED: 244 kt (452 km/h)
RADIUS OF ACTION: 198 nm (367 km)

ARMAMENT:
INTERNAL GUNS: four 7.62 mm M60C machine guns
HARDPOINTS: seven
MAX WEAPON LOAD: 1633 kg (3600 lb)
REPRESENTATIVE WEAPONS: AIM-9 AAM; Mk.80-series bombs; FFAR pods; gun pods; external fuel tank

DIMENSIONS:
LENGTH: 12.7 m (41 ft 7 in)
WINGSPAN: 12.2 m (40 ft 0 in)
HEIGHT: 4.6 m (15 ft 2 in)

VARIANTS & OPERATORS:
OV-10A: Colombia, Morocco, Philippines, Venezuela
OV-10C: Philippines
OV-10D: Colombia
OV-10E: Venezuela
OV-10F: Indonesia

FEATURES:
Twin-boom tail; podded fuselage; two Garrett T76 turboprops; fuselage stores sponsons

Saab JAS 39 Gripen SWEDEN

Interceptor, attack, and recce aircraft

First flown on December 9, 1988, the first multirole Gripen was delivered in 1993. Prototype JAS 39B flown April 29, 1996. Sweden has ordered 204. Sold to South Africa (new build), Czech Republic, and Hungary (leased Swedish aircraft).

SPECIFICATION:

ACCOMMODATION: JAS 39A/C/X, pilot; JAS 39B/D/XT, student and instructor
MAX SPEED: supersonic
RADIUS OF ACTION: 432 nm (800 km)

ARMAMENT:

INTERNAL GUNS: one 27 mm BK27 cannon
HARDPOINTS: six (plus wingtips)
MAX WEAPON LOAD: 4120 kg (9080 lb)
REPRESENTATIVE WEAPONS: AIM-9, AIM-120 AAMs; AGM-65 Maverick; RBS 15F; DWS 39; bombs; FFAR pods; ECM and recce pods; external fuel tanks

DIMENSIONS:

LENGTH: 14.1 m (46 ft 3 in)
WINGSPAN: 8.4 m (27 ft 7 in)
HEIGHT: 4.5 m (14 ft 9 in)

VARIANTS & OPERATORS:

Czech Republic, Hungary, South Africa (JAS 39X/XT), Sweden (JAS 39A/B/C/D)

FEATURES:

Canard foreplane; delta main wing; one Volvo RM12 (GE F404) turbofan
Not to be confused with Rafale and Typhoon

SEPECAT Jaguar FRANCE/UK

Close-air-support fighter

First prototype Jaguar (*E = Ecole*, or trainer) flown September 8, 1968. First production aircraft flew November 1971. France bought 200 and the UK 202. Sold to Ecuador, India (license-built by HAL, still in production), Nigeria, and Oman. RAF and Omani aircraft upgraded to GR.3A and T.4 configuration. Over 620 produced. OSD for RAF is 2007.

SPECIFICATION:

ACCOMMODATION: Jaguar A/ES/IM/IS/OS/S/SN, pilot; Jaguar B/BN/E/EB/IB/OB, student and instructor
MAX SPEED: M1.6 (917 kt, 1699 km/h)
RADIUS OF ACTION: 760 nm (1408 km)

ARMAMENT:

INTERNAL GUNS: two 30 mm Aden cannon
HARDPOINTS: five (plus overwing pylons)
MAX WEAPON LOAD: 4536 kg (10,000 lb)
REPRESENTATIVE WEAPONS: Magic, ASRAAM, AIM-9 AAMs; Sea Eagle ASM; AS.37 Martel ARM; bombs; FFAR pods; ECM and recce pods; external fuel tanks

DIMENSIONS:

LENGTH: 16.8 m (55 ft 2 in)
WINGSPAN: 8.7 m (28 ft 6 in)
HEIGHT: 4.9 m (16 ft 1 in)

VARIANTS & OPERATORS:

Ecuador (Jaguar EB/ES), India (Jaguar IB/IM/IS), Nigeria (Jaguar BN/SN), Oman (Jaguar OB/OS), RAF (Jaguar B [T.2/4] / S [GR.1/3/3A])

FEATURES:

Shoulder/swept wing; two Rolls-Royce/Turbomeca Adour 804/811 turbofans; square lateral intakes; Jaguars A/B/E have pointed nose, others a wedge nose; Jaguar IM has Agave radar nose
Not to be confused with Mitsubishi F-1 and T-2

Shenyang J-6/F-6 (MiG-19) "Farmer" CHINA

Interceptor fighter

The J-6 (exported as F-6 and FT-6 trainer) is the Chinese-built version of Russia's MiG-19, first flown in September 1953. The MiG-19 entered Soviet service in 1954, and Russian production of about 2500 ceased in 1959. The first Chinese J-6 (MiG-19S) flew in December 1961. Several thousand J-6 and variants built by Guizhou and Shenyang up to early 1980s.

SPECIFICATION:

ACCOMMODATION: J-6/F-6, pilot; FT-6, student and instructor
MAX SPEED: 738 kt (1452 km/h)
RADIUS OF ACTION: 370 nm (685 km)

ARMAMENT:

INTERNAL GUNS: two/three 30 mm NR-30 cannon
HARDPOINTS: up to eight
MAX WEAPON LOAD: about 500 kg (1123 lb) plus external fuel tanks
REPRESENTATIVE WEAPONS: AIM-9 AAM (Pakistan); FFAR pods; bombs

DIMENSIONS:

LENGTH: 14.6 m (48 ft 2 in)
WINGSPAN: 9.0 m (29 ft 8 in)
HEIGHT: 3.9 m (12 ft 8 in)

VARIANTS & OPERATORS:

J-6: China
F-6: Egypt, Iran, North Korea, Sudan, Tanzania, Zambia
FT-6: Bangladesh, Egypt, North Korea, Pakistan

FEATURES:

Fin-mounted tailplane; mid/swept wing; two Shenyang WP6 (R-9BF) turbojets; nose intake

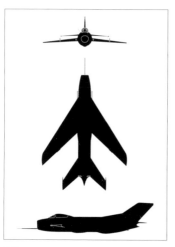

Shenyang J-8 "Finback" CHINA

Air superiority fighter

First prototype J-8 flown on July 5, 1969, but development delayed. J-8/J-8 I in production 1979–1987 (100+). J-8B first flew on June 12, 1984, and 24 reported in service by 1993. J-8B and C production continues and J-8 upgrade developing.

SPECIFICATION:

ACCOMMODATION: pilot
MAX SPEED: M2.2
RADIUS OF ACTION: 432 nm (800 km)

ARMAMENT:
INTERNAL GUNS: one 23 mm Type 23-3 twin-barrel cannon
HARDPOINTS: seven
MAX WEAPON LOAD: about 5400 kg (11,902 lb)
REPRESENTATIVE WEAPONS: PL-2B, PL-7, R-27 Alamo AAMs; bombs; rockets; ECM and recce pods; external fuel tanks

DIMENSIONS:
LENGTH: 21.6 m (70 ft 10 in)
WINGSPAN: 9.3 m (30 ft 8 in)
HEIGHT: 5.4 m (17 ft 9 in)

VARIANTS & OPERATORS:
China

FEATURES:
Tailed delta configuration; swept fin; ventral fin; two Liyang WP13A II turbojets; side slab intakes
Not to be confused with MiG-21 and J-7/F-7

SOKO J-22 Orao (Eagle) ROMANIA/YUGOSLAVIA

(BOSNIA AND HERZEGOVINA)

Ground-attack and reconnaissance aircraft

Joint Romanian/Yugoslav project initiated in 1970. Prototype flew on October 31, 1974 (one in each country), with two-seater flying on January 29, 1977, with 138 delivered. No longer in Romanian service. Yugoslav aircraft now in service with Bosnia and Herzegovina and Serbia.

SPECIFICATION:

ACCOMMODATION: see above
MAX SPEED: 586 kt (1086 km/h)
RADIUS OF ACTION: 248 nm (460 km)

ARMAMENT:
INTERNAL GUNS: two 23 mm twin-barrel cannon
HARDPOINTS: five
MAX WEAPON LOAD: 1500 kg (3307 lb)
REPRESENTATIVE WEAPONS: AAMs; 250 kg or 500 kg bombs; FFAR pods; external fuel tanks

DIMENSIONS:
LENGTH: 14.9 m (48 ft 11 in); trainer, 15.4 m (50 ft 6 in)
WINGSPAN: 9.3 m (30 ft 6 in)
HEIGHT: 4.5 m (14 ft 0 in)

VARIANTS & OPERATORS:
IJ-22/INJ-22 Orao 1: Tactical recce version, some two-seater conversion trainers
NJ-22 Orao: Two-seater tactical recce version, some with afterburning Vipers
J-22 Orao 2: Single-seater attack version, some with afterburning Vipers; first flown October 20, 1983

FEATURES:
Shoulder/swept wing; twin Rolls-Royce Viper turbojets; short pointed nose
Not to be confused with G-4 Super Galeb

Sukhoi Su-17/-20/-22 "Fitter-D/K" RUSSIA

Ground-attack and recce fighter

Evolved from the Su-7, the Su-17 featured V-G outer wings and the prototype flew on August 2, 1966. Ground-attack, recce, and trainer versions were developed. The Su-20 and -22 were used exclusively as export designations. Over 2900 Su-17/-20/-22 "Fitters" were produced.

SPECIFICATION:

ACCOMMODATION: all but Su-22U/UM, pilot; Su-22U/UM3, student and instructor
MAX SPEED: M2.09
RADIUS OF ACTION: about 550 nm (1017 km)

ARMAMENT:
INTERNAL GUNS: two 30 mm NR-30 cannon
HARDPOINTS: nine
MAX WEAPON LOAD: 4250 kg (9370 lb)
REPRESENTATIVE WEAPONS: Kh-23 Kerry, Kh-25 Karen, Kh-28 Kyle AGMs; bombs; rockets; external fuel tanks

DIMENSIONS:
LENGTH: 18.8 m (61 ft 6 in)
WINGSPAN: spread, 10.0 m (32 ft 10 in); swept, 8.8 m (28 ft 9 in)
HEIGHT: 5.0 m (16 ft 5 in)

VARIANTS & OPERATORS:
Angola (Su-22M4/ UM3), Azerbaijan (Su-17M), Libya (Su-20/-22M/U/UM3), Peru (Su-20/-22MU/UM3), Poland (Su-22M4/UM3), Syria (Su-22M/M4/UM3), Turkmenistan (Su-17M/UM3), Ukraine (Su-17M3/M4/UM3), Uzbekistan (Su-17M3/UM3), Vietnam (Su-22M3/M4/UM3), Yemen (Su-20/Su-22M/UM3)

FEATURES:
V-G wing; one Lyulka AL-21F-3 turbojet; nose intake

Sukhoi Su-24 "Fencer" RUSSIA

Bomber and recce/EW aircraft

An F-111 look-alike, the Su-24 prototype first flew in January 1970; by 1980, production was running at 70 per year. Also operates as "buddy" tanker. About 1000 Su-24s produced to date.

SPECIFICATION:

ACCOMMODATION: pilot and WSO
MAX SPEED: M2.18
RADIUS OF ACTION: about 565 nm (1050 km)

ARMAMENT:
INTERNAL GUNS: one 30 mm six-barrel cannon
HARDPOINTS: nine
MAX WEAPON LOAD: 8000 kg (17,635 lb)
REPRESENTATIVE WEAPONS: Kh-23 Kerry, Kh-25ML Karen, Kh-25MP Kegler, Kh-29ovod Kingbolt, Kh-29 Kedge, Kh-58 Kilter AGMs; bombs; rockets; AAR pod; external fuel tanks

DIMENSIONS:
LENGTH: 24.5 m (80 ft 5 in)
WINGSPAN: spread, 17.6 m (57 ft 10 in); swept, 10.4 m (34 ft 0 in)
HEIGHT: 5.0 m (16 ft 3 in)

VARIANTS & OPERATORS:
Algeria (Su-24MK/MR), Angola (Su-24), Azerbaijan (Su-24), Belarus (Su-24MK/MR), Iran (Su-24MK), Kazakhstan (Su-24/MR), Libya (Su-24MK), Russia (Su-24/MP/MR), Syria (Su-24MK), Ukraine (Su-24M/MP/MR), Uzbekistan (Su-24/MR)

FEATURES:
V-G wing; two Saturn/Lyulka AL-21F-3A turbojets; lateral intakes; ventral fins
Not to be confused with F-111

Sukhoi Su-25 "Frogfoot" RUSSIA

Close-air-support aircraft

Prototype Su-25 first flown on February 22, 1975. Initial production in Tbilisi, Georgia, ended by 1989, but about 50 built/partially built aircraft remain unsold and Su-25 Scorpion upgrade was developed. Russian production at Ulan-Ude finished 1992, and Su-39 upgrade developed. About 1000 Su-25s produced to date.

SPECIFICATION:

ACCOMMODATION: Su-25/T/TM/Su-39, pilot; Su-25UB/UBK/UTG, student and instructor
MAX SPEED: 526 kt (975 km/h)
RANGE: 675 nm (1250 km)

ARMAMENT:
INTERNAL GUNS: one 30 mm AO-17A two-barrel cannon
HARDPOINTS: 10
MAX WEAPON LOAD: 4400 kg (9700 lb)
REPRESENTATIVE WEAPONS: R-3S Atoll, R-60 Aphid AAMs; Kh-23 Kerry, Kh-25 Karen, Kh-29 Kedge AGMs; LGBs; bombs; rockets; 23 mm gun pod; external fuel tanks

DIMENSIONS:
LENGTH: 15.5 m (50 ft 11 in)
WINGSPAN: 14.4 m (47 ft 1 in)
HEIGHT: 4.8 m (15 ft 9 in)

VARIANTS & OPERATORS:
Angola (Su-25/UB), Armenia (Su-25), Azerbaijan (Su-25), Belarus (Su-25/UBK), Bulgaria (Su-25/UBK), Dem. Rep. of Congo (Su-25), Eritrea (Su-25K), Gambia (Su-25), Georgia (Su-25/UBK/T/TM/Su-39), Iran (Su-25), Kazakhstan (Su-25), North Korea (Su-25/UBK), Peru (Su-25), Russia (Su-25/UB/UTG/T/TM/Su-39), Turkmenistan (Su-25/UBK), Ukraine (Su-25/UBK/UTG), Uzbekistan (Su-25)

FEATURES:
Shoulder/slightly swept wing; ECM pod wingtips; two Soyuz/Gavrilov R-195 turbojets; lateral intakes and jetpipes

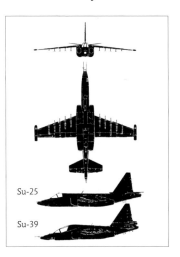

Su-25

Su-39

Sukhoi Su-27 "Flanker" RUSSIA

Air superiority fighter and ground-attack aircraft

Prototype Su-27 "Flanker-B" first flown on May 20, 1977, and developed as a long-range heavy fighter, as well as an operational trainer ("Flanker-C") Su-27UB. Further developments described in other entries. Exported and to be built under license in China as J-11.

SPECIFICATION:

ACCOMMODATION: Su-27, pilot; Su-27UB, student and instructor
MAX SPEED: M2.35 (1350 kt, 2500 km/h)
RADIUS OF ACTION: 810 nm (1500 km)

ARMAMENT:
INTERNAL GUNS: one 30 mm GSh-30-1 cannon
HARDPOINTS: eight (plus wingtips)
MAX WEAPON LOAD: 4000 kg (8818 lb)
REPRESENTATIVE WEAPONS: R-27 Alamo, R-33 Amos, R-60 Aphid, R-73 Archer AAMs; bombs; rockets; 23 mm gun pod; external fuel tanks

DIMENSIONS:
LENGTH: 21.9 m (71 ft 11 in)
WINGSPAN: 14.7 m (48 ft 3 in)
HEIGHT: 5.9 m (19 ft 5 in)

VARIANTS & OPERATORS:
Angola (Su-27), Belarus (Su-27/SK/UB), China (Su-27/SK/UB), Ethiopia (Su-27), Kazakhstan (Su-27/UB), Russia (Su-27/UB), Ukraine (Su-27/UB), Uzbekistan (Su-27/UB), Vietnam (Su-27/UB)

FEATURES:
Twin fins; shoulder/swept wing; two Saturn/Lyulka AL-31F turbofans; intakes under fuselage/wing; ventral fins; tailcone between jetpipes

Sukhoi Su-30/-33 "Flanker" RUSSIA

Air superiority fighter and ground-attack aircraft (Su-30MKI pictured)

Originally the Su-27PU, the tandem two-seater Su-30 first flew on December 31, 1989, as a long-range interceptor. Su-30M "Flanker-F" is multirole version. Su-30MKI "Flanker-H" features canards. Su-33 (Su-27K "Flanker-D") is carrier-borne version.

Su-30M

SPECIFICATION:

ACCOMMODATION: pilot and WSO
MAX SPEED: M2.35 (1350 kt, 2500 km/h)
RADIUS OF ACTION: 810 nm (1500 km)

ARMAMENT:

INTERNAL GUNS: one 30 mm GSh-30-1 cannon
HARDPOINTS: 10 (plus wingtips)
MAX WEAPON LOAD: 8000 kg (17,635 lb)
REPRESENTATIVE WEAPONS: R-27 Alamo, R-73 Archer, R-77 Adder AAMs; Kh-29 Kedge, Kh-31 Krypton, Kh-59 Kazoo AGMs; Raduga 3M80E ASM; bombs; rockets; external fuel tanks

DIMENSIONS:

LENGTH: 21.9 m (71 ft 11 in)
WINGSPAN: 14.7 m (48 ft 3 in)
HEIGHT: 5.9 m (19 ft 5 in)

VARIANTS & OPERATORS:

Algeria (Su-30MKA), China (Su-30MKK "Flanker-G"), India (Su-30MK/MKI/PU), Malaysia (Su-30MKM), Russia (Su-30/M/-33), Venezuela (Su-30MK?), Vietnam (Su-30MK?)

FEATURES:

Twin fins; shoulder/swept wing; retractable canards in LERX; two Saturn/Lyulka AL-31F turbofans; intakes under fuselage/wing; ventral fins; tailcone between jetpipes

Sukhoi Su-32/-33U/-34 "Fullback" RUSSIA

Long-range fighter/attack aircraft

Originally the Su-27IB with side-by-side seating, the Su-34 first flew on December 18, 1993. This configuration developed as Su-32 for export attack, carrier versions and Su-33UB (Su-27KUB) carrier-borne trainer version. Su-34 is Russian Air Forces version.

SPECIFICATION:

ACCOMMODATION: Su-32/-34, pilot and WSO; Su-33UB, student and instructor
MAX SPEED: M1.8 (1025 kt, 1900 km/h)
RADIUS OF ACTION: 601 nm (1113 km)

ARMAMENT:

INTERNAL GUNS: one 30 mm GSh-30-1 cannon
HARDPOINTS: 10 (plus wingtips)
MAX WEAPON LOAD: 8000 kg (17,635 lb)
REPRESENTATIVE WEAPONS: R-73 Archer, R-77 Adder AAMs; ASMs; LGBs; bombs; external fuel tanks

DIMENSIONS:

LENGTH: 23.3 m (76 ft 7 in)
WINGSPAN: 14.7 m (48 ft 3 in)
HEIGHT: 6.5 m (21 ft 4 in)

VARIANTS & OPERATORS:

Russia (Su-33UB/-34)

FEATURES:

Twin fins; shoulder/swept wing; canard foreplanes; two Saturn/Lyulka AL-31F turbofans; intakes under fuselage/wing; ventral fins; tailcone between jetpipes

Sukhoi Su-35/-37 "Flanker-E" RUSSIA

All-weather counter-air fighter (Su-35 pictured)

The Su-35, originally Su-27M, first flew on June 28, 1988. Planned for Russian service but not produced; marketed for export. The Su-37 was a technology demonstrator for vectored-thrust jetpipes, flown in April 1996.

Su-35

SPECIFICATION:

ACCOMMODATION: pilot
MAX SPEED: M2.35 (1350 kt, 2500 km/h)
RANGE: 2160+ nm (4000+ km)

ARMAMENT:
INTERNAL GUNS: one 30 mm GSh-30-1 cannon
HARDPOINTS: 12 (plus wingtips)
MAX WEAPON LOAD: 8200 kg (18,077 lb)
REPRESENTATIVE WEAPONS: R-27 Alamo, R-40 Acrid, R-60 Aphid, R-73 Archer, R-77 Adder AAMs; Kh-25ML Karen, Kh-25MP Kegler, Kh-29 Kedge, Kh-31 Krypton, Kh-59 Kazoo AGMs; LGBs; PGMs; bombs; rocket; ECM pods; external fuel tanks

DIMENSIONS:
LENGTH: 22.2 m (72 ft 9 in)
WINGSPAN: 15.2 m (49 ft 9 in)
HEIGHT: 6.4 m (20 ft 10 in)

VARIANTS & OPERATORS:
Su-35 (and Su-33UB trainer) in service in small numbers with Russia; Indonesia ordered two in 2003

FEATURES:
Twin fins; shoulder/swept wing; canard foreplanes; two Saturn/Lyulka AL-35F turbofans; intakes under fuselage/wing; ventral fins; tailcone between jetpipes

Tupolev Tu-22M "Backfire" RUSSIA

MRA bomber and EW aircraft

The V-G Tu-22M was first flown on August 30, 1969, and the production Tu-22M-2 entered Russian service in 1975, followed by improved M-3 version in 1983. Tu-22MP is an EW/escort jammer aircraft, and MR is for maritime recce. Production ceased in 1992 after 497 built.

SPECIFICATION:

ACCOMMODATION: two pilots, navigator, WSO
MAX SPEED: M1.88 (1080 kt, 2000 km/h)
RADIUS OF ACTION: 1300 nm (2410 km)

ARMAMENT:
INTERNAL GUNS: one 23 mm GSh-23M twin-barrel cannon
WEAPONS BAY: internal, plus two hardpoints
MAX WEAPON LOAD: 24,000 kg (52,910 lb)
REPRESENTATIVE WEAPONS: Kh-22 Kitchen ASM; Kh-15P Kickback SRAM; Kh-31 Krypton, Kh-35 Kayak AGMs; bombs; mines

DIMENSIONS:
LENGTH: 42.5 m (139 ft 4 in)
WINGSPAN: spread, 34.3 m (112 ft 6 in); swept, 23.3 m (76 ft 5 in)
HEIGHT: 11.0 m (36 ft 3 in)

VARIANTS & OPERATORS:
Russia (Tu-22M/MR), Ukraine (Tu-22M)

FEATURES:
Low V-G wing; two Samara/Kuznetsov NK-25 turbofans in fuselage; lateral intakes
Not to be confused with B-1 and Tu-160 "Blackjack"

Tupolev Tu-95/-142 "Bear" RUSSIA

Long-range bomber and MRA aircraft

The Tu-95 prototype first flew on November 12, 1952, and became operational in Russian service in 1956, with Tu-95MS6 ("Bear-H6") in service from 1984. First Tu-142 ASW version flown July 1968, with the Tu-142M ("Bear-F Mod 2") entering service in 1972. Final aircraft built in 1994.

SPECIFICATION:

ACCOMMODATION: two pilots, four WSOs, one gunner
MAX SPEED: 499 kt (925 km/h)
RADIUS OF ACTION: 3455 nm (6400 km)

ARMAMENT:
INTERNAL GUNS: one/two 23 mm cannon
HARDPOINTS: two plus internal weapon bay
MAX WEAPON LOAD: about 11,000 kg (24,244 lb)
REPRESENTATIVE WEAPONS: Kh-55 Kent, Kh-101 ALCMs; Kh-35 Kayak ASM; bombs; mines; sonobuoys

DIMENSIONS:
LENGTH: 49.1 m (161 ft 2 in)
WINGSPAN: 50.0 m (164 ft 2 in)
HEIGHT: 13.3 m (43 ft 8 in)

VARIANTS & OPERATORS:
India (Tu-142M), Russia (Tu-95/MR/MS/Tu-142)

FEATURES:
Tall fin; shoulder/swept wing; four Samara/ Kuznetsov NK-12MP turboprops; nose radome on Tu-95MS; underfuselage radome on Tu-142M

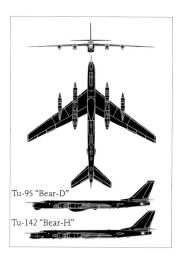

Tu-95 "Bear-D"

Tu-142 "Bear-H"

Tupolev Tu-160 "Blackjack" RUSSIA

Long-range bomber

First flown on December 18 or 19, 1981, and the production Tu-160s entered Soviet service in the Ukraine in May 1987 and in Russia in 1992. After the dissolution of the Soviet Union, eight Ukrainian aircraft eventually returned to Russia. About 32 of 100 planned aircraft built to 1992, when production ceased. Plans for further low-rate production progress slowly.

SPECIFICATION:

ACCOMMODATION: two pilots, two WSOs
MAX SPEED: M2.05 (1200 kt, 2220 km/h)
RADIUS OF ACTION: 1080nm (2000km)

ARMAMENT:
INTERNAL GUNS: none
WEAPONS BAYS: two internal
MAX WEAPON LOAD: 40,000 kg (88,185 lb)
REPRESENTATIVE WEAPONS: Kh-55 Kent, Kh-101 ALCMs; Kh-15P Kickback SRAM

DIMENSIONS:
LENGTH: 54.1 m (177 ft 6 in)
WINGSPAN: spread, 55.7 m (182 ft 9 in); swept, 35.6 m (116 ft 10 in)
HEIGHT: 13.1 m (43 ft 0 in)

VARIANTS & OPERATORS:
Russia

FEATURES:
V-G wing blended to fuselage; four Samara NK-321 turbofans under fuselage
Not to be confused with B-1 and Tu-22 M "Backfire"

Vought (N-G) A-7 Corsair II USA

Attack aircraft

Based on F-8 Crusader, the first A-7A flew on September 27, 1965. In USN service from 1966 and USAF service from 1968, all now withdrawn. A-7A/B/Cs powered by P&W TF30, A-7D/E/H/J by Allison (Rolls-Royce) TF41 (Spey). Last of 1541 delivered in 1982, with last remanufactured A-7P finished in 1985.

SPECIFICATION:

ACCOMMODATION: A-7E/H, pilot; TA-7C/H, student and instructor
MAX SPEED: 600 kt (1112 km/h)
RADIUS OF ACTION: about 700 nm (1296 km)

ARMAMENT:

INTERNAL GUNS: one 20 mm M61 cannon
HARDPOINTS: eight
MAX WEAPON LOAD: 6805 kg (15,000 lb)
REPRESENTATIVE WEAPONS: AIM-9 AAMs; LGBs; PMGs; Mk.80-series bombs; FFAR pods; external fuel tanks

DIMENSIONS:

LENGTH: 14.1 m (46 ft 1 in)
WINGSPAN: 11.8 m (38 ft 9 in)
HEIGHT: 4.9 m (16 ft 0 in)

VARIANTS & OPERATORS:

TA-7C: Greece, Thailand
A-7E: Greece, Thailand
A-7H: Greece
TA-7H: Greece

FEATURES:

Shoulder/swept wing; one Allison TF41 (Spey) turbofan; chin intake in nose

Xian H-6 (Tu-16) "Badger" CHINA/RUSSIA

Medium bomber/MRA aircraft (H-6 pictured)

The H-6 is the Tu-16, first flown (as Tu-88) on April 27, 1952, built under license in China. Used by both PLAAF and APN. Chinese production apparently ceased in the late 1980s, but may have resumed at a low rate.

SPECIFICATION:

ACCOMMODATION: two pilots, one navigator/bombardier, three gunners
MAX SPEED: 566 kt (1050 km/h)
RANGE: 3885nm (7200 km)

ARMAMENT:

INTERNAL GUNS: seven 23 mm AM-23 cannon
BOMB BAYS: one internal plus two hardpoints
MAX WEAPON LOAD: 9000 kg (19,800 lb)
REPRESENTATIVE WEAPONS: Kh-26 Kingfisher ASM; nuclear and conventional bombs

DIMENSIONS:

LENGTH: 34.8 m (114 ft 2 in)
WINGSPAN: 33.0 m (108 ft 3 in)
HEIGHT: 10.4 m (34 ft 0 in)

VARIANTS & OPERATORS:

China (H-6, H-6/DU/U)

FEATURES:

Mid/swept wing with trailing-edge fairings; two Mikulin RD-3M-500 turbojets; wingroot intakes; glazed nose

Tu-16

Military Training Aircraft

Aermacchi (Alenia Aerospace) M-311 ITALY

Basic jet trainer (M-311 pictured)

First flown on April 10, 1981, this tandem-seat jet trainer was aimed at crossing the top end of the turboprop trainer market and the lower end of the jet trainer market. Only two customers bought the S.211, with the last of 60 delivered in 1991. Production rights to Aermacchi 1997. In 2005, Aermacchi revealed the updated version, redesignated M-311, with digital avionics and an uprated JT15D-5C engine. Avionics demonstrator (converted S.211) flown June 1, 2005.

SPECIFICATION:

ACCOMMODATION: student and instructor
MAX SPEED: 400 kt (740 km/h)
RANGE: internal fuel, 740 nm (1370 km)

ARMAMENT:
INTERNAL GUNS: none
HARDPOINTS: five
MAX WEAPON LOAD: 1000 kg (2205 lb)
REPRESENTATIVE WEAPONS: bombs; FFAR pods; gun pods; external fuel tanks

DIMENSIONS:
LENGTH: 9.8 m (32 ft 4 in)
WINGSPAN: 8.5 m (27 ft 10 in)
HEIGHT: 3.7 m (12 ft 3 in)

VARIANTS & OPERATORS:
S.211A: Philippines, Singapore
M-311: no orders as of January 2007

FEATURES:
Mid/swept wing; lateral intakes; one P&WC JT-15D-5C turbofan; tandem canopy
Not to be confused with Alpha Jet, IA.63 Pampa, and Kawasaki T-4

S.211

Aermacchi (Alenia Aerospace) MB-326 ITALY

Advanced trainer/light attack aircraft

Prototype MB-326 first flown on December 10, 1957. License-built as AT-26 Xavante by EMBRAER of Brazil and as Impala I/II by Atlas (Denel) in South Africa. Total of 736 built.

SPECIFICATION:

ACCOMMODATION: MB-326/L, student and instructor; MB-326K, pilot
MAX SPEED: 496 kt (871 km/h)
RADIUS OF ACTION: 145 nm (268 km)

ARMAMENT (MB-326K SERIES):

INTERNAL GUNS: two 30 mm DEFA cannon
HARDPOINTS: six (plus wingtip tanks)
MAX WEAPON LOAD: 1814 kg (4000 lb)
REPRESENTATIVE WEAPONS: Magic AAMs; AS 11/12 AGMs; bombs; FFAR pods; gun and recce pods; external fuel tanks

DIMENSIONS:

LENGTH: 10.7 m (35 ft 0 in)
WINGSPAN: 10.8 m (35 ft 7 in)
HEIGHT: 3.7 m (12 ft 2 in)

VARIANTS & OPERATORS:

MB-326: Argentina, Brazil, Ghana, Paraguay, Togo, Tunisia, Zambia
MB-326K series: Ghana, Tunisia
MB-326L series: Tunisia

FEATURES:

Low/straight wing; one Rolls-Royce Viper 632 turbojet; wingtip tanks

Aermacchi (Alenia Aerospace) MB-339 ITALY

Advanced FLI trainer/light attack aircraft

Prototype MB-339 first flown on August 12, 1976. MB-339CD/FD series feature digital avionics. Order book (including deliveries) is 237.

SPECIFICATION:

ACCOMMODATION: student and instructor
MAX SPEED: 500 kt (926 km/h)
RADIUS OF ACTION: 255 nm (472 km)

ARMAMENT:
INTERNAL GUNS: none
HARDPOINTS: six (plus wingtip tanks)
MAX WEAPON LOAD: 1814 kg (4000 lb)
REPRESENTATIVE WEAPONS: Magic, AIM-9 AAMs;
AGM-65 Maverick; Marte ASM; bombs; FFAR pods;
gun and recce pods; external fuel tanks

DIMENSIONS:
LENGTH: 11.2 m (36 ft 10 in)
WINGSPAN: 11.2 m (36 ft 10 in)
HEIGHT: 3.9 m (12 ft 11 in)

VARIANTS & OPERATORS:
MB-339A series: Eritrea, Ghana, Italy, Malaysia,
Peru, UAE (Dubai)
MB-339C series: Eritrea, Italy, Malaysia
MB-339FD: Venezuela
MB-339PAN: Italy

FEATURES:
Low/straight wing; raised canopy; one Rolls-Royce
Viper 680 turbojet; wingtip tanks
Not to be confused with AT-3, C-101, HJT-36,
IAR-99, K-8, L-39/159 series, and MiG-AT

Aermacchi (Alenia Aerospace) M-346 ITALY

Advanced jet trainer

A comprehensively redesigned and Westernized version of the Russo-Italian Yak-130D development (which see) to meet requirements of the Eurotrainer group. The prototype Yak-130D first flew on April 25, 1996. Aermacchi announced M-346 version in July 2000. First of three Italian prototypes flew on July 15, 2004 with initial production predicted from 2007.

SPECIFICATION:

ACCOMMODATION: student and instructor
MAX SPEED: 585 kt (1083 km/h)
RANGE: internal fuel, 1020 nm (1889 km)

ARMAMENT:
INTERNAL GUNS: none
HARDPOINTS: nine (including wingtips)
MAX WEAPON LOAD: 3000 kg (6614 lb)
REPRESENTATIVE WEAPONS: AAMs; AGMs; FFAR pods; gun pods; external fuel tanks

DIMENSIONS:
LENGTH: 11.5 m (37 ft 9 in)
WINGSPAN: 9.7 m (31 ft 10 in)
HEIGHT: 4.9 m (16 ft 4 in)

VARIANTS & OPERATORS:
M-346: none (as of January 2007)

FEATURES:
Low/swept wing; tandem cockpit; two Honeywell F124-GA-200 turbofans; underwing root intakes/exhausts

Aermacchi (SIAI-Marchetti) SF.260 ITALY

Aerobatic and weapons trainer

Designed as a civil trainer and first flown July 15, 1964; first military version, SF.260M, flown on October 10, 1970. The SF.260TP, powered by an Allison (now R-R) 250-B17D turbo-prop engine, first flown in 1980. Over 650 of all types built. Italy to replace surviving 21 SF.260AM with 30 new-production SF.260EA aircraft.

SPECIFICATION:

ACCOMMODATION: student and instructor
MAX SPEED: 235 kt (436 km/h)
RANGE: 890 nm (1650 km)

ARMAMENT:
INTERNAL GUNS: none
HARDPOINTS: two or four
MAX WEAPON LOAD: 300 kg (661 lb)
REPRESENTATIVE WEAPONS: FFAR pods, gun pods, target-towing kit, external fuel tanks

DIMENSIONS:
LENGTH: 7.1 m (23 ft 3 in)
WINGSPAN: 8.3 m (27 ft 4 in)
HEIGHT: 2.4 m (7 ft 11 in)

VARIANTS & OPERATORS:
SF.260AM: Italy
SF.260C: Tunisia
SF.260D: Belgium, Turkey
SF.260E: Italy, Mauritania, Mexico, Uruguay, Venezuela
SF.260F: Zimbabwe
SF.260M: Belgium, Indonesia, Zambia, Zimbabwe
SF.260TP: Ethiopia, Philippines, Zambia, Zimbabwe
SF.260W: Chad, Indonesia, Libya, Tunisia, Uganda, Zimbabwe

FEATURES:
Swept fin; low/straight wing with dihedral; wingtip tanks; side-by-side cockpit; one Textron Lycoming O-540-E4A5 piston engine

Aero Vodochody L-29 Delphin CZECH REPUBLIC

Basic/advanced jet trainer

Prototype XL-29 first flown on April 5, 1959, with first production aircraft flying in April 1963. Large orders from Soviet Union and Warsaw Pact, plus others. Total of 3665 built, with production ending in 1974.

SPECIFICATION:

ACCOMMODATION: student and instructor
MAX SPEED: 42 kt (820 km/h)
RANGE: 480 nm (894 km)

ARMAMENT:

INTERNAL GUNS: none
HARDPOINTS: two (plus wingtip tanks)
MAX WEAPON LOAD: 260 kg (573 lb)
REPRESENTATIVE WEAPONS: bombs; FFAR pods; external fuel tanks

DIMENSIONS:

LENGTH: 10.8 m (35 ft 5 in)
WINGSPAN: 10.3 m (33 ft 9 in)
HEIGHT: 3.1 m (10 ft 3 in)

VARIANTS & OPERATORS:

L-29: Azerbaijan, Georgia, Ghana, Mali, Romania, Syria

FEATURES:

T-tail; mid/straight wing; one M 701c turbojet; wingtip tanks

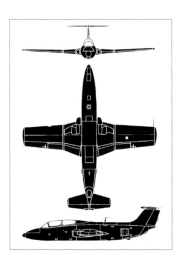

Aero Vodochody L-39/-139/-59/-159 CZECH REPUBLIC

Advanced jet trainer and light attack aircraft

L-39 first flown on November 4, 1968, and selected to replace L-29 in the Soviet Union. L-39Z series are armed. L-139 has Honeywell TFE731 engine. L-39MS/L-59 has improved Czech engine. A total 2938 of all versions built. Work on L-159 ALCA (Advanced Light Combat Aircraft) began in 1992. Two-seater L-159B flown August 2, 1997; first production L-159A flown October 20, 1999.

SPECIFICATION:

ACCOMMODATION: L-39/-59/-159B, student and instructor; L-159A, pilot
MAX SPEED: L-39/-139/-59, 340 kt (630 km/h); L-159, 505 kt (936 km/h)
RADIUS OF ACTION: L-39/-139/-59, 401 nm (743 km); L-159, 380 nm (705 km)

ARMAMENT (L-159A):
INTERNAL GUNS: none
HARDPOINTS: seven (plus wingtip tanks)
MAX WEAPON LOAD: 2340 kg (5159 lb)
REPRESENTATIVE WEAPONS: AAMs; AGMs; PGMs, bombs or FFAR pods; external fuel tanks; gun, ECM, or designator pods

DIMENSIONS (L-39/-139/-59):
LENGTH: 12.1 m (39 ft 9 in)
WINGSPAN: 9.5 m (31 ft 3 in)
HEIGHT: 4.8 m (15 ft 8 in)

DIMENSIONS (L-159):
LENGTH: 12.7 m (41 ft 9 in)
WINGSPAN: 9.5 m (31 ft 3 in)
HEIGHT: 4.8 m (15 ft 8 in)

VARIANTS & OPERATORS:
L-39: Azerbaijan, Russia, Turkmenistan
L-39C: Afghanistan, Algeria, Armenia, Cambodia, Cuba, Czech Republic, Ethiopia, Krygizia, Lithuania, North Korea, Russia, Slovak Republic, Ukraine, Vietnam, Yemen
L-39ZA: Algeria, Angola, Bangladesh, Bulgaria, Czech Republic, Lithuania, Nigeria, Romania, Slovak Republic, Syria, Uganda
L-39ZO: Ghana, Hungary, Libya, Syria
L-59: Egypt, Tunisia
L-159A/B ALCA: Czech Republic

FEATURES:
Low/straight wing; wingtip tanks; one turbofan engine (AI 25 TL in L-39; DV-2 in L-39MS/-59; Honeywell F124-GA-100 in L-159); intakes behind canopy; long pointed nose
Not to be confused with AT-3, C-101, HJT-36, IAR-99, K-8, MB-339, and MiG-AT

L-39

Avione IAR-99 Soim ROMANIA

Basic/advanced jet trainer/light attack aircraft

Prototype flown on December 21, 1985, with production of 20 from 1988. Elbit is working with Avione on an avionics/cockpit upgrade for a further 18.

SPECIFICATION:

ACCOMMODATION: IAR-99, student and instructor
MAX SPEED: 467 kt (865 km/h)
RANGE: 593 nm (1100 km)

ARMAMENT:
INTERNAL GUNS: removable ventral 23 mm GSh-23 cannon pod
HARDPOINTS: four
MAX WEAPON LOAD: 2000 kg (4408 lb)
REPRESENTATIVE WEAPONS: bombs; FFAR pods; gun pods; external fuel tanks

DIMENSIONS:
LENGTH: 11.0 m (36 ft 1 in)
WINGSPAN: 9.8 m (32 ft 4 in)
HEIGHT: 3.9 m (12 ft 9 in)

VARIANTS & OPERATORS:
IAR-99: Romania

FEATURES:
Low/straight wing; raised cockpit; one Rolls-Royce Viper 632 turbojet; wingroot intakes
Not to be confused with AT-3, C-101, HJT-36, K-8, L-39/159 series, MB-339, and MiG-AT

BAC (BAE Systems) 167 Strikemaster UK

Basic/advanced jet trainer/light attack aircraft

Derived from BAC 145 Jet Provost T.5 (now withdrawn), the first BAC 167 Strikemaster was flown on October 26, 1967. A total of 155 were built.

SPECIFICATION:

ACCOMMODATION: student and instructor
MAX SPEED: 467 kt (865 km/h)
RANGE: 593 nm (1100 km)

ARMAMENT:
INTERNAL GUNS: two 7.62 mm FN machine guns
HARDPOINTS: eight (plus wingtip tanks)
MAX WEAPON LOAD: 1360 kg (3000 lb)
REPRESENTATIVE WEAPONS: bombs; FFAR pods; recce pods; external fuel tanks

DIMENSIONS:
LENGTH: 11.0 m (36 ft 1 in)
WINGSPAN: 9.8 m (32 ft 4 in)
HEIGHT: 3.9 m (12 ft 9 in)

VARIANTS & OPERATORS:
Côte d'Ivoire, Ecuador (Mk.89), Sudan (Mk.90)

FEATURES:
Low/straight wing; side-by-side cockpit; one Rolls-Royce Viper 535 turbojet; lateral intakes
Not to be confused with A-37, T-37, and Kiran

BAE Systems (HSA) Hawk 50/60/100 UK

Advanced jet trainer (Hawk Mk.128 (T.2) pictured)

The prototype HS.1182 Hawk was first flown on August 21, 1974, and entered RAF service as the Hawk T.1 (Series 50) in 1976. Followed by 60 and 100 series, plus U.S. Navy T-45 Goshawk (which see). More than 900 have been ordered across all versions.

Hawk 100 series

SPECIFICATION:

ACCOMMODATION: student and instructor
MAX SPEED: 575 kt (1065 km/h)
RADIUS OF ACTION: 345 nm (638 km)

ARMAMENT:
INTERNAL GUNS: none
HARDPOINTS: five (plus wingtips)
MAX WEAPON LOAD: 3000 kg (6614 lb)
REPRESENTATIVE WEAPONS: centerline 30 mm gun pod; AIM-9 AAM; AGM-65 Maverick AGM; bombs; FFAR pods; CBLS; external fuel tanks

DIMENSIONS:
LENGTH: 10.8 m (35 ft 4 in)
WINGSPAN: 9.4 m (30 ft 9 in)
HEIGHT: 4.0 m (13 ft 1 in)

VARIANTS & OPERATORS:
Series 50: Finland, Indonesia, Kenya, UK
Series 60: Kuwait, Saudi Arabia, South Korea, UAE (Abu Dhabi/Dubai), Zimbabwe
Series 100: Australia, Bahrain, Canada, India, Indonesia, Malaysia, Oman, South Africa, Switzerland (no longer in service), UAE (Abu Dhabi), UK

FEATURES:
Low/swept wing; tandem cockpit; single Rolls-Royce/Turbomeca Adour turbofan
Not to be confused with T-45 and Super Galeb

BAE Systems (HSA)/Boeing (McDD) T-45 Goshawk

UK/USA

Intermediate/advanced jet trainer

The prototype of the carrier-capable T-45 Goshawk was first flown on April 16, 1988, with T-45A deliveries to USN from 1992 and T-45C (with glass cockpit) from 1997. A total of 187 are planned.

SPECIFICATION:

ACCOMMODATION: student and instructor
MAX SPEED: 575 kt (1065 km/h)
RADIUS OF ACTION: 345 nm (638 km)

ARMAMENT:
INTERNAL GUNS: none
HARDPOINTS: three
MAX WEAPON LOAD: n/a
REPRESENTATIVE WEAPONS: bombs; FFAR pods; external fuel tanks

DIMENSIONS:
LENGTH: 12.0 m (35 ft 4 in)
WINGSPAN: 9.4 m (30 ft 10 in)
HEIGHT: 4.3 m (14 ft 0 in)

VARIANTS & OPERATORS:
U.S. Navy

FEATURES:
Low/swept wing; tandem cockpit; arrester hook; nose leg catapult strut; single Rolls-Royce/Turbomeca Adour turbofan
Not to be confused with Hawk and Super Galeb

Beagle (BAE Systems) Bulldog 120 UK

Primary trainer

First flight of Beagle-built Bulldog on May 19, 1969, and first RAF Bulldog T.1 version flown on January 30, 1973. Last RAF Bulldogs withdrawn 2001. A total of 184 built.

SPECIFICATION:

ACCOMMODATION: student and instructor
MAX SPEED: 210 kt (389 km/h)
RANGE: 540 nm (1000 km)

ARMAMENT:
INTERNAL GUNS: none
HARDPOINTS: two
MAX WEAPON LOAD: 290 kg (640 lb)
REPRESENTATIVE WEAPONS: FFAR pod; gun pod; SAR equipment

DIMENSIONS:
LENGTH: 7.1 m (23 ft 3 in)
WINGSPAN: 10.0 m (33 ft 0 in)
HEIGHT: 2.3 m (7 ft 6 in)

VARIANTS & OPERATORS:
Kenya (Model 127), Lebanon (Model 126), Malta (ex-RAF T.1)

FEATURES:
Low/straight wing with slight dihedral; side-by-side cockpit; fixed tricycle undercarriage; one Avco Lycoming IO-360-A1B6 piston engine
Not to be confused with CT4 Airtrainer

Beech (Raytheon) T-34 Mentor USA

Primary trainer/light strike aircraft

First flight of the Beech Model 45 (Continental O-470-13A piston engine) was on December 2, 1948; YT-34A USAF version first flew in May 1950. USAF took 450 T-34A and USN 423 T-34Bs. First flight of YT-34C Turbo-Mentor on September 21, 1973. By April 1990, 1465 T-34s delivered from U.S. plus 50 Fuji T-3s, license-built in Japan.

SPECIFICATION:

ACCOMMODATION: student and instructor
MAX SPEED: 280 kt (518 km/h)
RANGE: 708 nm (1311 km)

ARMAMENT (T-34C-1):
INTERNAL GUNS: none
HARDPOINTS: four
MAX WEAPON LOAD: 544 kg (1200 lb)
REPRESENTATIVE WEAPONS: AGM-22 AGM; practise bombs; FFAR pod; gun pod

DIMENSIONS:
LENGTH: 8.8 m (28 ft 8 in)
WINGSPAN: 10.2 m (33 ft 4 in)
HEIGHT: 2.9 m (9 ft 7 in)

VARIANTS & OPERATORS:
T-34A/B: Argentina, Bolivia Colombia, Indonesia
VT-34A: Venezuela
T-34C: Algeria, Argentina, Ecuador, Gabon, Indonesia, Morocco, Peru, Taiwan, Uruguay, USA
Fuji T-3: Japan

FEATURES:
Low/straight wing with dihedral; tandem cockpit; one P&WC PT6A-25 turboprop (T-34C)
Not to be confused with EMB-312/-314, KT-1 Woong-Bee, PC-7/-9, Pillan, T-6, and T-34

T-34C

CASA (EADS) C-101 Aviojet SPAIN

Basic/advanced trainer/attack aircraft

First flight of the C-101 prototype was on June 27, 1977, and 88 C-101s (E.25 Mirlo) were delivered to Spain. Assembled under license in Chile by ENAER. Production ended in 1997 at 151 aircraft.

SPECIFICATION:

ACCOMMODATION: student and instructor
MAX SPEED: 450 kt (834 km/h)
RANGE: 260 nm (482 km)

ARMAMENT (A-36):

INTERNAL GUNS: provision for ventral gun pack (one 20 mm cannon or two 7.62 mm machine guns)
HARDPOINTS: six
MAX WEAPON LOAD: 2250 kg (4960 lb)
REPRESENTATIVE WEAPONS: AIM-9 AAM; AGM-65 Maverick, bombs; FFAR pods; external fuel tanks

DIMENSIONS:

LENGTH: 12.5 m (41 ft 0 in)
WINGSPAN: 10.6 m (34 ft 9 in)
HEIGHT: 4.2 m (13 ft 11 in)

VARIANTS & OPERATORS:

C-101BB: Chile (T-36)
C-101CC: Chile (A-36), Jordan
C-101EB: Spain

FEATURES:

Low/straight wing; lateral intake; tandem cockpit; one Honeywell TFE731 turbofan
Not to be confused with AT-3, HJT-36, IAR-99, K-8, L-39/-159 series, MB-339, and MiG-AT

Cessna T-37 "Tweety Bird" USA

Basic/advanced trainer/attack aircraft

First flown on October 12 ,1954, the T-37 remains the basic jet trainer of the USAF and others. Prototype YAT-37D attack version flown October 22, 1963, and produced as A-37 Dragonfly. Production of 1272 T-37/A-37 aircraft ended in 1977.

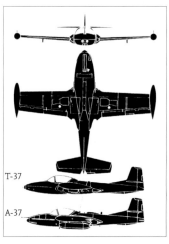

T-37

A-37

SPECIFICATION:

ACCOMMODATION: A-37, two pilots; T-37, student and instructor
MAX SPEED: 455 kt (843 km/h)
RANGE: 399 nm (740 km)

ARMAMENT (A-37):
INTERNAL GUNS: one 7.62 mm GAU-2B/A minigun
HARDPOINTS: eight (plus wingtip tanks)
MAX WEAPON LOAD: 2574 kg (5680 lb)
REPRESENTATIVE WEAPONS: Mk.81/82 bombs; FFAR pods; gun pods; external fuel tanks

DIMENSIONS:
LENGTH: 8.6 m (28 ft 3 in)
WINGSPAN: 10.9 m (35 ft 10 in)
HEIGHT: 2.7 m (8 ft 10 in)

VARIANTS & OPERATORS:
A-37B: Chile, Colombia, Ecuador, Guatemala, Honduras, Peru, El Salvador, South Korea, Uruguay
T-37B/C: Bangladesh, Colombia, Germany, Greece, Morocco, Pakistan, South Korea, Turkey, USA

FEATURES:
Low/straight wing; wingtip tanks; wingroot intakes; side-by-side cockpit; one GE J85-GE-17A turbojet
Not to be confused with Strikemaster and Kiran

Dassault/Dornier Alpha Jet FRANCE/GERMANY

Advanced trainer/close-air-support aircraft

The first prototype (of four) was flown on October 26, 1973, and entered service with France (as a trainer) and Germany (CAS now withdrawn). Production of 504 Alpha Jets ended in 1991.

SPECIFICATION:

ACCOMMODATION: student and instructor
MAX SPEED: 560 kt (1038 km/h)
RANGE: 315 nm (583 km)

ARMAMENT:
INTERNAL GUNS: one 30 mm DEFA or 27 mm Mauser cannon in underfuselage pod
HARDPOINTS: five
MAX WEAPON LOAD: 2500 kg (5510 lb)
REPRESENTATIVE WEAPONS: Magic, AIM-9 AAMs; AGM-65 Maverick; Mk.81/82 bombs; FFAR pods; recce and gun pods; external fuel tanks

DIMENSIONS:
LENGTH: 11.8 m (38 ft 6 in)
WINGSPAN: 9.1 m (29 ft 10 in)
HEIGHT: 4.2 m (13 ft 9 in)

VARIANTS & OPERATORS:
Belgium, Cameroon, Egypt, France, Morocco, Nigeria, Portugal, Qatar, Thailand, Togo, UK

FEATURES:
Shoulder/swept wing; lateral intakes; tandem cockpit; two SNECMA/Turbomeca Larzac 04-C6/20 turbofans
Not to be confused with IA63 Pampa and Kawasaki T-4

Embraer EMB-312 Tucano BRAZIL

Turboprop trainer (S312 Tucano T.1 pictured)

Powered by a PT6A turboprop, the EMB-312 Tucano first flew on August 16, 1980, and entered Brazilian service in 1983. Shorts produced a modified version with the Honeywell TPE331 turboprop as the S312 Tucano T.1 for RAF. A stretched version, EMB-314, became the EMB-314M/AT-29 for Brazil. A total of 650 produced, plus demonstrators.

SPECIFICATION:

ACCOMMODATION: student and instructor
MAX SPEED: 280 kt (519 km/h)
RANGE: 995 nm (1843 km)

ARMAMENT:
INTERNAL GUNS: none
HARDPOINTS: four
MAX WEAPON LOAD: 1000 kg (2204 lb)
REPRESENTATIVE WEAPONS: Mk.81 250 lb bombs; FFAR pods; gun pods; practise bombs

DIMENSIONS:
LENGTH: 9.9 m (32 ft 4 in)
WINGSPAN: 11.1 m (36 ft 6 in)
HEIGHT: 3.4 m (11 ft 2 in)

VARIANTS & OPERATORS:
EMB-312: Angola, Argentina, Brazil, Colombia, Egypt, France, Honduras, Iran, Paraguay, Peru, Venezuela
S312: Kenya, Kuwait, RAF

FEATURES:
Low/tapered wing; blown tandem canopy; one P&WC PT6A-25C turboprop
Not to be confused with KT-1 Woong-Bee, PC-7/-9, Pillan, T-6, and T-34

EMB-312

S312

ENAER T-35 Pillan CHILE

Basic trainer

First flown on March 6, 1981, deliveries to Chile began in 1985. Exported to Spain and around Latin America. Single-seater and turboprop versions developed but not sold. Production of 146 to 1991, plus eight ordered in 1998.

SPECIFICATION:

ACCOMODATION: student and instructor
MAX SPEED: 241 kt (446 km/h)
RANGE: 680 nm (1260 km)

ARMAMENT:
INTERNAL GUNS: none
HARDPOINTS: none
MAX WEAPON LOAD: N/A
REPRESENTATIVE WEAPONS: N/A

DIMENSIONS:
LENGTH: 8.8 m (29 ft 0 in)
WINGSPAN: 11.1 m (36 ft 6 in)
HEIGHT: 2.6 m (8 ft 8 in)

VARIANTS & OPERATORS:
Chile, Dominican Republic, Ecuador, Guatemala, Panama, Paraguay, El Salvador, Spain

FEATURES:
Low/tapered wing; blown tandem canopy; one Textron Lycoming IO-540-K1K5 piston engine
Not to be confused with EMB-312/-314, KT-1 Woong-Bee, PC-7/-9, T-6, and T-34

FMA (LMAA) IA 63/AT-63 Pampa ARGENTINA

Basic/advanced jet trainer

The prototype IA 63 Pampa first flew on October 6, 1984, with deliveries to Argentina from 1987. In 2001, AT-63 light attack variant launched at Paris Air Show. Production of 18 IA 63s, with 20 orders for AT-63.

SPECIFICATION:

ACCOMODATION: student and instructor
MAX SPEED: 445 kt (825 km/h)
RANGE: 1090 nm (2018 km)

ARMAMENT:
INTERNAL GUNS: none
HARDPOINTS: seven
MAX WEAPON LOAD: 2290 kg (5047 lb)
REPRESENTATIVE WEAPONS: AAMs; AGMs; bombs, FFAR pods; gun pods; external fuel tanks

DIMENSIONS:
LENGTH: 10.9 m (35 ft 9 in)
WINGSPAN: 9.7 m (31 ft 9 in)
HEIGHT: 4.3m (14 ft 1 in)

VARIANTS & OPERATORS:
Argentina

FEATURES:
Shoulder/straight wing; tandem canopy; one Honeywell TFE731-2-2N turbofan; lateral intakes
Not to be confused with Alpha Jet and Kawasaki T-4

HAIC JL-8/K-8 Karakorum 8 CHINA

Basic jet trainer/light attack aircraft

Originally a collaborative project with Pakistan, the first K-8 flew on November 21, 1990. Six pre-production K-8s delivered to Pakistan from 1994. Re-engined with Russian AI-25 engine as JL-8 for Chinese use. As of January 2007, over 140 delivered out of an order book of 184+.

SPECIFICATION:

ACCOMMODATION: student and instructor
MAX SPEED: 512 kt (950 km/h)
RANGE: internal fuel, 842 nm (1560 km)

ARMAMENT:

INTERNAL GUNS: one 23 mm cannon in centerline gun pod
HARDPOINTS: four
MAX WEAPON LOAD: 943 kg (2080 lb)
REPRESENTATIVE WEAPONS: PL-7 AAM; bombs; FFAR pods; external fuel tank

DIMENSIONS:

LENGTH: 11.6 m (38 ft 1 in)
WINGSPAN: 9.6 m (34 ft 7 in)
HEIGHT: 4.2 m (13 ft 10 in)

VARIANTS & OPERATORS:

China, Egypt, Morocco, Myanmar, Namibia, Pakistan, Sri Lanka, Zimbabwe, Zambia

FEATURES:

Low/tapered wing; tandem cockpit; one Honeywell TFE731 or Progress AI-25 turbofan; lateral intakes
Not to be confused with AT-3, C-101, HJT-36, IAR-99, L-39/-159 series, MB-339, and MiG-AT

Hindustan Aeronautics Ltd. HJT-16 Kiran INDIA

Basic/advanced jet trainer

The prototype Kiran first flew on September 4, 1964, with deliveries of the Mk.I version to India from 1968. Mk.IA featured one hardpoint under each wing; the Mk.II had two. Production reached 250 of all versions.

SPECIFICATION:

ACCOMODATION: student and instructor
MAX SPEED: 463 kt (858 km/h)
RANGE: 332 nm (615 km)

ARMAMENT (MK II):
INTERNAL GUNS: two 7.62 mm machine guns
HARDPOINTS: four
MAX WEAPON LOAD: 1000 kg (2204 lb)
REPRESENTATIVE WEAPONS: 250 kg bombs; FFAR pods; CBLS; external fuel tanks

DIMENSIONS:
LENGTH: 10.2 m (33 ft 7 in)
WINGSPAN: 10.7 m (35 ft 1 in)
HEIGHT: 3.6 m (11 ft 11 in)

VARIANTS & OPERATORS:
India

FEATURES:
Low/mid/straight wing; side-by-side canopy; one Rolls-Royce Viper 11 (Mk.I/IA) or Orpheus 701 turbojet (Mk.II)
Not to be confused with Strikemaster, A-37, T-37

Hindustan Aeronautics Ltd. HJT-36 Sitara INDIA

Basic jet trainer

Work on this Kiran replacement began 1997. Requirement for Indian Air Force (187) and Navy (24) approved in January 2001. Initial contract (16 for IAF) announced February 2003. First flown on March 7, 2003. Deliveries to start before end 2007.

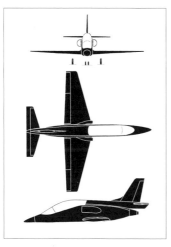

SPECIFICATION:

ACCOMODATION: student and instructor
MAX SPEED: 378 kt (700 km/h)
RANGE: 540 nm (1000 km)

ARMAMENT:
INTERNAL GUNS: none
HARDPOINTS: four plus centerline
MAX WEAPON LOAD: 1000 kg (2204 lb)
REPRESENTATIVE WEAPONS: gun pods; rocket pods; bombs; external tanks

DIMENSIONS:
LENGTH: 10.9 m (35 ft 11 in)
WINGSPAN: 10.0 m (32 ft 9 in)
HEIGHT: 4.4 m (14 ft 5 in)

VARIANTS & OPERATORS:
Indian Air Force
Indian Navy

FEATURES:
Low/swept wing; tandem canopy; swept tail; one Saturn AL-55 turbofan; bifurcated intakes behind canopy
Not to be confused with AT-3, C-101, IAR-99, K-8, L-39/-159 series, MB-339, and MiG-AT

Kawasaki T-4 JAPAN

Intermediate jet trainer

First flight of XT-4 on July 29, 1985, with deliveries from 1988. Equips JASDF Blue Impulse aerobatic team. Similar to Alpha Jet in appearance. Production of 212 complete.

SPECIFICATION:

ACCOMMODATION: student and instructor
MAX SPEED: 560 kt (1038 km/h)
RANGE: 900 nm (1668 km)

ARMAMENT:
INTERNAL GUNS: none
HARDPOINTS: three
MAX WEAPON LOAD: N/A
REPRESENTATIVE WEAPONS: ECM pods; towed targets; external fuel tanks

DIMENSIONS:
LENGTH: 13.0 m (42 ft 8 in)
WINGSPAN: 9.9 m (32 ft 7 in)
HEIGHT: 4.6 m (15 ft 1 in)

VARIANTS & OPERATORS:
T-4: Japan

FEATURES:
Tall fin; shoulder/swept wing; tandem cockpit; two Ishikawajima-Harima F3-IHI-30 turbofans; lateral intakes
Not to be confused with Alpha Jet and IA 63 Pampa

KAI (Daewoo) KT-1 Woong-Bee SOUTH KOREA

Basic/advanced trainer/attack aircraft

The KTX-1 prototype first flew on December 12, 1991, and the KT-1 was ordered into production in 1999 (85 on order plus seven for Indonesia). An FAC version, KOX-1, is being developed (20 required).

SPECIFICATION:

ACCOMMODATION: student and instructor
MAX SPEED: 350 kt (648 km/h)
RANGE: 900 nm (1668 km)

ARMAMENT:
INTERNAL GUNS: none
HARDPOINTS: four
MAX WEAPON LOAD: N/A
REPRESENTATIVE WEAPONS: FFAR pods; gun pods; external fuel tanks

DIMENSIONS:
LENGTH: 10.3 m (33 ft 8 in)
WINGSPAN: 10.6 m (34 ft 9 in)
HEIGHT: 3.7 m (12 ft 0 in)

VARIANTS & OPERATORS:
KT-1: South Korea, Indonesia

FEATURES:
Low/straight wing; tandem cockpit; one P&WC PT6A-62A turboprop
Not to be confused with EMB-312/-314, Pillan, PC-7, PC-9, PC-21, T-6, and T-34

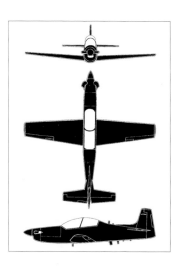

KAI T-50 (TA-50) Golden Eagle SOUTH KOREA

Advanced jet trainer/light attack aircraft

Initiated in 1992 by Samsung (now KAI) with assistance from Lockheed Martin (as offset for RoKAF F-16 program). Maiden flight on August 20, 2002, and three others since flown (including one LIFT version). First 25 T-50s ordered by RoKAF in December 2003, with 50 more ordered (T-50 and TA-50) December 2006. Offered for export as F-5/T-38 replacement.

SPECIFICATION:

ACCOMMODATION: student and instructor
MAX SPEED: M1.5
RANGE: 1400 nm (2592 km)

ARMAMENT (LIFT/A-50):
INTERNAL GUNS: 20 mm Gatling-type cannon (in port LERX)
HARDPOINTS: seven (including wingtips)
MAX WEAPON LOAD: 4309 kg (9500 lb)
REPRESENTATIVE WEAPONS: AIM-9 AAMs; AGM-65 Maverick; cluster munitions; ACMI pod; external fuel tanks

DIMENSIONS:
LENGTH: 13.1 m (43 ft 1 in)
WINGSPAN: 9.5 m (31 ft 0 in)
HEIGHT: 4.9 m (16 ft 2 in)

VARIANTS & OPERATORS:
T-50: South Korea

FEATURES:
Similar to F-16—swept wing (with LERX) and fin; tandem cockpit; intakes under LERX; one GE F404-GE-102 turbofan
Not to be confused with Mitsubishi F-2 and F-16

Lockheed AT/T-33 (CT-133 Silver Star) USA

Basic/advanced jet trainer

Derived from the P-80 Shooting Star, the prototype TF-80C was first flown on March 22, 1948, and later redesignated T-33. Lockheed produced 5691 aircraft. License-built by Canadair as the CT-133 Silver Star (656) and Kawasaki of Japan (210), the last of which flew in 1959.

SPECIFICATION:

ACCOMMODATION: student and instructor
MAX SPEED: 486 kt (900 km/h)
RANGE: 1169 nm (2165 km)

ARMAMENT (AT-33):
INTERNAL GUNS: two 0.50 in M3 machine guns
HARDPOINTS: wingtip tanks only
MAX WEAPON LOAD: N/A
REPRESENTATIVE WEAPONS: N/A

DIMENSIONS:
LENGTH: 11.5 m (37 ft 8 in)
WINGSPAN: 11.8 m (38 ft 10 in)
HEIGHT: 3.5 m (11 ft 8 in)

VARIANTS & OPERATORS:
T-33A: Bolivia, Thailand
AT-33A: Mexico
AT-33AN Silver Star: Bolivia
CT-33SF: Bolivia

FEATURES:
Low/straight wing; tandem cockpit; one Allison J-23 or Rolls-Royce Nene turbojet; low lateral intakes

Mitsubishi T-2 JAPAN

Advanced jet trainer

Japan's first supersonic trainer flew on July 20, 1971, and entered JASDF service in 1975. The last of 96 aircraft delivered in 1988. Similar to Jaguar E in appearance.

SPECIFICATION:

ACCOMMODATION: pilot
MAX SPEED: M1.6
RADIUS OF ACTION: N/A

ARMAMENT:
INTERNAL GUNS: one 20 mm JM61 cannon
HARDPOINTS: five
MAX WEAPON LOAD: 2721 kg (5997 lb)
REPRESENTATIVE WEAPONS: bombs; FFAR pods; external fuel tanks

DIMENSIONS:
LENGTH: 17.8 m (58 ft 6 in)
WINGSPAN: 7.9 m (25 ft 10 in)
HEIGHT: 4.4 m (14 ft 2 in)

VARIANTS & OPERATORS:
Japan

FEATURES:
Shoulder/swept wing; two Rolls-Royce/Turbomeca Adour 108 turbofans; rear ventral fins
Not to be confused with Jaguar

Nanchang CJ-6A (Yak-18 "Max") CHINA

Basic trainer

First Yak-18 prototype flown in 1945, it was progressively developed to the Yak-18T, with some 8000 of all versions produced. China license-produced the Yak-18 (as CJ-5) from 1954, then further developed it as the Nanchang CJ-6 and CJ6-A, building 1796 by 1986. BT-6 is the Bangladesh designation for the type.

SPECIFICATION:

ACCOMMODATION: student and instructor
MAX SPEED: 155 kt (286 km/h)
RANGE: max fuel, 372 nm (690 km)

ARMAMENT:
INTERNAL GUNS: none
HARDPOINTS: none
MAX WEAPON LOAD: N/A
REPRESENTATIVE WEAPONS: N/A

DIMENSIONS:
LENGTH: 8.5 m (27 ft 9 in)
WINGSPAN: 10.2 m (33 ft 5 in)
HEIGHT: 3.2 m (10 ft 8 in)

VARIANTS & OPERATORS:
Yak-18A: Mali
Yak-18T: Armenia, Lithuania
BT-6: Bangladesh, Sri Lanka, Zambia
CJ-6/6A: Albania, China, Ecuador, North Korea

FEATURES:
Straight wing; straight fin and tailplane; one Zhuzhou (SMPMC) HS6A radial engine; large tandem canopy

Northrop (N-G) T-38 Talon USA

Supersonic jet trainer

A private venture, the T-38 Talon prototype first flew on April 10, 1959, and entered USAF service in 1961. Developed into the F-5 series fighters. T-38C upgrade by McDonnell Douglas (Boeing) ordered in 1996—over 200 delivered. Last of 1187 Talons delivered in 1972.

SPECIFICATION:

ACCOMMODATION: student and instructor
MAX SPEED: M1.23+
RANGE: internal fuel, 955 nm (1700 km)

ARMAMENT:
INTERNAL GUNS: none
HARDPOINTS: one (AT-38B only)
MAX WEAPON LOAD: N/A
REPRESENTATIVE WEAPONS: N/A

DIMENSIONS:
LENGTH: 14.1 m (46 ft 4 in)
WINGSPAN: 7.7 m (25 ft 3 in)
HEIGHT: 3.9 m (12 ft 10 in)

VARIANTS & OPERATORS:
Germany (T-38A), South Korea (T-38), Turkey (T-38A), USA (T-38A/B/C, AT-38B)

FEATURES:
Low tailplane; low/swept wing; two GE J85 turbojets

PAC Mushshak (Saab MFI-17 Supporter) PAKISTAN (SWEDEN)

Light trainer/observation aircraft

First flown as MFI-17 on April 9, 1973. Built under license in Pakistan as Mushshak, then upgraded as Shabaz and Super Mushshak Agile. Over 295 built.

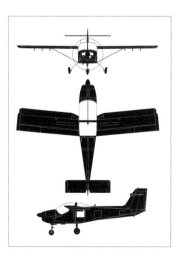

SPECIFICATION:

ACCOMMODATION: student and instructor (plus one other)
MAX SPEED: 196 kt (363 km/h)
RANGE: internal fuel, N/A

ARMAMENT:
INTERNAL GUNS: none
HARDPOINTS: none
MAX WEAPON LOAD: N/A
REPRESENTATIVE WEAPONS: N/A

DIMENSIONS:
LENGTH: 7.0 m (22 ft 11 in)
WINGSPAN: 8.8 m (29 ft 0 in)
HEIGHT: 2.6 m (8 ft 6 in)

VARIANTS & OPERATORS:
Mushshak: Iran, Pakistan, Syria
Super Mushshak: Oman, Pakistan, Saudi Arabia
MFI-17: Uganda, Zambia

FEATURES:
High tailplane; shoulder/slightly forward-swept wing; fixed tricyle undercarriage; one Textron Lycoming IO-360 piston engine

Pacific Aerospace CT4 Airtrainer NEW ZEALAND

Basic trainer

A redesign of the Victa Aircruiser (first flown February 12, 1972); 114 CT4A/B trainers built by 1977. CT4C turboprop prototype (not produced). CT4E with bigger engine in production from 1998 with 24 orders.

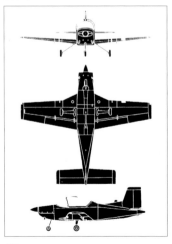

SPECIFICATION:

ACCOMMODATION: student and instructor
MAX SPEED: 230 kt (426 km/h)
RANGE: internal fuel, 520 nm (963 km)

ARMAMENT:
INTERNAL GUNS: none
HARDPOINTS: none
MAX WEAPON LOAD: N/A
REPRESENTATIVE WEAPONS: N/A

DIMENSIONS:
LENGTH: 7.3 m (23 ft 9 in)
WINGSPAN: 7.9 m (26 ft 0 in)
HEIGHT: 2.6 m (8 ft 6 in)

VARIANTS & OPERATORS:
New Zealand (CT4E), Thailand (CT4A/B/E)

FEATURES:
Low/tapered wing; side-by-side cockpit; fixed tricyle undercarriage; one Textron Lycoming AEIO-540 piston engine
Not to be confused with Bulldog

Pilatus PC-7 Turbo Trainer SWITZERLAND

Basic trainer

The PC-7 first flew on August 18, 1978, with deliveries from December 1978. The Mk.II M version flown September 28, 1992, the 60 SAAF version was named Astra. A total of 448 PC-7s and 66 PC-7 Mk.IIs built.

SPECIFICATION:

ACCOMMODATION: student and instructor
MAX SPEED: 270 kt (500 km/h)
RANGE: internal fuel, 1420 nm (2630 km)

ARMAMENT:

INTERNAL GUNS: none
HARDPOINTS: four (locally installed on Iranian aircraft)
MAX WEAPON LOAD: N/A
REPRESENTATIVE WEAPONS: N/A

DIMENSIONS:

LENGTH: 9.8 m (32 ft 1 in)
WINGSPAN: 10.4 m (34 ft 1 in)
HEIGHT: 3.2 m (10 ft 6 in)

VARIANTS & OPERATORS:

PC-7: Angola, Austria, Bolivia, Botswana, Chad, Chile, France, Guatemala, Iran, Malaysia, Mexico, Myanmar, Netherlands, Switzerland, UAE (Abu Dhabi), Uruguay
PC-7 Mk.II: Brunei, Malaysia, South Africa

FEATURES:

Low/tapered wing; tandem cockpit; one P&WC PT6A-62 turboprop
Not to be confused with EMB-312/-314, KT-1 Woong-Bee, PC-9, Pillan, T-6, and T-34

Pilatus PC-9 Advanced Turbo Trainer SWITZERLAND

Advanced turboprop trainer

Derived from the PC-7, the PC-9 was first flown on May 7, 1984, with deliveries from 1986. The PC-9 Mk.II version was developed by Raytheon (Beech) as T-6A Texan II (which see). PC-9M has enlarged dorsal fairing (and cockpit layout) of PC-7 Mk II. Over 260 PC-9s built, plus U.S. production.

SPECIFICATION:

ACCOMMODATION: student and instructor
MAX SPEED: 320 kt (593 km/h)
RANGE: internal fuel, 830 nm (1537 km)

ARMAMENT:

INTERNAL GUNS: none
HARDPOINTS: provision for six
MAX WEAPON LOAD: N/A
REPRESENTATIVE WEAPONS: N/A

DIMENSIONS:

LENGTH: 10.3 m (32 ft 3 in)
WINGSPAN: 10.1m (33 ft 2 in)
HEIGHT: 3.3 m (10 ft 9 in)

VARIANTS & OPERATORS:

PC-9: Angola, Cyprus, Myanmar, Saudi Arabia, Switzerland
PC-9/A: Australia
PC-9M: Bulgaria, Croatia, Ireland, Oman, Slovenia

FEATURES:

Enlarged dorsal fin; low/tapered wing; tandem cockpit; one P&WC PT6A-62 turboprop
Not to be confused with EMB-312/-314, KT-1 Woong-Bee, PC-7, Pillan, T-6, and T-34

Pilatus PC-21 SWITZERLAND

Advanced turboprop trainer

Development began in 1999 and prototype PC-21 was first flown on July 1, 2002. Based on PC-7/-9 experience but with 21st-century design, materials, and technology. Intended for advanced pilot training and pilot/WSO weapons training at turboprop (rather than jet) costs. Initial markets seen in Australia, South Africa, and UK. Switzerland ordered six PC-21s in February 2007.

SPECIFICATION:

ACCOMMODATION: student and instructor
MAX SPEED: 370 kt (685 km/h)
RANGE: internal fuel, 720 nm (1333 km)

ARMAMENT:
INTERNAL GUNS: none
HARDPOINTS: one centerline and four wing-stores stations
MAX EXTERNAL LOAD: 1150 kg (2535 lb)
REPRESENTATIVE WEAPONS: N/A

DIMENSIONS:
LENGTH: 11.5 m (36 ft 11 in)
WINGSPAN: 9.12 m (29 ft 11 in)
HEIGHT: 3.8 m (12 ft 4 in)

VARIANTS & OPERATORS:
PC-21: on order for Singapore (November 2006)
Switzerland: six on order

FEATURES:
Low/tapered wing; swept fin and tailplane; tandem cockpit; one P&WC PT6A-68B turboprop
Not to be confused with KT-1 Woong-Bee and T-6A Texan II

RAC-MiG Advanced Trainer (MiG-AT) RUSSIA

Advanced jet trainer

One of two designs selected for evaluation as successor to L-29/L-39 in
Russian service. Prototype first flew
March 16, 1996. Several variants proposed with Russian or French engines/
avionics. No production order yet, but
three development aircraft flown.
Concentrating on export market.

SPECIFICATION:

ACCOMMODATION: student and instructor
MAX SPEED: 540 kt (1000 km/h)
RANGE: 647 nm (1200 km)

ARMAMENT:

INTERNAL GUNS: none
HARDPOINTS: seven
MAX WEAPON LOAD: 2000 kg (4410 lb)
REPRESENTATIVE WEAPONS: AAMs; AGMs; bombs;
FFAR pods; gun pods; external fuel tanks

DIMENSIONS:

LENGTH: 12.0 m (39 ft 5 in)
WINGSPAN: 10.2 m (33 ft 4 in)
HEIGHT: 4.4 m (14 ft 6 in)

VARIANTS & OPERATORS:

Russia (prototypes only)

FEATURES:

Low/tapered wing with wingroot engine pods; two
Turbomeca-SNECMA Larzac 04-R20 turbofans;
tandem canopy
Not to be confused with AT-3, C-101, HJT-36,
IAR-99, K-8, L-39/-159 series, and MB-339

Raytheon (Beech) T-6 Texan II USA

Advanced turboprop trainer

Derived from the PC-9 (which see) under an agreement between Pilatus and Raytheon (Beech) to bid for joint USAF/USN JPATS requirement. Selected in June 1995. Production prototype T-6A flown July 15, 1998; first deliveries from March 2000. Requirement for USAF (454) and USN (328), with export sales to Canada (24, designated CT-156 Harvard II) and to Greece (45). Armed T-6B version being promoted.

SPECIFICATION:

ACCOMMODATION: student and instructor
MAX SPEED: 316 kt (585 km/h)
RANGE: internal fuel, 850 nm (1574 km)

ARMAMENT (T-6B):
INTERNAL GUNS: none
HARDPOINTS: three under each wing
MAX WEAPON LOAD: 1040 kg (2293 lb)
REPRESENTATIVE WEAPONS: N/A

DIMENSIONS:
LENGTH: 10.3 m (32 ft 3 in)
WINGSPAN: 10.1 m (33 ft 2 in)
HEIGHT: 3.3 m (10 ft 9 in)

VARIANTS & OPERATORS:
T-6A: Greece, USN, USAF
CT-156: Canada

FEATURES:
Enlarged dorsal fin; low/tapered wing; tandem cockpit; one P&WC PT6A-68 turboprop
Not to be confused with EMB-312/-314, KT-1 Woong-Bee, PC-7/-9, Pillan, and T-34

Saab 105 (Sk 60) SWEDEN

Basic/advanced jet trainer/light attack and recce aircraft

The prototype Saab 105 was first flown on June 29, 1963, and 190 were built for Sweden, 106 of which have been re-engined with FJ44 turbofans. Austria took 40 105ÖE (or 105XT) versions with GE J85 turbojets.

SPECIFICATION:

ACCOMMODATION: student and instructor
MAX SPEED: 432 kt (1800 km/h)
RANGE: internal fuel, 1350 nm (2500 km)

ARMAMENT:
INTERNAL GUNS: none
HARDPOINTS: six
MAX WEAPON LOAD: 700 kg (1543 lb)
REPRESENTATIVE WEAPONS: bombs; FFAR pods; gun pods

DIMENSIONS:
LENGTH: 10.8 m (35 ft 4 in)
WINGSPAN: 9.5 m (31 ft 2 in)
HEIGHT: 2.7 m (8 ft 9 in)

VARIANTS & OPERATORS:
Austria (105ÖE), Sweden (Sk 60)

FEATURES:
Shoulder/swept wing; side-by-side cockpit; two Williams-Rolls FJ44 turbofans

Slingsby T67 Firefly UK

Basic trainer

The current T67 series are composite-built versions of the original wooden T67A (itself a license-built Fournier RF6B first flown in 1980). The first T67M military variant flew on December 5, 1982, and is available with various engine configurations. Used for military training in the UK, but aircraft are civilian owned and operated. To 1999, 265 had been built and Jordan ordered 16 T67M-260s in 2001.

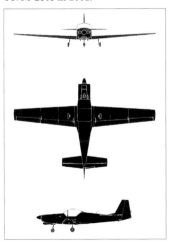

SPECIFICATION:

ACCOMMODATION: student and instructor
MAX SPEED: 195 kt (361 km/h)
RANGE: 407 nm (753 km)

ARMAMENT:
INTERNAL GUNS: none
HARDPOINTS: none
MAX WEAPON LOAD: N/A
REPRESENTATIVE WEAPONS: N/A

DIMENSIONS:
LENGTH: 7.6 m (24 ft 10 in)
WINGSPAN: 10.6 m (34 ft 9 in)
HEIGHT: 2.4 m (7 ft 9 in)

VARIANTS & OPERATORS:
T67M-160: UK
T67M-200: Bahrain, Belize
T67M-260: Jordan, UK

FEATURES:
Low wing; side-by-side cockpit; one Textron Lycoming AEIO-540-D4A4 piston engine; fixed tricycle undercarriage

SOCATA (Aerospatiale) TB 30 Epsilon FRANCE

Basic trainer

The TB 30 Epsilon prototype first flew on December 22, 1979, and, as a result of initial trials, the design was refined. Entered French service in 1984. A total of 174 were built.

SPECIFICATION:

ACCOMMODATION: student and instructor
MAX SPEED: 281 kt (530 km/h)
RANGE: N/A

ARMAMENT:
INTERNAL GUNS: none
HARDPOINTS: four
MAX WEAPON LOAD: 300 kg (661 lb)
REPRESENTATIVE WEAPONS: FFAR pods; gun pods; practise bomb carriers

DIMENSIONS:
LENGTH: 7.6 m (24 ft 10 in)
WINGSPAN: 7.9 m (26 ft 0 in)
HEIGHT: 2.7 m (8 ft 9 in)

VARIANTS & OPERATORS:
TB30: France, Portugal, Togo

FEATURES:
Low wing; tandem cockpit; one Textron Lycoming AEIO-540-L1B5D piston engine

SOKO G-4 Super Galeb BOSNIA AND HERZEGOVINA

Armed jet trainer

The prototype Super Galeb was first flown on July 17, 1978, entering service with Yugoslavia in 1981. Armed during the 1991 war with Croatia. Exact number built remains unkown.

SPECIFICATION:

ACCOMMODATION: student and instructor
MAX SPEED: M0.9
RANGE: 701 nm (1300 km)

ARMAMENT:
INTERNAL GUNS: one GSh-23L twin barrel cannon in ventral pack
HARDPOINTS: four
MAX WEAPON LOAD: 2053 kg (4526 lb)
REPRESENTATIVE WEAPONS: R-60 Aphid, R-73T Archer AAMs; AGM-65B Maverick; bombs; FFAR pods; external fuel tanks

DIMENSIONS:
LENGTH: 12.2 m (40 ft 2 in)
WINGSPAN: 9.9 m (32 ft 5 in)
HEIGHT: 4.3 m (14 ft 1 in)

VARIANTS & OPERATORS:
Bosnia and Herzegovina (Republika Srpska), Montenegro, Myanmar, Serbia

FEATURES:
Tailplane anhedral; low/swept wing; tandem canopy; one Rolls-Royce Viper 632 turbojet; lateral intakes

Yakovlev Yak-130 RUSSIA/ITALY

Advanced jet trainer

Developed in partnership between Russia's Yakovlev (now owned by Irkut) and Aermacchi of Italy as a potential replacement for Russia's L-29/L-39 trainers, the Yak-130D development aircraft first flew on April 25, 1996. Design was refined and each partner took their own variant forward as Yak-130 and M-346 (which see). First series-configured Yak-130 flew on April 30, 2004.

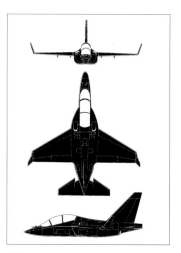

SPECIFICATION:

ACCOMMODATION: student and instructor
MAX SPEED: 572 kt (1060 km/h)
RANGE: 1079 nm (2000 km)

ARMAMENT:
INTERNAL GUNS: none
HARDPOINTS: seven (plus optional wingtips)
MAX WEAPON LOAD: 3000 kg (6614 lb)
REPRESENTATIVE WEAPONS: AAMs; AGMs; FFAR pods; gun pods; external fuel tanks

DIMENSIONS:
LENGTH: 11.5 m (37 ft 9 in)
WINGSPAN: 9.7 m (31 ft 10 in)
HEIGHT: 4.8 m (15 ft 8 in)

VARIANTS & OPERATORS:
Yak-130: Russia (expected)

FEATURES:
Low/swept wing; tandem cockpit; two ZMKB Progress AI-222-25 (DV-2S/RD-35) turbofans; underwing root intakes/exhausts; bevelled nose chine
Not to be confused with M-346

Combat Support Aircraft

Airbus A310 MRTT FRANCE/GERMANY/SPAIN/UK

AAR tanker/transport

Developed by Europe's Airbus Industrie as an AAR tanker variant of the A310 airliner (aka MRT), the first (of four) MRTT conversions for Germany flew on December 20, 2003. Canada ordered a similar conversion for two of its CC-150 Polaris MRTs in late 2001.

SPECIFICATION:

PAYLOAD/ACCOMMODATION: 3 or 4 flight crew plus 214 passengers or 36 tonnes cargo
DISPOSABLE FUEL: 28,000 kg (61,729 lb)
MAX SPEED: M0.8
RANGE: 4800 nm (8889 km)

DIMENSIONS:
LENGTH: 47.4 m (155 ft 5 in)
WINGSPAN: 43.9 m (144 ft 0 in)
HEIGHT: 15.8 m (51 ft 10 in)

VARIANTS & OPERATORS:
A310MRT/MRTT: Canada, Germany

FEATURES:
Low/swept wing; two GE CF6 turbofans; underwing AAR pods and/or tail-mounted AAR boom

Airbus A330 MRTT FRANCE/GERMANY/SPAIN/UK

AAR tanker/transport

The MRTT version of the Airbus A330 is based on the -200 series aircraft. Bid into the UK's FSTA program by AirTanker (a consortium of EADS, Rolls-Royce, Thales, and FR Aviation), the A330-200 was selected in January 2004 but, as of January 2007, no formal contract signed, due to complex PFI contract negotiations. Original ISD was 2008 but has now slipped. Australia selected the A330 in April 2004, signing in December 2004. Delivery is due 2009-11. EADS, teamed with Northrop Grumman, is bidding the KC-330 variant to USA.

SPECIFICATION:

PAYLOAD/ACCOMMODATION: 3 or 4 flight crew plus up to 379 passengers
MAX FUEL: 111,270 kg (245,300 lb)
MAX SPEED: M0.82
RANGE: 9000 nm (16,668 km)

DIMENSIONS:
LENGTH: 59.7 m (195 ft 10 in)
WINGSPAN: 60.3 m (197 ft 10in)
HEIGHT: 17.9 m (58 ft 8 in)

VARIANTS & OPERATORS:
Australia: A330-203 MRTT (five aircraft ordered)
UK: A330-200 (about 16 aircraft required)

FEATURES:
Low/swept wing with winglets; twin underwing Rolls-Royce 700-series turbofans; swept tailfin; low/swept tailplane; wide-body fuselage; underwing FR Mk 32-900 series refuelling pods and (on RAAF version) rear fuselage AAR boom

Airtech CN-235M INDONESIA/SPAIN

Transport/MPA (HC-235A (HC-144A) pictured)

A collaborative venture between IPTN of Indonesia (now Dirgantara) and CASA (EADS) of Spain, the prototype CN-235 first flew on November 11, 1983, entering service in both countries in 1991. MPA variant (HC-235A) selected for U.S. Coast Guard's Deepwater program in 2002. First aircraft delivered December 2006. As of January 2007, CASA had sold 173 aircraft and Dirgantara (IPTN) 77, covering military and civil variants.

SPECIFICATION:

PAYLOAD/ACCOMMODATION: 2 flight crew and 1 loadmaster plus 46 paratroopers or 6000 kg (13,227 lb) cargo
SENSORS (MPA): search radar, FLIR turret, ESM/DAS
ARMAMENT (M-SERIES): six underwing hardpoints for ASMs or ASW torpedoes
MAX SPEED: 240 kt (445 km/h)
RANGE: 2400 nm (4445 km)

DIMENSIONS:
LENGTH: 21.4 m (70 ft 2 in)
WINGSPAN: 25.9 m (84 ft 8 in)
HEIGHT: 8.2 m (26 ft 10 in)

VARIANTS & OPERATORS:
CN-235: Spain, USA
CN-235-10: Spain
CN-235M: Botswana, Brunei, Colombia, Gabon, Saudi Arabia, Turkey, UAE (Abu Dhabi)
CN-235M-100: Chile, Ecuador, Indonesia, Morocco, Oman, Papua New Guinea, South Africa, South Korea, Spain
CN-235M-200: Colombia, France, Thailand
CN-235M-220: Malaysia, Pakistan, South Korea, Thailand
CN-235M-300: Austria, Ecuador
CN-235MP: Ireland, Venezuela
CN-235MP Persuader: Ecuador
CN-235MPA: Indonesia
HC-235A: USA (HC-144A)

FEATURES:
High tail; shoulder/tapered wing; two GE CT7-9C turboprops; fuselage undercarriage fairings

Alenia G222 (C-27) ITALY

Tactical transport

First G222 flown on July 18, 1970,
Italy took delivery of the first
military transport version in 1976.
Sold in several versions to several
countries, including R-R Tyne-
engined version for Libya and C-27
Spartan for USAF (now withdrawn).
Production ceased in 1993 after
111 built.

SPECIFICATION:

PAYLOAD/ACCOMMODATION: 3 flight crew and
1 loadmaster plus 53 troops, 40 paratroopers, or
9000 kg (19,840 lb) cargo
MAX SPEED: 291 kt (540 km/h)
RANGE: 740 nm (1371 km)

DIMENSIONS:
LENGTH: 22.7 m (74 ft 5 in)
WINGSPAN: 28.7 m (94 ft 2 in)
HEIGHT: 9.8 m (32 ft 2 in)

VARIANTS & OPERATORS:
C-27A: Colombia
G222: Argentina, Thailand, Tunisia, Venezuela
G222T: Libya
G222AAA: Italy
G222RM: Italy
G222TCM: Italy
G222VS: Italy

FEATURES:
High tail; shoulder/tapered wing; two GE
T64-GE-P4D turboprops; fuselage undercarriage
fairings

Alenia/Lockheed Martin C-27J Spartan ITALY/USA

Tactical transport

A collaborative venture between Alenia and Lockheed Martin, the C-27J merges engines, avionics, and systems from the C-130J with the G222. Prototype C-27J (a converted G222) first flown on September 24, 1999. First Italian C-27J (of 12) delivered in January 2007.

SPECIFICATION:

PAYLOAD/ACCOMMODATION: 2 flight crew and 1 loadmaster plus 53 troops, 40 paratroopers, or 10,000 kg (22,046 lb) cargo
MAX SPEED: 325 kt (602 km/h)
RANGE: 1350 nm (2500 km)

DIMENSIONS:
LENGTH: 22.7 m (74 ft 5 in)
WINGSPAN: 28.7 m (94 ft 2 in)
HEIGHT: 9.8 m (32 ft 2 in)

VARIANTS & OPERATORS:
C-27J: Bulgaria, Greece, Italy, Lithuania, Romania

FEATURES:
High tail; shoulder/tapered wing; two Rolls-Royce AE 2100D2 turboprops; fuselage undercarriage fairings

Antonov An-12 (Y-8) "Cub" UKRAINE

Tactical transport

Derived from the An-10 airliner, the An-12 was first flown with NK-4 turboprops in 1958, and later re-engined with Ivchenko AI-20A/M turbprops. In service from 1959, some 900 were built to 1973, including an EW version. Widely exported and license-built in China as the Y-8.

SPECIFICATION:

PAYLOAD/ACCOMMODATION: 5 flight crew and 1 rear gunner plus 90 troops, 60 paratroopers, or 20,000 kg (44,090 lb) cargo
MAX SPEED: 419 kt (777 km/h)
RANGE: 1942 nm (3600 km)

DIMENSIONS:
LENGTH: 33.1 m (108 ft 7 in)
WINGSPAN: 38.0 m (124 ft 8 in)
HEIGHT: 12.2 m (40 ft 0 in)

ARMAMENT:
Two 23 mm NK-23 cannon in tail turret

VARIANTS & OPERATORS:
An-12: Azerbaijan, Ethiopia, Kazakhstan, Russia, Turkmenistan, Ukraine, Uzbekistan, Yemen
Y-8: China, Myanmar, Sudan, Tanzania

FEATURES:
High tail; shoulder/tapered wing; anhedral on outer wing panels; four Ivchenko AI-20 turboprops; fuselage undercarriage fairings

Antonov An-24 "Coke," An-26 "Curl," An-32 "Cline"

UKRAINE

Tactical transport/freighter/survey aircraft (An-26 "Curl" pictured)

The prototype An-24 was first flown on December 20, 1959, and entered service from 1963. Production of about 1200 ended in 1979, although continued in China (as Y-7) into the mid-1990s. The An-26 freighter (Y-7H-500 in China) first shown in 1969. The An-32 is derived from the An-26 and first flew on July 9, 1976; 346 produced to 1997.

SPECIFICATION:

PAYLOAD/ACCOMMODATION: 5 or 6 flight crew plus (An-24) 36–44 passengers or (An-26) 4500 kg (9920 lb) cargo; An-32, 3 or 4 flight crew plus 50 passengers, 42 paratroops, or 7500 kg (16,525 lb) cargo

MAX SPEED: An-24, 243 kt (450 km/h); An-32, 286 kt (530 km/h)

RANGE: An-24, 296 nm (550 km); An-32, 971 nm (1800 km)

DIMENSIONS (AN-24):
LENGTH: 23.5 m (77 ft 2 in)
WINGSPAN: 29.2 m (95 ft 9 in)
HEIGHT: 8.3 m (27 ft 3 in)

DIMENSIONS (AN-32):
LENGTH: 23.7 m (77 ft 8 in)
WINGSPAN: 29.2 m (9 ft 9 in)
HEIGHT: 8.7 m (28 ft 8 in)

VARIANTS & OPERATORS:
An-24: Afghanistan, Armenia, Azerbaijan, Belarus, Cambodia, China, Cuba, Kazakhstan, Laos, Mali, Mongolia, North Korea, Romania, Russia, Slovak Republic, Syria, Turkmenistan, Ukraine, Uzbekistan
An-26: Afghanistan, Angola, Belarus, Bulgaria, Cape Verde, Chad, China, Cuba, Czech Republic, Ethiopia, Hungary, Kazakhstan, Laos, Libya, Lithuania, Madagascar, Mali, Mongolia, Mozambique, Namibia, Nicaragua, Niger, Poland, Romania, Russia, Serbia, Slovak Republic, Syria, Ukraine, Uzbekistan, Vietnam, Yemen, Zambia
An-32: Afghanistan, Angola, Armenia, Bangladesh, Equatorial Guinea, Ethiopia, India, Libya, Mexico, Peru, Russia, Sri Lanka, USA

FEATURES:
Dihedral tail; shoulder/tapered wing; (An-24/-26) two Progress/Ivchenko AI-24A or (An-32) two AI-20D5 turboprops

Antonov An-70 UKRAINE

Wide-body transport/freighter

The prototype An-70 first flew on December 16, 1994, and was lost on February 10, 1995. Second prototype flown April 24, 1997, with third prototype (An-70T commercial) variant due to fly in 2002, but still had not flown by 2006. Production of ten authorized 1999, but Russian interest evaporated in 2004. Some commercial and military interest remains, but project appears stagnated as of December 2006.

SPECIFICATION:

PAYLOAD/ACCOMMODATION: 3 flight crew and 1 loadmaster plus provision for 300 troop seats, 214 stretchers, or 47,000 kg (103,615 lb) cargo
MAX SPEED: 432 kt (800 km/h)
RANGE: 4319 nm (8000 km)

DIMENSIONS:
LENGTH: 40.7 m (133 ft 7 in)
WINGSPAN: 44.1 m (144 ft 7 in)
HEIGHT: 16.4 m (53 ft 9 in)

VARIANTS & OPERATORS:
An-70: Russia, Ukraine (in limbo)

FEATURES:
Shoulder/tapered wing; four Progress/Ivchenko D27 propfans with eight-bladed propellers; fuselage undercarriage fairings

BAE Systems (HSA) Nimrod MR.2/MRA.4 UK

MPA and ASW aircraft (Nimrod MRA.4 pictured)

Derived from the de Havilland Comet 4C airliner to become the HS.801 Nimrod, the prototype first flew May 23, 1967, and entered RAF service from 1969. 49 Nimrods were built (46 MR.1 and three R.1 ELINT aircraft), of which 35 MR.1s were converted to MR.2 standard. Of these, one has been converted to R.1 standard and 12 MR.2s are now being remanufactured to MRA.4 configuration. First flight on August 26, 2004. ISD is now 2012.

SPECIFICATION:

PAYLOAD/ACCOMMODATION: 3 flight crew and 9 mission specialists
HARDPOINTS: one under each wing for Harpoon ASMs or AIM-9 AAMs (two per wing for MRA.4); fuselage sonobuoy launchers; lower-fuselage bomb bay for mines, depth charges, or Stingray torpedoes, for a max payload of 6120 kg (13,500 lb)
MAX SPEED: 500 kt (926 km/h)
FERRY RANGE: 5000 nm (9265 km)

DIMENSIONS (MR.2):
LENGTH: 39.4 m (129 ft 1 in)
WINGSPAN: 35.0 m (114 ft 10 in)
HEIGHT: 9.1 m (29 ft 8 in)

VARIANTS & OPERATORS:
Nimrod R.1: UK
Nimrod MR.2P: UK
Nimrod MRA.4: UK

FEATURES:
Fin-top ESM pod; mid/swept wings; wingtip ESM pods; four Rolls-Royce Spey Mk.207 (MR.2) or BMW R-R BR710 (MRA.4) turbofans in wing root; tail MAD boom

Nimrod MR.2

BAE Systems (Vickers) VC10 C.1K & K.3/4 UK

Transport/tanker aircraft (VC10 K.3 pictured)

Derived from the civil VC10, first flown on June 29, 1962, and entered RAF service from 1965. The RAF took 14 VC10 C.1 transports, 13 of which later converted to C.1K tanker/transports. Later ex-civil airliners converted to VC10 K.2 (5, now withdrawn), K.3 (4), and K.4 (5) tankers. OSD will depend on arrival in service of A330 FSTA.

SPECIFICATION:

PAYLOAD/ACCOMMODATION: 4/5 flight crew plus (C.1K) plus 137–146 passengers
MAX SPEED: VC10 C.1K, 494 kt (914 km/h); VC10 K.3/4, 494 kt (914 km/h)
RANGE: 4692 nm (8690 km)

DIMENSIONS (VC10 C.1K):
LENGTH: 48.4 m (158 ft 8 in)
WINGSPAN: 44.6 m (146 ft 2 in)
HEIGHT: 12.0 m (39 ft 6 in)

DIMENSIONS (VC10 K.3/4):
LENGTH: 52.3 m (171 ft 8 in)
WINGSPAN: 44.6 m (146 ft 2 in)
HEIGHT: 12.0 m (39 ft 6 in)

VARIANTS & OPERATORS:
VC10 C.1K: UK
VC10 K.3/4: UK

FEATURES:
Swept T-tail; low/swept wings; underwing AAR pods; four rear-fuselage Rolls-Royce Conway Mk.301 turbofans

Beriev (BETAIR) Be-200 Altair RUSSIA

Multirole amphibian

Derived from the A-40/Be-42, which first flew in A-40 guise December 8, 1986, the slightly smaller Be-200 made its "official" first flight on October 17, 1998. Developed as a firefighting water bomber, the Be-200 has been considered for SAR and ASW duties. Most likely military use may be as Russian Border Guards patrol aircraft. Five firm orders from Russia's Ministry of Emergency Situations, as of October 2003, and some export interest expressed.

SPECIFICATION:

PAYLOAD/ACCOMMODATION: 2 flight crew, plus mission specialists, with maximum payload of 7500 kg (16,534 lb) of cargo or 72 passengers plus 2 cabin crew
MAX LEVEL SPEED: 388 kt (720 km/h)
RANGE: 2078 nm (3850 km)

DIMENSIONS:
LENGTH: 31.4 m (103 ft 1 in)
WINGSPAN: 38.8 m (107 ft 6.5 in)
HEIGHT: 8.9 m (29 ft 2.5 in)

VARIANTS & OPERATORS:
Be-200ChS: Russia

FEATURES:
T-tail; shoulder/swept wing with winglets, underwing floats; two upper rear-fuselage-mounted ZMKB Progress D-436TP turbofans; optional nose AAR probe

Beriev (Ilyushin) A-50 "Mainstay" RUSSIA

AEW&C aircraft

Developed from the Il-76 (which see) as an AEW&C aircraft, the prototype A-50 was first flown on December 19, 1978. Has Liana or Vega-M Shmell-II AEW radar in rotating radome above fuselage. About 28 produced.

SPECIFICATION:

PAYLOAD/ACCOMMODATION: 5 flight crew and 10 systems operators
MAX SPEED: 425 kt (785 km/h)
RANGE: 2753 nm (5100 km)

DIMENSIONS:
LENGTH: 46.6 m (152 ft 10 in)
WINGSPAN: 50.5 m (165 ft 8 in)
HEIGHT: 14.8 m (48 ft 5 in)

VARIANTS & OPERATORS:
A-50: China, Russia

FEATURES:
T-tail; shoulder/swept wing; four Aviadvigatel D-30KP-2 turbofans; radar "flying saucer" above rear fuselage; fuselage undercarriage fairings

Boeing (McDonnell Douglas) C-17 Globemaster III USA

Strategic transport aircraft

Developed as C-X from early 1980s, the C-17A first flew September 15, 1991, with first deliveries to USAF from 1993. USAF has over 100 of 120 ordered. Four Boeing-owned aircraft leased to RAF will be bought, plus a fifth. 60 more ordered for USAF in 2002. Ordered by Australia and selected by Canada and NATO (for a "pool" operation) in 2006.

SPECIFICATION:

PAYLOAD/ACCOMMODATION: 2 flight crew and 1 loadmaster, plus 154 passengers, 102 paratroops, or a max of 76,655 kg (169,000 lb) of cargo
MAX SPEED: M0.77
RANGE: 2400 nm (8704 km)

DIMENSIONS:
LENGTH: 53.0 m (174 ft 0 in)
WINGSPAN: 51.7 m (169 ft 9 in)
HEIGHT: 16.8 m (55 ft 1 in)

VARIANTS & OPERATORS:
C-17A: Australia, Canada, NATO, UK, USA

FEATURES:
T-tail; shoulder/swept wing with winglet tips; four wing-mounted P&W F117-PW-100 (PW2040) turbofans; fuselage undercarriage sponsons

Boeing E-3 Sentry AWACS USA

AEW&C aircraft

Based on the airframe of the Boeing 707-320B airliner fitted with AN/APY-1 "flying saucer" radome over the rear fuselage, the first prototype, designated EC-137D, first flew on February 5, 1972. The first E-3A Sentry flew in 1975 and entered USAF service in 1977. British, French, and Saudi E-3s powered by CFM56 turbofans. Production ceased in 1992 with 68 built. Many being upgraded.

SPECIFICATION:

PAYLOAD/ACCOMMODATION: 4 flight crew plus 13 mission specialists
MAX SPEED: 460 kt (853 km/h)
ENDURANCE: over 11 h

DIMENSIONS:
LENGTH: 46.6 m (152 ft 11 in)
WINGSPAN: 44.4 m (145 ft 9 in)
HEIGHT: 12.7 m (41 ft 9 in)

VARIANTS & OPERATORS:
E-3A: NATO, Saudi Arabia
E-3B/C: USAF
E-3D: UK
E-3F: France

FEATURES:
Low/swept wing; radome over rear fuselage; four P&W TF33-PW-100 or CFM International F108 (CFM 56) turbofans, two under each wing

Boeing E-6B Mercury TACAMO II USA

Communications relay aircraft

Based on the airframe of the E-3 Sentry and fitted with an AVLF communications-relay system, the first prototype E-6 flew on June 1, 1987. It replaced EC-130Q Hercules TACAMO in USN service from 1989. A total of 16 produced. Since upgraded, the last being redelivered in December 2006.

SPECIFICATION:

PAYLOAD/ACCOMMODATION: 4 flight crew plus 8 mission specialists
MAX SPEED: 530 kt (981 km/h)
ENDURANCE: over 15 h

DIMENSIONS:
LENGTH: 46.6 m (152 ft 11 in)
WINGSPAN: 45.2 m (148 ft 2 in)
HEIGHT: 12.9 m (42 ft 5 in)

VARIANTS & OPERATORS:
E-6A: USN

FEATURES:
Low/swept wing; radome over rear fuselage; four CFM International F108-CF-100 (CFM56-2A-2) turbofans, two under each wing

Boeing 737 AEW&C (Wedgetail) USA

Airborne early warning and control

The Boeing 737 AEW&C Wedgetail aircraft is based on the Boeing Business Jet (C-40B/C in U.S. service), using the fuselage of the 737-700 with the strengthened wing and undercarriage of the 737-800. It is fitted with a Northrop Grumman MESA radar mounted above the rear fuselage and a 10-station mission fit internally. Selected by Australia in 1999, four ordered in December 2000 with two options exercised in

2004. First flown in Wedgetail configuration on May 20, 2004, all six aircraft should be delivered to the RAAF by the end of 2008. Turkey ordered four similar aircraft in June 2002, with South Korea ordering four in November 2006.

SPECIFICATION:

PAYLOAD/ACCOMMODATION: 3 or 4 flight crew plus up to 10 mission systems crew
MAX FUEL: 32,825 kg (72,367 lb)
MAX SPEED: M0.82
RANGE: 5985 nm (11,084 km)

DIMENSIONS:
LENGTH: 33.6 m (102 ft 6 in)
WINGSPAN: 35.8 m (117 ft 5 in)
HEIGHT: 12.6 m (41 ft 3 in)

VARIANTS & OPERATORS
Boeing 737 AEW&C: Australia (Wedgetail), South Korea, Turkey

FEATURES:
Low/swept wing with winglets; twin underwing CFM56-7 series turbofans; swept tailfin; low/swept tailplane; numerous blade antennae above and below fuselage plus MESA fore-and-aft radar antenna with narrow "mushroom" top above rear fuselage and rear underfuselage strakes; undernose and lower tail fairings for ECM antenna

Boeing E-767 AWACS/KC-767 tanker USA

AWACS and tanker aircraft (KC-767 pictured)

Based on the airframe of the Boeing 767-200ER airliner and fitted with the AN/APY-2 radar, the first prototype E-767 (for Japan) flew on October 10, 1994. With four E-767s in service, Japan plans to buy four more, plus four of the KC-767 AAR tanker variant. Italy has bought four KC-767s, while USAF plans to acquire the type remain in limbo, pending the outcome of the KC-X program in mid-2007.

SPECIFICATION:

PAYLOAD/ACCOMMODATION: AWACS – 2 flight crew plus up to 19 mission specialists
MAX SPEED: over 434 kt (805 km/h)
RANGE: 5000 nm (9260 km)

DIMENSIONS:
LENGTH: 48.5 m (159 ft 2 in)
WINGSPAN: 47.6 m (156 ft 1 in)
HEIGHT: 15.8 m (52 ft 0 in)

VARIANTS & OPERATORS:
E-767: Japan
KC-767: Italy, Japan

FEATURES:
Low/swept wing; "flying saucer" radome over rear fuselage (on E-767); two GE CF6-80C2B6FA turbofans; tail AAR boom (on KC-767) plus underwing AAR pods

E-767

Boeing C-135 series USA

Special-mission aircraft (RC-135U pictured)

As well as the KC-135, the USAF bought 88 non-tanker C-135s. These were adapted for special missions including airborne command post, ELINT, radio relay, range monitoring, SIGINT, trials, weather reconnaissance, and VIP transport. The major variants (albeit built in small numbers) are detailed below.

RC-135V

SPECIFICATION:

PAYLOAD/ACCOMMODATION: 4 flight crew plus various mission specialists
MAX SPEED: EC-135K, 530 kt (982 km/h); RC-135V, 535 kt (991 km/h)
RANGE: EC-135K, 2997 nm (5552 km); RC-135V, 4913 nm (9100 km)

DIMENSIONS (EC-135K):
LENGTH: 41.5 m (136 ft 3 in)
WINGSPAN: 39.9 m (130 ft 10 in)
HEIGHT: 12.3 m (40 ft 7 in)

DIMENSIONS (RC-135V):
LENGTH: 49.9 m (163 ft 9 in)
WINGSPAN: 44.4 m (145 ft 8 in)
HEIGHT: 12.9 m (42 ft 4 in)

VARIANTS & OPERATORS:
C-135B/C/E, EC-135E/K/N, RC-135S Cobra Ball, RC-135U Combat Sent, RC-135V Rivet Joint, TC-135W, WC-135C/W: all in U.S. service

FEATURES:
Low/swept wing; various non-standard radomes/antennae on nose and fuselage; four P&W J57 turbojets, P&W TF33 (JT3D), or (on all -U/-V/-W versions) CFM International F108 (CFM56) turbofans, two under each wing

Boeing KC-135 Stratotanker USA

AAR tanker aircraft

Based on Boeing's Model 367-80, which spawned the Model 707 airliner (USAF: C-137; USN: C-18), with a wider-diameter fuselage. First flew on July 15, 1954, the KC-135 Stratotanker is fitted with the flying boom refuelling system. Boeing and IAI sold tanker conversions of the 707 airliner. The KC-135 has been in USAF service since 1957, taking 732 Stratotankers (of which the KC-135R is the major variant today).

SPECIFICATION:

PAYLOAD/ACCOMMODATION: 4 flight crew plus 1 boom operator
MAX SPEED: 530 kt (982 km/h)
RANGE: 2997 nm (5552 km)

DIMENSIONS:
LENGTH: 41.5 m (136 ft 3 in)
WINGSPAN: 39.9 m (130 ft 10 in)
HEIGHT: 12.3 m (40 ft 7 in)

VARIANTS & OPERATORS:
C-135FR: France
KC-135E: USAF
KC-135R: France, Singapore, Turkey, USAF
KC-135T: USAF
KC-137: Brazil, Venezuela
KC-707: Israel
KE-3A: Saudi Arabia
707 tanker: Australia, Chile, Colombia, Iran, Italy, Peru, South Africa, Spain

FEATURES:
Low/swept wing; flying boom under rear fuselage (some aircraft have underwing refuelling pods); four CFM International F108 (CFM56) or P&W TF33 (JT3D) turbofans

CASA (EADS) C-212 Aviocar SPAIN

Light multirole transport (C-212-300 pictured)

First flown on March 26, 1971, the C-212 has evolved through four major variants. It has been adapted for roles including transport, paratrooper, freighter, ambulance, photographic aircraft, ELINT/ECM and ASW/MPA. Production of Series 100 (153 built) and Series 200 (211 built) ended. Over 460 Series 300/ 400 for military/civil use sold. Built under license in Indonesia by Dirgantara.

C-212-200

SPECIFICATION (Series 300/400):

PAYLOAD/ACCOMMODATION: 2 flight crew plus 25 passengers or 2700 kg (5952 lb) of freight
MAX SPEED: 200 kt (370 km/h)
RANGE: 233 nm (431 km)
WEAPONS: when carried, two fuselage hardpoints for machine gun or rocket pods for 250 kg (551 lb) each

DIMENSIONS:
LENGTH: 16.1 m (53 ft 0 in)
WINGSPAN: 20.3 m (66 ft 6 in)
HEIGHT: 6.6 m (21 ft 8 in)

VARIANTS & OPERATORS:
C-212-100: Chile, Colombia, Indonesia, Portugal, Spain, Thailand
C-212-200: Angola, Argentina, Chile, Colombia, Indonesia, Mexico, Panama, Paraguay, South Africa, Spain, Sweden, Thailand, Uruguay, USA (C-41A), Venezuela, Zimbabwe
C-212-300: Angola, Argentina, Botswana, Chile, Colombia, France, Lesotho, Panama, Portugal, South Africa, Thailand
C-212-300MP: Angola
C-212-400: Dominican Republic, Ecuador, Lesotho, Paraguay, Suriname, Venezuela
C-212-400MP: Venezuela

FEATURES:
Shoulder/straight wing; winglets on Series 300/400 aircraft; two Honeywell TPE331-10R-513C turboprops

CASA (EADS) C-295 SPAIN

Multirole transport

Derived from the CN-235M, the C-295M was first flown on November 28, 1997. Like the C-212 and CN-235M, can be adapted for roles including tactical transport, paratrooper, freighter, and MPA. Spain ordered nine in April 1999 and a market of 300 is foreseen.

SPECIFICATION:

PAYLOAD/ACCOMMODATION: 2 flight crew plus up to 78 passengers, 48 paratroopers, or 7500 kg (16,535 lb) of freight
MAX SPEED: 260 kt (481 km/h)
RANGE: 728 nm (1348 km)

DIMENSIONS:
LENGTH: 24.4 m (80 ft 2 in)
WINGSPAN: 25.8 m (84 ft 8 in)
HEIGHT: 8.6 m (28 ft 2 in)

VARIANTS & OPERATORS:
C-295: Algeria, Brazil, Finland, Jordan, Poland, Portugal, Spain

FEATURES:
Shoulder/tapered wing; fuselage undercarriage fairings; two P&WC PW127G turboprops

Dassault (Breguet) Atlantic 1 & 2 FRANCE

ASW/MPA (Atlantique 2 pictured)

First flown, as Breguet BR 1150, on October 21, 1961, the Franco-German Atlantic 1 entered French Navy service in 1965. German, Italian, and Pakistani aircraft since upgraded. Production of Atlantic 1 (87 built) ended 1974. France converted 28 to Atlantique 2 configuration, the first of which entered service in 1990.

Atlantic 1

SPECIFICATION (Atlantic 1):

PAYLOAD/ACCOMMODATION: 2 flight crew plus 10 mission crew
MAX SPEED: 300 kt (556 km/h)
RANGE: 4200 nm (7778 km)
WEAPONS: bomb bay for bombs, depth charges, or homing torpedoes; underwing hardpoints for rockets and ASMs

DIMENSIONS:
LENGTH: 31.8 m (104 ft 2 in)
WINGSPAN: 36.3 m (119 ft 1 in)
HEIGHT: 11.3 m (37 ft 2 in)

VARIANTS & OPERATORS:
Atlantic 1: Germany (being phased out), Italy, Pakistan
Atlantique 2: France

FEATURES:
Straight/mid-wing; ECM dome atop fin; tail MAD boom; two SNECMA-built Rolls-Royce Tyne RTy.20 Mk.21 turboprops

de Havilland Canada (Bombardier) DHC-5 Buffalo

CANADA

All-weather STOL transport

Developed from the DHC-4, the DHC-5 prototype first flew with GE CT-64 turboprops on April 9, 1964, and served in Canadian and U.S. army (later USAF) as well as being widely exported (with GE CT-82 turboprops). Production (126 built) ended in 1986.

SPECIFICATION:

PAYLOAD/ACCOMMODATION: 2 flight crew and crew chief, plus 41 troops, 35 paratroops, or 8164 kg (18,000 lb) of freight
MAX SPEED: 252 kt (467 km/h)
RANGE: 225 nm (415 km)

DIMENSIONS:
LENGTH: 24.1 m (79 ft 0 in)
WINGSPAN: 29.3 m (96 ft 0 in)
HEIGHT: 8.7 m (28 ft 8 in)

VARIANTS & OPERATORS:
DHC-5D: Brazil, Canada (CC-115), Ecuador, Egypt Indonesia, Kenya, Mexico, Sudan, Tanzania

FEATURES:
High wing; T-tail; two GE CT-82-4 turboprops

Douglas DC-3 Dakota/C-47 Skytrain USA

Multirole transport (Turbo-67 pictured)

The ubiquitous DC-3 Dakota first flew on December 18, 1935, and the last Douglas-built version (total 10,629) was completed in 1946. Many others built in Russia and China as the Li-2. Some aircraft have been converted to turboprop power in the USA (Basler Turbo-67) and South Africa (C-47TP).

DC-3/C-47

SPECIFICATION:

PAYLOAD/ACCOMMODATION: 2 flight crew and 21 passengers
MAX SPEED: 199 kt (368 km/h)
RANGE: 1306 nm (2420 km)

DIMENSIONS:
LENGTH: 19.6 m (64 ft 5 in)
WINGSPAN: 28.9 m (95 ft 0 in)
HEIGHT: 5.2 m (16 ft 11 in)

VARIANTS & OPERATORS:
C-47: Greece, Honduras, Indonesia, Madagascar, Mexico, South Africa, Thailand, Venezuela
C-47TP: South Africa
Dakota C.III: UK (BBMF)
Turbo AC-47: Colombia
Turbo-67: Bolivia, Colombia, El Salvador, Guatemala, Malawi, Mali, Mauritania, Thailand, USA

FEATURES:
Low/tapered wing; tailwheel undercarriage; two Wright Cyclone GR-1820-G102A or P&W Twin Wasp R-1830-S1C3G piston engines, or P&WC PT6A-65AR/-67R turboprops

Embraer EMB-145 (R-99) BRAZIL

Surveillance aircraft

The EMB-145 is derived from the ERJ-145 regional airliner, which first flew on November 17, 1995. The EMB-145SA (R-99A) is an AEW and surveillance aircraft equipped with the Erieye dorsal radar (five ordered), and the EMB-145RS (R-99B) is a remote-sensing variant (three ordered) for Brazil's SIVAM program. Greece and Mexico have ordered variants.

SPECIFICATION:

PAYLOAD/ACCOMMODATION: 2 flight crew and 4-6 mission systems operators
MAX SPEED: 450 kt (833 km/h)
RANGE: 1600 nm (2963 km)

DIMENSIONS:
LENGTH: 29.9 m (98 ft 0 in)
WINGSPAN: 20.0 m (65 ft 9 in)
HEIGHT: 6.8 m (22 ft 2 in)

VARIANTS & OPERATORS:
EMB-145MP: Mexico
EMB-145RS: Brazil
EMB-145SA: Brazil, Greece, Mexico

FEATURES:
Low/swept wing; T-tail; dorsal radar antenna (R-99A); belly-mounted radome and fuselage antenna just forward of wing root (R-99B); two rear-fuselage-mounted Rolls-Royce/Allison AE 3007A1 turbofans

Fokker F27/Fokker 50/60 THE NETHERLANDS

MPA and transport aircraft (F27 Troopship pictured)

The prototype F27 first flew on November 24, 1955, while the follow-on Fokker 50 flew December 28, 1985. A successful civil airliner (Friendship), the F27 was adapted as a military transport (Troopship) and the MPA role (Maritime Enforcer). It was built under license in the USA as the Fairchild-Hiller FH-227. The Fokker 50 and 60 were modern equivalents, falling victim to the bankruptcy of the manufacturer in 1996–97. Production of the F27 (786 built) ended 1986; the Fokker 50/60 (209) in 1997.

SPECIFICATION:

PAYLOAD/ACCOMMODATION: 2 flight crew and 52 passengers, 6261 kg (13,804 lb) freight or (for MPA variant) 4–6 mission systems operators
HARDPOINTS (MPA): 2 x 907 kg (2000 lb) fuselage; 6 x underwing—inner 295 kg (650 lb), center 680 kg (1500 lb), and outer 113 kg (250 lb)
WEAPONS: MPA, homing torpedoes; depth charges; AGMs; ASMs; external fuel tanks
MAX SPEED: F27 series, 259 kt (480 km/h); Fokker 50, 282 kt (522 km/h)
RANGE: MPA—F27 series, 2698 nm (5000 km); Fokker 50, 1700 nm (3148 km)

DIMENSIONS (F27 SERIES):
LENGTH: 23.6 m (77 ft 3 in)
WINGSPAN: 29.0 m (95 ft 2 in)
HEIGHT: 8.7 m (28 ft 6 in)

DIMENSIONS (FOKKER 50):
LENGTH: 25.3 m (82 ft 10 in)
WINGSPAN: 29.0 m (95 ft 2 in)
HEIGHT: 8.3 m (27 ft 3 in)

VARIANTS & OPERATORS:
F27: Algeria, Angola, Argentina, Bolivia, Finland, Ghana, Guatemala, Iceland, Indonesia, Iran, Myanmar, Pakistan, Peru, Philippines, Senegal, Spain, Thailand, USA (C-31A)
Fokker 50: Indonesia, Netherlands, Singapore, Taiwan, Tanzania, Thailand
FH-227: Myanmar

FEATURES:
High/tapered wing; dorsal fin fillet; two wing-mounted Rolls-Royce Dart Mk.552 (F-27/FH-227) or two P&WC PW125B (Fokker 50/60) turboprops; some MPAs have belly radome

Fokker 50

Grumman (N-G) OV-1 Mohawk USA

Observation aircraft

First flown on April 14, 1959, as an observation and intelligence-gathering platform for the U.S. Army. Progressively upgraded but now withdrawn from service. Some transferred to Argentina and South Korea (now withdrawn). Production of the Mohawk (380 built) ended in 1970.

SPECIFICATION:

PAYLOAD/ACCOMMODATION: 2 flight crew and specialized mission equipment and cameras
MAX SPEED: 265 kt (491 km/h)
HARDPOINTS: two under each wing for sensor pods and external fuel tanks
RANGE: 878 nm (1627 km)

DIMENSIONS:
LENGTH: 12.5 m (41 ft 0 in)
WINGSPAN: 14.6 m (48 ft 0 in)
HEIGHT: 3.9 m (12 ft 8 in)

VARIANTS & OPERATORS:
OV-1D: Argentina

FEATURES:
Mid/slightly-swept wing; bulged side-by-side canopy in nose; triple fin; two wing-mounted Lycoming T53-L-701 turboprops

Grumman (N-G) S-2T Tracker USA

MPA & ASW aircraft

A carrier-borne ASW aircraft for the USN, the Tracker was first flown on December 4, 1952, as the XS2F-1. Widely exported and progressively upgraded, including re-engining with turboprops by Marsh Aviation. Production of the Tracker (1269 built) ended in 1967.

SPECIFICATION:

PAYLOAD/ACCOMMODATION: 2 flight crew and 2 mission specialists
HARDPOINTS: three under each wing for bombs, torpedoes, rockets, and external fuel tanks, plus bomb bay for homing torpedoes and depth charges for a max payload of 2182kg (4810 lb)
MAX SPEED: 260 kt (481 km/hr)
RANGE: 1390 nm (2581 km)

DIMENSIONS:

LENGTH: 13.3 m (43 ft 6 in)
WINGSPAN: 22.1 m (72 ft 7 in)
HEIGHT: 5.1 m (16 ft 7 in)

VARIANTS & OPERATORS:

S-2T: Argentina, Taiwan

FEATURES:

Tapered shoulder wing; bulged side-by-side canopy; two wing-mounted (S-2E) Wright R-1820-82 radial engines or (S-2T) AlliedSignal (Garrett) TPE331-15AW turboprops

IAI (Boeing) Phalcon 707 ISRAEL

AEW aircraft

Specifically developed for Chile, this is an IAI conversion of a Boeing 707-385C airliner fitted with the Phalcon solid-state phased-array radar located in antennas located in the nose and large forward fuselage panniers. First flown on May 12, 1993, and delivered to Chile in 1995, where it is called "Condor." One built.

SPECIFICATION:

PAYLOAD/ACCOMMODATION: 3 flight crew and 13 mission specialists
MAX SPEED: 545 kt (1010 km/h)
RANGE: 5000 nm (9265 km)

DIMENSIONS:
LENGTH: 46.6 m (152 ft 11 in)
WINGSPAN: 44.4 m (145 ft 9 in)
HEIGHT: 12.9 m (42 ft 5 in)

VARIANTS & OPERATORS:
Phalcon 707: Chile

FEATURES:
Swept/low wing; four wing-mounted P&W JT3D-7 turbofans; large nose radome; forward fuselage side panniers with radomes fore and aft

Ilyushin Il-38 "May" RUSSIA

MPA and ASW aircraft

Derived from the Il-18D "Coot" airliner (which see), this MPA version first flew on September 27, 1961, and serves with the naval air arms of India and Russia. Now in process of receiving a sensor upgrade. A total of 57 built.

SPECIFICATION:

PAYLOAD/ACCOMMODATION: 3 flight crew plus 9 mission specialists; specialized ASW and surveillance sensor payloads
MAX SPEED: 390 kt (722 km/h)
RANGE: 3887 nm (7200 km)

DIMENSIONS:

LENGTH: 39.6 m (129 ft 10 in)
WINGSPAN: 37.4 m (122 ft 8 in)
HEIGHT: 10.2 m (33 ft 4 in)

VARIANTS & OPERATORS:

Il-38: India, Russia

FEATURES:

Tapered/low wing; with four wing-mounted Ivchenko AI-20M turboprops; round radome under forward fuselage; tail MAD boom

Ilyushin Il-76MD "Candid-B" & Il-78M "Midas" RUSSIA

Transport and tanker aircraft (Il-78MK pictured)

This military transport (also built as the Il-76 civil freighter—which see), first flew on March 25, 1971. It has been developed into into the A-50 "Mainstay" AEW&C version by Beriev (which see) and also the "Midas" three-point AAR tanker. Over 850 of all versions built.

SPECIFICATION:

PAYLOAD/ACCOMMODATION: 5 flight crew and 2 loadmasters, plus 47,000 kg (103,615 lb) freight; "Midas" has two underwing and one rear-fuselage AAR pods
MAX SPEED: 459 kt (850 km/h)
RANGE: 2051 nm (3800 km)
WEAPONS: twin 23 mm GSh-23 guns in tail turret

DIMENSIONS:
LENGTH: 46.6 m (152 ft 10 in)
WINGSPAN: 50.5 m (165 ft 8 in)
HEIGHT: 14.8 m (48 ft 5 in)

VARIANTS & OPERATORS:
Il-76: Algeria, Angola, Armenia, Belarus, China, India, Iran, Libya, North Korea, Russia, Syria, Ukraine, Yemen
Il-78: Algeria, India, Russia, Ukraine

FEATURES:
T-tail; shoulder/swept wing; four Aviadvigatel D-30KP-2 turbofans under wings; glazed lower nose with radome under forward fuselage

Il-76

Kawasaki C-1A JAPAN

Transport aircraft

The first prototype XC-1 military transport first flew on November 12, 1970. The EC-1 ECM training version with a large bulbous nose radome and two smaller forward fuselage side radomes was converted from one transport. A total of 31 built.

SPECIFICATION:

PAYLOAD/ACCOMMODATION: 5 flight crew plus 11,900 kg (26,235 lb) freight
MAX SPEED: 435 kt (806 km/h)
RANGE: 1810 nm (3353 km)

DIMENSIONS:
LENGTH: 29.0 m (95 ft 2 in)
WINGSPAN: 30.6 m (100 ft 5 in)
HEIGHT: 26.5 m (86 ft 11 in)

VARIANTS & OPERATORS:
C-1A: Japan
EC-1: Japan

FEATURES:
T-tail; shoulder/swept wing; two Mitsubishi (P&W) JT8D-M-9 turbofans under wings

Lockheed S-3B Viking USA

Carrier-borne ASW aircraft

Prototype first flown January 21, 1972, and entered USN service in 1974. A total of 187 S-3As built, including five US-3A COD versions and one KS-3A dedicated AAR tanker. First flight of developed S-3B on September 13, 1984; 122 A-models brought up to this standard (in service), plus 16 to ES-3B EW standard (now withdrawn). Planned withdrawal by 2009.

SPECIFICATION:

PAYLOAD/ACCOMMODATION: 2 flight crew and 2/3 mission specialists
MAX SPEED: 450 kt (834 km/h)
RANGE: 2000 nm (3706 km)
HARDPOINTS: one under each wing for mines, Harpoon/SLAM ASMs, external tanks, or "buddy" AAR pod; fuselage sonobuoy launchers; fuselage bomb bay for mines, depth charges, or torpedoes

DIMENSIONS:
LENGTH: 16.3 m (53 ft 4 in)
WINGSPAN: 20.9 m (68 ft 8 in)
HEIGHT: 6.9 m (22ft 9 in)

VARIANTS & OPERATORS:
S-3B: USA (40 aircraft in six squadrons)

FEATURES:
Shoulder/swept wing; two underwing-mounted GE TF34-GE-2 turbofans; retractable MAD tail boom; bulged side-by-side canopy

Lockheed U-2S USA

High-altitude recce aircraft

The prototype "Dragon Lady" was first flown on August 4, 1955, and an unspecified number built for USAF and CIA use. The U-2R flew in 1967 and 12 were procured. Another 37 versions built from 1979, comprising 16 U-2Rs, one U-2RT trainer, 16 TR-1As, two TR-1B trainers, and two ER-2s for NASA. From 1994, remaining aircraft re-engined as U-2S/ TU-2S and have undergone a cockpit avionics upgrade.

SPECIFICATION:

PAYLOAD/ACCOMMODATION: U-2S, pilot; TU-2S, pilot and instructor
MAX SPEED: 673+ kt (692+ km/h)
RANGE: 2605+ nm (4830+ km)
HARDPOINTS: one under each wing for mission pods of various sensor equipment, plus fuselage-mounted sensors

DIMENSIONS:
LENGTH: 19.2 m (63 ft 0 in)
WINGSPAN: 31.4 m (103 ft 0 in)
HEIGHT: 4.9 m (16 ft 0 in)

VARIANTS & OPERATORS:
U-2S: USA
TU-2S: USA

FEATURES:
Shoulder/tapered wing; some aircraft have wing pods; one GE F118-GE-101 turbofan; various radomes/antennas, depending on configuration

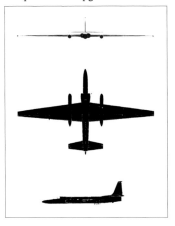

Lockheed Martin C-130A/B/E/H Hercules USA

Transport & special-mission aircraft (C-130B pictured below, C-130K bottom)

Rightfully known as "ubiquitous," the prototype YC-130 first flew on August 23, 1954, and entered USAF service in 1956. The C-130 was developed through many versions and specialized variants and sold worldwide. All USAF, USN, and USMC versions of the Hercules (other than the J model—which see) will receive an Avionics Modernization Program. 2156 first-generation Hercules (not the J model) were built, comprising two YC-130s, 231 C-130As, 230 C-130Bs, 491 C-130Es, 1089 C-130Hs, 113 L-100 civil freighters.

SPECIFICATION:

PAYLOAD/ACCOMMODATION: 5 flight crew plus (standard) 94 troops, 64 paratroopers, or 19,356 kg (42,673 lb) freight or (-30 models) 128 troops, 92 paratroops, or 17,645 kg (38,900 lb) freight
MAX SPEED: 325 kt (602 km/h)
RANGE: 4250 nm (7876 km)

DIMENSIONS:
LENGTH: standard, 29.8 m (97 ft 9 in); -30 models, 34.4 m (112 ft 9 in)
WINGSPAN: 40.4 m (132 ft 7 in)
HEIGHT: 11.7 m (38 ft 3 in)

VARIANTS & OPERATORS:
Algeria (C-130H/H-30, L-100-30), Angola (L-100-30), Argentina (C-130B/H, KC-130H, L-100-30), Australia (C-130H, EC-130H), Austria (C-130K), Bangladesh (C-130B), Belgium (C-130H), Bolivia (C-130B/H), Botswana (C-130F), Brazil (C-130E/H, KC-130H), Cameroon (C-130H/H-30), Canada (C-130E/H/H-30, KC-130H), Chad (C-130A/H/H-30), Chile (C-130B/H), Colombia (C-130B/H), Ecuador (C-130B/H, L-100-30), Egypt (C-130H/

KC-130H pictured below

H-30, VC-130H), Ethiopia (C-130B), France (C-130H/H-30), Gabon (C-130H, L-100-30), Greece (C-130B/H), Honduras (C-130A), Indonesia (C-130B/H/H-30, KC-130B, L-100-30), Iran (C-130E/H), Iraq (C-130E), Israel (C-130E/H, EC-130, KC-130H), Japan (C-130H), Jordan (C-130H), Kuwait (L-100-30), Libya (C-130H,

L-100-20/-30), Malaysia (C-130H/H-30, KC-130H), Mexico (C-130A/E/K/K-30, L-100-30), Morocco (C-130H, KC-130H), Netherlands (C-130H-30/K), New Zealand (C-130H), Niger (C-130H), Nigeria (C-130H/H-30), Norway (C-130H), Oman (C-130H), Pakistan (C-130B/E, L-100), Peru (L-100-20), Philippines (C-130B/H, L-100-20), Portugal (C-130H/H-30), Romania (C-130B/H), Saudi Arabia (C-130E/H/H-30, KC-130H, VC-130H, L-100-30), Singapore (C-130H, KC-130B/H), South Africa (C-130B), South Korea (C-130H/H-30), Spain (C-130H/ H-30, KC-130H), Sri Lanka (C-130K), Sudan (C-130H), Sweden (C-130H), Taiwan (C-130H/HE), Thailand (C-130H/H-30), Tunisia (C-130B/H), Turkey (C-130B/E), UAE/Abu Dhabi (C-130H), UAE/Dubai (C-130H-30, L-100-30), Uruguay (C-130B), UK (C-130K/ K-30), USA (AC-130H/U [see earlier separate entry], C-130E/H/T, EC-130E/H, HC-130H/N/P, KC-130F/R/T/T-30, LC-130H/R, MC-130E/H/P, NC-130A/H), Venezuela (C-130H), Yemen (C-130H)

FEATURES:
Shoulder/straight wing; with four wing-mounted Allison (R-R) T56-A-15 turboprops; underwing fuel tanks; lower fuselage undercarriage fairings

C-130H

Lockheed Martin C-130J/J-30 Super Hercules USA

Transport & special-mission aircraft (C-130J Hercules C.5 pictured)

The first "next-generation" C-130J Hercules II (or Super Hercules) flew April 5, 1996 (a USAF evaluation aircraft). The UK placed the first formal order for 15 C-130J-30s (Hercules C.4) and 10 C-130Js (Hercules C.5). In the USA, the Air National Guard and Air Force Reserve Command took the first USAF aircraft. As of late 2006, 186 Super Hercules were on order and 143 delivered.

SPECIFICATION:

PAYLOAD/ACCOMMODATION: 2 flight crew plus loadmaster with (C-130J) 94 troops, 64 paratroopers, or 18,955 kg (41,790 lb) freight or (C-130J-30) 128 troops, 92 paratroops, or 17,264 kg (38,061 lb) freight
MAX SPEED: 348 kt (645 km/h)
RANGE: 2835 nm (5250 km)

DIMENSIONS:
LENGTH: C-130J, 29.8 m (97 ft 9 in); C-130J-30, 34.4 m (112 ft 9 in)
WINGSPAN: 40.4 m (132 ft 7 in)
HEIGHT: 11.7 m (38 ft 3 in)

VARIANTS & OPERATORS:
C-130J: Italy, UK, USAF
C-130J-30: Australia, Denmark, Italy, UK, USAF
EC-130J: USAF
HC-130J: U.S. Coast Guard
KC-130J: USMC
WC-130J: USAF

FEATURES:
Shoulder/straight wing; four wing-mounted Rolls-Royce (Allison) AE2100D3 turboprops; lower fuselage undercarriage fairings

Lockheed Martin C-5 Galaxy USA

Bulk military freighter (C-5M pictured)

First flown on June 30, 1968, the C-5A Galaxy entered USAF service in 1969, with the improved C-5B from 1984. A third iteration, the C-5M, is now under development involving an avionics upgrade and new engines. First flown on June 19, 2006. A total of 81 C-5As and 50 C-5Bs built.

SPECIFICATION:

PAYLOAD/ACCOMMODATION: 5 flight crew plus 118,387 kg (261,000 lb) freight
MAX SPEED: 496 kt (919 km/h)
RANGE: 5618 nm (10,411 km)

DIMENSIONS:
LENGTH: 75.5 m (247 ft 10 in)
WINGSPAN: 67.9 m (222 ft 8 in)
HEIGHT: 19.8 m (65 ft 1 in)

VARIANTS & OPERATORS:
C-5A/B/C/M: USA

FEATURES:
T-tail; shoulder/swept wing; four GE TF39-GE-1C turbofans under wings (on A/B/C models) and GE CF6-80C2 turbofans (on C-5M); lower fuselage undercarriage fairings

C-5B

Lockheed Martin P-3 Orion USA

MPA/ASW and special-mission aircraft (AP-3C pictured)

Converted from the Electra airliner, the first YP-3A flew on November 25, 1959, and entered USN service in 1962. The P-3A and B models were followed by the P-3C plus three update configurations. Sold widely, many Orions are being further upgraded. A total of were 650 built.

P-3C

SPECIFICATION:

PAYLOAD/ACCOMMODATION: 3 flight crew and 7 mission specialists
MAX SPEED: 411 kt (761 km/h)
RANGE: 2070 nm (3835 km)
HARDPOINTS: three under each wing for mines, Harpoon/SLAM ASMs, or AIM-9 AAMs; rear fuselage sonobuoy launchers; fuselage bomb bay for mines, depth charges, or torpedoes for a max payload of 3290 kg (7252 lb)

DIMENSIONS:
LENGTH: 35.6 m (116 ft 10 in)
WINGSPAN: 30.4 m (99 ft 8 in)
HEIGHT: 10.3 m (33 ft 8 in)

VARIANTS & OPERATORS:
Argentina (P-3B), Australia (AP-3C, EP-3C, P-3W), Brazil (P-3AM), Canada (CP-140 Aurora, CP-140A Arcturus), Chile (P-3A, UP-3A), Germany (P-3C), Greece (P-3B), Iran (P-3F), New Zealand (P-3K), Norway (P-3C/N), Pakistan (P-3C), Portugal (P-3P), South Korea (P-3B/C), Spain (P-3A/B), Thailand (P-3T, UP-3T), USA (VP-3A, P-3C, EP-3E, NP-3C/D)

FEATURES:
Low/tapered wing; four wing-mounted Allison (Rolls-Royce) T56-A-14 turboprops; tail MAD boom; various radomes and antennas for special-mission aircraft

McDonnell Douglas KC-10A Extender USA

Tanker/transport aircraft

Based on the DC-10-30F airliner, the first KC-10A flew on July 12, 1980, and entered USAF service in 1981. A number now equipped to carry Flight Refuelling Mk32B AAR pods. Last of 60 Extenders delivered in 1990. In 1995, the Netherlands took delivery of two KDC-10 tankers converted from civil airliners but essentially similar to the Extender.

SPECIFICATION:

PAYLOAD/ACCOMMODATION: 3 flight crew and boom operator plus 76,843 kg (169,409 lb) cargo
MAX SPEED: 530 kt (982 km/h)
RANGE: 3797 nm (7032 km)
HARDPOINTS: one under each wing for AAR pods

DIMENSIONS:
LENGTH: 55.3 m (182 ft 7 in)
WINGSPAN: 50.4 m (165 ft 4 in)
HEIGHT: 17.7 m (58 ft 1 in)

VARIANTS & OPERATORS:
KC-10A: USA
KDC-10: Netherlands

FEATURES:
Low/swept wing; two wing-mounted and one fin-mounted GE CF6-50C2 turbofans; advanced aerial refuelling boom under tail; some underwing AAR pods

Northrop Grumman E-2C Hawkeye USA

AEW and control aircraft

The prototype E-2A first flew October 21, 1960, followed by E-2B upgrade and prototype E-2C on January 20, 1971. AEW radar progressively improved from AN/APS-120 through -125, -138, -139 to AN/APS-145. Latest version known as Hawkeye 2000. Modest exports. 211 built/on order.

SPECIFICATION:

PAYLOAD/ACCOMMODATION: 2 flight crew plus 3 mission specialists
MAX SPEED: 338 kt (626 km/h)
FERRY RANGE: 1541 nm (2854 km)

DIMENSIONS:
LENGTH: 17.6 m (57 ft 9 in)
WINGSPAN: 24.6 m (80 ft 7 in)
HEIGHT: 5.6 m (18 ft 4 in)

VARIANTS & OPERATORS:
E-2C: Egypt, France, Japan, Mexico, Singapore, USN
E-2D Advanced Hawkeye: USN (on order)
E-2T: Taiwan
TE-2C: USN

FEATURES:
Four fins; tapered wing; two wing-mounted Allison (Rolls-Royce) T56-A-427 turboprops; "flying saucer" rotodome above fuselage

Northrop Grumman (Boeing) E-8 Joint STARS USA

Ground-surveillance/battle-management aircraft

Converted from Boeing 707-300 series airliners and fitted with AN/APY-3 SLAR in canoe fairing under forward fuselage, the first flight of E-8A full-scale development aircraft in Joint STARS configuration was December 22, 1988. In addition to two E-8A development aircraft and one E-8C permanent testbed, a total of 17 E-8C production aircraft delivered.

SPECIFICATION:

PAYLOAD/ACCOMMODATION: 4 flight crew plus 18 mission specialists (plus some reserve crew for long missions)
MAX SPEED: M0.84
ENDURANCE: 11 h on internal fuel

DIMENSIONS:
LENGTH: 46.6 m (152 ft 11 in)
WINGSPAN: 44.4 m (145 ft 9 in)
HEIGHT: 12.9 m (42 ft 6 in)

VARIANTS & OPERATORS:
E-8A/C: USAF

FEATURES:
Swept wing; four underwing-mounted P&W TF33-P-102C turbofans; canoe radome below forward fuselage

Raytheon (Beech) C-12 & RC-12 Guardrail USA

Transport and ELINT aircraft (RC-12 pictured)

Two distinct military variants have evolved from the Beech (Super) King Air 200, which first flew on October 27, 1972: the C-12 Huron utility transports for the USAF (UC-12 for the USN/USMC) and the RC-12 Guardrail special-mission aircraft for the U.S. Army. Over 1789 aircraft (of all variants) built.

RC-12

SPECIFICATION:

PAYLOAD/ACCOMMODATION: 2 flight crew plus (UC/C-12) 7 passengers or (RC-12) various mission specialists
MAX SPEED: 292 kt (541 km/h)
RANGE: 1850 nm (3426 km)

DIMENSIONS:
LENGTH: 13.4 m (43 ft 10 in)
WINGSPAN: 16.6 m (54 ft 6 in)
HEIGHT: 4.5 m (14 ft 10 in)

VARIANTS & OPERATORS:
King Air 200: Algeria, Argentina, Bolivia, Botswana, Burkina Faso, Chile, Colombia, Ecuador, Israel, Malaysia, Mexico, Morocco, New Zealand, South Africa, Sri Lanka, Thailand, Togo, Turkey, Uruguay, Venezuela
C-12A/R/AP Huron: Greece
C-12C/D/F Huron: USAF
C-12R: U.S. Army
UC-12B/F/M: USN, USMC
RC-12D/K: Israel, U.S. Army
RC-12F/H/N/P/Q: U.S. Army

FEATURES:
T-tail; tapered wing; two wing-mounted P&WC PT6A-42 turboprops; RC-12 has wingtip tanks and various wing- and fuselage-mounted radomes and antenna sets (depending on variant)

Raytheon (Bombardier) Sentinel R.1 USA

Ground-surveillance aircraft

Raytheon Systems Limited was chosen as the UK MoD's ASTOR requirement in June 1999, using Bombardier Global Express airframes, with an ASARS-2 ground surveillance radar system with SAR/MTI modes. An aerodynamically representative airframe was flown August 3, 2001, with the first production airframe (ZJ690) making its maiden flight on May 26, 2004. Sentinel entered RAF service with 5 Sqn in early 2007.

SPECIFICATION:

PAYLOAD/ACCOMMODATION: 2 flight crew plus 3 mission specialists
MAX SPEED: 505 kt (935 km/h)
RANGE: 5320 nm (9852 km)

DIMENSIONS:
LENGTH: 30.3 m (99 ft 5 in)
WINGSPAN: 28.7 m (94 ft 0 in)
HEIGHT: 8.2 m (26 ft 1 in)

VARIANTS & OPERATORS:
Sentinel R.1: RAF (5)

FEATURES:
Low/swept wing with winglets; two tail-mounted Rolls-Royce Deutschland BR710 turbofans; swept T-tail with swept anhedral; dorsal radome on forward fuselage; ventral canoe antenna
Not to be confused with Cessna 750 Citation X, Gulfstream Aerospace Gulfstream IV, or Gulfstream V

Saab 340 AEW&C (S 100B Argus) SWEDEN

Transport and AEW&C aircraft

Derived from the Saab 340 airliner, which first flew on January 25, 1983, the AEW&C (S 100B) version first flew (minus Ericsson PS-890 Erieye SLAR antenna) on January 17, 1994. Six ordered for Swedish Air Force, plus one 340B for royal/VIP duties. Production ceased in 1999 with 459 built, including the three test aircraft.

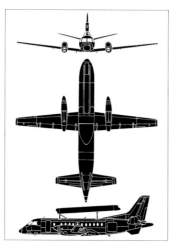

SPECIFICATION:

PAYLOAD/ACCOMMODATION: 2+1 flight crew plus (VIP) about 20 passengers or (S 100B) up to 10 mission specialists
MAX SPEED: 272 kt (504 km/h)
RANGE: 940 nm (1566 km)

DIMENSIONS:
LENGTH: 19.7 m (64 ft 8 in)
WINGSPAN: 21.4 m (70 ft 4 in)
HEIGHT: 6.9 m (22 ft 6 in)

VARIANTS & OPERATORS:
S 340B: Sweden
S 340 AEW&C: Sweden

FEATURES:
Tapered wing; two wing-mounted GE CT7-5A2 turboprops; above-fuselage lateral antenna for radar; rear fuselage ventral fins

ShinMaywa US-1A/US-2 JAPAN

SAR amphibian (US-2 pictured)

First flown on October 16, 1974, 17 have been delivered to the JMSDF (first delivery 1975), with a further four planned. Now being upgraded with new mission system and new Rolls-Royce AE2100J turbo-props. First flown as US-1A*kai* on December 18, 2003, and now re-designated US-2.

US-1

SPECIFICATION:

PAYLOAD/ACCOMMODATION: 9 crew plus 20 seated survivors
MAX SPEED: 276 kt (511 km/h)
RANGE: 2060 nm (3817 km)

DIMENSIONS:
LENGTH: 33.5 m (109 ft 9 in)
WINGSPAN: 33.1 m (108 ft 9 in)
HEIGHT: 9.9 m (32 ft 8 in)

VARIANTS & OPERATORS:
US-1A/US-2: Japan

FEATURES:
T-tail; tapered wing; four wing-mounted GE T64-IHI-10J turboprops (Rolls-Royce AE2110Js on US-2); bulged nose radome; underwing floats

465

Transall C.160 FRANCE/GERMANY

Transport aircraft (C.160 NGR pictured)

Developed by the European Transall (Transporter Allianz) group, the first prototype C.160 flew on February 25, 1963. The first production batch of 169 aircraft completed by 1972. First of a second series (C.160NG) for France flown on April 9, 1981, and 29 completed by 1985.

C.160D

SPECIFICATION:

PAYLOAD/ACCOMMODATION: 3 flight crew plus 93 seated troops, 61–88 paratroops, or up to 8000 kg (17,637 lb) cargo; assorted mission specialists for C.160G/H versions
MAX SPEED: 277 kt (513 km/h)
RANGE: 2750 nm (5095 km)

DIMENSIONS:
LENGTH: 32.4 m (106 ft 3 in)
WINGSPAN: 40.0 m (131 ft 3 in)
HEIGHT: 11.6 m (38 ft 3 in)

VARIANTS & OPERATORS:
C.160D: Germany, Turkey
C.160G Gabriel: France
C.160H Asarté: France
C.160NGR: France
C.160R: France

FEATURES:
High/tapered wing; two wing-mounted Rolls-Royce Tyne RTy.20 Mk.22 turboprops; various antenna/radomes on C.160G Gabriel

Military
Helicopters

Aerospatiale (Eurocopter) SA 313/315
Alouette II/Lama FRANCE
General-purpose helicopter

First flown as the Sud-Aviation SE 3130 on March 12, 1955, the Alouette II became the SA 313 under Aerospatiale. The SA 315B Lama has the reinforced airframe of the SA 313 with rotor system and Artouste engine of the SA 316 (which see). License-built in Brazil by Helibras as the Gaviao, in India by HAL as the Cheetah, and in Romania by IAR-Brazov. With the Astazou engine, the Alouette II is re-designated SA 318C. A total of 1534 Aloutte IIs (of all versions) were built.

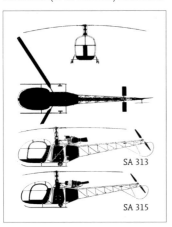

SA 313

SA 315

SPECIFICATION:

ACCOMMODATION: 1 pilot plus 4 passengers or 1135 kg (2500 lb) external sling load
MAX SPEED: 110 kt (205 km/h)
RANGE: 278 nm (51 km)

DIMENSIONS:
MAIN ROTOR DIAMETER: 11.0 m (36 ft 2 in)
LENGTH: 12.9 m (42 ft 5 in)
HEIGHT: 3.1 m (10 ft 2 in)

VARIANTS & OPERATORS:
SA 313: Guinea-Bissau
SA 315B: Angola (Lama), Argentina (Lama), Bolivia (Gaviao and Lama), Ecuador (Lama), Morocco (Lama), India (Cheetah), Namibia (Cheetah), Nepal (Cheetah), Pakistan (Lama), Peru (Lama), Togo (Lama)
SA 318C: Belgium, Cameroon, Senegal, Turkey

FEATURES:
Bubble canopy; open rear fuselage; single Turbomeca Artouste IIC.6/IIIB (SA 313/315) or Astazou IIA (SA 318) turboshaft; skid undercarriage

Aerospatiale (Eurocopter) SA 316/319 Alouette III FRANCE

General-purpose helicopter

First flown as the Sud-Aviation SE 3160 on February 28, 1959, the Alouette III became the SA 316 under Aerospatiale. A development of the Alouette II with a larger cabin, greater power, improved equipment, and higher performance. SA 319B Alouette III is powered by the Astazou engine. The SA 316/319B has been license-built in India (as the Chetak), Romania (IAR-316), and Switzerland. A total of 1455 Alouette IIIs were built.

SA 316

SA 319

SPECIFICATION:

ACCOMMODATION: 1 pilot plus 6 passengers plus 750 kg (1650 lb) external sling load
MAX SPEED: 113 kt (210 km/h)
RANGE: 290 nm (540 km)

ARMAMENT (WHEN FITTED):

INTERNAL GUNS: cabin-mounted 7.62 mm machine gun or 20 mm MG 151/20 cannon
HARDPOINTS: up to four on cabin-mounted pylons
REPRESENTATIVE WEAPONS: four AS 11 or two AS 12 missiles

DIMENSIONS:

MAIN ROTOR DIAMETER: 11.0 m (36 ft 2 in)
LENGTH: 12.8 m (42 ft 1 in)
HEIGHT: 3.0 m (9 ft 10 in)

VARIANTS & OPERATORS:

SA 316 (SE 3160): Argentina, Austria, Burundi, Chad, China, Ecuador, Ethiopia, France, Gabon, Guinea-Bissau, India (Chetak & Lancer), Jordan, Lebanon, Malaysia, Malta, Mauritius (Chetak), Morocco, Namibia (Chetak), Nepal (Chetak), Netherlands, Pakistan (IAR-316 and SA 316), Portugal, Romania (IAR-316), Senegal, South Africa, Swaziland, Switzerland, Tunisia, Venezuela, Zimbabwe
SA 319: Albania, Austria, Belgium, Cameroon, France, Greece, India, South Korea

FEATURES:

Rounded, glazed nose; single Turbomeca Artouste IIIB (SA 316) or Astazou XIV (SA 319) turboshaft; wheeled undercarriage

Aerospatiale (Eurocopter) SA 321 Super Frelon FRANCE

Heavy-duty helicopter

Derived from the smaller Frelon, the Super Frelon (originally designated SE 3210) first flew December 7, 1962. Developed in troop carrier and naval ASW versions, it was license-produced in China as the Changhe Z-8. Over 100 Super Frelons were built.

SPECIFICATION:

ACCOMMODATION: 3 flight crew plus 27–30 passengers or 5000 kg (11,023 lb) internal or external cargo
MAX SPEED: 148 kt (275 km/h)
RANGE: 549 nm (1020 km)

ARMAMENT (SA 321G/H):

HARDPOINTS: up to four
REPRESENTATIVE WEAPONS: four homing torpedoes or two AM-39 Exocet ASMs

DIMENSIONS:

MAIN ROTOR DIAMETER: 18.9 m (62 ft 0 in)
LENGTH: 23.0 m (75 ft 7 in)
HEIGHT: 6.8 m (22 ft 2 in)

VARIANTS & OPERATORS:

SA 321: France, Libya
Z-8: China

FEATURES:

Boat-hull bottom to fuselage; nose radome; rear-fuselage sponsons; three Turbomeca Turmo IIIC turboshafts; wheeled undercarriage

Aerospatiale (Eurocopter) SA 330 Puma FRANCE

Medium transport helicopter

Developed for a French Army requirement, the prototype Puma flew on April 15, 1965. Chosen for the RAF, Westland and Aerospatiale jointly produced the Puma for the RAF. License-built in Romania, assembled in Indonesia and remanufactured in South Africa (as the Oryx). Production ceased 1987 with 697 Pumas built.

SA 330E

SPECIFICATION:

ACCOMMODATION: 2 (+1) flight crew plus 16–20 passengers or 3200 kg (7055 lb) external slung cargo
MAX SPEED: 158 kt (294 km/h)
RANGE: 309 nm (572 km)

ARMAMENT (PUMA SOCAT):
INTERNAL GUNS: Giat 20 mm cannon in undernose turret
HARDPOINTS: up to four on cabin pylons
REPRESENTATIVE WEAPONS: AAMs; ATGWs; 57 mm or 70 mm rocket pods

DIMENSIONS:
MAIN ROTOR DIAMETER: 15.0 m (49 ft 2 in)
LENGTH: 18.5 m (59 ft 6 in)
HEIGHT: 5.1 m (16 ft 10 in)

VARIANTS & OPERATORS:
Argentina (SA 330L), Cameroon (SA 330C), Ethiopia (SA 330H, IAR-330), France (SA 330B/Ba), Gabon (SA 330C), Guinea Republic (IAR-330L), Indonesia (NAS 330J/L/SM), Kenya (SA 330H, IAR-330L), Kuwait (SA 330F), Lebanon (SA 330L), Malawi (SA 330J), Mexico (SA 330S), Morocco (SA 330C/F/G), Oman (SA 330J), Pakistan (SA 330J), Philippines (SA 330L), Portugal (SA 330S), Romania (IAR-330, SOCAT), Spain (SA 330H/J), Sudan (IAR-330L), UAE (SA 330C, IAR-330L), UK (SA 330E Puma HC.1)

FEATURES:
Air intakes over cabin; rear-fuselage sponsons; two Turbomeca Turmo IVC turboshafts; wheeled undercarriage; tailplane to port of boom; tail rotor to right

Aerospatiale (Eurocopter) SA 341/342 Gazelle FRANCE

Light utility helicopter (SA 342M pictured)

The Gazelle prototype was first flown on April 7, 1967, and the SA 341 became part of the Westland/Aerospatiale joint program (with the SA 330 Puma and WG 13 Lynx for the French and British services). Features a Fenestron enclosed tail rotor. The SA 342 has an improved powerplant and highter take-off weight. License-built by Soko in the former Yugoslavia. Over 800 Gazelles of all versions built.

SA 341

SPECIFICATION:

ACCOMMODATION: 1 or 2 flight crew plus 3 passengers
MAX SPEED: 167 kt (310 km/h)
RANGE: 194 nm (360 km)

ARMAMENT (SA 342L/M):
HARDPOINTS: up to four on cabin pylons
REPRESENTATIVE WEAPONS: Mistral AAMs; AS 11, AS 12, or HOT ATGWs; 2.75 in or 67 mm rocket pods

DIMENSIONS:
MAIN ROTOR DIAMETER: 10.5 m (34 ft 5 in)
LENGTH: 12.0 m (39 ft 4 in)
HEIGHT: 3.1 m (10 ft 3 in)

VARIANTS & OPERATORS:
Angola (SA 342L), Bosnia and Herzegovina (SA 341H, SA 342L), Burundi (SA 342L), Cameroon (SA 342L), China (SA342L), Cyprus (SA 343L), Ecuador (SA 342K/L), Egypt (SA 342K/L), France (SA 341F, SA 342L/M), Gabon (SA 342L), Guinea Rep. (SA 342L), Ireland (SA 342L), Kuwait (SA 342L), Lebanon (SA 342L), Libya (SA 342L), Montenegro (SA 342L), Morocco (SA 342K,L), Qatar (SA 342L), Serbia (SA 341H, SA 342L), Syria (SA 342L), UAE (Abu Dhabi—SA 342J/L), UK (SA 341B Gazelle AH.1)

FEATURES:
Glazed cabin; one Turbomeca Astazou IIIA (SA 341) or Astazou XIVM (SA 342L) turboshaft with upturned exhaust; skid undercarriage; Fenestron in tailboom

Agusta (A-W) A 109 ITALY

Light utility helicopter (A109LUH pictured)

The prototype A 109A, powered by an Allison 250 turboshaft engine, was first flown on August 4, 1971, with deliveries starting in 1976. Progressively developed (including reengining with PW 206 or Arriel) and sold widely on both civil and military markets. Over 600 A 109s of all versions built or on order.

A 109A

SPECIFICATION:

ACCOMMODATION: 1 or 2 flight crew plus 6 or 7 passengers
MAX SPEED: 168 kt (311 km/h)
RANGE: 352 nm (652 km)

ARMAMENT (A 109CM/HA):
INTERNAL GUNS: cabin-mounted 7.62 mm or 12.7 mm machine gun
HARDPOINTS: two lateral pylons
MAX WEAPON LOAD: 600 kg (1322 lb)
REPRESENTATIVE WEAPONS: TOW ATGWs; 2.75 in or 81 mm rocket pods; 12.7 mm machine gun pod

DIMENSIONS:
MAIN ROTOR DIAMETER: 11.0 m (36 ft 1 in)
LENGTH: 11.4 m (37 ft 6 in)
HEIGHT: 3.5 m (11 ft 6 in)

VARIANTS & OPERATORS:
Argentina (A 109A), Belgium (A 109BA), Ghana (A 109), Greece (A 109E Power), Italy (A 109A/A-II/ C/CM/E Power), Malaysia (A 109E Power, LUH), Nigeria (A 109E Power, LUH), Peru (A 109K2), South Africa (A 109LUH), Sweden (A 109M/Hkp15), Turkey (A 109A), UAE (Dubai—A 109K2), UK (A 109A/E Power), USA (MH-68 Sting Ray), Venezuela (A 109A)

FEATURES:
Slender fuselage; tailboom has upper and ventral fin; port tail rotor; two Allison 250-C turboshafts; retractable wheel undercarriage

Agusta (A-W) A 129 Mangusta ITALY

Light attack helicopter

The Mangusta prototype first flew on September 11, 1983, with deliveries starting in 1990. Standard tandem cockpit and powered by two Gem 1004 turboshafts. Multirole and shipborne plus international versions (with T800 turboshafts) developed but not sold. Only 60 A 129s built to date.

SPECIFICATION:

ACCOMMODATION: 2 flight crew
MAX SPEED: 159 kt (294 km/h)
RANGE: 303 nm (561 km)

ARMAMENT:

INTERNAL GUNS: 20 mm cannon in nose turret on CBT version
HARDPOINTS: four pylons
MAX WEAPON LOAD: 1000 kg (2204 lb)
REPRESENTATIVE WEAPONS: Stinger or Mistral AAMs; TOW ATGWs; 2.75 in, 70 mm, or 81 mm rocket pods; 12.7 mm machine gun or 20 mm cannon pods

DIMENSIONS:

MAIN ROTOR DIAMETER: 11.9 m (39 ft in)
LENGTH: 14.3 m (46 ft 10 in)
HEIGHT: 2.3 m (9 ft 0 in)

VARIANTS & OPERATORS:

A 129: Italy (upgraded to A129CBT)

FEATURES:

Tandem cockpit; port tail rotor; two Rolls-Royce Gem 1004 (A 129) or LHTEC T800-LHT-800 (A 129 International) turboshafts; fixed-wheel undercarriage

AgustaWestland Industries (EHI) EH 101 Merlin ITALY/UK

Multirole helicopter (Merlin HC.3 pictured)

Evolved as a joint project between Agusta of Italy and the UK's Westland to produce a Sea King replacement helicopter from 1981. First EH 101 (the first preproduction aircraft—PP1) flown on October 9, 1987. Nine PP aircraft flown in three main configurations: naval, utility, and civil. The Merlin HM.1 ASW entered Royal Navy service in 2002. A total of 112 EH 101s built or on order.

Merlin HM.1

SPECIFICATION:

ACCOMMODATION: 2 pilots plus specialized mission crew or 30 passengers (Series 300) or 30–45 troops
MAX SPEED: 167 kt (309 km/h)
RADIUS OF ACTION: SAR, 350 nm (648 km)

ARMAMENT:

INTERNAL GUNS: provision for a nose-mounted 0.5 n (12.7 mm) machine gun chin turret
HARDPOINTS: four (plus optional two)
MAX WEAPON LOAD: four torpedoes = 960 kg (2116 lb)
REPRESENTATIVE WEAPONS: Marte Mk 2 ASMs; Sting Ray, Mk 46, or MU90 torpedoes; depth charges; FFAR pods

DIMENSIONS:

MAIN ROTOR DIAMETER: 18.6 m (61 ft 0 in)
LENGTH: 22.8 m (74 ft 10 in)
HEIGHT: 6.6 m (21 ft 9 in)

VARIANTS & OPERATORS:

Series 100: Denmark (SAR), Italy (ASW/ASVW = Mk 110; AEW = Mk 112), UK (Merlin HM.1 = Mk 111)
Series 300: Commercial passenger version—no orders as yet
Series 400: Italy (Utility = Mk 410), Portugal, UK (Merlin HC.3 = Mk 411)
Series 500: Japan (Tokyo Police = Mk 510)
AW320: Canada (CH-149 Cormorant)

FEATURES:

Starboard tailplane; port tail rotor; three Rolls-Royce/Turbomeca RTM 322-01/8 (UK versions) or GE T700-GE-T6A/A1 (Canadian/Italian versions) turboshafts; retractable undercarriage

Bell AH-1 HueyCobra/SuperCobra USA

Attack helicopter

The Model 209 AH-1G HueyCobra
first flew on September 7, 1965, and
was a dedicated helicopter gunship,
seeing service in the Vietnam War.
Evolved and upgraded as an ATGW-
armed anti-tank helicopter, and built
under license in Japan (AH-1S) and
Taiwan (AH-1W). The USMC is now
upgrading 180 AH-1W SuperCobras
to the AH-1Z configuration. Over
2060 of all variants built.

AH-1W

SPECIFICATION:

ACCOMMODATION: 2 flight crew
MAX SPEED: 222 kt (411 km/h)
RADIUS OF ACTION: 125 nm (232 km)

ARMAMENT (AH-1Z):
INTERNAL GUNS: M197 20 mm cannon in nose
turret
HARDPOINTS: six pylons
MAX WEAPON LOAD: 1556 kg (3430 lb)
REPRESENTATIVE WEAPONS: Sidewinder AAMs;
TOW or Hellfire ATGWs; Maverick AGMs; 2.75 in
rocket pods; 12.7 mm machine gun or 20 mm
cannon pods

DIMENSIONS:
MAIN ROTOR DIAMETER: 14.6 m (48 ft 0 in)
LENGTH: 17.7 m (58 ft 0 in)
HEIGHT: 4.4 m (14 ft 7 in)

VARIANTS & OPERATORS:
AH-1E: Bahrain, Israel
AH-1F: Bahrain, Israel, Jordan, Pakistan, South
Korea
AH-1J: Iran, South Korea
AH-1P: Turkey
AH-1S: Israel, Japan, Turkey
AH-1W: Taiwan, Turkey, USA
AH-1Z: USA (not yet in service)
TAH-1P: Bahrain, Turkey

FEATURES:
Lateral intakes behind tandem cockpit; port tail
rotor; two GE T700-GE-401 turboshafts; skid
undercarriage

Bell UH-1 Iroquois/Bell 204/205 USA

Utility helicopter

The first XH-40 prototype flew October 22, 1956, and, after development as Model 204, the UH-1A Iroquois entered U.S. Army service in 1959. Later versions were designated UH-1B/C/E/F/L/M, HH-1K, and TH-1F/L, all affectionately known as "Huey." The Model 205 (UH-D/H/V, EH-1H and HH-1H) had a longer fuselage and flew August 16, 1961. License-built in Germany, Italy, Japan and Taiwan, almost 10,000 of all UH-1/204/205 variants were built.

UH-1D

SPECIFICATION:

ACCOMMODATION: 2 flight crew plus 8 passengers (204) and 11–14 passengers (205)
MAX SPEED: UH-1C, 128 kt (238 km/h)
RANGE: UH-1C, 332 nm (615 km)

ARMAMENT (UH-1D; OPTIONAL):
INTERNAL GUNS: 7.62 mm, 12.7 mm machine guns or 20 mm cannon in cabin
HARDPOINTS: four pylons
MAX WEAPON LOAD: N/A
REPRESENTATIVE WEAPONS: 2.75 in, 68 mm, 71 mm, 81 mm rocket pods; 12.7 mm machine gun or 20 mm cannon pods

DIMENSIONS:
MAIN ROTOR DIAMETER: 14.6 m (48 ft 0 in)
LENGTH: 16.4 m (53 ft 11 in)
HEIGHT: 4.1 m (13 ft 5 in)

VARIANTS & OPERATORS:
AB 204ASW/B: Turkey, Yemen
205A/AB 205/A/B: Albania, Brazil, Greece, Indonesia, Iran, Italy, Libya, Macedonia, Mexico, Morocco, Myanmar, Oman, Pakistan, Thailand, Tunisia, Turkey, Zambia
UH-1B: Paraguay
UH-1D: Germany
UH-1H: Argentina, Australia, Bolivia, Bosnia and Herzegovina, Brazil, Chile, Colombia, Dominican Republic, Georgia, Greece, Guatemala, Honduras, Iraq, Japan, Jordan, Lebanon, Macedonia, New Zealand, Pakistan, Panama, Papua New Guinea, Paraguay, Peru, Philippines, South Korea, Spain, Thailand, Tunisia, Turkey, Uruguay, USA, Venezuela
UH-1J: Japan
UH-1M: El Salvador
UH-1V: Bosnia and Herzegovina, USA

FEATURES:
Squat fuselage; tail rotor—port on 204, starboard on 205; one Lycoming T53-L turboshaft; skid undercarriage

Bell UH-1N Iroquois/Bell 212/AB 212 USA

Utility helicopter (UH-1N pictured)

Derived from the UH-1H/Model 205, fitted with two PT6T turboshafts in Turbo Twin Pac configuration, the first Model 212 (UH-1N) flew April 16, 1969, and entered service in 1970. License-built by Agusta in Italy (AB 212), versions include AB 212ASW and AB 212EW. Almost 500 of all variants built. USN/USMC ordered a SLEP for 43 UH-1Ns in July 2006.

AB 212

SPECIFICATION:

ACCOMMODATION: 2 flight crew plus up to 14 passengers
MAX SPEED: 100 kt (185 km/h)
RANGE: 227 nm (420 km)

DIMENSIONS:

MAIN ROTOR DIAMETER: 14.7 m (48 ft 2 in)
LENGTH: 17.6 m (57 ft 3 in)
HEIGHT: 4.5 m (14 ft 10 in)

VARIANTS & OPERATORS:

212/AB 212: Angola, Argentina, Austria, Bahrain, Bangladesh, Brunei, Colombia, Ecuador, Greece, Guatemala, Iran, Italy, Jordan, Lebanon, Libya, Mexico, Morocco, Oman, Panama, Peru, Saudi Arabia, Sri Lanka, Sudan, Thailand, Turkey, UAE (Dubai), Uruguay, UK, Yemen, Zambia
212ASW/AB 212ASW: Greece, Iran, Italy, Peru, Spain, Thailand, Turkey, Venezuela
AB 212EW: Greece, Turkey
HH-1N: USA
UH-1N: Colombia, Tunisia, USA
UH-1Y: USA

FEATURES:

Above-cabin intakes; starboard tail rotor; two P&WC PT6T-3B turboshafts in Turbo Twin Pac; skid undercarriage

Bell UH-1Y Iroquois USA

Utility helicopter

Derived from the USMC's UH-1N, the first 10 of 100 helicopters required are being remanufactured from UH-1Ns, with 90 being new-build. The UH-1Y is re-engined with two GE T700 turboshaft engines and features a four-blade main rotor and a new tailboom structure, sharing 84% commonality with the AH-1Z Super-Cobra attack helicopter. First flown as YUH-1Y on December 20, 2001, with the first production aircraft rolled out on September 27, 2006.

SPECIFICATION:

ACCOMMODATION: 2 flight crew plus up to 8 troops or 6 litters
MAX SPEED: 198 kt (366 km/h)
RANGE: 350 nm (648 km)

ARMAMENT:

INTERNAL GUNS: 0.50 in (12.7 mm) or 7.62 mm machine guns or 7.62 mm GAU-17A minigun
HARDPOINTS: one pylon each side of fuselage, each with two hardpoints
REPRESENTATIVE WEAPONS: podded machine guns/cannon, 2.75 in (68 mm) FFAR pods

DIMENSIONS:

MAIN ROTOR DIAMETER: 14.6 m (48 ft 0 in)
LENGTH: 17.9 m (58 ft 4 in)
HEIGHT: 4.4 m (14 ft 7 in)

VARIANTS & OPERATORS:

UH-1Y: USMC

FEATURES:

Above-cabin intakes; four-blade main rotor; port tail rotor; two General Electric T700-GE-401C turboshafts; skid undercarriage
Not to be confused with any other UH-1/Bell 205/212/412 product

Bell 214 USA

Utility helicopter

The basic Model 214A, which first flew on March 15, 1974, was developed for Iran, with the 214ST (Stretched Twin) flying in February 1977. Bell later developed the 214ST as a commercial Super Transport, retaining the designator letters. Over 400 214s were built.

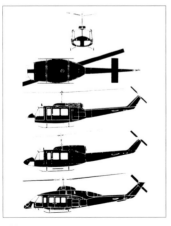

SPECIFICATION:

ACCOMMODATION: 2 flight crew plus up to 18 passengers
MAX SPEED: 140 kt (259 km/h)
RANGE: 439 nm (813 km)

DIMENSIONS:
MAIN ROTOR DIAMETER: 15.8 m (52 ft 0 in)
LENGTH: 18.9 m (62 ft 2 in)
HEIGHT: 4.8 m (15 ft 10 in)

VARIANTS & OPERATORS:
214A/C: Iran
214B: UAE (Dubai)
214ST: Brunei, Oman, Peru, Thailand

FEATURES:
Streamlined; stretched fuselage; starboard tail rotor; two GE CT7-2A turboshafts; skid or wheeled undercarriage

Bell RH-70/Bell 407 USA

Armed reconnaissance helicopter

Developed from the commercial Bell 407, the RH-70 was selected as the US Army's future armed reconnaissance helicopter (ARH) in July 2005. Bell 407 first flown April 21, 1994, and Bell's ARH demonstrator flew July 20, 2006. The first ten LRIP RH-70s funded in FY07, with a requirement for 480. First deliveries to U.S. Army scheduled for February 2008, to replace the OH-58 Kiowa series. A variant has been offered to India.

SPECIFICATION:

ACCOMMODATION: 2 flight crew plus up to 3 passengers
MAX SPEED: 128 kt (237 km/h)
RANGE: 195 nm (362 km)

ARMAMENT:
INTERNAL GUNS: none planned
HARDPOINTS: one pylon each side of fuselage
REPRESENTATIVE WEAPONS: podded 0.5 in (12.7 mm) or 7.62 mm machine guns, 2.75 in (68 mm) FFAR pods, AGM-114 Hellfire ATGWs

DIMENSIONS:
MAIN ROTOR DIAMETER: 10.7 m (35 ft 0 in)
LENGTH: 12.7 m (41 ft 9 in)
HEIGHT: 3.6 m (11 ft 10 in)

VARIANTS & OPERATORS:
RH-70: U.S. Army, U.S. National Guard

FEATURES:
Undernose E-O turret; four-blade main rotor; port tail rotor; one Honeywell HTS900-1-4D turboshaft; swept tailfins; mid-section horizontal stabilizer with swept endplate fins; skid undercarriage
Not to be confused with any other OH-58/Bell 206/406/407 variant

Bell 412/AB 412 USA

Utility helicopter

The Model 412 is essentially a 212 with a four-bladed rotor (which can be retrofitted to 212s), first flying in August 1979. Production transferred to Canada in 1989. License-built by IPTN in Indonesia and by Agusta (as the AB 412) in Italy. Over 580 Model 412s of all variants were built.

SPECIFICATION:

ACCOMMODATION: 1 or 2 flight crew plus up to 14 passengers
MAX SPEED: 122 kt (226 km/h)
RANGE: 402 nm (745 km)

ARMAMENT (AB 412 GRIFFON):
INTERNAL GUNS: 12.7 mm machine gun turret under nose
HARDPOINTS: two pylons
MAX WEAPON LOAD: N/A
REPRESENTATIVE WEAPONS: Sea Skua ASMs; TOW ATGWs; 2.75 in or 81 mm rocket pods; 25 mm cannon pods

DIMENSIONS:
MAIN ROTOR DIAMETER: 14.0 m (46 ft 0 in)
LENGTH: 17.1 m (56 ft 2 in)
HEIGHT: 4.6 m (15 ft 0 in)

VARIANTS & OPERATORS:
412: Chile, Colombia, Eritrea, Ghana, Guatemala, Lesotho, South Korea, Sri Lanka, Sweden (Hkp 11), Thailand, Venezuela
412CP: Italy (HP/SP/EM-4)
412EP: Algeria, Botswana, Cyprus, El Salvador (Centella), Jamaica, Lesotho, Mexico, Pakistan, Philippines, Saudi Arabia, Slovenia, Tanzania, Thailand, Turkey, UAE (Sharjah), UK (Griffin HT.1/HAR.2), Venezuela
412HP: Canada (CH-146 Griffon), Italy, Peru, Poland, Slovenia, Thailand, UAE (Dubai)
412SP: Bahrain, Botswana, Cyprus, Gabon, Honduras, Italy, Lesotho, Netherlands, Norway, Philippines, Slovenia, Venezuela, UAE (Abu Dhabi), Zimbabwe

FEATURES:
Above-cabin intakes; starboard tail rotor; two P&WC PT6T-3B turboshafts in Turbo Twin Pac; skid or wheeled undercarriage

Bell OH-58D Kiowa/Bell 406CS USA

Light attack/scout helicopter

The OH-58D was derived from the OH-58A/B/C (Model 206 Jetranger, which see) under the U.S. AHIP program. The prototype first flew on October 6, 1983, with deliveries to U.S. Army from 1985. Many upgraded to Kiowa Warrior configuration. A similar version developed for export as Model 406CS Combat Scout. Some 439 OH-58D/406CSs were built or on order.

SPECIFICATION:

ACCOMMODATION: 2 pilots
MAX SPEED: 122 kt (226 km/h)
RANGE: 130 nm (241 km)

ARMAMENT:
HARDPOINTS: two pylons
MAX WEAPON LOAD: N/A
REPRESENTATIVE WEAPONS: Stinger AAMs; Hellfire ATGWs; 2.75 in rocket pods; 0.5 in (12.7 mm) machine gun pod

DIMENSIONS:
MAIN ROTOR DIAMETER: 10.7 m (35 ft 0 in)
LENGTH: 12.6 m (41 ft 2 in)
HEIGHT: 3.9 m (12 ft 10 in)

VARIANTS & OPERATORS:
406CS: Saudi Arabia
OH-58D: Taiwan, USA
TH-57: Ecuador, USA, Venezuela
TH-67A: Taiwan, USA

FEATURES:
MMS above rotor head; "tadpole" fuselage; port tail rotor; one Rolls-Royce (Allison) 250-C30R turboshaft; skid undercarriage

Bell/Boeing V-22 Osprey USA

Utility tilt-rotor aircraft

Based on the Bell XV-15 program, the JVX project proceeded as joint Bell/Boeing partnership. The first V-22 prototype made its maiden flight on March 19, 1989. The first MV-22B for the USMC flown in April 1999. First CV-22 delivered to USAF Special Operations Command in September 2005, when full production authorized. USMC expects to deploy first unit, VMM-263, in 2007. A five-year Multi-Year Production contract expected late 2007, covering 150 aircraft.

SPECIFICATION:

ACCOMMODATION: 2 pilots plus crew chief and up to 24 combat-equipped troops
MAX SPEED: 305 kt (565 km/h)
RANGE: VTO, 515 nm (953 km)

ARMAMENT:

INTERNAL GUNS: possibly a 7.62 mm or 0.5 in (12.7 mm) machine gun in nose turret

DIMENSIONS:

TOTOR DIAMETER: 11.6 m (38 ft 1 in)
LENGTH: wings folded, 19.2 m (63 ft 0 in)
HEIGHT: nacelles vertical, 6.7 m (22 ft 1 in)

VARIANTS & OPERATORS:

CV-22B: USAF—50 required for special operations
CV-22B: USN—48 required for C-SAR
MV-22B: USMC—360 required for transport

FEATURES:

Twin fins; two Rolls-Royce (Allison) T406-AD-400 turboshafts in rotating nacelles at wingtips; retractable wheeled undercarriage

Boeing (Hughes/McDD) AH-64 Apache USA

Attack/recce helicopter (WAH-64D Apache AH.1 pictured)

The Hughes YAH-64 prototype first flew on 30 September 1975. The first AH-64A entered U.S. Army service in January 1984. The D model, with a Longbow MMW radar above the rotorhead, entered U.S. Army service 1998. License-built by Fuji in Japan and in UK by AgustaWestland as WAH-64D, reengined with Rolls-Royce/Turbomeca RTM 322 engines. Over 1069 Apaches of all versions built or on order. Most AH-64As remanufactured to AH-64D Apache Longbow configuration.

SPECIFICATION:

ACCOMMODATION: 2 pilots
MAX SPEED: 197 kt (365 km/h)
RANGE: AH-64D, 220 nm (407 km)

ARMAMENT:

INTERNAL GUNS: M230 30 mm Chain Gun in undernose mounting
HARDPOINTS: four (plus two planned) pylons
MAX WEAPON LOAD: N/A
REPRESENTATIVE WEAPONS: Mistral, Sidewinder, Starstreak or Stinger AAMs; Hellfire ATGWs; 2.75 in FFAR pods

DIMENSIONS:

MAIN ROTOR DIAMETER: 14.6 m (48 ft 0 in)
LENGTH: 17.8 m (58 ft 3 in)
HEIGHT: AH-64D, 4.9 m (16 ft 3 in)

VARIANTS & OPERATORS:

AH-64A: Israel, Japan, Saudi Arabia, UAE (Abu Dhabi), USA
AH-64D: Egypt, Greece, Israel, Kuwait, Netherlands, Singapore, USA
WAH-64D: UK (Apache AH.1)

FEATURES:

Tandem cockpit; two GE T700-GE-701C turboshafts; port tail rotor; fixed wheeled undercarriage

AH-64A

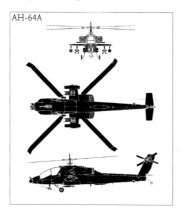

Boeing CH-46 Sea Knight/Vertol 107 USA

Transport helicopter (CH-46 pictured)

Originally the Vertol Model 107, the twin-rotor prototype first flew on April 22, 1958. Entered USMC service in 1961 and was progressively upgraded. Built under license by Kawasaki in Japan. A total of 700 helicopters of all versions built.

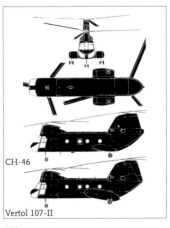

CH-46

Vertol 107-II

SPECIFICATION:

ACCOMMODATION: 3 flight crew plus 25 troops
MAX SPEED: 144 kt (267 km/h)
RANGE: 206 nm (383 km)

ARMAMENT:
INTERNAL GUNS: pintle-mounted 0.5 in (12.7 mm) machine gun

DIMENSIONS:
ROTOR DIAMETER: CH-46D, 15.5 m (51 ft 0 in)
LENGTH: 25.7 m (84 ft 4 in)
HEIGHT: 5.1 m (16 ft 8 in)

VARIANTS & OPERATORS:
107: Japan, Saudi Arabia, Sweden (Hkp4)
CH-46E: USMC, USN
HH-46D: USMC

FEATURES:
Twin-rotor configuration; two GE T58-GE-11 turboshafts; rear-fuselage sponsons; fixed tricycle wheeled undercarriage

Boeing CH-47 Chinook USA

Transport helicopter (Chinook CH-47C+ pictured)

The YCH-47A Chinook first flew September 21, 1961. Built under license by Kawasaki of Japan and Meridionali of Italy. The U.S. Army re-manufactured 479 CH-47A/B/Cs to D model configuration from 1982, now being upgraded to CH-47F ICH standard. SOCOM MH-47E variants being upgraded to MH-47G. HH-47 is new USAF C-SAR heli-copter in 2006. Over 1200 Chinooks built or on order.

CH-47D

SPECIFICATION:

ACCOMMODATION: 2 pilots plus crew chief plus 33–55 troops
MAX SPEED: 154 kt (285 km/h)
RADIUS OF ACTION: MH-47E, 505 nm (935 km)

ARMAMENT:
INTERNAL GUNS: two or three pintle-mounted 7.62 mm M134 Miniguns or 0.5 in (12.7 mm) machine guns in cabin

DIMENSIONS:
ROTOR DIAMETER: 18.3 m (60 ft 0 in)
LENGTH: 30.1 m (98 ft 11 in)
HEIGHT: 5.7 m (18 ft 11 in)

VARIANTS & OPERATORS:
234MLR Chinook: Taiwan
414 Chinook HC.2/2A: UK
CH-47C: Egypt, Iran, Morocco, UAE (Abu Dhabi)
CH-47C+: Italy
CH-47D: Australia, Egypt, Greece, Netherlands, Singapore, South Korea, Spain, Thailand, USA
MH-47D/E: USA
CH-47F: USA
CH-47SD: Greece, Singapore, Taiwan
CH-47J/JA: Japan
HH-47: USA
MH-47G: USA

FEATURES:
Twin-rotor configuration; two Honeywell (Lycoming) T55-L-712 turboshafts; fuselage sponsons; fixed wheeled undercarriage

Denel (Atlas) AH-2A Rooivalk SOUTH AFRICA

Attack helicopter

Designed as a Combat Support Helicopter for the SAAF (hence its previous designation, CSH-2), the prototype Rooivalk (Red Kestrel) first flew February 11, 1990. It uses many reverse-engineered and locally built components from the dynamics system of the SA 330 Puma. A second prototype was followed by a pre-production aircraft, with the SAAF ordering a dozen. The Rooivalk is being actively promoted for export.

SPECIFICATION:

ACCOMMODATION: 2 pilots
MAX SPEED: PAH-1, 167 kt (309 km/h)
RANGE: 720 nm (1335 km)

ARMAMENT:
INTERNAL GUNS: F2 20 mm cannon in undernose turret
HARDPOINTS: six pylons (three on each stub wing)
MAX WEAPON LOAD: 2032 kg (4480 lb)
REPRESENTATIVE WEAPONS: Mistral AAMs; Mokapa ATGWs; 68 mm FFAR pods

DIMENSIONS:
MAIN ROTOR DIAMETER: 15.6 m (51 ft 1 in)
LENGTH: 18.7 m (61 ft 5 in)
HEIGHT: 5.2 m (17 ft 0 in)

VARIANTS & OPERATORS:
AH-2A: SAAF

FEATURES:
Tandem cockpit; starboard tail rotor; port tailplane; two Turbomeca Makila 1K2 turboshafts; fixed wheeled undercarriage

Eurocopter AS 532 Cougar (Super Puma) & EC 725 Cougar RESCO FRANCE

Medium transport helicopter

The AS 332 Super Puma (with the Makila engine), first flew September 13, 1978. Military versions redesignated AS 532 Cougar in 1990. The AS 532UL Horizon has a battlefield surveillance radar. License-built in Indonesia by Dirgantara (IPTN) and TAI in Turkey, assembled in Spain by EADS/CASA. Some SA 330s remanufactured as (AS 332) Oryx in South Africa. Over 686 Super Pumas/Cougars built or on order.

AS 332

SPECIFICATION:

ACCOMMODATION: 2 (+1) flight crew plus 21 passengers or 4500 kg (9920 lb) external slung cargo
MAX SPEED: 170 kt (315 km/h)
RANGE: 656 nm (1215 km)

ARMAMENT: (OPTIONAL)
HARDPOINTS: two pylons
REPRESENTATIVE WEAPONS: Exocet ASMs; FFAR pods; 20 mm cannon or 12.7 mm machine gun pods; homing torpedoes

DIMENSIONS:
MAIN ROTOR DIAMETER: Cougar Mk II, 16.2 m (53 ft 1 in)
LENGTH: 19.5 m (63 ft t 11 in)
HEIGHT: 5.0 m (16 ft 5 in)

VARIANTS & OPERATORS:
Argentina (AS 332B), Brazil (AS 332M, AS 532UE), Bulgaria (AS 352AL), Cameroon (AS 332L), Chile (AS 332B/M), China (AS 332L), Ecuador (AS 332B), France (AS 332C/L, AS 532A2 RESCO/UL, EC 725 RESCO), Germany (AS 532UL), Greece (AS 332C1, AS 532SC), Iceland (AS 332L1), Indonesia (NAS 332B/L1), Japan (AS 332L, EC 725), Jordan (AS 332M), Kuwait (AS 532SC), Malawi (AS 332), Mexico (AS 332L), Morocco (AS 332L2), Nepal (AS 332L), Netherlands (AS 532U2), Oman (AS 332C/L), Saudi Arabia (AS 532AL/A2), Singapore (AS 332M, AS 532UL), Slovenia (AS 352L), South Africa (Oryx), Spain (AS 332B/M, AS 532AL/UC/UL), Sweden (AS 532/Hkp 10), Switzerland (AS 332M, AS532UL), Turkey (AS 532AL/UL), UAE (Abu Dhabi—AS 332B/M), Venezuela (AS 332B, AS 532), Zimbabwe (AS 532)

FEATURES:
Air intakes over cabin; rear-fuselage sponsons; two Turbomeca Makila 1A2 turboshafts; retractable wheeled undercarriage; starboard tailplane; port tail rotor

Eurocopter AS 550/555 Ecureuil/Fennec FRANCE

Light utility helicopter

First flight of AS 350 Ecureuil (Squirrel), powered by a Lycoming LTS101 engine, June 27, 1974. Second prototype Ecureuil flew with production-standard Turbomeca Arriel 1A engine in February 1975. A twin-engined version, designated AS 355, flew on September 28, 1979. Military versions produced after 1990 redesignated AS 550/555 Fennec respectively. Built under license in Brazil; China's CHAIC Z-11 appears a copy. Over 2250 AS 350/550/555s built or on order.

SPECIFICATION:

ACCOMMODATION: 1 pilot and second front seat plus 4 passengers or 907 kg (2000 lb) cargo sling
MAX SPEED: 155 kt (287 km/h)
RANGE: 362 nm (670 km)

ARMAMENT (AS 550C3):
HARDPOINTS: two
MAX WEAPON LOAD: N/A
REPRESENTATIVE WEAPONS: TOW ATGMs; one torpedo; FFAR pods; 7.62 mm or 12.7 mm machine gun or 20 mm cannon pods

DIMENSIONS:
MAIN ROTOR DIAMETER: 10.7 m (35 ft 1 in)
LENGTH: 12.9 m (42 ft 5 in)
HEIGHT: 3.4 m (10 ft 11 in)

VARIANTS & OPERATORS:
Albania (AS 350B), Algeria (AS 355N), Argentina (AS 350BA, AS 555MN), Australia (AS 350BA), Benin (AS 350B), Botswana (AS 350B/BA), Brazil (HB 350B/BA/L1, HB 355FS/F2), Burkina Faso (AS 350B), Burundi (AS 350B), Cambodia (AS 350B), Central African Rep. (AS 350B), Chile (AS 350B, AS 255F), China (Z-11), Colombia (AS 555SN), Comoros (AS 350B), Denmark (AS 550C2), Djibouti (AS 355F), Ecuador (AS 350B), France (AS 350B/BA, AS 355F/U, AS 550U2, AS 555AN/UN), Gabon (AS 350B, AS 355F), Guinea Rep. (AS 350B), Ireland (AS 355N), Jamaica (AS 355N), Jordan (AS 350B), Malawi (AS 350B), Malaysia (AS 555SN), Mali (AS 350B), Mauritius (AS 555), Mexico (AS 355F, AS 550), Nepal (AS 350B), Paraguay (HB 350B), Morocco (AS 355F), Singapore (AS 550A2/C2), Thailand (AS 350B/BA), Tunisia (AS 350B), UAE (Abu Dhabi—AS 350B/C3), UK (AS 355BA Squirrel HT.1/2, AS 355F1 Twin Squirrel), Uruguay (HB 355F2), Venezuela (AS 355F)

FEATURES:
Starboard tail rotor; one Turbomeca Arriel 1D1 or 2B (AS 350/550) or two Turbomeca Arrius 1A turboshafts (AS 355/555); skid undercarriage

Eurocopter AS 565 Panther (Dauphin 2) FRANCE

General-purpose helicopter

First flight of AS 365N Dauphin 2 on March 31, 1979. Developed for several naval, army, and air force roles. Bought by U.S. Coast Guard as AS 366G1 (HH-65 Dolphin). Redesignated as AS 565 Panther in 1990. Built under license in China by HAMC as the Z-9. Over 500 Dauphin 2/Panthers of all variants built or on order.

SPECIFICATION:

ACCOMMODATION: 1 pilot and second front seat plus up to 12 passengers or 1600 kg (3525 lb) cargo sling
MAX SPEED: 155 kt (287 km/h)
RANGE: 464 nm (859 km)

ARMAMENT (AS 365N):
HARDPOINTS: four on two pylons
MAX WEAPON LOAD: N/A
REPRESENTATIVE WEAPONS: AS-15TT ASMs, torpedoes; 7.62 mm or 12.7 mm machine gun or 20 mm cannon pods

DIMENSIONS:
MAIN ROTOR DIAMETER: 11.9 m (39 ft 2 in)
LENGTH: 13.7 m (45 ft 0 in)
HEIGHT: 4.1 m (13 ft 4 in)

VARIANTS & OPERATORS:
Angola (AS 565AA/UA), Argentina (AS 365N), Brazil (AS 565UB), Bulgaria (AS 565MB), Cambodia (AS 365), Cameroon (AS 365N), Côte d'Ivoire (AS 365C), China (Z-9), Dominican Rep. (AS365N), France (AS 365F/N, AS 565MA), Greece (AS 365N), Iceland (AS 365N), Ireland (AS 365F), Israel (AS 565SA), Mexico (AS 365, AS 565SB), Morocco (AS 365N, AS 565SB), Saudi Arabia (AS 365N, AS 565SA), Switzerland (AS 365N), UAE (Abu Dhabi —AS 565SB), UAE (Dubai—AS 365N), UK (AS 365N), Uruguay (AS 365N), USA (HH-65 Dolphin)

FEATURES:
Fenestron tail rotor; two Turbomeca Arriel 1C2 or 2C turboshafts; retractable wheeled undercarriage

AS 565 SA

491

Eurocopter AS 665 Tigre/Tiger FRANCE/GERMANY

Multirole combat helicopter

The prototype of the Franco-German AS 665 Tigre/Tiger multirole combat helicopter first flew April 27, 1991. Original requirement for 427 (France 75 HAP, 140 HAC and Germany 212 PAH-2, now UHT) reduced and now 160 (80 per each), with prospect of future orders. Australia ordered Tiger in 2001 with Spain following in 2003 (first aircraft delivered to both customers in 2004). First deliveries to France in March 2005 and to Germany in April 2005.

SPECIFICATION:

ACCOMMODATION: 2 pilots
MAX SPEED: 175 kt (322 km/h)
RANGE: 432 nm (800 km)

ARMAMENT:
INTERNAL GUN: HAP/HCP, Giat 30 mm cannon in undernose turret
HARDPOINTS: four on two pylons
MAX WEAPON LOAD: N/A
REPRESENTATIVE WEAPONS: Mistral or Stinger AAMs; Hellfire (RAAF), HOT or Trigat ATGWs; FFAR pods; 12.7 mm machine gun or 20 mm cannon pods; external fuel tanks

DIMENSIONS:
MAIN ROTOR DIAMETER: 13.0 m (42 ft 8 in)
LENGTH: 15.8 m (51 ft 10 in)
HEIGHT: 4.3 m (14 ft 2 in)

VARIANTS & OPERATORS:
Tiger UHT: Germany (80 ordered)
Tigre HAD: France (40 ordered), Spain (24 ordered)
Tigre HAP: France (40 ordered)
Tigre HCP: Australia (22 ordered)

FEATURES:
Tandem cockpit; twin-finned tailplanes; starboard tail rotor; two MTU/Rolls-Royce/Turbomeca MTR 390 turboshafts; fixed wheeled undercarriage

Hindustan Aeronautics Ltd. Dhruv ALH INDIA

Multirole utility helicopter

Designed in India, with German assistance, the first prototype ALH flew on August 20, 1992. The Indian Air Force requires 60 utility Dhruvs, the Indian Army 120, while the Indian Navy and the Coast Guard will have 120 and seven naval variants respectively. The first seven production aircraft were delivered in April 2002. As of 2006, some 45 aircraft delivered.

SPECIFICATION:

ACCOMMODATION: 2 pilots plus 12–14 passengers or 1500 kg (3307 lb) external cargo sling
MAX SPEED: 178 kt (330 km/h)
RANGE: 432 nm (800 km)

ARMAMENT:

INTERNAL GUNS: provision for 20 mm cannon under nose
HARDPOINTS: four on two pylons
MAX WEAPON LOAD: N/A
REPRESENTATIVE WEAPONS: AAMs; ASMs; ATGWs; torpedoes; depth charges; 68 mm or 71 mm FFAR pods; 12.7 mm machine gun or 20 mm cannon pods

DIMENSIONS:

MAIN ROTOR DIAMETER: 13.2 m (43 ft 4 in)
LENGTH: 15.9 m (52 ft 1 in)
HEIGHT: 4.9 m (16 ft 1 in)

VARIANTS & OPERATORS:

Druhv, utility: India, Nepal
Druhv, naval: India

FEATURES:

Side-by-side cockpit; twin-finned tailplanes; starboard tail rotor; two Turbomeca TM 333-2B turboshafts; skid undercarriage (utility); retractable wheeled undercarriage (naval)

Kaman SH-2G Super Seasprite USA

Naval helicopter

First flown on July 2, 1959, 184 early SH-2A/B models were built 1961–63. All converted to twin-T58 UH-2C configuration, some later modified as LAMPS Mk1 (SH-2D). Returned to production 1981 as the SH-2F for the USN and all C models were upgraded to F models. Only six SH-2Gs with two T700 engines built new for the USN, but 18 SH-2Fs were converted to SH-2Gs. Withdrawn from U.S. service by June 2001. Export sales of G models are converted SH-2Fs, but New Zealand ordered four new-builds.

SPECIFICATION:

ACCOMMODATION: 2 pilots plus tactical coordinator
MAX SPEED: 138 kt (256 km/h)
RANGE: 478 nm (885 km)

ARMAMENT:
INTERNAL GUNS: provision for 7.62 mm machine gun in cabin
HARDPOINTS: two pylons
MAX WEAPON LOAD: N/A
REPRESENTATIVE WEAPONS: Maverick AGMs, Penguin or Sea Skua ASMs; Hellfire ATGWs; torpedoes; external fuel tanks

DIMENSIONS:
MAIN ROTOR DIAMETER: 13.5 m (44 ft 4 in)
LENGTH: 16.1 m (52 ft 9 in)
HEIGHT: 4.6 m (15 ft 0 in)

VARIANTS & OPERATORS:
SH-2G: Australia, Egypt, New Zealand, Poland

FEATURES:
Side-by-side cockpit; port tail rotor; two GE T700-GE-401 turboshafts; retractable wheeled undercarriage

Kamov Ka-25 "Hormone" RUSSIA

Naval helicopter

The prototype Ka-25 "Hormone" first flew in 1961 and featured a pair of coaxial main rotors, with no tail-boom. The main version ("Hormone-A") is a shipborne ASW helicopter; the "Hormone-B" is configured to provide over-the-horizon targeting information for ship-launched cruise missiles. The "Hormone-C" is a specialized SAR version. About 140 were built between 1966 and 1973.

SPECIFICATION:

ACCOMMODATION: 2 pilots plus up to 12 passengers or fewer mission specialists
MAX SPEED: 119 kt (220 km/h)
RANGE: 216 nm (400 km)

ARMAMENT:
HARDPOINTS: two weapons bays
MAX WEAPON LOAD: N/A
REPRESENTATIVE WEAPONS: torpedoes; depth charges; external fuel tanks

DIMENSIONS:
ROTOR DIAMETER: each, 15.7 m (51 ft 8 in)
LENGTH: 9.7 m (31 ft 9 in)
HEIGHT: 5.4 m (17 ft 8 in)

VARIANTS & OPERATORS:
Ka-25 "Hormone": India, Ukraine
Ka-25BSh "Hormone-A": Syria
Ka-25BShZ "Hormone": Russia
Ka-25PL "Hormone-A": Russia, Vietnam
Ka-25PS "Hormone-C": Russia
Ka-25T "Hormone-B": Russia

FEATURES:
Side-by-side cockpit; undernose radome; triple fin configuration; two Glushenkov GTD-3F turboshafts; fixed wheeled undercarriage

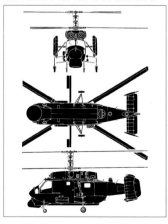

Kamov Ka-27/-28/-32 "Helix-A/-D/-C" RUSSIA

Naval helicopter (Ka-32T pictured)

A prototype "Helix-A," designated Ka-25-2, first flew on August 8, 1973, and featured a dipping-sonar facility. Later redesignated Ka-27, the main production "Helix-A" usually operated in pairs, flying from larger ships and carriers. The Ka-27PS "Helix-D" was a dedicated SAR version and the Ka-28 was the export designation for the "Helix-A"; the civil variant was designated Ka-32 "Helix-C." About 267 Ka-27/-28s were built.

Ka-27

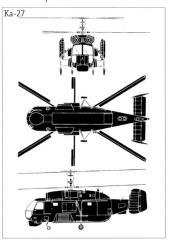

SPECIFICATION:

ACCOMMODATION: 2 pilots plus 1 mission specialist
MAX SPEED: 146 kt (270 km/h)
RANGE: 432 nm (800 km)

ARMAMENT:
HARDPOINTS: one weapons bay
MAX WEAPON LOAD: Ka-28, 1000 kg (2205 lb)
REPRESENTATIVE WEAPONS: torpedoes; depth charges; bombs; external fuel tanks

DIMENSIONS:
ROTOR DIAMETER: each, 15.9 m (52 ft 2 in)
LENGTH: 11.3 m (38 ft 0 in)
HEIGHT: 5.5 m (17 ft 10 in)

VARIANTS & OPERATORS:
Ka-27 "Helix": Algeria, Ukraine
Ka-27PL "Helix-A": Russia
Ka-27PS "Helix-D": Russia
Ka-28 "Helix": China, India, Vietnam
Ka-32T "Helix-C": Algeria, Laos, South Korea, USA, Vietnam

FEATURES:
Side-by-side cockpit; undernose radome; triple fin configuration; two Klimov TV3-117V turboshafts; fixed wheeled undercarriage

Kamov Ka-29/-31 "Helix-B" RUSSIA

Naval assault helicopter

A prototype "Helix-B," designated Ka-252TB, first flew on July 28, 1976, and was later redesignated Ka-29TB. Entered service from 1985. The Ka-31 (formerly known as the Ka-29RLD) was a specialized AEW/EW variant sold to India. About 61 Ka-29/-31s were built.

SPECIFICATION:

ACCOMMODATION: 2 pilots plus (Ka-29) 16 assault troops or (Ka-31) mission specialists
MAX SPEED: 151 kt (280 km/h)
RANGE: 248 nm (460 km)

ARMAMENT:
INTERNAL GUNS: 7.62 mm machine gun on starboard door
HARDPOINTS: four on outrigger pylons plus weapons bay
MAX WEAPON LOAD: 1800 kg (3968 lb)
REPRESENTATIVE WEAPONS: AT-6 Spiral ATGWs; torpedoes; bombs; rocket pods; 23 mm or 30 mm gun pods; external fuel tanks

DIMENSIONS:
ROTOR DIAMETER: each, 15.9 m (52 ft 2 in)
LENGTH: 11.3 m (38 ft 0 in)
HEIGHT: 5.4 m (17 ft 8 in)

VARIANTS & OPERATORS:
Ka-29TB "Helix-B": Russia
Ka-31: India

FEATURES:
Wider side-by-side cockpit; nose pitot tube; triple fin configuration; two Klimov TV3-117V turboshafts; fixed wheeled undercarriage

Kamov Ka-50/-52 "Hokum-A/-B" RUSSIA

Close-support helicopter

The single-seat prototype "Hokum," designated V-80, first flew on June 17, 1982, and was later redesignated Ka-50. The subject of much evaluation (against the Mi-28 "Havoc") and export promotion. It appears Russian Air Force has authorized further limited production of the Ka-50. The Ka-52 features a side-by-side cockpit.

SPECIFICATION:

ACCOMMODATION: Ka-50, 1 pilot on Zvelda K-37-800 ejection seat; Ka-52, 2 pilots on same ejection seats
MAX SPEED: 210 kt (390 km/h)
RANGE: 595 nm (1100 km)

ARMAMENT:

INTERNAL GUNS: 30 mm cannon on starboard fuselage
HARDPOINTS: four pylons on stub wings
MAX WEAPON LOAD: 3000 kg (6610 lb)
REPRESENTATIVE WEAPONS: AA-11 Archer AAMs; AS-12 Kegler ARMs; AT-6 ATGWs; 80 mm or 122 mm rocket pods; FAB-500 bombs; external fuel tanks

DIMENSIONS:

ROTOR DIAMETER: each, 14.5 m (47 ft 7 in)
LENGTH: 16.0 m (52 ft 6 in)
HEIGHT: 4.9 m (16 ft 2 in)

VARIANTS & OPERATORS:

Ka-50 "Hokum-A": Russia
Ka-52 "Hokum-B": Russia

FEATURES:

E-O fairings under nose; small twin-fin tailplane; single main fin; two Klimov TV3-117VMA turboshafts; retractable wheeled undercarriage

Kawasaki OH-1 JAPAN

Scout/observation helicopter

The prototype XOH-1 was first flown on August 6, 1996. Features Fenestron-type tail fan and E-O sensor mounted forward of rotor mast below main rotor. Of a requirement of 150–200 for the JGSDF, 28 (including four flying prototypes) have been ordered to FY06. First deliveries in 2003.

SPECIFICATION:

ACCOMMODATION: 2 pilots
MAX SPEED: 150 kt (277 km/h)
RANGE: 297 nm (550 km)

ARMAMENT:

HARDPOINTS: two pylons under each stub-wing
MAX WEAPON LOAD: 132 kg (291 lb)
REPRESENTATIVE WEAPONS: Type 91 IR-guided AAMs

DIMENSIONS:

MAIN ROTOR DIAMETER: 11.6 m (38 ft 1 in)
LENGTH: 12.0 m (39 ft 4 in)
HEIGHT: 3.4 m (11 ft 2 in)

VARIANTS & OPERATORS:
OH-1: Japan

FEATURES:
Tandem cockpit; Fenestron-type tail rotor in main fin; two Mitsubishi TS1-10QT turboshafts; fixed wheeled undercarriage

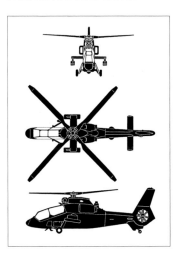

MD Helicopters (Hughes/McDD) MD 500/530 Defender USA

Scout/attack helicopter

First flown as the Hughes OH-6A Cayuse (Model 500) February 27, 1963, developed into civil MD 500 by 1968. The MD 500D flew 1984. Specialized military variants developed while AH-6/MH-6 versions used by U.S. Special Forces, known as "Little Birds." Built under license by Kawasaki in Japan and BredaNardi in Italy. Development of the NOTAR applied to the design led to MD 520N, MD 600N and MH-90 Enforcer (Explorer). Over 1430 (OH-6A to MD 530F) were built.

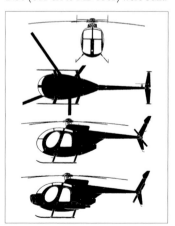

SPECIFICATION:

ACCOMMODATION: 1 or 2 pilots plus up to 4 passengers or 907 kg (2000 lb) external slung cargo
MAX SPEED: 130 kt (241 km/h)
RANGE: 213 nm (428 km)

ARMAMENT:
HARDPOINTS: two pylons under stub-wings
MAX WEAPON LOAD: N/A
REPRESENTATIVE WEAPONS: Stinger AAMs; TOW ATGWs; 2.75 in FFAR pods; 7.62 mm machine gun pods

DIMENSIONS:
MAIN ROTOR DIAMETER: 8.0 m (26 ft 4 in)
LENGTH: 7.6 m (24 ft 0 in)
HEIGHT: 2.6 m (8 ft 8 in)

VARIANTS & OPERATORS:
Argentina (MD 500C/D/M, MD 530F), Belgium (MD 520N), Chile (MD 530F), Colombia (MD 500/D/E/M, MD 530F), Costa Rica (MD 500E), El Salvador (MD 500D/E), Finland (MD 500D/E), Honduras (MD 500D), Italy (NH 500D/E/M/MC/MD), Japan (OH-6D/DA/J), Jordan (MD 500D), Kenya (MD 500D/MD/MD-TOW/ME), Malta (NH 500HM), Mexico (MD 500E, MD 530F/MG), North Korea (MD 500D/E), Philippines (MD 520MG), South Korea (MD 500MD/MD-TOW), Spain (MD 500), Taiwan (MD 500MD), Turkey (MD 600N), USA (AH-6J, TH-6B, TH-6J)

FEATURES:
"Tadpole" cabin; slim tail boom with T-tail; port tail rotor (NOTAR on MD 520/600N and MH-90); one Rolls-Royce (Allison) 250-C20B turboshaft; skid undercarriage

Mil Mi-6 "Hook" RUSSIA

Heavy transport helicopter

At the time of its first flight on June 5, 1957, the Mi-6 was the world's largest helicopter. Developed to the Mi-10 "Flying Crane" and Mi-22 "Hook-C" command support helicopters. More than 800 built for civil and military use, ending in 1981.

SPECIFICATION:

ACCOMMODATION: 5 flight crew plus 70 combat troops or 8000 kg (17,637 lb) external slung cargo
MAX SPEED: 162 kt (300 km/h)
RANGE: 540 nm (1000 km)

ARMAMENT:
INTERNAL GUNS: some have 12.7 mm nose-mounted machine gun

DIMENSIONS:
MAIN ROTOR DIAMETER: 35.0 m (114 ft 10 in)
LENGTH: 41.7 m (136 ft 11 in)
HEIGHT: 9.9 m (32 ft 4 in)

VARIANTS & OPERATORS:
Mi-6 "Hook-A": China, Kazakhstan, Laos, Russia, Ukraine, Uzbekistan
Mi-6VKP "Hook-B": Russia, Ukraine
Mi-6AYa (Mi-22) "Hook-C": Russia, Ukraine, Uzbekistan

FEATURES:
Long fuselage/tailboom; starboard tail rotor; stub wings; two Soloviev D-25 V (TV-2BM) turboshafts; fixed wheeled undercarriage

Mil Mi-8/-17/-171/-172 "Hip" RUSSIA

Heavy assault helicopter (Mi-8, this page, and Mi-17, opposite, pictured)

The first prototype Mi-8 "Hip-A" was flown on June 24, 1961. Production undertaken by Mil (Moscow), Ulan-Ude, and Kazan. Many variants were developed and the second-generation "Hip," designated Mi-17 "Hip-H," using an Mi-8 airframe and Mi-14 powerplant and dynamic components, first flew on August 17, 1975, but designated Mi-8MT for Russian service. There are many versions and subvariants under varying Mi-8/-17 designations, plus the Mi-9 "Hip-G" dedicated airborne command post variant. Further improved versions (Mi-171/172) continue to be developed. This helicopter family has been widely exported, with over 11,000 (about 3700 Mi-8T and 7300 Mi-17) built by Ulan-Ude and 7300 Mi-8/-17/171/-172 from Kazan.

Mi-8

Mi-17

SPECIFICATION:

ACCOMMODATION: 2 pilots and (Mi-8T "Hip-C") up to 24 troops and (Mi-17-1V) up to 30 troops, or 3000 kg (6614 lb) external cargo sling
MAX SPEED: 135 kt (250 km/h)
RANGE: 545 nm (1010 km)

ARMAMENT (MI-8TB "HIP-E"):

INTERNAL GUNS: one 12.7 mm machine gun in nose
HARDPOINTS: six on outrigger pylons
MAX WEAPON LOAD: N/A
REPRESENTATIVE WEAPONS: AT-2 Swatter ATGWs; 57 mm rocket pods

DIMENSIONS:

MAIN ROTOR DIAMETER: 21.3 m (69 ft 10 in)
LENGTH: overall, rotors turning, 25.3 m (83 ft 1 in)
HEIGHT: overall, rotors turning, 5.5 m (18 ft 2 in)

VARIANTS & OPERATORS:

Mi-8 "Hip": Afghanistan, Albania, Algeria, Angola, Azerbaijan, Belarus, Bhutan, Bosnia and Herzegovina, Burkina Faso, Cambodia, Croatia, Cuba, Czech Republic, Egypt, Estonia, Ethiopia, Finland, Georgia, Ghana, Guinea-Bissau, Hungary, India, Iran, Kazakhstan, Kyrgystan, Laos, Latvia, Libya, Lithuania, Macedonia, Maldives, Mali, Mexico, Moldova, Mongolia, Montenegro, Mozambique, Namibia, North Korea, Peru, Poland, Romania, Russia, Serbia, Slovak Republic, Sudan, Syria, Tajikistan, Turkmenistan, Ukraine, USA, Uzbekistan, Vietnam, Yemen

Mi-9 "Hip-G": Armenia, Belarus, Czech Republic, Kazakhstan, Russia, Ukraine
Mi-17 "Hip-H": Algeria, Angola, Armenia, Bangladesh, Bosnia and Herzegovina, Bulgaria, Burkina Faso, Cambodia, China, Colombia, Croatia, Cuba, Czech Republic, Djibouti, Eritrea, Ethiopia, Georgia, Hungary, India, Indonesia, Iraq, Kazakhstan, Kenya, Kyrgystan, Laos, Macedonia, Mexico, Myanmar, Nepal, Nicaragua, Pakistan, Peru, Poland, Romania, Rwanda, Slovak Republic, Sri Lanka, Syria, Turkey, Uganda, USA, Uzbekistan, Venezuela, Vietnam, Zambia
Mi-171 "Hip": Algeria, Angola, Czech Republic, Ecuador, Indonesia, Iran, Malaysia, Myanmar, Nigeria, Pakistan, Slovak Republic, Yemen
Mi-172: Tajikistan

FEATURES:

Round windows on military cabin; square windows on civil variants; starboard tail rotor on Mi-8; port tail rotor on Mi-17; two Klimov TV2-117AG (Mi-8) and TV3-117MT (Mi-17) turboshafts; fixed wheeled undercarriage
Not to be confused with Mil-14 "Haze"; Aerospatiale SA 330; Eurocopter AS.332/532 Super Puma/Cougar

Mil Mi-14 "Haze" RUSSIA

Attack/assault helicopter

Essentially an Mi-8 with a boat-hull lower fuselage (in the manner of a Sea King) and Mi-17 engines. First flown in September 1969, the "Haze" was developed for ASW and SAR work. At least 250 were produced.

SPECIFICATION:

ACCOMMODATION: 2 pilots and 2 mission specialists plus up to 10 survivors
MAX SPEED: 124 kt (230 km/h)
RANGE: 612 nm (1135 km)

ARMAMENT (MI-14PL "HAZE-A"):
HARDPOINTS: N/A
MAX WEAPON LOAD: N/A
REPRESENTATIVE WEAPONS: torpedoes; depth charges; nuclear depth bomb

DIMENSIONS:
MAIN ROTOR DIAMETER: 21.9 m (69 ft 10 in)
LENGTH: 25.3 m (83 ft 1 in)
HEIGHT: 6.9 m (22 ft 9 in)

VARIANTS & OPERATORS:
Mi-14: Georgia, Ukraine, USA
Mi-14PL "Haze-A": Bulgaria, Ethiopia, Libya, North Korea, Poland, Russia, Syria
Mi-14PS "Haze-C": Poland, Russia

FEATURES:
Round windows on cabin; boat-type hull; rear fuselage sponsons; port tail rotor; two Klimov TV3-117MT turboshafts; retractable wheeled undercarriage

Mil Mi-24/-25/-35 "Hind" RUSSIA

Attack/assault helicopter

First prototype flown on September 19, 1969, and entered service from 1972. Progressively developed with various sensor and armament fits. Export designations are Mi-25 and Mi-35. Russia now upgrading Mi-24P "Hind-F" to Mi-24PN standard. More than 2500 Mi-24 "Hinds" of all variants produced, many now being upgraded. Remains in production.

SPECIFICATION:

ACCOMMODATION: pilot and WSO
MAX SPEED: Mi-24P, 172 kt (320 km/h)
COMBAT RADIUS: Mi-24P on internal fuel, 86 nm (160 km)

ARMAMENT:

INTERNAL GUNS: one 12.7 mm four-barrel machine gun in undernose turret (Mi-24/25); twin-barrel 23 mm gun (Mi-35)
HARDPOINTS: four pylons on stub wings, and twin rails under endplate
MAX WEAPON LOAD: Mi-24P, 2400 kg (5291 lb); Mi-35M, 2860 kg (6305 lb)
REPRESENTATIVE WEAPONS: AAMs; ATGWs; rockets; bombs

DIMENSIONS (MI-35M):

MAIN ROTOR DIAMETER: 17.2 m (56 ft 5 in)
LENGTH: rotors turning, 21.3 m (69 ft 10 in)

VARIANTS & OPERATORS:

Mi-24 "Hind": Afghanistan, Angola, Armenia, Azerbaijan, Belarus, Bulgaria, Burundi, Chad, Czech Republic, Ethiopia, Georgia, Guinea Republic, Hungary, Ivory Coast, Kazakhstan, Kyrgystan, Libya, Macedonia, Mexico, Mozambique, Namibia, Nigeria, North Korea, Poland, Peru, Russia, Rwanda, Slovak Republic, Sri Lanka, Sudan, Syria, Tajikistan, Turkmenistan, Uganda, Ukraine, USA, Uzbekistan, Vietnam, Yemen, Zimbabwe
Mi-24K "Hind-G2": Armenia, Macedonia, Russia, Ukraine
Mi-24RKR "Hind-G1": Armenia, Russia, Ukraine
Mi-25: India
Mi-35: Angola, Burkina Faso, Cyprus, Czech Republic, India, Indonesia, Sri Lanka, Venezuela

FEATURES:

Tandem cockpit; undernose sensor fairings on some versions; port tail rotor; two Klimov TV3-117MT turboshafts; fixed wheeled undercarriage

Mil Mi-28 "Havoc" RUSSIA

Attack helicopter

First prototype flew on November 10, 1982, and was considered an "Apache look-alike." Basic Mi-28A selected for preseries production but not initiated. Mi-28N "Night Hunter" developed and, by mid-2004, production of 50 was authorized, starting in February 2005. ISD estimated for 2006/7.

SPECIFICATION:

ACCOMMODATION: 2 pilots
MAX SPEED: 162 kt (300 km/h)
RANGE: 234 nm (435 km)

ARMAMENT:
INTERNAL GUNS: one 30 mm cannon in undernose turret
HARDPOINTS: two pylons under each stub-wing
MAX WEAPON LOAD: 11,500 kg (24,961 lb)
REPRESENTATIVE WEAPONS: Vikhr, Igla-V, or AT-6 Spiral ATGWs; 80 mm or 122 mm rocket pods; 23 mm cannon pods; mine dispensers

DIMENSIONS:
MAIN ROTOR DIAMETER: 17.2 m (56 ft 5 in)
LENGTH: 17.0 m (55f t 10 in)
HEIGHT: 4.7 m (15 ft 5 in)

VARIANTS & OPERATORS:
Mi-28 "Havoc": Russia

FEATURES:
Angular fuselage; starboard tail rotor; port tailplane; two laterally mounted Klimov TV3-117VMA turboshafts; fixed wheeled undercarriage

NH Industries NH 90 FRANCE/GERMANY/ITALY/NETHERLANDS/

Medium transport/naval helicopter (NH 90 TTH pictured)

The first of five prototype NH 90s (NATO Helicopter for the 1990s) flew in France on December 18, 1995. Originally a four-nation collaborative venture, Portugal joined in 2001. Two versions are being developed: the tactical transport helicopter (TTH) and the NATO frigate helicopter (NFH). As of 2006, there are 357 firm orders. New Zealand selected NH 90 in March 2005, Spain in May 2005, and Belgium in December 2005. There are options on a further 120.

NH 90 TTH

NH 90 NFH

SPECIFICATION:

ACCOMMODATION: 2 flight crew plus mission specialists (NFH) or 14–20 troops (TTH)
MAX SPEED: 157 kt (291 km/h)
RANGE: 650 nm (1203 km)

ARMAMENT:
INTERNAL GUNS: 7.62 mm machine gun(s) in door mountings
HARDPOINTS: two pylons
MAX WEAPON LOAD: 4600 kg (10,143 lb)
REPRESENTATIVE WEAPONS: ASV, Marte Mk 2/S ASMs; ASW torpedoes, depth charges

DIMENSIONS:
MAIN ROTOR DIAMETER: 16.3 m (53 ft 5 in)
LENGTH: 19.6 m (64 ft 2 in)
HEIGHT: 4.1 m (13 ft 5 in)

VARIANTS & OPERATORS:
NH90: Oman
NH 90 NFH: France, Italy, Netherlands, Norway
NH 90 TTH: Australia (MRH90), Finland, France, Germany, Greece, Italy, Netherlands, Portugal, Sweden (Hkp 14)
NH90 TTH (ETT-1): Italy

FEATURES:
Side-by-side cockpit; port tail rotor; starboard tailplane; two RTM 322 or GE T700-T6E turboshafts; fuselage sponsons for retractable wheeled undercarriage
Not to be confused with AgustaWestland AW139; Eurocopter AS332/532 Super Puma/Cougar; Sikorsky S-92

PZL Šwidnik (Mil) Mi-2 "Hoplite" RUSSIA/POLAND

Light helicopter

First flown in Russia on September 22, 1962, but production and marketing assigned to Poland in 1964. Built in ambulance, agricultural, naval, SAR, troop transport, combat support, and antitank versions. Over 5450 Mi-2s of all versions built.

SPECIFICATION:

ACCOMMODATION: 1 pilot plus up to 8 passengers
MAX SPEED: 113 kt (210 km/h)
RANGE: internal fuel, 237 nm (440 km)

ARMAMENT (MI-2U RP):

HARDPOINTS: four on outrigger pylons
MAX WEAPON LOAD: N/A
REPRESENTATIVE WEAPONS: AT-3 Sagger ATGWs or Strela 2 AAMs

DIMENSIONS:

MAIN ROTOR DIAMETER: 14.5 m (47 ft 7 in)
LENGTH: 17.4 m (57 ft 2 in)
HEIGHT: 3.8 m (12 ft 4 in)

VARIANTS & OPERATORS:

Mi-2: Algeria, Armenia, Azerbaijan, Czech Republic, Djibouti, Estonia, Georgia, Ghana, Hungary, Indonesia, Latvia, Mexico, Myanmar, North Korea, Peru, Poland, Russia, Slovak Republic, Syria, Ukraine, USA

FEATURES:

Short cabin; starboard tail rotor; two Isotov GTD-350 turboshafts; fixed wheeled undercarriage

PZL Šwidnik W-3 Sokol POLAND

Multipurpose helicopter

Clearly showing its Mi-2 grand-parentage, the prototype W-3 first flew on November 16, 1979; several versions were produced and other, one-off specialized variants evaluated. Over 124 W-3s built or on order.

SPECIFICATION:

ACCOMMODATION: 2 flight crew plus 12 passengers
MAX SPEED: 140 kt (260 km/h)
RANGE: 402 nm (745 km)

ARMAMENT (W-3W):

INTERNAL GUNS: twin-barrel 23 mm cannon (starboard side)
HARDPOINTS: four on cabin pylons
MAX WEAPON LOAD: N/A
REPRESENTATIVE WEAPONS: 57 mm or 80 mm rocket pods

DIMENSIONS:

MAIN ROTOR DIAMETER: 15.7 m (51 ft 6 in)
LENGTH: 18.8 m (61 ft 8 in)
HEIGHT: 5.1 m (16 ft 10 in)

VARIANTS: & OPERATORS

W-3 Sokol: Iraq, Myanmar, Poland
W-3A Sokol: Czech Republic
W-3P/RL: Poland
W-3RM Anakonda: Poland, Vietnam
W-3T: Poland
W-3W Sokol: Iraq, Poland

FEATURES:

Sharp nose; starboard tail rotor; two WSK-PZL Rzeszow PZL-10W turboshafts; fixed wheeled undercarriage

Sikorsky S-61/SH-3 Sea King USA

Amphibious ASW/SAR helicopter (ASH-3D pictured)

The prototype S-61 (initial military designation HSS-2) was first flown on March 11, 1959, and featured a boat-hull fuselage. It entered USN service in September 1961 (later being designated SH-3). Developed into several versions (including the S-61R/HH-3 Pelican) and license-built in Italy by Agusta, in Japan by Mitsubishi and the UK by Westland (which see). Over 1030 versions of the S-61/SH-3 were produced.

SPECIFICATION):

ACCOMMODATION: 2 pilots and 2 WSOs
MAX SPEED: 144 kt (267 km/h)
RANGE: 542 nm (1005 km)

ARMAMENT (SH-3D/H):
INTERNAL GUNS: provision for door-mounted 7.62 mm Miniguns
HARDPOINTS: four
MAX WEAPON LOAD: 381 kg (840 lb)
REPRESENTATIVE WEAPONS: AS 12, Marte Mk 2 or Exocet ASMs; torpedoes; depth charges

DIMENSIONS:
MAIN ROTOR DIAMETER: 18.9 m (62 ft 0 in)
LENGTH: 22.1 m (72 ft 8 in)
HEIGHT: 5.1 m (16 ft 10 in)

VARIANTS & OPERATORS:
Argentina (S-61D-4, ASH-3H, SH-3D/H), Brazil (ASH-3D/SH-3D), Canada (CH-124A/B), Denmark (S-61A), Egypt (AS-61), Iran (AS-61A-4, ASH-3D), Italy (AS-61A-4, ASH-3D/H, HH-3F Pelican), Japan (S-61A/AH, HSS-2B), Libya (AS-61A-4), Malaysia (AS-61N Nuri, S-61A-4 Nuri), Namibia (S-61L), Peru (ASH-3D), Saudi Arabia (AS-61A-4), Spain (H-3, SH-3), Tunisia (HH-3E), USA (NVH-3A, UH-3H, VH-3D), Venezuela (AS-61D)

FEATURES:
Boat-hull fuselage; port tail rotor; two GE T58-GE-10 turboshafts; outrigger sponsons for retractable wheeled undercarriage

Sikorsky S-65/CH-53 Sea Stallion USA

Assault transport helicopter

A step up from the S-61R/CH-3 and using some S-64 Skycrane components, the first CH-53A flew October 14, 1964, and entered USMC service as the Sea Stallion in 1966. Adopted by the USAF, the HH-53 was nicknamed "Super Jolly." The MH-53J Pave Low III is a SOCOM version. License-built in Germany by VFW-Fokker. Some 522 S-65/CH-53s of all versions were built.

SPECIFICATION:

ACCOMMODATION: 3 flight crew plus up to 37 troops
MAX SPEED: 170 kt (315 km/h)
RANGE: 468 nm (869 km)

ARMAMENT (MH-53J):
INTERNAL GUNS: three 7.62 mm or 0.5 in (12.7 mm) machine guns in fuselage and on ramp

DIMENSIONS:
MAIN ROTOR DIAMETER: 22.0 m (72 ft 3 in)
LENGTH: 26.9 m (88 ft 3 in)
HEIGHT: 7.6 m (24 ft 11 in)

VARIANTS & OPERATORS:
Germany (CH-53G), Iran (RH-53D), Israel (CH-53D Yasur 2000), USA (CH-53D, MH-53J/M)

FEATURES:
Long cabin with tail ramp; port tail rotor; starboard tailplane; two pod-mounted GE T64-GE-6 turboshafts; center-fuselage sponsons for retractable wheeled undercarriage

Sikorsky S-80/SH-53E Super Stallion USA

Assault and MCM helicopter

Essentially a three-engined version of the S-65/CH-53, the prototype S-80/CH-53E first flew March 1, 1974. The CH-53E Super Stallion replaced CH-53Ds in USMC service; in the USN, the MH-53E Sea Dragon replaced the RH-53D in the MCM role. U.S. versions being upgraded. Some 237 S-80/CH/MH-53s were produced. In January 2006, the USMC ordered a new-build model, CH-53K, as its next heavy-lift helicopter.

SPECIFICATION:

ACCOMMODATION: 3 flight crew plus up to 55 troops or various towed MCM devices
MAX SPEED: 170 kt (315 km/h)
RANGE: ferry, 1120 nm (2074 km)

ARMAMENT:
INTERNAL GUNS: provision for three 7.62 mm or 0.5 in (12.7 mm) machine guns in fuselage and on ramp
HARDPOINTS: two on sponsons
REPRESENTATIVE STORES: external fuel tanks

DIMENSIONS:
MAIN ROTOR DIAMETER: 24.1 m (79 ft 0 in)
LENGTH: 30.2 m (99 ft 0 in)
HEIGHT: 9.0 m (29 ft 5 in)

VARIANTS & OPERATORS:
Japan (MH-53EJ), USA (CH-53E, MH-53E)

FEATURES:
Long cabin with tail ramp; canted fin with port tail rotor; starboard tailplane; three GE T64-GE-416/-416A turboshafts; center-fuselage sponsons for retractable wheeled undercarriage

Sikorsky S-70A/UH-60 Black Hawk USA

Battlefield helicopter

First flown on October 17, 1974, the YUH-60A was winner of the U.S. Army's UTTAS competition in December 1976. The Black Hawk entered U.S. Army service in 1979 and has evolved into many specialized variants, including EW, medevac, C-SAR, and Special Forces. Sikorsky is now producing the latest UH-60M configuration. Export variants are designated S-70A, while the naval version is S-70B (SH-60; which see). As of January 2007, 2189 S-70A/wUH-60 versions have been built or are on order, with another 514 planned for U.S. forces.

UH-60A

SPECIFICATION:

ACCOMMODATION: 3 flight crew plus 11 troops or 4082 kg (9000 lb) external cargo sling
MAX SPEED: UH-60L/Q, 194 kt (359 km/h)
RANGE: with external tanks, 1200 nm (2222 km)

ARMAMENT (OPTIONAL):
INTERNAL GUNS: provision for two 7.62 mm miniguns or 0.5 in (12.7 mm) GECAL 50 machine guns in fuselage doors
HARDPOINTS: four mounted on the outrigger ESSS
MAX WEAPON LOAD: ESSS, 2268 kg (5000 lb)
REPRESENTATIVE WEAPONS: ESSS, Stinger AAMs; Hellfire ATGWs; 2.75 in FFAR pods; mine dispensers; ECM pods; external fuel tanks

DIMENSIONS:
MAIN ROTOR DIAMETER: 16.7 m (53 ft 8 in)
LENGTH: 19.8 m (64 ft 10 in)
HEIGHT: 5.1 m (16 ft 10 in)

VARIANTS & OPERATORS:
Argentina (S-70A), Australia (S-70A), Austria (S-70A), Bahrain (UH-60A/L), Brazil (S-70A, UH-60L), Brunei (S-70A), Chile (S-70A), China (S-70C), Colombia (UH-60A/L), Egypt (S-70A, UH-60L), Israel (S-70A, UH-60A), Japan (UH-60J), Jordan (S-70A, UH-60L), Malaysia (S-70A), Mexico (S-70A), Morocco (S-70A), Philippines (S-70A), Saudi Arabia (S-70A), South Korea (UH-60P), Taiwan (S-70C/C-6/C(M)), Thailand (S-70A, UH-60L), Turkey (S-70A), USA (EH-60A, HH-60G/H/J/L, MH-60G/K/L/S, UH-60A/L/M/Q, VH-60N)

FEATURES:
Side-by-side cockpit; square windows in fuselage; starboard tail rotor; full tailplane at base of fin; two GE T700-GE-700/-701 turboshafts; fixed wheeled undercarriage

Sikorsky S-70B/SH-60 Seahawk USA

Naval helicopter

Winner of the USN's LAMPS Mk III contest in 1977, the first YSH-60B (S-70B) Seahawk prototype flew on December 12, 1979. In USN service since 1983, the Seahawk has been developed into various specialized models for frigate and carrier-borne ASW, C-SAR, vertrep, and customs roles. Over 440 S-70B/SH-60s built or on order, with USN plans to buy up to 252 MH-60Rs.

SPECIFICATION:

ACCOMMODATION: 2 flight crew plus mission specialists or 4082 kg (9000 lb) external cargo sling
MAX SPEED: 160 kt (296 km/h)
RANGE: internal fuel, 319 nm (592 km)

ARMAMENT:

INTERNAL GUNS: (HH-60H) two 7.62 mm M60D machine guns in fuselage doors
HARDPOINTS: two on the rear fuselage
MAX WEAPON LOAD: N/A
REPRESENTATIVE WEAPONS: Mk 46/50/54 torpedoes; MCM equipment; ECM pods; external fuel tanks

DIMENSIONS:

MAIN ROTOR DIAMETER: 16.7 m (53 ft 8 in)
LENGTH: SH-60B, 12.3 m (40 ft 11 in)
HEIGHT: 5.2 m (17 ft 0 in)

VARIANTS & OPERATORS:

Australia (S-70B), Brazil (S-70B requested), Greece (S-70B), Japan (SH-60J/K), Singapore (S-70B on order), Spain (S-70B), Thailand (S-70B), Turkey (S-70B), USA (HH-60H/J, MH-60R/S, NSH-60B, SH-60B/F)

FEATURES:

Side-by-side cockpit; square windows in fuselage; starboard tail rotor; full tailplane at base of fin; two GE T700-GE-700/-701 turboshafts; fixed wheeled undercarriage (tailwheel further forward than UH-60)

SH-60B

Westland (A-W) WG.13 Lynx/Super Lynx UK

Naval and battlefield helicopter (Lynx AH.9 pictured)

The third type covered by the 1968 Westland/Aerospatiale joint program for the French and British services, the first of 13 WG.13 Lynx proto-types flew on March 21, 1971. Developed in army (battlefield) and naval versions, the first Royal Navy Lynx HAS.2 entered service in 1977. Upgraded and evolved (incuding BERP main rotors), the latest Super Lynx can be powered by the LHTEC CTS-800-4N engines. Over 430 Lynx/Super Lynx have been built or are on order. It will also form the new UK battlefield and maritime variant.

Naval Lynx

SPECIFICATION:

ACCOMMODATION: 1 pilot and 1 WSO (naval) or 2 pilots plus 10 troops (battlefield)
MAX SPEED: Army/Navy, 145 kt (269 km/h); Super Lynx, 138 kt (256 km/h)
RADIUS OF ACTION: Army/Navy, 292 nm (540 km); Super Lynx, 320 nm (593 km)

ARMAMENT:
INTERNAL GUNS: provision for door-mounted 7.62 mm GPMG or 0.5 in (12.7 mm) M3 machine gun
HARDPOINTS: two pylons (battlefield), or four (naval)
MAX WEAPON LOAD: 3949 kg (8707 lb) battlefield or 4618 kg (10,181 lb) naval
REPRESENTATIVE WEAPONS: battlefield—HOT, Hell-fire, or TOW ATGWs, FFAR pods, 7.62 mm machine gun or 20 mm cannon pods; naval-ASW—Mk 44/46, A244S, or Sting Ray torpedoes, depth charges; naval-ASV—Sea Skua, Penguin, or Marte ASMs, 7.62 mm machine guns or 20 mm cannon pods

DIMENSIONS (ARMY/NAVY):
MAIN ROTOR DIAMETER: 12.8 m (42 ft 0 in)
LENGTH: 15.1 m (49 ft 9 in)
HEIGHT: 3.5 m (11 ft 6 in)

DIMENSIONS (SUPER LYNX):
MAIN ROTOR DIAMETER: 12.8 m (42 ft 0 in)
LENGTH: 15.2 m (50 ft 0 in)
HEIGHT: 3.7 m (12 ft 0 in)

VARIANTS & OPERATORS:
Brazil (Super Lynx Mk 21A), Denmark (Super Lynx Mk 90B), France (Mk 4(FN)), Germany (Super Lynx Mk 88A/Mk 90B), Malaysia (Super Lynx 300), Netherlands (SH-14D), Norway (Mk 86), Nigeria (Mk 89), Oman (Super Lynx 300), Portugal (Mk 95), South Africa (Mk 64), South Korea (Mk 99/99A), Thailand (Super Lynx 300), UK (AH.7/9, HAS.3/ICE/S/SGM, HMA.7DEP, HMA.8/ACS/DAS/DSP, Mk 4X)

FEATURES:
Side-by-side cockpit; square windows in fuselage; port tail rotor; starboard tailplane; two Rolls-Royce Gem 42-1 turboshafts; skid (army) or fixed wheeled undercarriage (naval and AH.9)

Westland (A-W) WS-61 Sea King UK

Naval and battlefield helicopter (Sea King HC.4 pictured)

Westland acquired license to build/develop the S-61 (which see) in 1959, and first production Westland Sea King HAS.1 flew May 7, 1969. Several variants developed, including AEW, ASaC, ASW, ASV, and troop transport (Commando). Many variants upgraded including addition of BERP main rotors. Some 328 Sea King/Commando variants have been built by Westland in the UK.

SPECIFICATION:

ACCOMMODATION: 2 pilots plus 2 WSOs (ASW/ASVW) or 2 pilots plus 28 troops (Sea King HC.4/Commando) or 3628 kg (8000 lb) external slung cargo
MAX SPEED: 122 kt (226 km/h)
RANGE: Commando, 300 nm (556 km)

ARMAMENT:
INTERNAL GUNS: one 7.62 mm GPMG, starboard door mounted
HARDPOINTS: four
MAX WEAPON LOAD: N/A
REPRESENTATIVE WEAPONS: Sea Eagle or Exocet ASMs; Mk 46, A224S, Sting Ray torpedoes; depth charges

DIMENSIONS:
MAIN ROTOR DIAMETER: 18.9 m (62 ft 0 in)
LENGTH: 22.1 m (72 ft 8 in)
HEIGHT: 5.1 m (16 ft 10 in)

VARIANTS & OPERATORS:
Australia (Sea King Mk 50A/B), Belgium (Mk 48), Egypt (Commando Mk 1/2/2E), Germany (Mk 41), India (Mk 42B/C), Norway (Mk 43B), Pakistan (Mk 45), Qatar (Commando Mk 2/3), Sierra Leone (Commando Mk 2), UK (Sea King AEW.7 also known as ASaC.7), HAR.3/3A, HAS.6/6C, HC.4, HU.5/5SAR)

FEATURES:
Boat-hull fuselage; port tail rotor; two Rolls-Royce Gnome H.1400-1T turboshafts; outrigger sponsons for retractable wheeled undercarriage

Sea King HAR.3

Glossary of Acronyms and Terms

A-W	AgustaWestland (now wholly owned by Finmeccanica of Italy)
AAAW	Advanced AntiArmor Weapon (became Brimstone)
AAM	Air-to-Air Missile
AAR	Air-to-Air Refuelling
ACM	Advanced Cruise Missile, designation is AGM-129
ACMI	Air Combat Maneuvering Instrumentation (pod)
ADV	Air Defense Variant (of Tornado), RAF designations is Tornado F.2/2A, F.3 or EF.3
AEW	Airborne Early Warning
AEW&C	Airborne Early Warning and Control
AGM	Air-to-Ground Missile (also used in U.S. designations)
AH	Army Helicopter (UK designator)
AHIP	Army Helicopter Improvement Program (for U.S. Army OH-58 Kiowa)
AIDC	Aerospace Industrial Development Corporation (Taiwan)
AIM	Air Interception Missile (used in U.S. designations)
aka	also known as
ALARM	Air-Launched AntiRadar Missile
ALCM	Air-Launched Cruise Missile
ALH	Advanced Light Helicopter (HAL Druhvs)
AMRAAM	Advanced Medium-Range Air-to-Air Missile (designation is AIM-120)
An	Antonov (Russian design bureau)
APACHE	Armement Propulsée A CHarges Ejectables—French weapons dispenser weapon from which Storm Shadow/ SCALP EG weapons are derived
APN	Aviation of the People's Navy (China's naval air arm)
ARM	AntiRadar Missile
ASaC	Airborne Surveillance and Control (UK designator applied to what was the Sea King AEW.7, now ASaC.7)
ASM	AntiShip Missile
ASMP	Air-Sol-Moyenne Portée—French nuclear stand-off missile
ASRAAM	Advanced Short-Range Air-to-Air Missile
ASTOR	Airborne STand-Off Radar
ASV	Anti–Surface Vessel
ASVW	Anti–Surface Vessel Warfare
ASW	AntiSubmarine Warfare
ATF	Advanced Tactical Fighter
ATGW	AntiTank Guided Weapon
AVLF	Airborne Very Low Frequency—communications system used to communicate with submersed USN submarines
AWACS	Airborne Warning And Control System— the USAF program that spawned the E-3 Sentry and often incorrectly used as the aircraft name itself

B	Bomber (U.S. designation prefix)
BAC	British Aircraft Corporation
BAe	British Aerospace
BBMF	Battle of Britain Memorial Flight
Be	Beriev (Russian design bureau)
BERP	British Experimental Rotorcraft Program
C	Cargo (transport)—UK designator and U.S. prefix
CAC	Chengdu Aircraft Industrial Corporation (China)
CALCM	Conventional (-armed) Air-Launched Cruise Missile, designation is AGM-86C/D
CAS	Close Air Support (aka ground attack)
CBLS	Carrier, Bomb, Light Stores (a practise bomb carrier)
CFT	Conformal Fuel Tank (used on F-15)
CHAIC	CHanghe Aircraft Industries Corporation (China)
CIA	Central Intelligence Agency (U.S.)
COD	Carrier On-board Delivery
COIN	COunter INsurgency
C-SAR	Combat Search-And-Rescue
DAS	Defensive Aids Suite
DHI	Daewoo Heavy Industries (South Korea)
E-O	Electro-Optical equipment (FLIRs or laser rangefinder)
EADS	European Aeronautic and Defense Systems Company
EASA	European Aviation Safety Agency
ECM	Electronic CounterMeasures
ECR	Electronic Combat and Reconnaissance (variant of Tornado)
ELINT	Electronic Intelligence
EMD	Engineering, Manufacture, and Development (i.e. preproduction/preseries)
EMBRAER	EMpresa BRasiliera de AERonautica (Brazil)
ENAER	Empresa Nacional de AERonautica (Chile)
ESM	Electronic Support Measures
ESSS	External Stores Support System (for S-70A/UH-60)
EW	Electronic Warfare
EWO	Electronic Warfare Officer
F	Fighter (UK & U.S. designator)
FAC	Forward Air Control (or Controller)
FADEC	Full-Authority Digital Engine Control
FFAR	Folding-Fin Aerial Rocket (pod)
FLI	Fighter Lead-In (trainer)
FLIR	Forward-Looking InfraRed (thermal sensor)
FMA	Spanish acronym for Military Aircraft Factory, now Lockheed Martin Aircraft Argentina SA

FRY	Federal Republic of Yugoslavia		being AGM-154A (with 145 BLU-97/B bomblets), AGM-154B (with six BLU-108/B bomblets), and AGM-154C (with BROACH penetrating warhead)
FSD	Full-Scale Development		
FSTA	Future Strategic Tanker Aircraft (UK program)		
GE	General Electric (U.S.)	**JVX**	Joint Vertical eXperimental—the tiltrotor project that became the V-22 Osprey
GPMG	General Purpose Machine Gun (UK weapon)	**K**	Kerosene (tanker—UK designator)
GR	Ground-attack and Recconaissance (UK designator)	**Ka**	Kamov (Russian design bureau)
		KAI	Korean Aerospace Industries (South Korea)
HAC	Helicoptere Anti-Char (antitank helicopter), version of Tigre/Tiger	**LAMPS**	Light Airborne MultiPurpose System
HAI	Harbin Aircraft Industries (China)	**LANTIRN**	Low Altitude Navigation Targeting InfraRed at Night
HAL	Hindustan Aeronautics Limited (India)	**LERX**	Leading-Edge Root eXtension
HAMC	Harbin Aircraft Manufacturing Corporation (China)	**LGB**	Laser-Guided Bomb
HAP	Helicoptere d'Appui et de Protection (escort/fire support helicopter), version of Tigre/Tiger	**LHTEC**	Light Helicopter Turbine Engine Company (U.S.), joint venture between Rolls-Royce (formerly Allison) and Honeywell (formerly Garrett)
HARM	High-speed AntiRadar Missile, designation is AGM-88	**LHX**	Light Helicopter eXperimental (now the RAH-66)
HAS	Helicopter AntiSubmarine (UK designator)	**LIFT**	Lead-In Fighter Trainer
HC	Helicopter Cargo (UK designator)	**LOCAAS**	LOw-Cost Autonomous Attack System
HCP	Helicoptere de Combat Polyvalent (multirole combat helicopter) applied to Tigre/Tiger	**LRIP**	Low-Rate Initial Production
		MAD	Magnetic Anomoly Dectector
HMA	Helicopter, Maritime Attack (UK designator)	**MBB**	Messerschmitt Bolkow Blohm (Germany)
HOT	French ATGW acroynm from Haut subsonique Optiquement teleguide tire d'un Tube = subsonic optically tracked tube-launched [antitank missile]	**McDD**	McDonnell Douglas (U.S.)
		MCM	Mine CounterMeasures
		Medevac	Medical evacuation
		MESA	Multirole Electronically Scanned Array (radar—mounted on RAAF Boeing Wedgetail AEW&C aircraft)
HSA	Hawker Siddeley Aviation (UK)	**MFTS**	Military Flying Training System (UK program)
IAI	Israel Aircraft Industries		
ICAP (III)	Improved Capability (III)	**MiG**	Mikoyan-Gurevich (Russian design bureau)
ICH	Improved Cargo Helicopter (the CH-47F Chinook)	**Mi**	Mil (Russian design bureau)
IDS	InterDictor Strike (variant of Tornado)	**MLU**	Mid-Life Update
IOC	Initial Operating Capability	**MMS**	Mast-Mounted Sight
IOT&E	Initial Operational Test and Evaluation (USAF term)	**MMW**	MilliMetric (or MilliMeter) Wave (as AN/APG-78 Longbow radar for the AH-64D Apache Longbow helicopter)
ISD	In-Service Date	**MPA**	Maritime Patrol Aircraft
		MR	Maritime Reconnaissance (UK designator)
JASDF	Japanese Air Self-Defense Force (air force)		
JASSM	Joint Air-to-Surface Stand-off Missile, designation is AGM-158	**MRA**	Maritime Reconnaissance and Attack (UK designator)
JDAM	Joint Direct Attack Munition, a GPS-guidance package added to existing bomb bodies, designations being GBU-29 (with Mk.81 bomb), GBU-30 (Mk.82), GBU-31 (Mk.83), GBU-32 (Mk 84 or BLU-109/B), and GBU-35 (BLU-110/B)	**MRCA**	MultiRole Combat Aircraft (renamed Tornado)
		MRT	MultiRole Transport
		MRTT	MultiRole Tanker/Transport
		MTI	Moving Target Indication
		MTU	Motoren und Turbinen Union (Germany)
JGSDF	Japanese Ground Self-Defense Force (army)		
		N/A	Not Available
JMSDF	Japanese Maritime Self-Defense Force (navy)	**NBAA**	National Business Aviation Association
		N-G	Northrop Grumman (U.S.)
JPATS	Joint Primary Aircraft Training System (USAF/USN)	**NAMC**	Nanchang Aircraft Manufacturing Company (China)
JSF	Joint Strike Fighter (USAF/USN/USMC/RN/RAF)	**NASA**	National Aeronautics And Space Administration (U.S.)
JSOW	Joint Stand-Off Weapon, designations		

NATO	North Atlantic Treaty Organisation
NFH	Naval Frigate Helicopter (NH 90 variant)
NOTAR	NO TAil Rotor—patented tail-stabilization system developed for MD 500-type helicopter
OSD	Out-of-Service Date
P&W	Pratt & Whitney (U.S.)
P&WC	Pratt & Whitney Canada
PAC	Pakistan Aeronautical Complex
PAH	PanzerAbwehr-Hubschrauber (Army [anti-] tank helicopter)
Panavia	Tri-national consortium formed to produce Tornado, comprising MBB of Germany (now EADS/DASA), Aeritalia of Italy (now Alenia Aerospazio), and BAC (now BAE Systems)
PFI	Private Finance Initiative
PLAAF	People's Liberation Army—Air Force (China)
PGM	Precision-Guided Munition
PZL	Polskie Zaklady Lotnicze (Polish Aviation Factory)
Q	U.S. designation prefix for drone-configured aircraft
R	Radio (ELINT/SIGINT)—UK designator applied to versions of the Nimrod and Sentinel
R-R	Rolls-Royce
RAAF	Royal Australian Air Force
RAC-MiG	Russian Aircraft Corporation-MiG (RSK-MiG in Russian—the manufacturing organization teamed with the Mikoyan-Gurevich design bureau)
RAF	Royal Air Force
recce	Reconnaissance
RoA	Radius of Action
RoCAF	Republic of China (Taiwan) Air Force
RoKAF	Republic of Korea (South Korea) Air Force
S	Sikorsky (model designator, e.g., S-70)
SAAF	South African Air Force
SAR	Search-And-Rescue; Synthetic Aperture Radar
SCALP	Systéme de Croisiére conventional Autonome a Longue Portée de precision—French derivative of APACHE weapon
SDB	Small Diameter Bomb
SDD	System Design and Development (taken over from EMD)
SEPECAT	Societe Europeene de Production de l'Avion Ecole et Combat Appui Tactique = European company to produce the training and tactical combat aircraft; 50:50 Anglo-French company responsible for Jaguar, with BAC (now BAE Systems) and Breguet (now Dassault)
SIFICAP	SIstema de FIscalizacao e Controlo das Activades da Pesca—Portuguese acronym meaning System of Supervision and Fishing Activity Control; relates to EH 101 Mk 515
SIGINT	Signals Intelligence
SIVAM	SIstema de Vigilancia da AMazonia—Brazil's surveillance program for its Amazon region
SLAM	Stand-off Land Attack Missile, designation is AGM-84G
SLAM-ER	Stand-off Land Attack Missile—Expanded Response, designation is AGM-84H
SLAR	Sideways-Looking Airborne Radar
SLEP	Service (or Structural) Life Extension Program
SNECMA	Société Nationale d'Etude et de Construction de Moteurs d'Aviation (France)
SOCAT	Romanian acronym for the IAR-Brasov/Elbit upgrade of 24 IAR-330L Pumas with modern avionics and armament
SOCOM	US Special Operation Command
SRAM	Short-Range Attack Missile
STOL	Short Take-Off and Landing
STOVL	Short Take-Off Vertical Landing
Su	Sukhoi (Russian design bureau)
T	Trainer (UK designator)
TACAMO	TAke Charge And Move OuT—USN AVLF relay system
TOW	Tube-launched, Optically tracked, Wire-guided (ATGW), designation is BGM-71
TTH	Troop Transport Helicopter (NH 90 variant)
Tu	Tupolev (Russian design bureau)
UAE	United Arab Emirates
UHT	UnterstutzungHubschrauber Tiger—final antitank/fire support configuration of German Army Tiger, replacing original PAH-2
USAF	United States Air Force
USMC	United States Marine Corps
USN	United States Navy
UTTAS	Utility Tactical Transport Aircraft System
V-G	Variable-Geometry (i.e., swing-wing)
Vertrep	Vertical Replenishment (at sea)
VC	Vickers Commercial (as in VC 10)
VLF	Very Low Frequency radio transmission band
VTO	Vertical Take-Off
WCMD	Wind-Corrected Munition Dispenser, being an add-on to the CBU-78/B, CBU-87/B CEM, and CBU-98/B Gator cluster munitions
WSO	Weapons System Operator
X	U.S. designation prefix for experimental aircraft
Y	U.S. designation prefix for developmental aircraft

International Civil Aircraft Markings

AP	Pakistan		HL	Korea, South
A2	Botswana		HP	Panama
A3	Tonga Friendly Islands		HR	Honduras
A4O	Oman		HS	Thailand
A5	Bhutan		HV	Vatican
A6	United Arab Emirates		HZ	Saudi Arabia
A7	Qatar		H4	Solomon Islands
A8	Liberia			
A9C	Bahrain		I	Italy
B	China		JA	Japan
B-H	Hong Kong		JU	Mongolia
B-M	Macau/Macao		JY	Jordan
B	China—Taiwan		J2	Djibouti
			J3	Grenada
C	Canada		J5	Guinea Bissau
CC	Chile		J6	St. Lucia
CN	Morocco		J7	Dominica
CP	Bolivia		J8	St. Vincent and Grenadines
CS	Portugal			
CU	Cuba		LN	Norway
CX	Uruguay		LV	Argentina
C2	Nauru		LX	Luxembourg
C3	Andorra		LY	Lithuania
C5	Gambia		LZ	Bulgaria
C6	Bahamas			
C9	Mozambique		N	USA
D	Germany		OB	Peru
DQ	Fiji		OD	Lebanon
D2	Angola		OE	Austria
D4	Cape Verde Islands		OH	Finland
D6	Comoros		OK	Czech Republic
			OM	Slovakia
EC	Spain		OO	Belgium
EI	Eire		OY	Denmark, including Greenland and
EK	Armenia			Faroe Islands
EP	Iran			
ER	Moldova		P	Korea, North
ES	Estonia		PH	Netherlands
ET	Ethiopia		PJ	Netherlands Antilles
EW	Belarus		PK	Indonesia
EX	Kyrgyzstan		PP/PR/PT	Brazil
EY	Tajikistan		PZ	Suriname
EZ	Turkmenistan		P2	Papua New Guinea
E3	Eritrea		P4	Aruba
E5	Cook Islands			
			RA	Russian Federation
F	France		RDPL	Laos
			RP	Philippines
G	Great Britain			
			SE	Sweden
HA	Hungary		SP	Poland
HB	Switzerland and Liechtenstein		ST	Sudan
HC	Ecuador		SU	Egypt
HH	Haiti		SU-Y	Palestine
HI	Dominican Republic		SX	Greece
HK	Colombia		S2	Bangladesh

Prefix	Country
S5	Slovenia
S7	Seychelles
S9	Sao Tomè and Principe
TC	Turkey
TF	Iceland
TG	Guatemala
TI	Costa Rica
TJ	Cameroon
TL	Central African Republic
TN	Congo Brazzaville
TR	Gabon
TS	Tunisia
TT	Chad
TU	Ivory Coast
TY	Benin
TZ	Mali
T2	Tuvalu
T3	Kiribati
T7	San Marino
T8A	Palau
T9	Bosnia and Herzegovina
UK	Uzbekistan
UN	Kazakhstan
UR	Ukraine
VH	Australia
VN	Vietnam
VP-A	Anguilla
VP-B	Bermuda
VP-C	Cayman Islands
VP-F	Falkland Islands
VP-G	Gibraltar
VP-L	British Virgin Islands
VP-M	Montserrat
VQ-T	Turks and Caicos Islands
VT	India
V2	Antigua and Barbuda
V3	Belize
V4	St. Kitts and Nevis
V5	Namibia
V6	Micronesia
V7	Marshall Islands
V8	Brunei
XA/XB/XC	Mexico
XT	Burkina Faso
XU	Cambodia
XY	Myanmar
YA	Afghanistan
YI	Iraq
YJ	Vanuatu
YK	Syria
YL	Latvia
YN	Nicaragua
YR	Romania
YS	El Salvador
YU	Serbia and Montenegro
YV	Venezuela
Z	Zimbabwe
ZA	Albania
ZK	Cook Islands
ZK	New Zealand
ZP	Paraguay
ZS/ZU	South Africa
Z3	Macedonia
3A	Monaco
3B	Mauritius
3C	Equatorial Guinea
3D	Swaziland
3X	Guinea
4K	Azerbaijan
4L	Georgia
4R	Sri Lanka
4X	Israel
5A	Libya
5B	Cyprus
5H	Tanzania
5N	Nigeria
5R	Madagascar
5T	Mauritania
5U	Niger
5V	Togo
5W	Western Samoa
5X	Uganda
5Y	Kenya
6O	Somalia
6V	Senegal
6Y	Jamaica
7O	Yemen
7P	Lesotho
7Q	Malawi
7T	Algeria
8P	Barbados
8Q	Maldives
8R	Guyana
9A	Croatia
9G	Ghana
9H	Malta
9J	Zambia
9K	Kuwait
9L	Sierra Leone
9M	Malaysia
9N	Nepal
9Q/9T	Congo, Democratic Republic
9U	Burundi
9V	Singapore
9XR	Rwanda
9Y	Trinidad and Tobago

National Military Aircraft Markings

Afghanistan: Air Force

Albania: Air Force

Algeria: Air Force

Angola: Air Force

Argentina: Air Force and Army

Argentina: Navy

Argentina: Coast Guard

Armenia: Air Force

Australia: Air Force and Navy

Australia: Army

Australia: Low Visibility

Austria: Air Force

Azerbaijan: Air Force

Bahamas: Defence Force

Bahrain: Air Force and Navy

Bangladesh: Air Wing

Bangladesh: Army Aviation

Belarus: Air Force

Belgium: Air Force and Army

Belgium: Navy Flight

Belgium: Luchtkadetten

Belgium: Police

Belize: Defence Force

Benin: Armed Forces

Bhutan: Air Arm

Bolivia: Air Force

Bolivia: Army

Bosnia and Herzegovina: Air Force

Bosnia and Herzegovina: Serbian Republic

Botswana: Defence Force

Brazil: Air Force

Brazil: Navy 1

Brazil: Navy 2

Brazil: Army

Brazil: Low Visibility

Brunei: Air Force

Bulgaria: Air Force and Navy

Burkina Faso: Air Force

Burkina Faso: Alternate

Burundi: Army Air Arm

Cambodia: Air Force

Cameroon: Air Force

Cameroon: Government

Canada: Air Command

Canada: Low Visibility

Cape Verde: Air Force

Central African Republic: Air Arm

Chad: Air Arm

Chile: Air Force

Chile: Air Force Low Visibility

Chile: Navy

Chile: Army

Chile: Presidential/ VIP Transoirt

Chile: Carabineros

Chile: Carabineros (dark background)

China: Air Force and Navy

Colombia: Air Force, Navy, Army, & Police

Colombia: Low Visibility

Colombia: Navy

Comores: Air Arm

Congo: Air Force

Congo Democratic Republic: Air Force

Costa Rica: Public Security

Cote d'Ivoire: Air Force

Croatia: Air Force

Cuba: Air Force

Cyprus: Air Force

Czech Republic: Air Force

Czech Republic: Low Visibility

Czech Republic: Police

Denmark: Air Force, Navy and Army

Denmark: Army (Supplemental)

Djibouti: Air Force

Dominican Republic: Air Force

Ecuador: Air Force and Army

Ecuador: Navy

Egypt: Air Force and Navy

Egypt: Air Force (Special)

No marking

Egypt: VIP Transports

Equatorial Guinea: National Guard

Eritrea: Air Force

Estonia: Air Force

Estonia: Border Guard

Ethiopia: Air Force

Finland: Air Force and Army

France: Air Force, Army, Gendarmerie, and CEV

France: Navy

France: Gendarmerie (Supplemental)

Gabon: Air Force, Presidential Guard, & Army

Gabon: Gendarmerie

Gambia: Air Force

Georgia: Air Force

Germany: Air Force, Navy, and Army

Germany: Navy (Supplemental)

Germany: Navy (Supplemental: 2006 style)

Ghana: Air Force

Greece: Air Force, Navy, and Army

Greece: Navy Low Visibility

Greece: Coast Guard

Guatemala: Air Force

Guinea Bissau: Air Force

Guinea Republic: Air Force

Guyana: Defence Force

Haiti: Air Corps

Honduras: Air Force

Hungary: Air Force

Iceland: Coast Guard

India: Air Force and Army

India: Navy

India: Coast Guard

Indonesia: Air Force

Indonesia: Air Force Low Visibility

Indonesia: Navy

Indonesia: Army

Indonesia: Police

Iran: Air Force, Navy, and Army

Iraq: Air Force

Ireland: Air Corps

Israel: Air Force

Italy: Air Force, Army, Carabinieri, and Guardia di Finaza

Italy: Navy

 Italy: Capitanerie di Porto

 Italy: Low Visibility

 Jamaica: Defense Force

 Japan: Air Force, Navy, and Army

 Jordan: Air Force

 Kazakhstan: Air Force

 Kazakhstan: Government

 Kenya: Air Force

 Korea, North: Air Force

 Korea, South: Air Force

 Korea, South: Navy

 Korea, South: Army

 Kuwait: Air Force

 Kyrgyzstan: Air Force

 Laos: Air Force

 Latvia: Air Force

 Lebanon: Air Force

 Lesotho: Defense Force

 Liberia: Army

 Libya: Air Force, Navy, and Army

 Lithuania: Air Force

 Lithuania: National Defense Service

 Lithuania: Transport (Supplemental)

 Luxembourg: NATO AEW Force

Macedonia: Air Force

Macedonia: Alternative

Macedonia: Low Visibility

Madagascar: Air Force

Malawi: Air Force

 Malaysia: Air Force

 Malaysia: Low Visibility

 Malaysia: Government/VIP

 Malaysia: Air Force (Alternate)

 Malaysia: Navy

Malaysia: Fire and Rescue Department

 Mali: Air Force

 Malta: Armed Forces

 Mauritania: Air Force

 Mauritius: Coast Guard

Mexico: Air Force

Mexico: Low Visibility

Mexico: Navy

Mexico: Navy 2

Moldova: Air Force

Mongolia: Air Force

Morocco: Air Force and Gendarmerie

Mozambique: Air Force

Myanmar: Air Force

No marking

Namibia: Army

NATO: AEW Force

Nepal: Air Force

Netherlands: Air Force and Navy

Netherlands: Low Visibility

New Zealand: Air Force

New Zealand: Low Visibility 1

New Zealand: Low Visibility 2

Nicaragua: Air Force

Niger: National Squadron

Nigeria: Air Force

Nigeria: Government (Supplemental)

Nigeria: Navy

Norway: Air Force

Norway: Low Visibility

Oman: Air Force

Oman: Air Force (Simplified)

Oman: Low Visibility

Pakistan: Air Force and Army

Pakistan: Navy

Panama: Air Service

Papua New Guinea: Defense Force

Paraguay: Air Force

Paraguay: Navy

Peru: Air Force

Peru: Navy

Peru: Army

Peru: Police (Optional)

Philippines: Air Force

No marking

Philippines: Government

Philippines: Navy